Madrid

"All you've got to do is decide to go
and the hardest part is over.

So go!"

TONY WHEELER, COFOUNDER – LONELY PLANET

THIS EDITION WRITTEN AND RESEARCHED BY

Anthony Ham

Contents

Plan Your Trip 4

Explore Madrid 42

Understand Madrid 175

Survival Guide 201

Madrid Maps 229

LONELY PLANET / GETTY IMAGES ©

LONELY PLANET / GETTY IMAGES ©

(left) Flamenco show at Casa Patas (p73)

(above) Basilica de San Francisco El Grande (p64)

(right) *Jamón* (ham), tomatoes and peppers

DIEGO LEZAMA / GETTY IMAGES ©

Parque del Oeste & Northern Madrid p144

Salamanca p110

Malasaña & Chueca p121

Plaza Mayor & Royal Madrid p46

Sol, Santa Ana & Huertas p76

El Retiro & the Art Museums p90

La Latina & Lavapiés p62

Welcome to Madrid

No city on earth is more alive than Madrid, a beguiling place whose sheer energy carries a simple message: this city really knows how to live.

A Culinary Capital

Rising above the humble claims of its local cuisine, Madrid has evolved into one of the richest culinary capitals of Europe. This is a city that has wholeheartedly embraced all the creativity and innovation of Spain's gastronomic revolution. But this acceptance of the new is wedded to a passion for the enduring traditions of Spanish cooking (it's no coincidence that the world's oldest restaurant is found here), for the conviviality of the eating experience and for showcasing the infinite variety of food from every Spanish region. From tapas in sleek temples to all that's new to sit-down meals beneath centuries-old vaulted ceilings, eating in Madrid is a genuine pleasure.

Killing the Night

Madrid nights are the stuff of legend. The city may have more bars than any other city on earth, a collection of storied cocktail bars and nightclubs that combine a hint of glamour with non-stop *marcha* (action). But that only goes someway to explaining the appeal of after-dark Madrid. Step out into the night-time streets of many Madrid neighbourhoods and you'll find yourself swept along on a tide of people, accompanied by a happy crowd intent on dancing until dawn.

Beautiful Architecture

Madrid may not have the architectural cachet of Paris, the monumental history of Rome, or Barcelona's reputation for Modernista masterpieces. And no, there is no equivalent of the Eiffel Tower, Colosseum or La Sagrada Família that you can point to and say 'this is Madrid'. Madrid has nothing to be envious of when it comes to architecture. Instead, the broad sweep of architectural history provides a glorious backdrop to city life, from medieval mansions and royal palaces to the unimagined angles of Spanish contemporary architecture, from the sober brickwork and slate spires of Madrid baroque to the extravagant confections of the belle époque. Put simply, this is one beautiful city.

DIEGO LEZAMA / GETTY IMAGES ©

Why I Love Madrid

By Anthony Ham, Author

Ten years after I fell in love with Madrid and decided to call it home, the life that courses relentlessly through the streets here still produces in me a feeling that this is a place where anything can happen. Here is a place where the passions of Europe's most passionate country are the fabric of daily life, a city with music in its soul and an unshakeable spring in its step. But Madrid is also one of the most open cities on earth. As a result, it doesn't matter where you're from for the oft-heard phrase to ring true: 'If you're in Madrid, you're from Madrid'.

For more about our author, see p256.

Mercado de San Miguel (p54)

Madrid's Top 10

HEMIS / ALAMY ©

Museo del Prado *(p92)*

1 Spain's premier collection of Spanish and European art belongs among the elite of world art museums. Goya and Velázquez are the stars of the show in this beautiful museum that occupies pride of place along the city's grand boulevard, the Paseo del Prado. But the Prado's catalogue has such astonishing depth and breadth, from Rubens and Rembrandt to Botticelli and Bosch, that you'll require more than one visit to take it all in.

El Retiro & the Art Museums

Plaza Mayor *(p48)*

2 Madrid is distinguished by some extraordinarily beautiful plazas, but Plaza Mayor is easily the king. The plaza's constituent elements are easy to list: uneven cobblestones, perfectly proportioned porticoes, slate spires and facades in deep ochre offset by marvellous frescoes of mythic figures and wrought-iron balconies. But this stately square is the heartbeat of a city, the scene of so many grand events in Madrid's historical story and where the modern city most agreeably throngs with life. (STATUE OF PHILIP III)

Plaza Mayor & Royal Madrid

1

GUY VANDERELST / GETTY IMAGES ©

2

3

SANDRA RACCANELLO/SIME/4CORNERS ©

5

JEAN-PIERRE LESCOURRET / GETTY IMAGES ©

JEAN-PIERRE LESCOURRET / GETTY IMAGES ©

Tapas in La Latina

(p67)

3 One of the most important gastronomic streets in Spain, La Latina's Calle de la Cava Baja is lined with tapas bars. Some have elevated these tiny morsels into art forms, while others serve up specialties in traditional clay pots. Such is Madrid's love affair with tapas and the whole culture of enjoying them that even this long and graceful thoroughfare cannot contain the neighbourhood's tapas offerings. Nearby you'll find Madrid's best *tortilla de patatas* (potato and onion omelette), an egg-and-*jamón* (ham) dish beloved by the king…

La Latina & Lavapiés

Parque del Buen Retiro *(p106)*

4 The alter ego to Madrid's tableau of sound and movement, the Parque del Buen Retiro is one of our favourite corners of the city. Beautiful by any standards with eye-catching architectural monuments and abundant statues among the trees, El Retiro is where *madrileños* (people from Madrid) come to stroll in great numbers on weekends. As such it's one of the most accessible slices of local culture, at once filled with life and an escape from Madrid's frenetic pace.

El Retiro & the Art Museums

Centro de Arte Reina Sofía *(p101)*

5 In a city where world-class art galleries are everywhere, it takes something special for one painting to tower above the rest. But such is the strange and disturbing splendour of Picasso's *Guernica* that its claim to being Madrid's most extraordinary artwork is unrivalled. After decades of wandering the globe, it looks very much at home in the Centro de Arte Reina Sofía, alongside works by Salvador Dalí and Joan Miró. (EDIFICIO NOUVEL, ARCHITECT JEAN NOUVEL)

El Retiro & the Art Museums

Palacio Real *(p49)*

6 Built on the site where Madrid was born in the 9th century, Madrid's Palacio Real is one of the city's most significant (and most beautiful) buildings. Watching over a pretty square and shadowed by gorgeous ornamental gardens, the palace is a stately affair, combining grandeur, all the symbolism of an imperial past and unusual accessibility in the city's heart. The interior is as lavish and extravagant as you'd expect, a reminder of the glory days when Spanish royalty ruled the world.

Plaza Mayor & Royal Madrid

Malasaña & Chueca Nightlife *(p132)*

7 The legend of Madrid's hedonistic nights was born in the narrow, inner-city streets of Malasaña and Chueca. In gritty and grungy Malasaña, hard-living rock venues share punters with elegant 19th-century literary cafes. Next door in Chueca, a cool and predominantly gay clientele fill bars and nightclubs to capacity most nights. More than anywhere in the city, this is where locals come for a night out, and the diversity of what's on offer here is representative of a city whose contradictory impulses are legion. (PLAZA DE CHUECA)

Malasaña & Chueca

6

Museo Thyssen-Bornemisza *(p97)*

8 Of all Madrid's major art galleries, it is the Museo Thyssen-Bornemisza that most often appeals to the uninitiated. Here beneath one roof is seemingly every European painter of distinction from 13th-century religious art to zany 21st-century creations. There may just be one painting, or a handful of paintings from each artist, but the museum's broadbrush-strokes approach makes a visit here akin to a journey through all that has been refined and masterful during centuries of European art.

El Retiro & the Art Museums

Plaza Santa Ana & Night-Time Huertas *(p80)*

9 Nights around the Plaza Santa Ana and neighbouring *barrio* (district) of Huertas are long, loud and filled with variety. The plaza is both epicentre and starting point of so many epic Madrid nights, with outdoor tables a fabulous vantage point from which to take the pulse of the night and plan your journey through it. Within a short radius of the square, live music venues, old-style sherry bars and sleek rooftop lounge bars for sybarites will get your night going, with legendary Madrid nightclubs nearby.

 ***Sol, Santa Ana & Huertas***

9

BRUNO EHRS / CORBIS ©

10

MARCO CRISTOFORI / CORBIS ©

Ermita de San Antonio de la Florida *(p146)*

10 One of Madrid's best-kept secrets, the Ermita de San Antonio de la Florida is nonetheless one of the city's most significant artistic landmarks. Here in a small and otherwise nondescript hermitage in 1798, Goya, one of the city's most favoured adopted sons, painted a series of frescoes under royal orders; these extraordinary paintings remain exactly where he first painted them. Breathtaking in their vivid portrayal of Madrid life and the Miracle of St Anthony, they're definitely worth the trip across town to get here.

Parque del Oeste & Northern Madrid

What's New

Conde Duque

Out on the western fringe of Malasaña, Conde Duque has recently become one of the city's coolest corners. It's predominantly a night-time neighbourhood with great restaurants (Calle de San Bernardino) and nightlife (around Calle de Palma). Madrid's in and at times alternative crowd has suddenly realised what's going on, in the process creating a whole new buzz. (p132)

Calle de la Cava Baja Hotels

La Latina's beautiful and iconic Calle de la Cava Baja just got better: two ancient inns (Posada del Dragón and Posada del León de Oro) have been stunningly converted into two of Madrid's most exciting boutique hotels. (p169)

Vi Cool & Restaurante Sandó

Catalan master chef Sergi Arola has made Madrid his own with a series of restaurants but his latest offering, Vi Cool, is one of the most accessible with designer tapas in a bar-style setting. Basque master Juan Mari Arzak is also here, at Restaurante Sandó. (p81) and (p56)

Museo del Prado I

It always seemed an anomaly that one of the world's greatest art galleries was closed on a Monday. The Prado is now open seven days a week meaning you don't have to miss out on this world-class collection if Monday is your only day in town. (p92)

Museo del Prado II

In the process of restoring a painting that has been in Madrid's Museo del Prado since 1819, conservators have discovered a nearly exact copy of the *Mona Lisa,* painted by one of Leonardo da Vinci's favourite pupils at the same time as the original. (p92)

Praktik Metropol

Crowning one of the highest points in the city, the building on the corner of Gran Vía and Calle de la Montera has long been the preserve of budget *hostales*. The Praktik Metropol now offers stylish midrange rooms with some of Madrid's best downtown views. (p169)

Madrid Río

Madrid has spent billions turning its river into an oasis on the city-centre fringe. There's a summer beach, abundant greenery, bike paths and a beguiling sense of the city clawing back its green credentials. (p70)

Antiguo Cuartel de Conde Duque

One of Madrid's more dynamic cultural spaces, the 18th-century Antiguo Cuartel del Conde Duque, has been painstakingly restored to once again become of the city's architectural showpieces. (p125)

Airport Bus

The recently inaugurated Exprés Aeropuerto bus from the Estación de Atocha (or from Plaza de la Cibeles at night) just made life a whole lot easier (ie no metro stairs) if you're heading to the airport. (p202)

For more recommendations and reviews, see **lonelyplanet.com/madrid**

Need to Know

Currency
Euro (€)

Language
Spanish (Castellano)

Visas
Generally not required for stays of up to 90 days (not at all for members of EU or Schengen countries). Some nationalities need a Schengen visa.

Money
ATMs are widely available. Credit cards are accepted in most hotels, restaurants and shops.

Mobile Phones
Local SIM cards are widely available and can be used in European and Australian mobile phones. Other phones may need to be set to roaming.

Time
Western European (GMT/UTC plus one hour during winter, plus two hours during daylight-saving period).

Tourist Information
Centro de Turismo de Madrid (☎91 588 16 36; www.esmadrid.com; Plaza Mayor 27; ⌚9.30am-8.30pm; Ⓜ Sol) Main tourist office; other branches and information points around the city.

Your Daily Budget

Budget less than €80

➡ Dorm beds €15–20; *hostal* (budget hotel) doubles €50–70

➡ Three-course *menú del día* (daily set menu) lunches

➡ Plan sightseeing around 'free admission' times

Midrange €80–200

➡ Double room in midrange hotel €75–150

➡ Lunch and/or dinner in decent restaurants

➡ Use discount cards to keep costs down

Top End more than €200

➡ Double room in top-end hotel from €150

➡ Fine dining for lunch and dinner

Advance Planning

Three months before Reserve your hotel as early as you can.

One month before Book a table at Sergi Arola Gastro (p149), La Terraza del Casino (p81) or Viridiana (p107).

One week before Book online entry to the Museo del Prado (p92) to avoid queues on arrival.

Useful Websites

➡ **EsMadrid.com** (www.esmadrid.com) Tourist office's website.

➡ **LeCool** (www.lecool.com) Alternative, offbeat and avant-garde.

➡ **Lonely Planet** (www.lonelyplanet.com/madrid) An overview of Madrid with hundreds of useful links.

➡ **Turismo Madrid** (www.turismomadrid.es) Regional Comunidad de Madrid tourist office site.

WHEN TO GO

Spring and autumn are the best times to visit. Summer can be fiercely hot although it's a dry heat, while winters can be bitterly cold and snow is possible though rare.

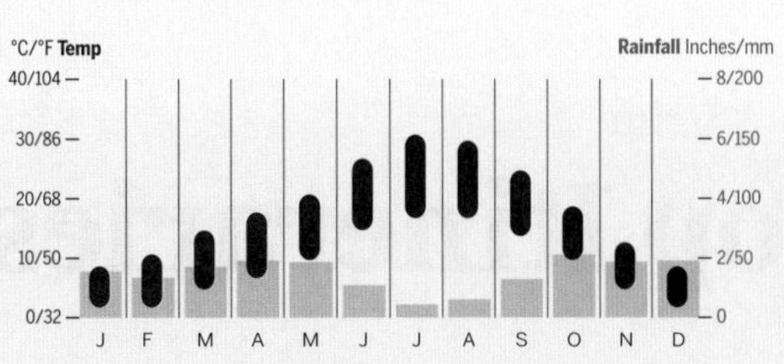

Arriving in Madrid

Barajas Airport Metro (6.05am to 2am), bus (24hr) and minibus to central Madrid; taxis around €25

Estación de Atocha (Atocha Train Station) Metro and bus to central Madrid from 6.05am to 2am; close to city centre; taxi from €7

Estacíon de Chamartín (Chamartín Train Station) Metro and bus to central Madrid from 6.05am to 2am; taxi around €10

Estación Sur de Autobuses (Bus Station) Metro and bus to central Madrid from 6.05am to 2am; taxi around €10

For much more on **arrival** see p202

Getting Around

Ten-trip Metrobús tickets cost €12.20 and are valid for journeys on Madrid's metro and bus network. Tickets can be bought from most newspaper kiosks and *estancos* (tobacconists), as well as in manned booths and ticket machines in metro stations.

➡ **Metro** The quickest and easiest way to get around. Runs 6.05am to 2am.

➡ **Bus** Extensive network but needs careful planning to make most of over 200 routes. Runs 6.30am to 11.30pm.

➡ **Taxi** Cheap fares by European standards; plentiful.

➡ **Walking** Compact city centre makes walking a good option, but hillier than first appears.

For much more on **getting around** see p204

Sleeping

Madrid is brimful of outstanding hotels, and prices here are often absurdly low when compared to other major European capitals. Advance reservations are always recommended to ensure you get the best deal.

Madrid is a worthy rival to Barcelona when it comes to stylish accommodation, with designer hotels within reach of most midrange travellers. Most midrange and top-end hotels range from tasteful and intimate boutique options to storied palaces of old-fashioned luxury.

Hostales are an excellent budget option, with private bathrooms and rock-bottom prices, while hostels are all about backpacker buzz and dorm-style sleeping.

Websites

➡ **Centro de Turismo de Madrid** (www.esmadrid.com)

➡ **Reserva Madrid** (www.reservamadrid.com)

➡ **Booking.com** (www.booking.com)

➡ **Atrapalo** (www.atrapalo.com)

➡ **Agoda** (www.agoda.es)

For much more on **sleeping** see p165

A CHEAP LUNCH

Madrid can be an expensive city in which to eat (at least €35 per person in most midrange restaurants), but a great way to sample home-style Spanish cooking without getting stung for à la carte prices is by ordering the weekday lunchtime *menú del día*, a fixed-price, three-course lunch that costs around €12. Lunch is the main meal of the day here and by eating big at lunchtime and ordering tapas in the evening you will spend surprisingly little on food.

Top Itineraries

Day One

Plaza Mayor & Royal Madrid (p46)

So many Madrid days begin in the **Plaza Mayor**, or perhaps nearby with a breakfast of *chocolate con churros* (chocolate with deep-fried doughnuts) at **Chocolatería de San Ginés**. Drop by the **Plaza de la Villa** and **Plaza de Oriente**, then stop for a coffee or wine at **Cafe de Oriente** and visit the **Palacio Real**.

Lunch Mercado de San Miguel (p54) is an innovative gastronomic space.

El Retiro & the Art Museums (p90)

Spend as much of the afternoon as you can at the **Museo del Prado**. When this priceless collection of Spanish and European masterpieces gets too much, visit the **Iglesia de San Jerónimo El Real** and **Caixa Forum**.

Dinner Restaurante Sobrino de Botín (p56) is the world's oldest restaurant.

Plaza Mayor & Royal Madrid (p46)

To kick off the night, perhaps take in a flamenco show at **Las Tablas**, followed by a leisurely drink at **Café del Real** or **Anticafé**. If you're up for a long night, **Teatro Joy Eslava** is an icon of the Madrid night.

Day Two

El Retiro & the Art Museums (p90)

Get to the **Centro de Arte Reina Sofía** early to beat the crowds, then climb up through sedate streets to spend a couple of hours soaking up the calm of the **Parque del Buen Retiro**. Wander down to admire the **Plaza de la Cibeles**.

Lunch Estado Puro (p109) is one of Madrid's most creative tapas bars.

Parque del Oeste & Northern Madrid (p144)

After lunch, catch the metro across town to admire the Goya frescoes in the **Ermita de San Antonio de la Florida**. **Templo de Debod** and **Parque del Oeste** are fine places for a stroll.

Dinner Casa Alberto (p81) is one of Madrid's most storied *tabernas*.

Sol, Santa Ana & Huertas (p76)

Begin the night at **Plaza de Santa Ana** for a drink or three at an outdoor table if the weather's fine. After another tipple at **La Venencia**, check out if there's live jazz on offer at wonderful **Café Central**, then have an after-show drink at **El Imperfecto**. The night is still young – **Costello Café & Niteclub** is good if you're in the mood to dance, **La Terraza del Urban** if you're in need of more sybaritic pleasures.

Day Three

El Retiro & the Art Museums (p90)

Begin the morning at the third of Madrid's world-class art galleries, the **Museo Thyssen-Bornemisza**. It's such a rich collection that you could easily spend the whole morning here. If you've time to spare, consider dipping back into the Prado or Reina Sofía.

Lunch Sula Madrid (p115) offers stunning tapas in an elegant setting.

Salamanca (p110)

Head out east to take a tour of the **Plaza de Toros** bullring, before dipping into the **Museo Lázaro Galdiano**. Spend the rest of the morning shopping along Calle de Serrano, Calle de José Ortega y Gasset and surrounding streets.

Dinner Naïa Restaurante (p68) has a lovely La Latina setting and fresh tastes.

La Latina & Lavapiés (p62)

As dusk approaches, make for La Latina and spend as long as you can picking your way among the tapas bars of **Calle de la Cava Baja** – even if you're not hungry, stop by for a beer or wine to soak up the atmosphere. A wine at **Taberna Tempranillo** and a mojito out on Plaza de la Paja at **Delic** should set you up for the night ahead.

Day Four

Sol, Santa Ana & Huertas (p76)

Start the day with some souvenir shopping at **Casa de Diego** and **Gil**. If you really love your art, **Real Academia de Bellas Artes de San Fernando** will nicely round out your experience of Madrid's exceptional art scene.

Lunch Albur (p126) or La Musa (p126) on Calle de Manuela Malasaña.

Malasaña & Chueca (p121)

You've been around almost long enough to be a local and it's therefore worth exploring the laneways of Malasaña between Calle Pez, Plaza Dos de Mayo and the Glorieta de Bilbao – stop off at **Lolina Vintage Café** along Calle del Espíritu Santo, **Café Manuela** on Calle de San Vincente Ferrer, and **Café Comercial**, as well as the **Museo de Historia** or **Museo del Romanticismo** en route.

Dinner La Tasquita de Enfrente (p126) is loved by celebrities and foodies.

Malasaña & Chueca (p121)

Get to know multifaceted Chueca from the dignified calm and boutiques of **Calle de Piamonte**, pass by **Plaza de Chueca** to watch the *barrio* (district) come to life, then get seriously into the cocktail bars along Calle de la Reina, followed by the legendary **Museo Chicote**. **El Junco Jazz Club** will leave you with great memories of the city.

If You Like...

City Squares

Plaza Mayor A perfectly proportioned centrepiece of Madrid life combining architecture with busy street life. (p48)

Plaza de Oriente The heart of Royal Madrid, with a royal palace, opera house, statues, gardens and some stunning facades. (p51)

Plaza de la Villa Compact, delightfully small and surrounded by impressive examples of Madrid's architectural centuries. (p53)

Plaza de Santa Ana Pretty architecture and a history of artistic endeavours meets a city intent on having a good time. (p80)

Plaza de la Paja On the site of the city's medieval market, it now wonderfully resembles a ramshackle village square. (p65)

Plaza de España A soaring and sober opening in the city centre watched over by a pair of Franco follies. (p52)

Architecture

Plaza de la Cibeles Madrid's grandest convergence of streets overlooked by extraordinary late-19th- and early 20th-century creations. (p103)

Caixa Forum Central Madrid's most striking symbol of Spain's revolution in contemporary architecture. (p103)

Convento de la Encarnación A beautiful example of Madrid's very own style of baroque

MARCP_DMOZ ON FLICKR / GETTY IMAGES ©

Antigua Estación de Atocha (p107)

architecture close to the Palacio Real. (p52)

Gran Vía A beguiling polyglot of facades with the Edificio Metrópolis the pick of a rather fine bunch. (p79)

San Lorenzo de El Escorial An at once sumptuous and sombre statement of imperial grandeur in the hills surrounding Madrid. (p155)

Antigua Estación de Atocha An artful conversion of Madrid's train station into a soaring structure that combines the traditional with the modern. (p107)

Centro de Arte Reina Sofía A fitting setting for a premier collection of contemporary art with the architecture itself a star attraction. (p101)

Palacio de Cristal An airy iron-and-glass relic overlooking a small lake in the heart of the Parque del Buen Retiro. (p106)

Restaurant Streets

Calle de la Cava Baja The richest pickings in Madrid for tapas with some highly regarded sit-down restaurants as well.

Calle de Manuela Malasaña At the northern end of Malasaña and lined with highly recommended restaurants.

Calle de la Libertad Deep in the *barrio* (district) of Chueca, with a range of cuisines, restaurants and eating experiences on offer.

Calle de Jorge Juan Only a couple of choices, but they're both worth crossing town for and could easily be combined for a night out.

Calle de San Bernardino An eclectic range of international restaurants at the lower end of Conde Duque.

Green Escapes

Parque del Buen Retiro Madrid's finest city park and scene of so much that's good about Madrid life. (p106)

Parque del Oeste Sloping stand of greenery northwest of the city centre with fine views and scarcely a tourist in sight. (p149)

Real Jardín Botánico An intimate oasis of exotic plants right alongside one of Madrid's busiest boulevards. (p103)

Casa de Campo Vast expanse of parkland west of downtown Madrid with the city's zoo, an amusement park and a cable car to get there. (p151)

Madrid Río Kilometres of developed parkland alongside Madrid's long-forgotten river.

Bastions of Culinary Tradition

Restaurante Sobrino de Botin The world's oldest restaurant and a mainstay of roasted meats and other traditional local specialties. (p56)

Lhardy The much-celebrated Madrid table where the great and good come for impeccable quality and service. (p82)

Posada de la Villa Decor evocative of an ancient Madrid inn, reliable cooking and repeat clientele. (p68)

Taberna La Bola One of the best places in town to try the Madrid specialty of *cocido a la madrileña* in a traditional bar-restaurant setting. (p57)

Casa Lucio Beloved by everyone, including the king and a cast of international celebrities, with assured cooking of Spanish staples. (p68)

For more top Madrid spots, see the following:

- Eating (p27)
- Drinking & Nightlife (p32)
- Entertainment (p35)
- Shopping (p40)

Casa Alberto A historic Huertas *taberna* (tavern) where the tapas are all about tradition and the sit-down meals include bull's tail. (p81)

Zalacaín The grand old señor of Madrid restaurants with an extraordinary wine list and upmarket cooking in the finest Spanish tradition. (p151)

Casa Revuelta The essence of the Madrid tapas experience with shouting waiters, old timers and terrific food. (p56)

Temples to Innovative Cooking

Estado Puro Tapas straight from the laboratory of some of Spain's finest and most innovative chefs. (p109)

Sergi Arola Gastro One of Madrid's most respected restaurants overseen by one of Spain's most respected chefs. (p149)

Restaurante Sandó Madrid kitchen of the celebrated Basque team of Juan Mari and Elena Arzak. (p56)

Vi Cool Master chef Ferran Adrìa's foray into reasonably priced tapas around halfway down the Huertas hill. (p81)

La Terraza del Casino Glorious setting and more state-of-the-art nouvelle cuisine from some of Spain's world-famous cooks. (p81)

Month by Month

TOP EVENTS

Fiestas de San Isidro Labrador May

Suma Flamenca June

Festimad May

Día Del Orgullo De Gays, Lesbianas Y Transexuales June

La Noche en Blanco September

January

Not much happens in Madrid until after 6 January, although the Christmas–New Year period can be high season in some hotels. Temperatures can be bitterly cold, but wonderfully clear, crisp days are also common.

Año Nuevo

Many *madrileños* (people from Madrid) gather in Puerta del Sol on Noche Vieja (New Year's Eve) to wait for the 12 *campanadas* (bell chimes), whereupon they try to stuff 12 grapes (one for each chime) into their mouths to mark Año Nuevo (New Year).

Reyes

On Día de los Reyes Magos (Three Kings' Day), three wise men lead the sweet-distributing frenzy of Cabalgata de Reyes. Horse-drawn carriages and floats make their way from the Parque del Buen Retiro to Plaza Mayor at 6pm on 5 January.

February

Usually the coldest month in Madrid, February always has a chill in the air. In warmer years, late February can be surprisingly mild, heralding the early onset of spring.

Carnaval

Carnaval spells several days of fancy-dress parades and merrymaking in many *barrios* (districts) across the Comunidad de Madrid, usually ending on the Tuesday, 47 days before Easter Sunday. Competitions for the best costume take place in the Círculo de Bellas Artes.

Festival Flamenco

A combination of big names and rising talents come together for five days of fine flamenco music in one of the city's theatres. The dates are movable, but big names are guaranteed.

March

Freezing temperatures can occur, but early spring sunshine can prompt restaurants to set up their outdoor tables. *Madrileños* often evacuate the city for Semana Santa (Holy Week), but it can still be high season for some hotels.

Jueves Santo

On Jueves Santo (Holy Thursday), local *cofradías* (lay fraternities) organise a colourful yet solemn religious processions. The main procession concludes by crossing Plaza Mayor to the Basílica de Nuestra Señora del Buen Consejo.

Viernes Santo

Viernes Santo (Good Friday) and Easter in general are celebrated with greater enthusiasm in some of the surrounding towns. Chinchón, Ávila and Toledo in particular, are known for their lavish Easter processions.

La Noche de los Teatros

On 'The Night of the Theatres', Madrid's streets become the stage for all manner of performances, with a focus on comedy and children's plays. It usually takes place on the last Saturday of March, and lasts from 5pm to midnight.

May

May is arguably Madrid's biggest month for festivals and with the weather warming up, it's one of our favourite times to be in the city.

Fiestas de San Isidro Labrador

The city's big holiday on 15 May, the Fiestas de San Isidro marks the feast day of its patron saint, San Isidro. Crowds gather in central Madrid to watch the colourful procession, which kicks off a week of cultural events across the city.

Festimad

This is the biggest of Spain's year-round circuit of major music festivals. Bands from all over the country and beyond converge on Móstoles or Leganés (on the MetroSur train network), just outside Madrid, for two days of indie music indulgence. It sometimes begins in April. (www.festimad.es)

Feria del Libro

The northeastern corner of the Parque del Buen Retiro is taken over by the Madrid Book Fair, with hundreds of stalls. It draws massive crowds with book signings and discounts of around 10%. (www.ferialibromadrid.com)

June

A select group of festivals usher in the Spanish summer. The city has a real spring in its step with warm weather and summer holidays just around the corner.

Suma Flamenca

A soul-filled flamenco festival in early June that draws some of the biggest names in the genre to theatres and some the better-known *tablaos* (flamenco venues), such as Casa Patas, Villa Rosa and Corral de la Morería. (www.madrid.org/sumaflamenca)

Día del Orgullo de Gays, Lesbianas Y Transexuales

The city's Gay and Lesbian Pride Festival and Parade take place on the last Saturday of the month. The extravagant floats begin on Plaza de la Independencia, passing along Gran Vía to Plaza de España. At all other times, Chueca is the place to be. (www.orgullogay.org or www.madridgaypride.com)

July

Madrid can really cook in July and the city's pace slows in response. That may have something do with the fact that those not at the beach are preparing to head there in August. Hotel prices often drop when things are quiet.

Veranos de la Villa

Half of Madrid evacuates to the beach in July, but those who remain are rewarded with concerts, opera, dance, theatre and exhibitions as part of 'Summers in the City'. Many take place at outdoor venues and the program starts in July and runs to the end of August. (veranosdelavilla.esmadrid.com/)

August

Temperatures soar and the city can be eerily quiet as locals flock to the coast or mountains. Many restaurants and other businesses close and some museums open reduced hours.

La Asunción

Also known as the Fiesta de la Virgen de la Paloma, 15 August is a solemn date in the city's religious calendar, celebrating the Assumption of the Virgin Mary. La Latina takes a hedonistic approach to it all with street parties.

September

Milder temperatures (although don't be surprised if summer spills over or winter makes an early appearance) and some fine festivals help to ease the city back into its customary clamour.

La Noche en Blanco

'The White Night' is when Madrid and many of its monuments, bars etc stay open all night with a citywide extravaganza of concerts and general revelry in 120 venues across the city. It's a participatory arts and culture festival and it rocks. (http://lanocheenblanco.esmadrid.com)

November

November is when Madrid's winter chill usually starts to bite. The city's jazz festival headlines an otherwise quiet month.

Festival Jazz Madrid

Madrid's annual jazz festival draws a prestigious cast of performers from across the globe and it's an increasingly important stop on the European jazz circuit. Venues vary, from the city's intimate jazz clubs to grander theatrical stages across town. (www.esmadrid.com/festivaljazzmadrid)

December

The run-up to Christmas sees the city brimful of festive spirit – crowds throng the city centre in astonishing numbers, many of them en route to the Plaza Mayor's Christmas market. There are high season prices in many hotels.

Navidad

The main family meal for Navidad (Christmas) is served on Nochebuena (Christmas Eve). Elaborate nativity scenes are set up in churches around the city and an exhibition is held in Plaza Mayor (otherwise taken over by a somewhat tacky, but wildly popular, Christmas market).

(Top) Fiestas de San Isidro Labrador (p21)
(Bottom) Reyes (Three Kings' Day; p20)

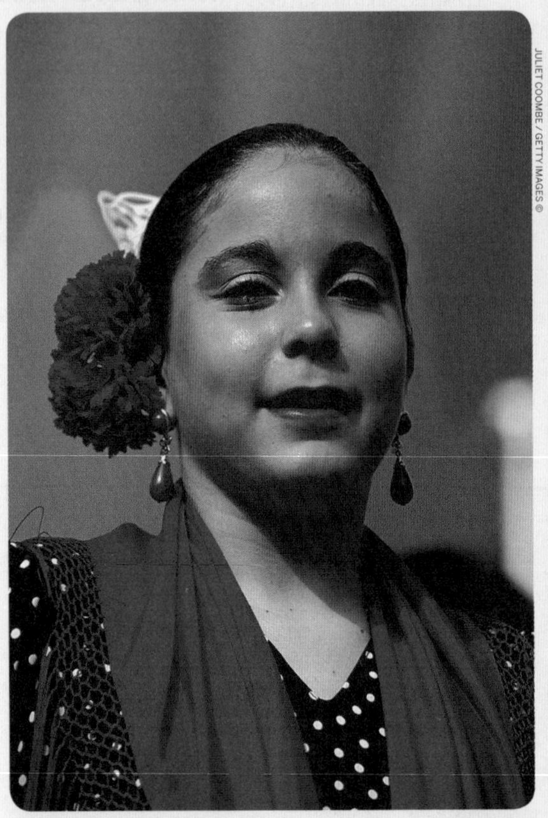

JULIET COOMBE / GETTY IMAGES ©

HITESH SAWLANI / GETTY IMAGES ©

With Kids

Madrid has plenty of child-friendly (and even a handful of excellent child-specific) sights and activities, and the city centre is relatively compact and easy to get around on foot (which is just as well because the metro can be a bit of an obstacle course for those with prams).

CARLOS DOMINIQUE / ALAMY ©

Parque de Atracciones (p151)

Child-Friendly Museums

Art Galleries

Most of Madrid's major art galleries have activities for children, although most will be in Spanish. Far more accessible are the museum guides designed specifically for kids – visit the museum bookshops first to see what's available.

Museo de Cera

Kids may not recognise all of the international figures rendered in wax form in this museum (p126) but there are enough footballers, actresses and international celebrities to get the kids excited about their visit. The 'Tren del Terror' shouldn't prove too scary for all but the youngest visitors. Apart from anything else, it's a reliable fallback option for a rainy day.

Museo de Ferrocarril

If your boy's a boy, he'll most likely love the **Museo del Ferrocarril** (☎902 228822; www.museodelferrocarril.org; Paseo de las Delicias 61; ⏰10am-3pm Tue-Thu, to 8pm Fri & Sat; adult/child €5.09/3.56; Ⓜ Delicias), Madrid's railway museum. Housed in the disused 1880s Estación de Delicias south of Lavapiés, this museum has about 30 pieces of rolling stock lined up along the platforms, ranging from the earliest steam locomotives to a sleeping car from the late 1920s. There are also dioramas of train stations, as well as model trains, tracks and other modelling products in the shop on the way out.

Parks & Playgrounds

Parque del Buen Retiro

Kids generally love the Parque del Buen Retiro (p106) as much as adults. There's ample lawn space in which they can run free, plus numerous playgrounds. Most get a kick out of the peacocks in the Jardines del Arquitecto Herrero Palacios. Renting a bike or a row boat are also great ways to pass the time, while there are occasionally puppet shows at various points around the park on weekends. There are two park information offices with details of what's possible, at the Casita del Pescador in the park's northeast and the Bosque del Recuerdo in the southwest.

NEED TO KNOW

- Bars and restaurants are now smoke-free and children are welcome in most.
- Metro maps show (with a wheelchair symbol) which stations have lifts.
- High chairs are increasingly common in restaurants.
- The *Guía del Ocio* (available from newspaper kiosks) has a 'Niños' section.
- 'El Madrid de los Niños' in *On Madrid* (with Friday's *El País* newspaper) is similar.

Playgrounds

Play areas for children are fairly thinly spread in central Madrid, but there are some decent playgrounds at the southern end of the Plaza de Oriente (p51) and two tiny playgrounds in the Plaza de Santa Ana (p80). North of the centre, Plaza Dos de Mayo in Malasaña has three playgrounds (with outdoor bars alongside from where you can keep watch), while Plaza de Olavide (p150) in Chamberí also has a couple, including one for kids aged eight and up.

Primarily for Kids

Zoo Aquarium de Madrid

Madrid's zoo (p151), out west of the city centre in the Casa de Campo, is a fine way to spend a day with your kids. Weekends can be busy, so try and visit during the week, although check the opening hours online before setting out. It might also be worth checking online the programme for the day (there are dolphin shows and the like) and planning your visit accordingly.

Parque de Atracciones

Rides for all ages are what this old-style amusement park (p151), also out west in the Casa de Campo, is all about. Long queues form on weekends, both at the rides and to get in, so either get here early or come another day if you can.

Warner Brothers Movie World

Disney World it ain't but this movie theme park (☎902 024100; www.parquewarner.com; San Martín de la Vega; hours vary; adult/child €39/30; Parque de Ocio), 25km south of central Madrid, has much to catch the attention. Entrance to the park is via Hollywood Boulevard, not unlike LA's Sunset Boulevard, whereafter you can choose between Cartoon World, the Old West, Hollywood Boulevard, Super Heroes (featuring Superman, Batman and the finks of Gotham City) and finally Warner Brothers Movie World Studios. Life-sized cartoon characters roam the grounds, and there are also rides and high-speed roller coasters. Opening times are complex; check before heading out. Tickets are cheaper if purchased online. Catch the *cercanías* train (line 3 for Aranjuez) from Atocha and get out at Parque de Ocio station.

Football

Children of a certain age will love the guided tour to the Estadio Santiago Bernabéu (p148), the home stadium of Real Madrid. It allows you to explore the place at your own speed. Better still, try for tickets to see a live game, an experience that your kids will remember for a lifetime.

Cable Car

This gentle cable-car ride (p149) is a worthwhile activity for its own sake, but it can also be a useful way to get out to the Casa de Campo. Never more than 40m above the ground and enclosed from the elements, it's an excursion that could be combined with a visit to the Templo de Debod (p147).

Shopping

Models

Model trains, plains and automobiles from Bazar Matey (p153) are brilliant little tokens to take home.

Baby Dolls

If your child loves a doll, the near-perfect babies from Así (p60) may just get you through an otherwise long day.

All Things Flamenco

For dancing shoes and polka-dot flamenco dresses, stop by Maty (p60) where the quality puts souvenir shops to shame.

Like a Local

In Madrid local knowledge is the difference between falling in love with the city and just passing through. Immerse yourself in the neighbourhoods of Malasaña and Chamberí, and in the local passion for tapas, chocolate con churros, mojitos and outdoor eating and drinking.

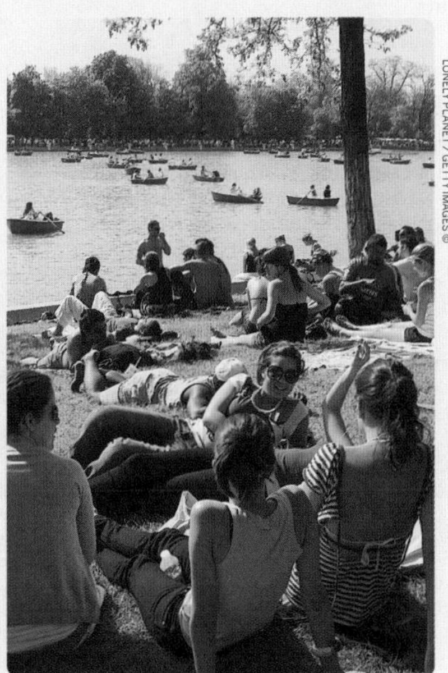

LONELY PLANET / GETTY IMAGES ©

Parque del Buen Retiro (p106)

A Madrid Sunday

Madrileños (people from Madrid) love their Sundays and although there are numerous variations on the theme, they usually go something like this. The day begins in the morning (early or otherwise) at the flea market of El Rastro (p66). Having shopped for bargains or simply reasserted one's right to partake of this age-old tradition, they then fan out into the bars of La Latina. It is customary at 1pm to order a vermouth (many of the bars have it on tap) to accompany the inevitable rounds of tapas, either as a precursor to lunch or as the main meal itself. Later, many gather in Plaza de la Puerta de Moros for an impromptu street party. But even more head to Parque del Buen Retiro (p106) to do everything from read the Sunday papers, take a boat ride on the lake or fall asleep (or all of the above) to have a picnic or wait for the drums to start.

Chamberí

Of all the *barrios* (districts) that encircle Madrid's city centre, Chamberí is the one where it's easiest to access life as locals live it away from tourist crowds. Plaza de Olavide is the hub of Chamberí life. Here, old men and women pass the day on park benches, small children tumble out into the plaza's playgrounds and queues form at the outdoor tables of the bars that encircle the plaza. Inside Bar Mentrida at No 3 you'll find a stirring photographic record of the plaza's history. There are some ageless old shops in the vicinity as well. Sunday morning is another good time to be here when Calle de Fuencarral (between the metro stations of Bilbao and Quevedo) is closed to cars and the whole neighbourhood comes out for a stroll.

Cafes of Malasaña

Back in the early 20th century, Malasaña was an important centre for Madrid's intellectual and cultural life, its cafes providing a meeting place for the great minds of the day. A handful of these cafes remain, among them Café Comercial (p132) and Café-Restaurante El Espejo (p133). But the spirit of that age continues and the clientele has since broadened out to include a broad cross-section of local society to the extent that the cafes of Malasaña, vintage and otherwise, are the essence of the neighbourhood and the secret of its unmistakeable *barrio* feel.

Ir de Tapear

To paraphrase Benito Pérez Galdós, a famous 19th-century Madrid writer, people of Madrid love to go out for a stroll so much that it almost counts as an occupation. That sense of a city unwilling to stay indoors finds its most agreeable expression in the tradition of *ir de tapear* (going out for tapas). Food may be the focal point of this popular tradition (and locals are passionate about their food), but it's also a vehicle (some might call it an excuse) for getting together with friends. Primarily an evening affair, or a lunch-and-afternoon event on weekends, it is one of the core elements of local life, a habit formed over the centuries and one that now is second nature to the vast majority of *madrileños*. Understanding the whole culture behind eating tapas in this way, and following suit, is an important step towards starting to think like a local.

The Terraza

An adjunct to the Madrid passion for passing the time with friends over tapas is the local love of the *terraza*, the outdoor tables that fill city squares and footpaths all across the city. Whenever the sun's out, even in winter (although this is generally a warm weather pastime), bar owners will set out their tables safe in the knowledge that locals will soon come to colonise them. People come and go, but it's not unusual if you're having a good time to begin in the afternoon and still be in residence hours later without really knowing where the time went, having in the meantime drunk and eaten your fill without having moved at all. Joining them is as easy as grabbing an empty chair as soon as it becomes available and thereafter defending it with your life.

Chocolate con Churros

In most places around the world, chocolate and deep-fried doughnuts would be a dessert. In Madrid this ultimate form of street food is many things, but it's most often breakfast, a hangover cure and/or an early-hours' cure for the munchies. As such it often serves a similar purpose to a 3am kebab in the UK. That's not to say that *madrileños* don't think twice about ordering *chocolate con churros* at other times of the day. It's just that the hours before dawn are when nothing else will do but this iconic street snack. Chocolatería de San Ginés (p58) is the most famous venue for this tradition. Elsewhere, El Brillante (p109) sometimes has queues forming when it opens at 6am, while Chocolatería Valor (p59) keeps much more reasonable hours.

A Passion for Mojitos

Cubans may have invented the mojito (a rum-based drink with sugar, fresh mint, crushed ice and lemon), but it has been a Madrid favourite for decades. Its popularity is such that any bar which produces sub-standard mojitos is unlikely to last for long in Madrid. Hemingway was perhaps the most famous spokesperson for the pedigree of the Madrid mojito, but ask any local and they're sure to know a bar that makes the mojito to perfection. Our pick? We can't decide between Museo Chicote (p136), Café Belén (p136) and Delic (p72).

Jamón (ham) with tomato, olives and peppers

Eating

Madrid has transformed itself into one of Europe's culinary capitals, not least because the city has long been a magnet for people (and cuisines) from all over Spain. Travel from one Spanish village to the next and you'll quickly learn that each has its own speciality; travel to Madrid and you'll find them all.

The Culture of Eating

Aside from the myriad tastes on offer, it's the buzz that accompanies eating in Madrid that defines the city as a memorable gastronomic experience. Here, eating is not a functional pastime to be squeezed in between other more important tasks; instead, it is one of life's great pleasures, a social event always taken seriously enough to allocate hours for the purpose and to be savoured like all good things in life. Treat it in the same way and you're halfway to understanding why *madrileños* (people from Madrid) are so passionate about their food.

Local Specialties

On the bleak *meseta* (plateau) of inland Spain, food in medieval Madrid was a necessity, good food a luxury, and the dishes that developed were functional and well suited to a climate dominated by interminable, bitterly cold winters. The city's traditional local cuisine is still dominated by these influences to a certain extent. At the same time, Madrid

NEED TO KNOW

Price Ranges

€	less than €10 per main course
€€	€10 to €20 per main course
€€€	more than €20 per main course

Opening Hours

- lunch 1pm to 4pm
- dinner 8.30pm to midnight or later

Tipping

A service charge is generally calculated into most bills in Madrid, so any further tipping is a matter of personal choice. Spaniards themselves are pretty stingy when it comes to tipping and often leave no more than €1 per person or nothing more than small change. If you're particularly happy, 5% on top would be fine.

Reservations

- Reservations for restaurants (not tapas bars) are strongly recommended on Friday and Saturday nights when many restaurants may have two sittings (one around 9pm, the second around 11pm); choose the latter unless you want to feel rushed.
- Reserving for lunch on Saturday or Sunday is also a good idea.

A Useful Resource

If you read Spanish, watch out for the annual (and indispensable) *Guía Metropoli – Comer y Beber en Madrid*. It's available from news kiosks for €11.90 and has reviews of over 1800 Madrid restaurants and bars by the food critics of *ABC* newspaper.

has wholeheartedly embraced dishes from across the country. The city has a thriving tapas culture and has become one of the biggest seafood-consuming cities in the world. Thus it is that Madrid has become one of the best places in the country to understand just why Spanish cuisine has taken the world by storm.

SOUPS & STEWS

When the weather turns chilly, that traditionally means in Madrid *sopa de ajo* (garlic soup) and *legumbres* (legumes) such as *garbanzos* (chickpeas), *judías* (beans) and *lentejas* (lentils). Hearty stews are the order of the day and there are none more hearty than *cocido a la madrileña*; it's a kind of hotpot or stew that starts with a noodle broth and is followed by, or combined with carrots, chickpeas, chicken, *morcilla* (blood sausage), beef, lard and possibly other sausage meats – there are as many ways of eating *cocido* as there are *madrileños*. *Repollo* (cabbage) sometimes makes an appearance. *Madrileños* love *cocido*. They dream of it while they're away from home and they wonder why it hasn't caught on elsewhere. There was even a hit song written about it in the 1950s. However, we'll put this as gently as we can: you have to be a *madrileño* to understand what all the fuss is about because it may be filling but it's not Spain's most exciting dish.

ROASTED MEATS

Madrid shares with much of the Spanish interior a love of roasted meats. More specifically, *asado de cordero lechal* (spring lamb roasted in a wood-fired oven) is a winter obsession in Madrid just as it is on much of the surrounding *meseta* of central Spain. Usually served with roasted potatoes (it's customary to also order a green salad to accompany the lamb and lighten things up a little), it's a mainstay in many of Madrid's more traditional restaurants. Less celebrated (it's all relative), is *cochinillo asado* (roast suckling pig) from the Segovia region northwest of Madrid.

SEAFOOD

Every day, tonnes of fish and other seafood are trucked in from Mediterranean and Atlantic ports to satisfy the *madrileño* taste for the sea to the extent that, remarkably for a city so far inland, Madrid is home to the world's second-largest fish market (after Tokyo). There's nothing you can't get here if you know where to look. From Galicia in Spain's Atlantic northwest, comes *pulpo gallego* (spicy boiled octopus cooked with oil, paprika and garlic) as well as all manner of weird-and-wonderful shellfish. From Asturias, Cantabria and the Basque Country come a passion for delicious *anchoas* (anchovies) and *bacalao* (cod), while Mediterranean Spain has mastered the art of seafood-laden rice dishes which *madrileños* have embraced as their own. The lightly fried fish of Andalucía rounds out an extraordinary banquet of seafood choice.

JAMÓN

An essential presence on many a Madrid table, and available from just about any

Madrid bar or restaurant, is the cured ham from the high plateau known as *jamón*. The *jamón* from Extremadura or Salamanca is widely considered to be the finest.

Spanish *jamón* is, unlike Italian prosciutto, a bold, deep red and well marbled with buttery fat. At its best, it smells like meat, the forest and the field. Like wines and olive oil, Spanish *jamón* is subject to a strict series of classifications. *Jamón serrano* refers to *jamón* made from white-coated pigs introduced to Spain in the 1950s. Once salted and semidried by the cold, dry winds of the Spanish sierra, most now go through a similar process of curing and drying in a climate-controlled shed for around a year. *Jamón serrano* accounts for approximately 90% of cured ham in Spain.

Jamón ibérico – more expensive and generally regarded as the elite of Spanish hams – comes from a black-coated pig indigenous to the Iberian Peninsula and a descendant of the wild boar. Gastronomically, its star appeal is its ability to infiltrate fat into the muscle tissue, thus producing an especially well-marbled meat. If the pig gains at least 50% of its body weight during the acorn-eating season, it can be classified as *jamón ibérico de bellota*, the most sought-after designation for *jamón*.

OTHER SPECIALTIES

The line between Spain-wide specialties and those from Madrid is decidedly blurred but most *madrileños* aren't too fussed whether the first *tortilla de patatas* (potato and onion omelette) was cooked in Madrid or elsewhere – all that matters is that it has become one of the best-loved dishes in the city. The same could also be said for *croquetas* (croquettes) and *patatas con huevos fritos* (baked potatoes with eggs, also known as *huevos rotos*).

Tapas

Nowhere is the national pastime of *ir de tapear* (going out to eat tapas) so deeply ingrained in local culture as much as it is in Madrid, where tapas are as much a social event as they are a much-loved culinary form. Anything can be a tapa, from a handful of olives or a slice of *jamón* on bread to a *tortilla de patatas* served in liquefied form. That's because tapas are the canvas upon which Spanish chefs paint the story of a nation's obsession with food, the means by which they show their fidelity to traditional Spanish tastes even as they gently nudge their compatriots in never-before-imagined directions. By making the most of very little, tapas serve as a link to the impoverished Spain of centuries past. By re-imagining even the most sacred Spanish staples, tapas are the culinary trademark of a confident country rushing headlong into the future.

ORDERING TAPAS

Too many travellers miss out on the joys of tapas because, unless you speak Spanish, the art of ordering can seem one of the dark arts of Spanish etiquette. Fear not – it's not as difficult as it first appears.

In many Madrid bars it couldn't be easier. With so many tapas varieties lined up along the bar, you either take a small plate and help yourself or point to the morsel you want. If you do this, it's customary to keep track of what you eat (by holding on to the toothpicks for example) and then tell the bar staff how many you've had when it's time to pay. Otherwise, many places have a list of tapas, either on a menu or posted up behind the bar. If you can't choose, ask for '*la especialidad de la casa*' (the house specialty) and it's hard to go wrong. Another way of eating tapas is to order *raciones* (literally 'rations'; large tapas servings) or *media raciones* (half-rations; smaller tapas servings). These plates and half-plates of a particular dish are a good way to go if you particularly like something and want more than a mere tapa. Remember, however, that after a couple of *raciones* you'll almost certainly be full; the *media ración* is a good choice if you want to experience a broader range of tastes. In some bars you'll also get a small (free) tapa when you buy a drink.

Vegetarians & Vegans

Pure vegetarianism remains something of an alien concept in most Spanish kitchens; cooked vegetable dishes, for example, often contain ham. That said, Madrid has a growing cast of vegetarian restaurants. Even in those restaurants that serve meat or fish dishes, salads are a Spanish staple and, in some places, can be a meal in themselves. You'll also come across the odd vegetarian paella, as well as dishes such as *verduras a la plancha* (grilled vegetables), *garbanzos con espinacas* (chickpeas and spinach), *patatas bravas* (potato chunks bathed in spicy tomato sauce) and the *tortilla de patatas*. The prevalence of legumes ensures that *lentejas* and *judías* are also easy to

MENÚ DEL DÍA

One great way to cap prices at lunchtime Monday to Friday is to order the *menú del día* (daily set menu), a three-course meal with water, bread and wine. These meals start from around €12, although €15 and up is increasingly the norm. You'll be given a menu with five or six entrées, the same number of mains and a handful of desserts – choose one from each category. The philosophy behind the *menú del día* is that, during the working week, few *madrileños* have time to go home to have their lunch. Taking a packed lunch is not the done thing, so the majority of people end up eating in restaurants, and all-inclusive three-course meals are as close as they can get to eating home-style food without breaking the bank.

track down, while *pan* (bread), *quesos* (cheeses), *alcachofas* (artichokes) and *aceitunas* (olives) are always easy to find. If vegetarianism is rare among Spaniards, vegans will feel as if they've come from another planet. However, some of the established vegetarian restaurants may have certain vegan dishes.

Eating by Neighbourhood

- **Plaza Mayor & Royal Madrid** Reasonable collection of restaurants and tapas bars.
- **La Latina & Lavapiés** Madrid's undisputed home of tapas.
- **Sol, Santa Ana & Huertas** Plenty of restaurants from Spain's regions.
- **El Retiro & the Art Museums** A couple of stand-out options between the galleries.
- **Salamanca** Terrific tapas and some refined sit-down restaurants.
- **Malasaña & Chueca** Arguably Madrid's widest choice of restaurants.
- **Parque del Oeste & Northern Madrid** Thinly spread but plenty of good places to eat.

Lonely Planet's Top Choices

Restaurante Sobrino De Botín (p56) The world's oldest restaurant and a bastion of tradition.

Sula Madrid (p115) Innovative cooking in superstylish surrounds.

Sergi Arola Gastro (p149) Home kitchen and cooking laboratory of Catalan wunderkind.

Estado Puro (p109) Tapas that push the boundaries of nouvelle Spanish cuisine.

Bazaar (p129) Style, substance and celebrities at budget prices.

Mercado de San Miguel (p54) Arguably Madrid's most varied gastronomic space.

Best Budget

Viva La Vida (p71)

Gastromaquia (p129)

Casa Mingo (p150)

Casa Revuelta (p56)

La Gloria de Montera (p82)

Best Midrange

La Musa (p126)

Vi Cool (p81)

Naïa Restaurante (p68)

Albur (p126)

Best Top End

Santceloni (p151)

Zalacaín (p151)

La Terraza del Casino (p81)

Cocido a la Madrileña

Taberna La Bola (p57)

Malacatín (p70)

Lhardy (p82)

Restaurante Los Galayos (p56)

Roast Lamb or Suckling Pig

Posada de la Villa (p68)

El Pedrusco (p150)

Restaurante Los Galayos (p56)

Tortilla de Patatas

Juana La Loca (p68)

Txirimiri (p68)

Bodega de la Ardosa (p150)

Las Tortillas de Gabino (p149)

Croquetas

Bar Melo's (p69)

Casa Julio (p127)

Casa Labra (p83)

Casa Alberto (p81)

Patatas Bravas

Las Bravas (p83)

Le Cabrera (p129)

Bodega de la Ardosa (p127)

Huevos Rotos

Almendro 13 (p71)

Casa Lucio (p68)

Rice & Paella

Costa Blanca Arrocería (p150)

Casa Perico (p126)

Albur (p126)

La Paella de la Reina (p130)

Chocolate con Churros

Chocolatería de San Ginés (p58)

Chocolatería Valor (p59)

El Brillante (p109)

Best for Vegetarians & Vegans

La isla del Tesoro (p127)

El Estragón (p70)

La Galette (p116)

Restaurante Integral Artemisa (p83)

Viva la Vida (p71)

Best Tapas

Biotza (p115)

Txacolina (p71)

Juana La Loca (p68)

La Colonial de Goya (p116)

Baco y Beto (p129)

Bocaito (p130)

Best Cooking Courses & Tours

Alambique (p130)

Letango Tours (p205)

Apunto – Centro Cultural del Gusto (p130)

Spanish Tapas Madrid (p205)

Kitchen Club (p130)

Cooking Club (p130)

Drinking & Nightlife

Nights in the Spanish capital are the stuff of legend. They're invariably long and loud most nights of the week, rising to a deafening crescendo as the weekend nears. And what Ernest Hemingway wrote of the city in the 1930s remains true to this day: 'Nobody goes to bed in Madrid until they have killed the night.'

Killing the Night

Madrid has more bars than any other city in the world, six, in fact, for every 100 inhabitants, and, wherever you are in town, there'll be a bar close by. But bars are only half the story. On any night in Madrid, first drinks, tapas and wines then segue easily into cocktail bars and the nightclubs that have brought such renown to Madrid as the unrivalled scene of all-night fiestas.

Cafes

Madrid's thriving cafe culture dates back to the early and mid-20th century, when old-style coffee houses formed the centrepiece of the country's intellectual life. Although many such cafes were torn down in the rush to modernisation, many that recall those times remain, with period architecture and an agreeably formal atmosphere; their clientele long ago broadened to encompass the entire cross-section of modern Madrid society. Added into the mix are some terrific and usually more casual modern cafes, although here, too, the principle remains the same: they're at once social and cultural meeting places, and places to escape from the often frenetic pace of city life.

THE SECRET LANGUAGE OF BEER

In the majority of bars you won't have much choice when it comes to beer, but thankfully Madrid's flagship beer, Mahou, goes down well and comes as both draught and bottled. Cruzcampo is a lighter beer. Otherwise, two Catalan companies, Damm and San Miguel, each produce about 15% of all Spain's beer. The most common order is a *caña*, a small glass of *cerveza de barril* (draught beer). A larger beer (about 300ml), more common in the hipper bars and clubs, usually comes in a *tubo* (a long, straight glass). The equivalent of a pint is a *pinta*, while a *jarra* refers to a jug of beer.

Cocktail Bars

The mojito (a rum-based drink with sugar, fresh mint, crushed ice and lemon) may have its origins in Cuba, but it has arguably become Madrid's favourite adopted son. As a consequence, the reputation of the city's cocktail bars can rise and fall according to the quality of its mojitos, and those that have lasted the distance have usually done so on the back of a mighty fine mojito. Other cocktails of breathtaking variety are also possible in the city's cocktail bars that range from slick and trendy temples to all that's new to storied bastions of tradition where bow-tied waiters and cocktail makers are as celebrated as the *famosos* (celebrities) who have visited down through the decades.

GETTING HOME

Madrid's extensive metro system can get you most places, but it grinds to a halt between 2am and 6.05am. If you're trying to get back to your hotel at these hours, there are two main options (apart from walking). The first is a taxi – although these hours attract a higher flag fall (€2.20 to €3.10) and per-kilometre rate (€1.20) than during daylight hours, it should rarely cost you more than €10 to get back to your hotel. The other option, the night buses known as *búhos* (owls), offer more than two dozen routes fanning out across the city from Plaza de la Cibeles. See p202 for further details.

Nightclubs

People here live fully for the moment. Today's encounter can be tomorrow's distant memory, perhaps in part because Madrid's nightclubs (also known as *discotecas*) rival any in the world. The best places are usually the megaclubs, with designer decor, designer people and, sometimes, with enough space for numerous dance floors, each with their own musical style to suit your mood. Themed nights are all the rage, so it's always worth checking in advance to see what flavour of the night takes your fancy.

Admission prices vary widely, depending on the time of night you enter, the way you're dressed and the number of people inside. The standard entry fee is €12, which usually includes the first drink, although megaclubs and swankier places charge a few euros more.

Drinking & Nightlife by Neighbourhood

- **Plaza Mayor & Royal Madrid** Plenty of nightclubs in the city centre.
- **La Latina & Lavapiés** Terrific for wine bars and fortifying tapas.
- **Sol, Santa Ana & Huertas** The epicentre of Madrid's night-time action.
- **El Retiro & the Art Museums** A daytime *barrio* (district) with little happening after dark.
- **Salamanca** A small collection of nightclubs.
- **Malasaña & Chueca** All-night neighbourhoods with terrific cocktail bars (Chueca) and fabulous cafes (Malasaña).
- **Parque del Oeste & Northern Madrid** Some nightlife focal points but thinly spread.

NEED TO KNOW

Opening Hours

- Local watering holes that serve as centres of community life usually open throughout the day from breakfast to last drinks.
- Trendier bars often get going around 8pm and stay open until 1am or 2am during the week, 3am on weekends.
- Nightclubs don't usually open until midnight or 1am and stay open until 6am. Some open all week, others from Thursday to Saturday.

Top Tips

- If you plan to stay out the whole night, sleeping the siesta the afternoon before could be the key to your staying power.
- Another essential element to surviving the long Madrid night is to never drink on an empty stomach – fill up on tapas or a late dinner wherever possible.
- Most *madrileños* (people from Madrid) take a localised approach to a night out – once they've begun to drink and otherwise settle into the night, they tend to move from one place to the next within the same *barrio*.
- Even those nightclubs that let you in for free will play catch up with hefty prices for drinks, so don't plan your night around looking for the cheapest ticket.

Lonely Planet's Top Choices

Café Comercial (p132) Madrid's most evocative old-world literary cafe.

The Roof (p84) Smooth bar for sophisticates high above Huertas.

La Venencia (p84) Timeless Huertas sherry bar that hasn't changed in decades.

Museo Chicote (p136) One of Europe's most celebrated cocktail bars.

Teatro Joy Eslava (p58) The pick of Madrid's city-centre nightclubs.

Chocolatería de San Ginés (p58) A Madrid institution whatever the hour.

Best Grand Old Cafes

Café-Restaurante el Espejo (p133)

Gran Café de Gijón (p133)

Café del Círculo de Bellas Artes (p84)

Café Manuela (p133)

Café de Ruiz (p134)

Cafe De Oriente (p58)

Best Mojitos

Café Belén (p136)

El Eucalipto (p72)

Dos Gardenias (p85)

Delic (p72)

Best Rooftop Terrazas (Open-air Bars)

La Terraza del Urban (p84)

Splash Óscar (p136)

Gaudeamus Café (p72)

Hotel de Las Letras (p170)

Best Cocktail Bars

Del Diego (p136)

Le Cabrera (p136)

Bar Cock (p136)

Mercado de la Reina Gin Club (p137)

La Escalera de Jacob (p74)

Real Café Bernabéu (p152)

Best Nightclubs

Kapital (p109)

Stella (p84)

Morocco (p135)

Why Not? (p138)

Best Gay & Lesbian

Café Acuarela (p137)

Why Not? (p138)

Black & White (p138)

Club 54 Studio (p138)

Liquid Madrid (p138)

Best Sherry & Wine Bars

Taberna Tempranillo (p72)

Casa Alberto (p81)

Taberna de Dolores (p85)

Bonnano (p73)

Best Squares for Open-Air Drinking

Plaza de Santa Ana (p80)

Paseo de la Castellana (p152)

Paseo de los Recoletos (p132)

Plaza de Olavide (p150)

Plaza de Oriente (p51)

Plaza de Chueca (p132)

Plaza de la Paja (p65)

Plaza Mayor (p48)

Best Old Tabernas

Casa Alberto (p81)

Casa Revuelta (p56)

Casa Labra (p83)

Antigua Casa Angel Sierra (p137)

Flamenco performance at Casa Patas (p73)

Entertainment

Madrid has a happening live music scene which owes a lot to the city's role as the cultural capital of the Spanish-speaking world. There's flamenco, world-class jazz and a host of performers of whom you may never have heard but may just be Spain's next big thing. For a dose of high culture, there's opera and zarzuela (satirical musical comedy).

NEED TO KNOW

Reservations

- Concert tickets for live music should always be made in advance – check venue websites for booking details.
- Mostly you can buy theatre tickets at the box office on the day of the performance, but for new or weekend shows book ahead. Try Taquilla Ultimo Minuto for discounted tickets.
- Tickets for Real Madrid football matches usually go on sale the Monday before a game at Gate 42 of the stadium on Calle de Conche de Espina. The all-important telephone number for booking tickets (which you later pick up at Gate 42) is ☎902 324 324, which only works if you're calling from within Spain.
- Tickets for most jazz clubs go on sale an hour or two before the scheduled performance start.

Opening Hours

- Theatre box offices are generally open from about 10am until 1pm and again from 5pm until the start of the evening's show.

Useful Websites

- In addition to checking the websites of individual live music venues, check out www.lanochenevivo.com.
- For a history of *zarzuela* in English, translations of *zarzuela* songs and storylines, CD and DVD reviews, and a critical look at current *zarzuela* (satirical musical comedy) shows, check out the terrific website zarzuela.net.

Flamenco

Madrid has numerous venues with nightly live performances, although seeing flamenco in Madrid can be expensive: at the *tablaos* (restaurants where flamenco is performed) expect to pay at least €30 just to see the show. The admission price usually includes your first drink, but you pay extra for meals (up to €50 per person) that, put simply, are rarely worth the money. For that reason, we suggest you eat elsewhere and simply pay for the show (after having bought tickets in advance), on the understanding that you won't have a front-row seat. For more on flamenco, see p199.

Jazz

Madrid was one of Europe's jazz capitals in the 1920s. It's taken a while, but it's once again among Europe's elite for live jazz. There's only a small number of places devoted exclusively to jazz, but the quality is world-class and the range of styles includes the kind of classic jazz designed to keep the purist happy as well as Latin, nu jazz and countless variations on the theme. Beyond the signature jazz venues, numerous multigenre live music stages broaden out the experience, often with a weekly jazz jam session. November's Festival Jazz Madrid is a great time for jazz enthusiasts to be in town.

Other Live Music

Madrid made its name as a live music city back in the 1980s, when drugs and rock music fuelled the decade-long fiesta known as *la movida madrileña* (the Madrid scene). At the height of *la movida*, an estimated 300 rock bands were performing in the bars of Malasaña alone. While

BOOKING CONCERT & THEATRE TICKETS

Outlets for online tickets to theatre and other live shows include:

- **Caixa Catalunya's Tel-Entrada** (☎902 101 212; www.telentrada.com)
- **El Corte Inglés** (p89) Click on 'Entradas' on its website.
- **Entradas.com** (www.entradas.com)
- **Fnac** (p61) Click on 'Entradas' on its website; it's mostly modern, big-name music groups.
- **Localidades Galicia** (☎91 531 91 31; www.bullfightticketsmadrid.com; Plaza del Carmen 1; ⏰9.30am-1pm & 4.30-7pm Mon-Sat, 9.30am-1pm Sun; Ⓜ Sol)
- **Servicaixa** (www.servicaixa.com) You can also purchase tickets in Servicaixa ATMs.
- **Taquilla Ultimo Minuto** (Map p242; www.taquillaultimominuto.com; Plaza del Carmen 1; ⏰5-8pm Wed, Thu & Sun, to 10pm Fri & Sat) Last-minute theatre tickets at up to 50% discount.
- **Ticketmaster** (www.ticketmaster.es) Tickets for major shows and sports.

LONELY PLANET / GETTY IMAGES ©

jazz at Populart (p87)

rock remains a Madrid mainstay and the doors of a handful of classic venues remain open, the live music scene now encompasses every genre imaginable. Many venues double as clubs where DJs follow the live acts, making it possible to start off the night with a great concert and stay on to party until late.

Classical Music & Opera

Madrid loves to party, but scratch beneath the surface and you'll find a thriving city of high culture, with venues dedicated to year-round opera and classical music. Orchestras from all over Europe perform regularly here, but Madrid's own **Orquesta Sinfónica** (www.osm.es) also performs (or accompanies) in the **Teatro Real** (Map p234; ☎902 24 48 48; www.teatro-real.com; Plaza de Oriente; Ⓜ Ópera) or Auditorio Nacional de Música (p153). The **Banda Sinfónica Municipal de Madrid** (www.muni madrid.es/bandasinfonica) plays at the Teatro Monumental (p87).

La Zarzuela

What began in the late 17th century as a way to amuse King Felipe IV and his court has become Spain's own unique theatre style. With a light-hearted combination of music and dance, and a focus on everyday people's problems, *zarzuelas* quickly became popular in Madrid, which remains the genre's capital. Although you're likely to have trouble following the storyline (*zarzuelas* are notoriously full of local references and jokes), seeing a *zarzuela* gives an entertaining look into local culture. The best place to catch a show is the Teatro de la Zarzuela (p87).

Dance

Spain's lively **Compañía Nacional de Danza** (☎91 354 50 53; www.cndanza.net) performs worldwide and has won accolades for its marvellous technicality and original choreography. Madrid is also home to the **Ballet Nacional de España** (☎91 517 99 99; balletnacional.mcu.es), a classical company known for its unique mix of ballet and traditional Spanish styles, including flamenco and *zarzuela*. When in town, both companies perform at venues that include the Teatro Real (p52) or Teatro de la Zarzuela (p87). One performer who frequently performs in Madrid is Sara Baras (www.sarabaras.com), a Cádiz-born performer whose soul-stirring flamenco ballet is unique.

Theatre

Madrid's theatre scene really gets going in autumn. Most shows are in Spanish and ticket prices start at around €10 and run up to €50.

Film

Plenty of cinemas offer *versión original* (VO; original version) films, which are shown in the original language with Spanish subtitles; otherwise foreign-language films are dubbed in mainstream cinemas. The highest concentrations of Spanish-language cinemas are on Gran Vía and Calle Fuencarral, between the Glorieta de Bilbao and Glorieta de Quevedo.

Spectator Sports

El Estadio Santiago Bernabéu (p148) is one of the world's great football arenas; watching a game here alongside 80,000 passionate Madridistas (Real Madrid supporters) will send chills down your spine. If you're lucky enough to be in town when Real Madrid wins a major trophy, head to Plaza de la Cibeles and wait for the all-night party to begin.

WHAT'S ON

- **EsMadrid Magazine** (www.esmadrid.com) Monthly tourist office listings.
- **Guía del Ocio** (www.guiadelocio.com) Weekly magazine available for €1 at news kiosks.
- **In Madrid** (www.in-madrid.com) Free monthly English-language expat publication.
- **La Netro** (www.madrid.lanetro.com) Comprehensive online guide.
- **Metropoli** (www.elmundo.es/metropoli) *El Mundo* newspaper's Friday supplement magazine.
- **On Madrid** (www.elpais.com) *El País* newspaper's Friday supplement.
- **What's on When** (www.whatsonwhen.com) The Madrid page covers the highlights of sport and cultural activities.

BULLFIGHTING

Love it or loathe it, bullfighting is a national institution. In the afternoons there are generally six bulls and three star *toreros* dressed in the dazzling *traje de luces* (suit of lights).

Many animal lovers feel bullfighting is immoral, and bullfights are vehemently opposed by numerous animal-welfare organisations, among them the World Society for the Protection of Animals (www.wspa.org.uk), the League Against Cruel Sports (www.leagueagainstcruelsports.org) and the Madrid-based Equanimal (www.equanimal.org). Although some regions of Spain, notably Catalonia, have banned bullfighting, there are no signs that Madrid will follow suit. Bullfighting's popularity has waned in the last few decades, especially among younger Spaniards, with some polls showing that three-quarters of Spaniards have no interest in the sport.

Madrid's other team, Atlético de Madrid (www.clubatleticodemadrid.com) has a cult following, attracts passionate support and fans of the *rojiblancos* (red-and-whites) declare theirs to be the real Madrid team.

Entertainment by Neighbourhood

- **Plaza Mayor & Royal Madrid** Plenty of cinemas, theatres and live music venues.
- **La Latina & Lavapiés** A small handful of flamenco and live music venues.
- **Sol, Santa Ana & Huertas** One of the best *barrios* for jazz, flamenco, theatre and live music.
- **El Retiro & the Art Museum** Football celebrations but not much else.
- **Salamanca** Upmarket nightclubs scattered thinly.
- **Malasana & Chueca** Quirky theatres and grungy live music stages.
- **Parque del Oeste & Northern Madrid** A heady mix of football and classical music.

Lonely Planet's Top Choices

Café Central (p86) One of the best jazz clubs on earth.

Sala El Sol (p86) Mythic Madrid stage for rock and other live acts.

Villa Rosa (p86) Top-notch flamenco behind an extravagantly tiled facade.

Estadio Santiago Bernabéu (p148) Legendary home stadium of Real Madrid.

Teatro de la Zarzuela (p87) Home theatre for Spain's home-grown operatic theatre.

Best Flamenco Venues

Corral de la Morería (p73)

Cardamomo (p87)

Las Tablas (p59)

Las Carboneras (p59)

Casa Patas (p73)

Café de Chinitas (p59)

Best Flamenco Festivals

Festival Flamenco (p20)

Suma Flamenca (p21)

Best for Flamenco Atmosphere

El Callejón (p85)

Almonte (p117)

El Rincón de Jeréz (p116)

Best Flamenco Beyond the Tablaos

BarCo (p139)

Clamores (p152)

ContraClub (p73)

El Juglar (p74)

Galileo Galilei (p152)

Best Jazz Clubs

Populart (p87)

El Berlín (p59)

El Junco Jazz Club (p136)

El Despertar (p74)

Segundo Jazz (p152)

Bogui Jazz (p139)

Best Jazz in Other Venues

Jazz Bar (p85)

BarCo (p139)

Clamores (p152)

Casa Pueblo (p87)

La Boca del Lobo (p87)

Zanzibar (p139)

Best Live Music Venues

Moby Dick (p152)

Café la Palma (p138)

Clamores (p152)

Costello Café & Niteclub (p86)

Honky Tonk (p152)

BarCo (p139)

Best for Classical Music & Opera

Teatro Real (p52)

Auditorio Nacional de Música (p153)

Fundación Juan March (p118)

Teatro Monumental (p87)

Best Theatres

Teatro Español (p87)

Teatro Alfil (p139)

Teatros del Canal (p152)

Teatro Pavón (p74)

Teatro Valle-Inclán (p74)

Shopping

Our favourite aspect of shopping in Madrid is the city's small boutiques and quirky shops. Often run by the same families for generations, they counter the overcommercialisation of mass-produced Spanish culture with everything from fashions to handcrafted abanicos (Spanish fans) and old-style ceramics to rope-soled espadrilles or gourmet Spanish food and wine.

Fashion

The world's most prestigious catwalks are clamouring for Spanish designers and with good reason. Spain's fashion industry, with Madrid as its capital, has a pedigree of bold colours and eye-catching designs born in the creative outpouring of *la movida madrileña* (the Madrid scene) in the 1980s. As such, even a cursory glance in the shop windows of Salamanca, Malasaña and Chueca in particular can be a revelation, confirming that there's so much more to *la moda española* (Spanish fashion) than Zara and Mango.

Souvenirs & Handicrafts

You could buy your friends back home a vividly coloured flamenco dress of the kind that hangs from the doorway of many a downtown Madrid souvenir shop. Then again, you could instead opt for a touch more class and take home an artfully designed *papier-mâché* figurine, a carefully crafted ceramic bowl made by the family potters of central Spain, or an intricately designed Spanish fan. And then there are guitars favoured by everyone from the Beatles to flamenco greats, stunning Spanish shawls, dresses from the shops where the flamenco greats get their gear...

Gourmet Foods

Nowhere is Spanish cuisine more accessible than in the city's purveyors of Spanish foods. At these places – at times traditional, at others representative of the revolution sweeping Spanish cooking – you can point to your favourite *jamón* (ham) or tub of olives and in no time they'll be packaged up and ready for that Retiro picnic or flight back home. Some are small specialist stores where the packaging is often as exquisite as the tastes on offer. Elsewhere, Madrid's markets have been transformed into vibrant spaces where you can eat as well as shop. Either way, there's no better place to understand Madrid's obsession with fine foods.

Shopping by Neighbourhood

- **Plaza Mayor & Royal Madrid** A little bit of everything.
- **La Latina & Lavapiés** Offbeat boutiques and a fabulous Sunday flea market.
- **Sol, Santa Ana & Huertas** Some of Madrid's best souvenirs.
- **El Retiro & the Art Museums** Museum gift and bookshops are the main drawcard.
- **Salamanca** The home of Spanish fashion.
- **Malasana & Chueca** Retro fashions (Malasaña) alongside more upmarket style (Chueca).
- **Parque del Oeste & Northern Madrid** Outposts of tradition aimed at a local market.

Lonely Planet's Top Choices

El Rastro (p66) Europe's largest flea market and Madrid's favourite Sunday pastime.

Mercado de Fuencarral (p140) Icon of retro Malasaña and its passion for down-and-dirty streetwear.

El Arco Artesanía (p60) Modern souvenirs with an art gallery aesthetic.

Helena Rohner (p75) Designer jewellery from catwalk to casual.

Agatha Ruiz de la Prada (p118) Candy bright colours from a Madrid fashion household name.

Antigua Casa Talavera (p60) Handpainted ceramics from small family kilns.

Best Spanish Fashion Icons

Camper (p118)

Custo Barcelona (p140)

Elisa Bracci (p142)

Loewe (p142)

Manolo Blahnik (p118)

Purificación García (p120)

Best Souvenirs & Handicrafts

Antigüedades Hom (p153)

Gil (p88)

México (p88)

Casa de Diego (p87)

Best Gourmet Food & Wine

Mantequería Bravo (p119)

Lhardy (p82)

Mercado de San Miguel (p54)

Bombonerías Santa (p119)

María Cabello (p88)

Oriol Balaguer (p118)

Best Children's Shops

Así (p60)

Biblioketa (p143)

Cuarto de Juegos (p119)

Bazar Matey (p153)

MacChinine (p143)

Best for English-language Books

Pasajes Librería Internacional (p153)

Petra's International Bookshop (p61)

J&J Books & Coffee (p141)

Altaïr (p153)

Fnac (p61)

Best Shopping Streets

Calle de Serrano

Calle de Fuencarral

Calle de José Ortega y Gasset

NEED TO KNOW

Opening Hours

➡ 10am to 2pm & 5pm to 8pm or 10am to 8pm Monday to Saturday.

➡ Some shops open are on Sundays.

Sales & Opening Hours

➡ The peak shopping season is during *las rebajas*, the annual winter and summer sales, when prices are slashed on just about everything. The winter sales begin around 7 January, just after Three Kings' Day, and last well into February. Summer sales begin in early July and last into August.

Taxes & Refunds

➡ Visitors are entitled to a refund of the IVA (value-added tax) on purchases costing more than €90.15 from any shop if the goods are taken out of the European Union (EU) within three months. Ask the shop for a cashback refund form at the point of purchase, then present the form at the customs booth for IVA refunds when you depart from Spain (or elsewhere from the EU).

Explore Madrid

MADRID'S **TOP SIGHTS**

Neighbourhoods at a Glance

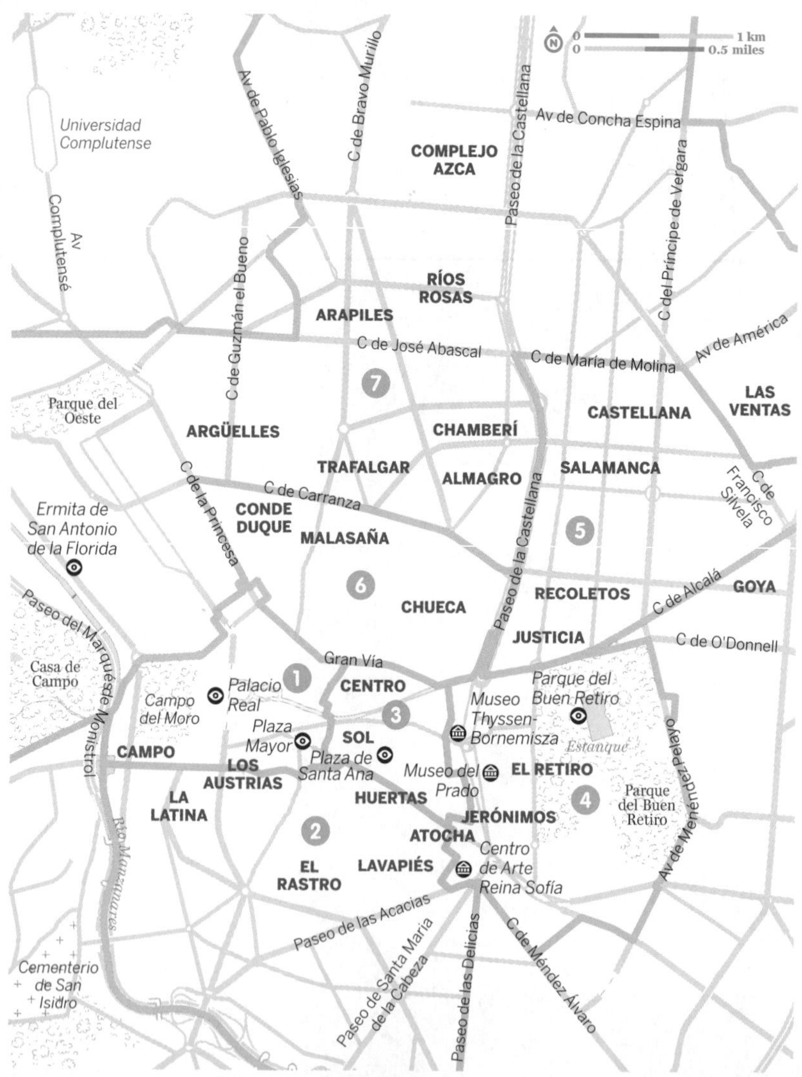

1 Plaza Mayor & Royal Madrid (p46)

The bustling, compact and medieval heart of the city is where Madrid's story began and the city became the seat of royal power. It's also where the splendour of imperial Spain was at its most ostentatious – think expansive palaces, ancient churches, elegant squares and imposing convents. It's an architectural highpoint of the city, with plenty of fine eating and shopping options thrown in for good measure.

2 La Latina & Lavapiés (p62)

La Latina combines Madrid's best selection of tapas bars, fine little boutiques and a medieval streetscape studded with elegant churches. Graceful Calle de la Cava Baja could just be our favourite street for tapas in town. Down the hill, Lavapiés is one of the city's oldest *barrios* (districts) and the heart of multicultural Madrid. Spanning the two neighbourhoods is the Sunday flea market of El Rastro.

3 Sol, Santa Ana & Huertas (p76)

These tightly packed streets are best known for nightlife that never seems to abate once the sun goes down, but there's so much more here than immediately meets the eye. At the Sol end of things, Madrid's beating heart, you'll find the sum total of all Madrid's personalities, with fabulous shopping, eating and entertainment options.

4 El Retiro & The Art Museums (p90)

From the Plaza de la Cibeles in the north, the buildings arrayed along the Paseo del Prado read like a roll-call of Madrid's most popular attractions. Temples to high culture include the Museo del Prado, Museo Thyssen-Bornemisza and Centro de Arte Reina Sofía which rank among the world's most prestigious art galleries. Up the hill to the east, the marvellous Parque del Buen Retiro helps to make this one of the most attractive areas of Madrid in which to spend your time.

5 Salamanca (p110)

The *barrio* of Salamanca is Madrid's most exclusive quarter. Like nowhere else in the capital, this is where stately mansions set back from the street share *barrio* space with designer boutiques from the big local and international fashionistas. Salamanca's sprinkling of fine restaurants, designer tapas bars and niche museums are also very much at home here.

6 Malasaña & Chueca (p121)

The two inner-city *barrios* of Malasaña and Chueca are where Madrid gets up close and personal. Here, it's more an experience of life as it's lived by *madrileños* (people from Madrid) than the traditional traveller experience of ticking off from a list of wonderful, if more static, attractions. These are *barrios* with attitude and personality, *barrios* where Madrid's famed nightlife, shopping and eating choices live and breathe and take you under the skin of the city.

7 Parque del Oeste & Northern Madrid (p144)

Madrid's north contains some of Madrid's most attractive *barrios,* including Chamberí which is a wonderful escape from downtown and offers unique insights into how locals enjoy their city. Parque del Oeste is a gorgeous expanse of green, while a series of fascinating sights – from Goya frescoes to an Egyptian temple – add considerable appeal.

Plaza Mayor & Royal Madrid

Neighbourhood Top Five

❶ Immersing yourself in the street life that courses across the cobblestones or taking up residence at an outdoor table surrounding the **Plaza Mayor** (p48), all the while enjoying one of Madrid's grandest architectural tableaus.

❷ Soaking up the grandeur at the **Palacio Real** (p49), Madrid's seat of royal power.

❸ Spending time in **Plaza de la Villa** (p53), one of Madrid's most architecturally rich corners.

❹ Stopping by for Madrid's best *chocolate con churros* at the **Chocolatería de San Ginés** (p58).

❺ Learning why locals are obsessed about food at **Mercado de San Miguel.** (p54).

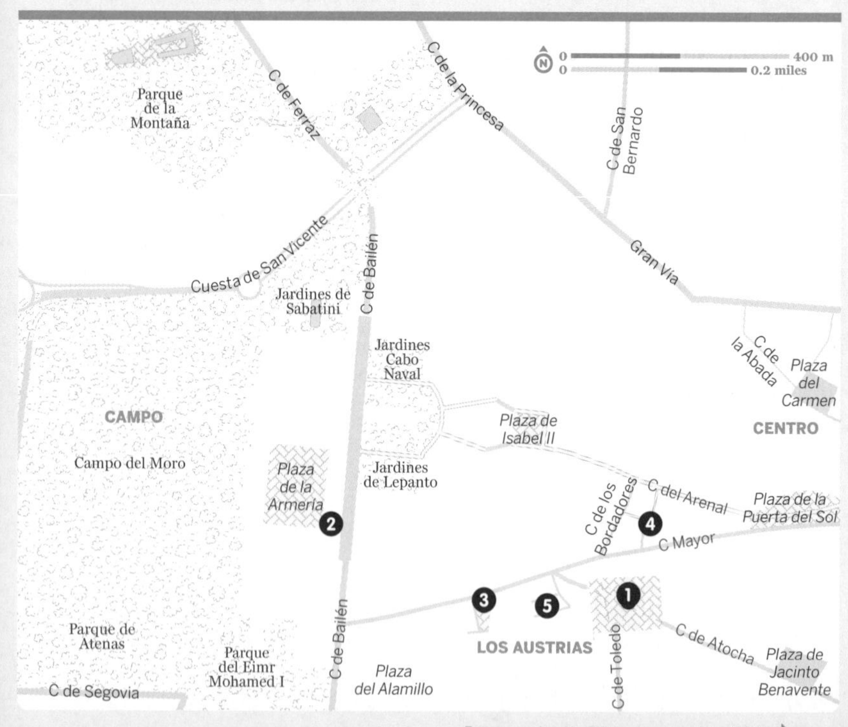

For more detail of this area see Map p234

Explore: Plaza Mayor & Royal Madrid

The Plaza Mayor is the hub of Madrid's most medieval quarter, an area known as Madrid de los Austrias, in reference to the Habsburg dynasty, which ruled Spain from 1517 to 1700. The plaza is a place both to admire and to get your bearings, the place where so many explorations of the neighbourhood (and wider city) begin. That's because it is at once the hub of neighbourhood life and the topographical highpoint of the *barrio* (district).

Build your day exploring this neighbourhood around this and other squares, which are lovely and quiet in the morning, and lively and pretty in the soft light of late afternoon. Running close to its northern edge, Calle Mayor connects Plaza Mayor with the rest of the neighbourhood, running down the hill past the wonderful Mercado de San Miguel to Plaza de la Villa, with tangled lanes of medieval origin twisting away on either side. Away to the north is the Plaza de Oriente, royal palace and cathedral. Linger in the plazas, which are as much touchstones of local life as stunning architectural showpieces.

Although it's no hard-and-fast rule, the shops, restaurants, bars and nightclubs tend to be concentrated at the eastern end of the neighbourhood, close to the Plaza Mayor, while the architectural highlights are more evenly spread.

Local Life

- **Hangout** The broad appeal of the neighbourhood is summed up by its two favourite meeting places: the stunningly converted Mercado de San Miguel (p54) and the timeless Chocolatería de San Ginés (p58).
- **Meeting Points** The equestrian statue of Felipe III in the centre of Plaza Mayor was moved here in 1848 and has ever since been a favoured meeting point for locals who arrange to meet 'under the balls of the horse'.
- **Shopping** Ignore the tacky souvenir shops that overflow from shopfronts across the centre: the small artisan shops on Plaza Mayor and elsewhere are well worth tracking down.
- **Nightclubs** Watch out for themed nights which might make Monday a better night to dance than the weekend.

Getting There & Away

- **Metro** A short step from Plaza Mayor, Sol metro station is one of the most useful in Madrid, with lines 1, 2 and 3 all passing through.
- **Metro** Ópera (lines 2 and 5) is another useful neighbourhood station – line 2 can carry you to the Paseo del Prado (leaving a short walk to the galleries), Parque del Buen Retiro or Salamanca in no time.

Lonely Planet's Top Tip

Treat Plaza Mayor as a place to soak up the atmosphere, and order a coffee or a glass of wine to justify your presence at one of the outdoor tables. But be aware it's expensive. Come here in the morning when the pressure to order something more substantial is minimal.

Best Places to Eat

- Mercado de San Miguel (p54)
- Restaurante Sobrino de Botín (p56)
- Taberna La Bola (p57)
- Casa Revuelta (p56)
- La Mar del Alabardero (p56)
- Restaurante Los Galayos (p56)

For reviews, see p54 

Best Places to Drink

- Café del Real (p58)
- Café de Oriente (p58)
- Anticafé (p58)
- Chocolatería de San Ginés (p58)
- Chocolatería Valor (p59)

For reviews, see p58

Best Places to Shop

- Antigua Casa Talavera (p60)
- El Arco Artesania (p60)
- Así (p60)
- Casa Hernanz (p60)
- El Flamenco Vive (p60)
- Maty (p60)

For reviews, see p60 

TOP SIGHTS
PLAZA MAYOR

It's easy to fall in love with Madrid in the Plaza Mayor. This is the monumental heart of the city and the grand stage for so many of the city's most important historical events. Here, Madrid's relentless energy courses across its cobblestones beneath ochre-hued apartments, wrought-iron balconies, frescoes and stately spires. This juxtaposition of endlessly moving city life and more static architectural attractions is Madrid in microcosm.

DON'T MISS...

- A Sense of History
- Spires & Slate Roofs
- Real Casa de la Panadería
- Markets

PRACTICALITIES

- Map p234
- Plaza Mayor
- M Sol

A Grand History

Ah, the history the plaza has seen! Inaugurated in 1619, its first public ceremony was suitably auspicious – the beatification of San Isidro Labrador (St Isidro the Farm Labourer), Madrid's patron saint. Thereafter it was as if all that was controversial about Spain took place in this square. Bullfights, often in celebration of royal weddings or births, with royalty watching on from the balconies and up to 50,000 people crammed into the plaza, were a recurring theme until 1878. Far more notorious were the *autos-da-fé* (the ritual condemnations of heretics during the Spanish Inquisition) followed by executions – burnings at the stake and deaths by garrotte on the north side of the square, hangings to the south. To see the plaza's epic history told in pictures, check out the carvings on the circular seats beneath the lamp posts.

A Less-Grand History

Not all the plaza's activities were grand events and, just as it is now surrounded by shops, it was once filled with food vendors. In 1673, King Carlos II issued an edict allowing the vendors to raise tarpaulins above their stalls to protect their wares and themselves from the refuse and raw sewage that people habitually tossed out of the windows above! Well into the 20th century, trams ran through Plaza Mayor.

Spires & Slate Roofs

The plaza was designed in the 17th century by Juan Gómez de Mora who, following the dominant style of the day, adopted a Herrerian style (named after Juan de Herrera, one of the towering architectural figures of the Spanish Renaissance). The slate spires and roofs are the most obvious expression of this pleasing and distinctively Madrid style, and their sombre hues are nicely offset by the warm colours of the uniformly ochre apartments and their 237 wrought-iron balconies.

Real Casa de la Panadería

The exquisite frescoes of the 17th-century Real Casa de la Panadería (Royal Bakery) rank among Madrid's more eye-catching sights. The present frescoes date to just 1992 and are the work of artist Carlos Franco, who chose images from the signs of the zodiac and gods (eg Cybele) to provide a stunning backdrop for the plaza. The frescoes were inaugurated to coincide with Madrid's 1992 spell as European Capital of Culture. The building now houses the city's main tourist office.

Markets

On Sunday mornings the plaza's arcaded perimeter is taken over by traders in old coins, banknotes and stamps. In December and early January the plaza is occupied by a hugely popular Christmas market selling fairground kitsch and nativity scenes of real quality.

DAVID TOMLINSON / GETTY IMAGES ©

TOP SIGHTS
PALACIO REAL

You can almost imagine how the eyes of Felipe V, the first of the Bourbon kings, lit up when the *alcázar* (Muslim-era fortress) burned down in 1734 on Madrid's most exclusive perch of real estate. His plan? Build a palace that would dwarf all its European counterparts. The resulting 2800-room royal palace never quite attained such a scale, but it's still an Italianate baroque architectural landmark of arresting beauty, an intriguing mix of the extravagant and restrained but unmistakeable elegance.

History's Tale

A little understanding of the Palacio Real's genesis and subsequent development will enhance your appreciation of what you see. The Italian architect Filippo Juvara (1678–1736), who had made his name building the Basilica di Superga and the Palazzo di Stupinigi in Turin, was called in to try and fulfil Felipe V's dream, but, like Felipe, he died without bringing the project to fruition. Upon Juvara's death, another Italian, Giovanni Battista Sacchetti, took over, finishing the job in 1764.

Farmacia Real

The Farmacia Real (Royal Pharmacy), the first set of rooms to the right at the southern end of the Plaza de la Armería courtyard, contains a formidable collection of medicine jars and stills for mixing royal concoctions; the royals were either paranoid or decidedly sickly.

DON'T MISS...

- History's Tale
- Farmacia Real
- Plaza de la Armería
- Salon del Trono
- Gasparini & Porcelana
- Comedor de Gala
- Jardines de Sabatini

PRACTICALITIES

- Map p234
- ☎91 454 88 00
- www.patrimonionacional.es
- Calle de Bailén
- adult/concession €10/5, guide/audioguide/pamphlet €7/4/1, EU citizens free 5-8pm Wed & Thu
- ⏰10am-8pm Apr-Sep, to 6pm Oct-Mar
- Ⓜ Ópera

PART-TIME PALACE

The Palacio Real is occasionally closed for state ceremonies and official receptions (the only way you'll know is if you turn up and it's closed), but the present king is rarely in residence – he and his family live in a smaller, less ostentatious palace just outside Madrid.

There are numerous places to have a drink close to the Palacio Real, among them La Mar del Alabardero (p56), Taberna del Alabardero (p56) and Taberna La Bola (p57). If you're after a coffee, there's no finer perch in Madrid than the outdoor tables of Café de Oriente (p58) that look out towards the palace. Not far away, Café del Real (p58) is one of our favourite places in Madrid for coffee, cake or a mojito.

BEST VIEWS

Some of the best views of the Palacio Real are from the northern end of the Plaza de Oriente, but less well known are the superlative views from the western side, the lush ornamental gardens of Campo del Moro.

Plaza de la Armería

The Plaza de la Armería (Plaza de Armas; Plaza of the Armoury) courtyard puts the sheer scale of the palace into perspective, and it's from here that Madrid's cathedral (Catedral de Nuestra Señora de la Almudena) takes on its most pleasing aspect. The colourful changing of the guard in full parade dress takes place at noon on the first Wednesday of every month (except August and September) between the palace and the cathedral, with a less extravagant changing of the guard inside the palace compound at the Puerta del Príncipe every Wednesday from 11am to 2pm. The plaza also provides access to the Armería Real (Royal Armoury), a hoard of weapons and striking suits of armour, mostly dating from the 16th and 17th centuries.

Salon del Trono

From the northern end of the Plaza de la Armería, the main stairway, a grand statement of imperial power, leads to the royal apartments and eventually to the Salón del Trono (Throne Room). The room is nauseatingly lavish with its crimson-velvet wall coverings complemented by a ceiling painted by the dramatic Venetian baroque master, Tiepolo, who was a favourite of Carlos III.

Gasparini & Porcelana

Close to the Throne Room, the Salón de Gasparini (Gasparini Room) has an exquisite stucco ceiling and walls resplendent with embroidered silks. The aesthetic may be different in the Sala de Porcelana (Porcelain Room), but the aura of extravagance continues with myriad pieces from the one-time Retiro porcelain factory screwed into the walls.

Comedor de Gala

In the midst of such extravagance, the spacious Comedor de Gala (Gala Dining Room) is where grand ceremonial occasions were once (and are still occasionally) held. The stately air is enhanced by the extravagant chandeliers, hoary old artworks on the walls and lavishly adorned archway.

Jardines de Sabatini

The French-inspired Jardines de Sabatini lie along the northern flank of the Palacio Real. They were laid out in the 1930s to replace the royal stables that once stood on the site. These quite formal gardens with fountains and small labyrinths offer a fine alternative view of the palace's northern facade.

SIGHTS

PLAZA MAYOR SQUARE

See p48.

PALACIO REAL PALACE

See p49.

PLAZA DE ORIENTE SQUARE

Map p234 (Plaza de Oriente; MÓpera) A royal palace that once had aspirations to be the Spanish Versailles. Sophisticated cafes watched over by apartments that cost the equivalent of a royal salary. The **Teatro Real**, Madrid's opera house and one of Spain's temples to high culture. Some of the finest sunset views in Madrid. Welcome to Plaza de Oriente, a living, breathing monument to imperial Madrid.

At the centre of the plaza, which the palace overlooks, is an equestrian statue of Felipe IV. Designed by Velázquez, it's the perfect place to take it all in with marvellous views wherever you look. If you're wondering how a heavy bronze statue of a rider and his horse rearing up can actually maintain that stance, the answer is simple: the hind legs are solid, while the front ones are hollow. That idea was Galileo Galilei's. Nearby are some 20 marble statues of mostly ancient monarchs. Local legend has it that these ageing royals get down off their pedestals at night to stretch their legs.

The adjacent **Jardines Cabo Naval**, a great place to watch the sun set, adds to the sense of a sophisticated oasis of green in the heart of Madrid.

CATEDRAL DE NUESTRA SEÑORA DE LA ALMUDENA CATHEDRAL

Map p234 (☎91 542 22 00; www.museocatedral.archimadrid.es; Calle de Bailén; cathedral & crypt by donation, museum adult/child €6/4; ⊙9am-8.30pm Mon-Sat, for Mass Sun, museum 10am-2.30pm Mon-Sat; MÓpera) Paris has Notre Dame and Rome has St Peter's Basilica. In fact, almost every European city of stature has its signature cathedral, a stand-out monument to a glorious Christian past. Not Madrid. Although the exterior of the Catedral de Nuestra Señora de la Almudena sits in harmony with the adjacent Palacio Real, Madrid's cathedral is cavernous and largely charmless within; its colourful, modern ceilings do little to make up for the lack of old-world gravitas that so distinguishes great cathedrals.

Carlos I first proposed building a cathedral here back in 1518, but building didn't actually begin until 1879. It was finally finished in 1992 and its pristine, bright-white neo-Gothic interior holds no pride of place in the affections of *madrileños* (people from Madrid).

It's possible to climb to the cathedral's summit, with fine views. En route you climb up through the cathedral's museum; follow the signs to the **Museo de la Catedral y Cúpola** on the northern facade, opposite the Palacio Real.

Just around the corner in Calle Mayor, the low-lying ruins of **Santa María de la Almudena** are all that remain of Madrid's first church, which was built on the site of Mayrit's Great Mosque when the Christians arrived in the 11th century.

And just down the hill beneath the cathedral's southern wall on Calle Mayor is the neo-Romanesque **crypt** with more than 400 columns, 20 chapels and fine stained-glass windows.

MURALLA ÁRABE WALLS

Map p234 (Cuesta de la Vega; MÓpera) Behind the cathedral apse and down Cuesta de la Vega is a short stretch of the original 'Arab Wall', the city wall built by Madrid's early-medieval Muslim rulers. Some of it dates as far back as the 9th century, when the initial Muslim fort was raised. Other sections date from the 12th and 13th centuries, by which time the city had been taken by the Christians. The earliest sections were ingeniously conceived – the outside of the wall was made to look dauntingly sturdy, while the inside was put together with cheap materials to save money. It must have worked, as the town was rarely taken by force. In summer the city council organises open-air theatre and music performances here. Just above the wall on Cuesta de la Vega, information panels show the original extent of the city walls superimposed on a modern map.

CAMPO DEL MORO GARDENS

Map p234 (☎91 454 88 00; www.patrimonionacional.es; Paseo de la Virgen del Puerto; ⊙10am-8pm Mon-Sat, 9am-8pm Sun & holidays Apr-Sep, 10am-6pm Mon-Sat, 9am-6pm Sun & holidays Oct-Mar; MPríncipe Pío) From this attractive park you can gain an appreciation of Madrid in its earliest days – it was from here, in what would become known as Campo del Moro (Moor's Field), that an Almoravid army laid siege to the city in 1110. The troops occupied all but the fortress (where the Palacio Real now stands), but the Christian garrison held on until the Almoravid fury abated and their forces retired south. The 20 hectares of gardens that now adorn the site were first laid in the 18th century, with major overhauls in 1844 and 1890. The gardens combine quiet corners that feel like an expansive private garden with the monumental grandeur designed to mimic the gardens surrounding the palace at Versailles; nowhere is the latter more in evidence than along the east–west **Pradera**, a lush lawn with the Palacio Real as its backdrop. The gardens' centrepiece, which stands halfway along the Pradera, is the elegant **Fuente de las Conchas** (Fountain of the Shells) designed by Ventura Rodríguez, the Goya of Madrid's 18th-century architecture scene. The only entrance is from Paseo de la Virgen del Puerto.

PLAZA DE RAMALES — SQUARE

Map p234 (MÓpera) This pleasant little triangle of open space is not without historical intrigue. Joseph Bonaparte ordered the destruction of the Iglesia de San Juanito to open up a pocket of fresh air in the then-crowded streets. It is believed Velázquez was buried in the church; excavations in 2000 revealed the crypt of the former church and the remains of various people buried in it centuries ago, but Velázquez was nowhere to be found. On the west side of the plaza is the **Escuela Superior de Música Reina Sofía** (Map p234; www.escuelasuperiordemusicareinasofia.es), a prestigious musical conservatory which sometimes hosts concerts.

TEATRO REAL — NOTABLE BUILDING

Map p234 (☎91 516 06 96; www.teatro-real.com; Plaza de Oriente; 50-/30-minute guided tour €5/3; ⊙10.30am-1pm Mon-Fri, 11am-1.30pm Sat, Sun & holidays; MÓpera) Backing onto the Plaza de Oriente, Madrid's signature opera house does not have the most distinguished of histories. The first theatre was built in 1708 on the site of public wash houses. Torn down in 1816, its successor was built in 1850 under the reign of Isabel II, whereafter it burned down and was later blown up in the civil war (when it was used as a powder store, resulting in the inevitable fireworks). It finally took its present neoclassical form in 1997 and, viewed from Plaza de Isabel II, it's a fine addition to the central Madrid cityscape; in Plaza de Oriente, however, it's somewhat overshadowed by the splendour of its surrounds. The 1997 renovations combined the latest in theatre and acoustic technology with a remake of the most splendid of its 19th-century decor. The guided tours (in Spanish) leave every half-hour.

PLAZA DE ESPAÑA — SQUARE

Map p234 (MPlaza de España) It's hard to know what to make of this curiously unprepossessing square. The 1953 **Edificio de España** (Spain Building) on the northeast side clearly sprang from the totalitarian recesses of Franco's imagination such is its resemblance to austere Soviet monumentalism, but there's also something strangely grand and pleasing about it. To the north stands the rather ugly and considerably taller 35-storey **Torre de Madrid** (Madrid Tower). In the square itself is a statue of Cervantes. At the writer's feet is a bronze statue of his immortal characters Don Quijote and Sancho Panza. The monument was erected in 1927. But Plaza de España is at its best down in its lower (southwestern) reaches, where abundant trees are remarkably successful in keeping Madrid's noise at bay.

CONVENTO DE LA ENCARNACIÓN — CONVENT

Map p234 (☎91 454 88 00; www.patrimonionacional.es; Plaza de la Encarnación 1; adult/concession €7/4, incl Convento de las Descalzas Reales €10/5, EU citizens free Wed & Thu afternoon; ⊙10am-2pm & 4-6.30pm Tue-Sat, 10am-3pm Sun; MÓpera) Founded by Empress Margarita de Austria, this 17th-century mansion built in the Madrid baroque style (a pleasing amalgam of brick, exposed stone and wrought iron) is still inhabited by nuns of the Augustine order. The large art collection dates mostly from the 17th century and among the many gold and silver reliquaries is one that contains the blood of San Pantaleón, which purportedly liquefies each year on 27 July. The convent also sits on a pretty plaza with lovely views down towards the Palacio Real.

CONVENTO DE LAS DESCALZAS REALES — CONVENT

Map p234 (Convent of the Barefoot Royals; www.patrimonionacional.es; Plaza de las Descalzas 3; adult/child €7/4, incl Convento de la Encarnación €10/5, EU citizens free Wed & Thu afternoon; ⊙10.30am-2pm & 4-6.30pm Tue-Sat, 10am-3pm Sun; MÓpera, Sol) The grim, prisonlike walls of this one-time palace keep modern Madrid at bay and offer no hint that behind the sober plateresque facade lies a sumptuous stronghold of the faith.

The compulsory guided tour (in Spanish) leads you up a gaudily frescoed Renaissance stairway to the upper level of the cloister. The vault was painted by Claudio Coello, one of the most important artists of the 17th-century Madrid School and whose works adorn San Lorenzo de El Escorial.

You then pass several of the convent's 33 chapels – a maximum of 33 Franciscan nuns is allowed to live here (perhaps because Christ is said to have been 33 when he died) as part of a closed order. These nuns follow in the tradition of the Descalzas Reales (Barefooted Royals), a group of illustrious women who cloistered themselves when the convent was founded in the 16th century. The first of these chapels contains a remarkable carved figure of a dead, reclining Christ, which is paraded in a moving Good Friday procession each year. At the end of the passage is the antechoir, then the choir stalls themselves. Buried here is Doña Juana – Carlos I's daughter who, in a typical piece of 16th-century collusion between royalty and the Catholic Church, commandeered the palace and had it converted into a convent. A *Virgen la Dolorosa* by Pedro de la Mena is seated in one of the 33 oak stalls.

In the former sleeping quarters of the nuns are some of the most extraordinary tapestries you're ever likely to see. Woven in the 17th century in Brussels, they include four based on drawings by Rubens. To produce works of this quality, four or five artisans could take up to a year to weave just 1 sq metre of tapestry.

The last tickets are sold an hour before closing time.

IGLESIA DE SAN GINÉS — CHURCH

Map p234 (Calle del Arenal 13; ⏲8.45am-1pm & 6-9pm Mon-Sat, 9.45am-2pm & 6-9pm Sun; MSol, Ópera) Due north of Plaza Mayor, San Ginés is one of Madrid's oldest churches: it has been here in one form or another since at least the 14th century. It is speculated that, prior to the arrival of the Christians in 1085, a Mozarabic community (Christians in Muslim territory) lived around the stream that later became Calle del Arenal and that their parish church stood on this site. What you see today was built in 1645 but largely reconstructed after a fire in 1824. The church houses some fine paintings, including El Greco's *Expulsion of the Moneychangers from the Temple* (1614), which is beautifully displayed; the glass is just 6mm from the canvas to avoid reflections. The church has stood at the centre of Madrid life for centuries; Spain's premier playwright Lope de Vega was married here and novelist Francisco de Quevedo was baptised in its font.

PLAZA DE LA VILLA & AROUND — SQUARE

(MÓpera) There are grander plazas in Madrid, but this intimate little square is one of Madrid's prettiest. Enclosed on three sides by wonderfully preserved examples of 17th-century Madrid-style baroque architecture (*barroco madrileño*), it was the permanent seat of Madrid's city government from the Middle Ages until recent years when Madrid's city council relocated to the grand Palacio de Comunicaciones on Plaza de la Cibeles (p103).

The 17th-century **Casa de la Villa** (old town hall), on the western side of the square, is a typical Habsburg edifice with Herrerian slate-tiled spires. First planned as a prison in 1644 by Juan Gómez de Mora, who also designed the Convento de la Encarnación (p52), its granite and brick facade is a study in sobriety. The final touches to the Casa de la Villa were made in 1693, although Juan de Villanueva, of Museo del Prado fame, made some alterations a century later. The **Salón del Pleno** (council chambers) were restored in the 1890s and again in 1986; the decoration is sumptuous neoclassical with late-17th-century ceiling frescoes. Ask at the Centro de Turismo de Madrid (p205) about guided tours to the Casa de la Villa. Look for the ceramic copy of Pedro Teixeira's landmark 1656 map of Madrid just outside the chambers.

On the opposite side of the square, the 15th-century **Casa de los Lujanes** is more Gothic in conception with a clear Mudéjar (a Moorish architectural style) influence. The brickwork tower was 'home' to the imprisoned French monarch François I and his sons after their capture during the Battle of Pavia (1525). As the star prisoner was paraded down Calle Mayor, locals are said to have been more impressed by the splendidly attired Frenchman than they were by his more drab captor, the Spanish Habsburg emperor Carlos I.

Currently closed to the public, the **Casa de Cisneros**, built in 1537 by the nephew of Cardinal Cisneros, a key adviser to Queen Isabel, is plateresque in inspiration, although it was much restored and altered at the beginning of the 20th century. The main door and window above it are what remains of the Renaissance-era building. It's now home to the **Salón de Tapices** (Tapestries Hall), adorned with exquisite 15th-century Flemish tapestries.

The section of Calle Mayor that runs past the plaza saw one of the most dramatic moments in the history of early 20th-century Madrid. On 31 May 1906, on the wedding day of King Alfonso XIII and Britain's Victoria Eugenia, a Catalan anarchist Mateu Morral threw a bomb concealed in a bouquet of flowers at the royal couple. Several bystanders died, but the monarch and his new wife survived, save for her blood-spattered dress. During the Spanish Civil War, Madrid's republican government briefly renamed the street Calle Mateu Morral.

Just down the hill from the plaza are the 18th-century baroque remakes of the **Iglesia del Sacramento**, the central church of the Spanish army, and the **Palacio del Duque de Uceda**, which is now used as a military headquarters (the Capitanía General), but is a classic of the Madrid baroque architectural style and was designed by Juan Gómez de Mora in 1608.

IGLESIA DE SAN NICOLÁS DE LOS SERVITAS — CHURCH

Map p234 (☎91 548 83 14; Plaza de San Nicolás 6; ⏲8am-1.30pm & 5.30-8.30pm Mon, 8-9.30am & 6.30-8.30pm Tue-Sat, 9.30am-2pm & 6.30-9pm Sun & holidays; Ⓜ Ópera) Tucked away up the hill from Calle Mayor, this intimate little church is Madrid's oldest surviving building of worship. It is believed to have been built on the site of Muslim Mayrit's second mosque. The most striking feature is the restored 12th-century Mudéjar bell tower, although much of the remainder dates in part from the 15th century. The vaulting is late Gothic while the fine timber ceiling, which survived a fire in 1936, dates from about the same period. Despite plateresque and baroque touches, much of the interior is a study in simplicity. The architect Juan de Herrera, one of the great architects of Renaissance Spain, was buried in the crypt in 1597.

FREE CONVENTO DEL CORPUS CRISTI — CONVENT

Map p234 (Las Carboneras; ☎91 548 37 01; Plaza del Conde de Miranda; ⏲9.30am-1pm & 4-6.30pm; Ⓜ Ópera) Architecturally nondescript but culturally curious, this church hides behind sober brickwork on the western end of a quiet square. A closed order of nuns occupies the convent building and, when Mass is held, the nuns gather in a separate area at the rear of the church. They maintain a centuries-old tradition of making sweet biscuits that can be purchased from the entrance just off the square on Calle del Codo.

BASÍLICA DE SAN MIGUEL — CHURCH

Map p234 (☎91 548 40 11; www.bsmiguel.es; Calle de San Justo 4; ⏲10.15am-1.15pm & 6-9pm Mon-Fri ; Ⓜ La Latina or Sol) Hidden away off Calle de Segovia, this basilica is something of a surprise. Its convex, late-baroque facade sits in harmony with the surrounding buildings of old Madrid. Among its fine features are statues representing the four virtues, and the reliefs of Justo and Pastor, the saints to whom the church was originally dedicated. The rococo and Italianate interior, completed by Italian architects in 1745, is another world altogether with gilded flourishes and dark, sombre domes.

PALACIO DE SANTA CRUZ — HISTORIC BUILDING

Map p234 (Plaza de la Provincia; Ⓜ Sol) Just off the southeastern corner of Plaza Mayor and dominating Plaza de Santa Cruz is this baroque edifice, which houses the **Ministerio de Asuntos Exteriores** (Ministry of Foreign Affairs) and hence can only be admired from the outside. A landmark with its grey slate spires, it was built in 1643 and initially served as the court prison.

EATING

TOP CHOICE MERCADO DE SAN MIGUEL — TAPAS €

Map p234 (www.mercadodesanmiguel.es; Plaza de San Miguel; tapas from €1; ⏲10am-midnight Sun-Wed, to 2am Thu-Sat; Ⓜ Sol) One of Madrid's oldest and most beautiful markets, the Mercado de San Miguel has undergone a stunning major renovation and bills itself as a 'culinary cultural centre'. Within the early-20th-century glass walls, the market has become an inviting space strewn with tables (difficult to nab) where you can enjoy the freshest food or a drink. Apart from the fresh fish corner, you can order tapas and sometimes more substantial plates at most of the counter-bars. **La Casa de Bacalao** (stall 17), for example, serves up a range

START PLAZA DE ORIENTE
END CONVENTO DE LAS DESCALZAS REALES
DISTANCE 2KM
DURATION TWO HOURS

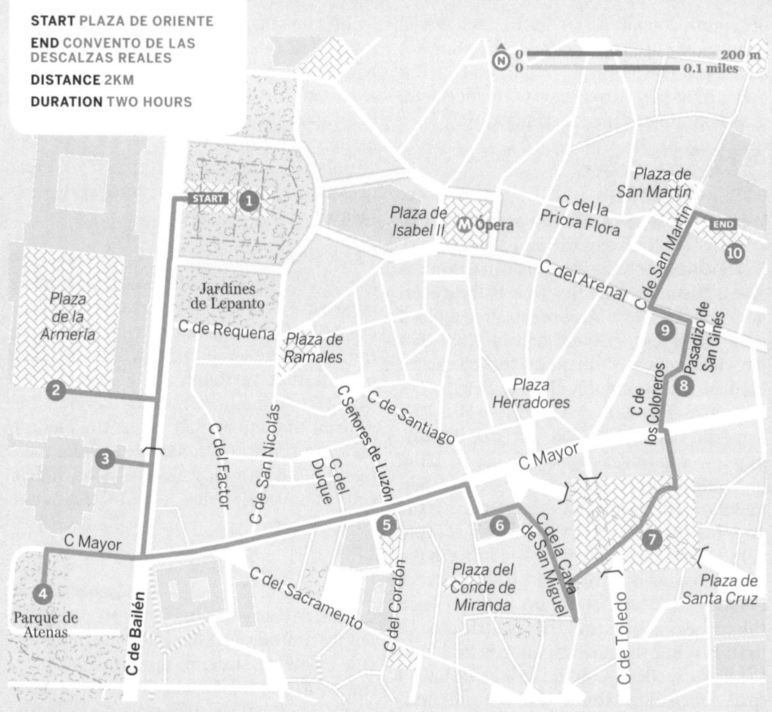

Neighbourhood Walk

Old Madrid

This walk takes you past the iconic architecture of imperial Madrid and into the heart of the modern city – two very different cities that often overlap.

Begin in 1 **Plaza de Oriente**, a splendid arc of greenery and graceful architecture which could be Madrid's most agreeable plaza. You'll find yourself surrounded by gardens, the Palacio Real and the Teatro Real, and *madrileños* (people from Madrid) at play. Overlooking the plaza, the 2 **Palacio Real** was Spain's seat of royal power for centuries. Almost next door is the 3 **Catedral de Nuestra Señora de la Almudena** which may lack the old-world gravitas of other Spanish cathedrals, but it's a beautiful part of the skyline.

From the cathedral, drop down to the 4 **Muralla Árabe**, then climb gently up Calle Mayor, pausing to admire the last remaining ruins of Madrid's first cathedral, Santa María de la Almudena, then on to 5 **Plaza de la Villa**, a cosy square surrounded on three sides by some of the best examples of Madrid baroque architecture. A little further up the hill and just off Calle Mayor, the 6 **Mercado de San Miguel**, one of Madrid's oldest markets, has become one of the coolest places to eat and mingle with locals in downtown Madrid.

Head down the hill along Cava de San Miguel, then climb up through the Arco de Cuchilleros to the 7 **Plaza Mayor**, one of Spain's grandest and most beautiful plazas. Down a narrow lane north of the plaza, 8 **Chocolatería de San Ginés** is justifiably famous for its *chocolate con churros* (deep-fried Spanish donuts with chocolate), the ideal Madrid indulgence at any hour of the day. Almost next door, along pedestrianised Calle del Arenal, there's the pleasing brick-and-stone 9 **Iglesia de San Ginés**, one of the longest-standing relics of Christian Madrid.

A short climb to the north, the 10 **Convento de las Descalzas Reales** is an austere convent with an extraordinarily rich interior. In the heart of downtown Madrid, it's a great place to finish up.

of tempting small toasts for €1 each, while an outpost of the classic Madrid restaurant **Lhardy** can be found at stalls 61 and 62. But everything here (from caviar to chocolate) is as tempting as the market is alive.

TOP CHOICE **RESTAURANTE SOBRINO DE BOTÍN** CASTILIAN **€€€**

Map p234 (☎91 366 42 17; www.botin.es; Calle de los Cuchilleros 17; mains €18.50-28; MLa Latina, Sol) It's not every day that you can eat in the oldest restaurant in the world (the *Guinness Book of World Records* has recognised it as the oldest – established in 1725) that has also appeared in many novels about Madrid, most notably Hemingway's *The Sun Also Rises*, and Frederick Forsyth's *Icon* and *The Cobra*. The secret of its staying power is fine *cochinillo* (roast suckling pig; €23.95) and *cordero asado* (roast lamb; €23.95) cooked in wood-fired ovens; the *angulas* (baby eels) at €101 a dish is probably beyond the reach of most. Eating in the vaulted cellar is a treat. Yes, it's filled with tourists. And yes, staff are keen to keep things ticking over and there's little chance to linger. But the novelty value is high and the food excellent. Contact Insider's Madrid (p205) for guided **tours** (The Botín Experience) of the restaurant.

CASA REVUELTA TAPAS **€**

Map p234 (☎91 366 33 32; Calle de Latoneros 3; tapas from €2.60; ⊙10.30am-4pm & 7-11pm Tue-Sat, 10.30am-4pm Sun, closed Aug; MSol, La Latina) Casa Revuelta puts out some of Madrid's finest tapas of *bacalao* (cod) bar none. While aficionados of Casa Labra (p83) may disagree, the fact that the octogenarian owner, Señor Revuelta, painstakingly extracts every fish bone in the morning and serves as a waiter in the afternoon wins the argument for us. Early on a Sunday afternoon, as the Rastro crowd gathers here, it's filled to the rafters, although locals who've been coming here for decades always manage to find room. It's also famous for its *callos* (tripe), *torreznos* (bacon bits) and *albóndigas* (meatballs).

RESTAURANTE SANDÓ CONTEMPORARY SPANISH **€€€**

Map p234 (☎91 547 99 11; www.restaurantesando.es; Calle de Isabel la Católica 2; mains €18-26, menú degustación €49; ⊙lunch & dinner Tue-Sat, lunch Sun; MSanto Domingo) He has taken his time opening a landmark restaurant in Madrid, but Juan Mari Arzak, one of Spain's most famous chefs, and his increasingly celebrated daughter Elena have finally set up shop just off the Plaza de Santo Domingo. Bringing Basque innovation to bear upon local tradition, their cooking is assured with dishes such as bites of beef with fresh garlic and pineapple. If you can't decide, try the *menú degustación* (tasting menu).

CASA MARÍA SPANISH **€€**

Map p234 (☎91 369 71 40; www.casamariaplazamayor.es; Plaza Mayor 23; tapas from €2.50, mains €13-19; ⊙10am-2am; MSol) A rare exception to the generally pricey and mediocre options that surround Plaza Mayor, Casa María combines professional service and a menu that effortlessly spans the modern and traditional. There's something for most tastes, with carefully chosen tapas, lunchtime stews and dishes such as sticky rice with lobster.

TAQUERÍA MI CIUDAD MEXICAN **€**

Map p234 (☎91 559 87 11; www.taqueriamiciudad.es; Calle de Hileras 5; tacos €1.50; MÓpera) This family-run Mexican bar has something of a cult following, serving up bite-sized tacos (the *cochinita pibil* is our favourite) washed down by fabulous margaritas (including those flavoured with tamarind). It's wildly popular on weekend nights, staying open until 1.30am.

TABERNA DEL ALABARDERO SPANISH **€€**

Map p234 (☎91 547 25 77; www.grupolezama.es; Calle de Felipe V 6; bar raciones €5.50-24.50, restaurant mains €17-27; MÓpera) This fine old Madrid *taberna* (tavern) is famous for its croquettes, fine *jamón* (ham), *montaditos de jamón* (small rolls of cured ham) and *montaditos de bonito* (small rolls of cured tuna) in the bar, while out the back the more classic cuisine includes *rabo de toro estofado* (bull's tail, served with honey, cinnamon, mashed potato and pastry with herbs; €20.10). Prices aren't cheap, but Madrid's notoriously fussy diners generally accept that it's worth it. Its sister restaurant around the corner in Plaza de Oriente, **La Mar del Alabardero** (Map p234; ☎91 541 33 33; www.grupolezama.es; Plaza de Oriente 6; mains €11-21; Ópera), is renowned for its high-quality seafood and rice dishes.

RESTAURANTE LOS GALAYOS SPANISH **€€**

Map p234 (☎91 366 30 28; www.losgalayos.net; Calle de Botoneros 5; mains €14-25; ⊙1pm-

12.30am; Ⓜ Sol) Most of the restaurants surrounding Plaza Mayor are tourist traps, but Los Galayos, a few steps off the plaza's southeastern corner, is an exception. Renowned for its *cocido* (meat and chickpea stew; €18; lunch only), it's a good place to sample traditional local cooking from around Spain. One of the house specialties is beef tenderloin cooked to your liking at your table on a stone slab.

TABERNA LA BOLA MADRILEÑO €€

Map p234 (☎91 547 69 30; www.labola.es; Calle de la Bola 5; mains €16-24; ⏲lunch & dinner Mon-Sat, lunch Sun, closed Aug; Ⓜ Santo Domingo) In any poll of food-loving locals seeking the best and most traditional Madrid cuisine, Taberna La Bola (going strong since 1870 and run by the sixth generation of the Verdasco family) always features near the top. We're inclined to agree and, if you're going to try *cocido a la madrileña* (€19.50) while in Madrid, this is a good place to do so. It's busy and noisy and very Madrid. It also serves other Madrid specialities, such as *callos* (tripe) and *sopa castellana* (garlic soup).

KITCHEN STORIES SPANISH €

Map p234 (☎91 366 97 71; www.kitchenstories.es; Calle de los Cuchilleros 3; mains €5.40-16.50; ⏲noon-1am; Ⓜ Sol, La Latina) Cafe, restaurant and food store in one, Kitchen Stories, at the foot of the Arco de Cuchilleros stairs, is a refreshing break from the often classical cooking in the area, with a bright modern space and Spanish flavours blended with international tastes, with everything from Thai vegetable curry to roast beef.

YERBABUENA VEGETARIAN €€

Map p234 (☎91 548 08 11; www.yerbabuena.ws; Calle de los Bordadores 3; mains €10-17.50; 🖉; Ⓜ Sol or Ópera) Cheerful bright colours, a full range of vegetarian staples (soya-bean burgers, biological rice and homemade yoghurt) and plenty of creatively conceived salads add up to one of central Madrid's best restaurants for vegetarians and vegans.

CASA CIRIACO MADRILEÑO €€

Map p234 (☎91 548 06 20; Calle Mayor 84; mains from €12; ⏲lunch & dinner Thu-Tue, closed Aug; 📶👪; Ⓜ Ópera) One of the *grande dames* of the Madrid restaurant scene, Casa Ciriaco has witnessed attempted assassinations (of King Alfonso XIII in 1906) and was immortalised by the Spanish writer Valle-Inclán who set part of his novel *Luces de Bohemia* here. Its legend made, it now puts all its energies into fine *madrileño* cooking from seafood to hearty meat dishes and *cocido a la madrileña* on Tuesdays.

MUSEO DEL JAMÓN SPANISH €

Map p234 (☎91 531 45 50; www.museodeljamon.com; Calle Mayor 7; raciones from €2.50; ⏲8am-midnight; Ⓜ Sol) Famous for having appeared in Pedro Almodóvar's 1997 film *Carne Trémula* (Live Flesh), and equally beloved by first-time visitors to Spain for the sight of hundreds of hams hanging from the ceiling, Museo del Jamón is definitely a local landmark. Prices for a *ración/bocadillo* (large tapas serving/filled roll) start at €2.50/1.50 and can go much higher depending on the quality of the *jamón*.

ALGARABÍA LA RIOJA €

Map p234 (☎91 542 41 31; Calle de la Unión 8; mains €14-20, set menu €35; ⏲lunch & dinner Mon-Fri, dinner Sat, closed Feb and for lunch Aug; 📶; Ⓜ Ópera) You know the wines of La Rioja, but the food of this northern Spanish region is also filled with flavour. The cuisine here is all about home-cooking and choosing the *menú de degustación* is a great way to get an overview of the regional specialties. The *croquetas* (croquettes) have a loyal following and, not surprisingly, the wine list is excellent.

BANGKOK THAI RESTAURANT THAI €

Map p234 (☎91 559 16 96; 1st fl, Calle de los Bordadores 15; mains €6.50-12.50; ⏲noon-4pm & 8pm-midnight; Ⓜ Sol, Ópera) Great Thai food, reasonable prices, good service and a Thai-style dining area make for a terrific meal in the heart of town. If you're lucky, you'll get one of the tables overlooking the busy

MERCADO DE SAN MIGUEL

The Mercado de San Miguel has become almost too popular for its own good and, as a consequence, lunchtime and evenings can be uncomfortably crowded. Although it's always busy and snaffling a table or a bar stool is invariably a game of chance, we recommend coming for a late lunch or early dinner from 5pm to 7pm when there's usually far more room to move.

LOCAL KNOWLEDGE

BOCADILLO DE CLAMARES

One of the lesser-known culinary specialties of Madrid is a *bocadillo de calamares* (a baguette-style roll filled to bursting with deep-friend calamari). You'll find them in many bars in the streets surrounding Plaza Mayor and neighbouring bars along Calle de los Botaderos off Plaza Mayor's south-eastern corner. At around €2.50, it's the perfect street snack.

pedestrian thoroughfare of Calle del Arenal. In addition to its à la carte choices, it offers a well-priced *menú del día* (daily set menu; €11.60) that's available for lunch seven days a week, a *menú de noche* (evening set menu; €15) and a *menú de degustación* (€19.50). Opening hours are particularly friendly to non-Spanish stomachs.

CERVECERÍA 100 MONTADITOS SPANISH €

Map p234 (www.100montaditos.com; Calle Mayor 22; montaditos €1-2; MSol) This bar with outlets all across the city serves up no fewer than 100 different varieties of mini-*bocadillos* that span the full range of Spanish staples, such as chorizo, *jamón*, tortilla, a variety of cheeses and seafood, in more combinations than you could imagine. Each one costs a princely €1 to €2 and four will satisfy most stomachs. You order at the counter and your name is called in no time. Menus are available in English.

DRINKING & NIGHTLIFE

CAFÉ DEL REAL COCKTAIL BAR, CAFE

Map p234 (Plaza de Isabel II 2; 9am-1am Mon-Thu, to 3am Fri & Sat; MÓpera) A cafe and cocktail bar in equal parts, this intimate little place serves up creative coffees and a few cocktails to the soundtrack of chill-out music. The best seats are upstairs, where the low ceilings, wooden beams and leather chairs are a great place to pass an afternoon with friends.

CHOCOLATERÍA DE SAN GINÉS CAFE

Map p234 (Pasadizo de San Ginés 5; 9.30am-7am; MSol) One of the grand icons of the Madrid night, this *chocolate con churros* (Spanish donuts with chocolate) cafe sees a sprinkling of tourists throughout the day, but locals usually pack it out in their search for sustenance on their way home from a nightclub sometime close to dawn. It closes for only two hours a day, and only then to give it a quick scrub. Only in Madrid...

TEATRO JOY ESLAVA CLUB

Map p234 (Joy Madrid; 913663733; www.joy-eslava.com; Calle del Arenal 11; admission €12-15; 11.30pm-6am; MSol) The only things guaranteed at this grand old Madrid dance club (housed in a 19th-century theatre) are a crowd and the fact that it'll be open (it claims to have operated every single day for the past 29 years). The music and the crowd are a mixed bag, but queues are long and invariably include locals and tourists, and even the occasional *famoso* (celebrity). Every night's a little different. Loco Monday kicks off the week in spectacular fashion, Thursday is student night, Friday's 'Fabulush' is all about glamour and there's even the no-alcohol, no-smoking 'Joy Light' on Saturday evenings (5.30pm to 10pm) for those aged between 14 and 17. Throw in occasional live acts and cabaret-style performances on stage and it's a point of reference for Madrid's professional party crowd.

CAFE DE ORIENTE CAFE

Map p234 (Plaza de Oriente 2; 8.30am-1.30am Mon-Thu, 9am-2.30am Fri & Sat, 9am-1.30am Sun; MÓpera) The outdoor tables of this distinguished old cafe are among the most sought-after in central Madrid, providing as they do a front-row seat for the beautiful Plaza de Oriente, with the Palacio Real as a backdrop. The building itself was once part of a long-gone, 17th-century convent and the interior feels a little like a set out of Mittel europa. It's the perfect spot for a coffee when the weather's fine.

ANTICAFÉ CAFE

Map p234 (Calle de la Unión 2; 7pm-2am Mon-Thu, 7pm-2.30am Fri, 5pm-2.30am Sat, 5pm-midnight Sun; MÓpera) Bohemian kitsch in the best sense is the prevailing theme here and it runs right through the decor, regular cultural events (poetry readings and concerts) and, of course, the clientele. As such, it won't be to everyone's taste, but we rather think that it adds some much-needed variety to the downtown drinking scene. Coffees are as popular as the alcohol, although that rather strange predilection wears off as the night progresses.

EL CAFÉ DE LA OPERA CAFE

Map p234 (☎91 542 63 82; www.elcafedelaopera.com; Calle de Arrieta 6; ⏰8am-midnight; Ⓜ Ópera) Opposite the Teatro Real, this classic before-performance cafe has one unusual requirement for would-be waiters – they have to be able to sing opera. They break into song from around 9.30pm, when you'll fork out a minimum €54 for a meal – not bad value if you don't have tickets for the show across the road.

CHOCOLATERÍA VALOR CAFE

Map p234 (www.chocolateriasvalor.es; Postigo de San Martín; ⏰9am-10.30pm Sun, 8am-10.30pm Mon-Thu, 8am-1am Fri, 9am-1am Sat; Ⓜ Callao) It may be Madrid tradition to indulge in *chocolate con churros* around sunrise on your way home from a nightclub, but for everyone else who prefers a more reasonable hour, this is possibly the best *chocolatería* in town. It serves traditional *churros,* but they're only the side event to the astonishing array of chocolates in which to dip them. Our favourite has to be *cuatro sentidos de chocolate* (four senses of chocolate; €7.95), but we'd happily try everything on the menu to make sure.

OBA OBA NIGHTCLUB, LIVE MUSIC

Map p234 (obaoba.es; Calle de Jacometrezo 4; ⏰11.30pm-5.30am Wed-Sun; Ⓜ Callao) This nightclub is Brazilian down to its G-strings, with live music most nights and dancing till dawn most nights of the week. You'll find plenty of Brazilians in residence, which is the best recommendation we can give for the music and the authenticity of its caipirinhas.

☆ ENTERTAINMENT

CINESA CAPITOL CINEMA

Map p234 (☎902 333 231; www.cinesa.es; Gran Vía 41; Ⓜ Callao) One of the stalwarts of the Madrid cinema scene – expect Hollywood more than art house.

CAFÉ DE CHINITAS FLAMENCO

Map p234 (☎91 547 15 02; www.chinitas.com; Calle de Torija 7; admission incl drink €32; ⏰shows 8pm & 10.30pm Mon-Sat; Ⓜ Santo Domingo) One of the most distinguished *tablaos* (flamenco venues) in Madrid, drawing in everyone from the Spanish royal family to Bill Clinton, Café de Chinitas has an elegant setting and top-notch flamenco performers. You can order a meal off the menu (around €50 per person) or simply have a drink (coffee costs €5!). It may attract loads of tourists, but flamenco aficionados also give it top marks. Reservations are highly recommended.

LAS CARBONERAS FLAMENCO

Map p234 (☎91 542 86 77; www.tablaolascarboneras.com; Plaza del Conde de Miranda 1; admission €30; ⏰shows 8.30pm & 10.30pm Mon-Thu, 8.30pm & 11pm Fri & Sat; Ⓜ Ópera, Sol, La Latina) Like most of the *tablaos* around town, this place sees far more tourists than locals, but the quality is nonetheless unimpeachable. It's not the place for gritty, soul-moving spontaneity, but it's still an excellent introduction and one of the few places that flamenco aficionados seem to have no complaints about.

LAS TABLAS FLAMENCO

Map p234 (☎91 542 05 20; www.lastablasmadrid.com; Plaza de España 9; admission €27; ⏰shows 10.30pm Sun-Thu, 8pm & 10pm Fri & Sat; Ⓜ Plaza de España) Las Tablas has a reputation for quality flamenco and reasonable prices; it could just be the best choice in town. Most nights you'll see a classic flamenco show, with plenty of throaty singing and soul-baring dancing. Antonia Moya and Marisol Navarro, leading lights in the flamenco world, are regular performers here.

CAFÉ BERLIN JAZZ

Map p234 (☎91 521 57 52; Calle de Jacometrezo 4; admission €8; ⏰7pm-2.30am Tue-Sun Sep-Jul; Ⓜ Callao, Santo Domingo) Café Berlín was something of a Madrid jazz stalwart since the 1950s but it has recently broadened its horizons to take in a bit of flamenco, soul and other genres. The art-deco interior ads to the charm and the headline acts can come from a who's who of world jazz; in the past Al Foster (Miles Davis' drummer), Santiago de Muela and the Calento Jazz Orchestra have all taken to the stage. The headline acts take to the stage at 11.30pm on Fridays and Saturdays, with other performances sprinkled throughout the week.

SHOPPING

ANTIGUA CASA TALAVERA — CERAMICS

Map p234 (Calle de Isabel la Católica 2; ⏲10am-1.30pm & 5-8pm Mon-Fri, 10am-1.30pm Sat; Ⓜ Santo Domingo) The extraordinary tiled facade of this wonderful old shop conceals an Aladdin's cave of ceramics from all over Spain. This is not the mass-produced stuff aimed at the tourist market, but comes from the small family potters of Andalucía and Toledo, ranging from the decorative (tiles) to the useful (plates, jugs and other kitchen items). The old couple who run the place are delightful.

EL ARCO ARTESANÍA — HANDICRAFTS

Map p234 (www.artesaniaelarco.com; Plaza Mayor 9; ⏲11am-9pm; Ⓜ Sol, La Latina) This original shop in the southwestern corner of Plaza Mayor sells an outstanding array of homemade designer souvenirs, from stone and glass work to jewellery and home fittings. The papier mâché figures are gorgeous, but there's so much else here to turn your head.

MATY — FLAMENCO

Map p234 (☎91 531 32 91; www.maty.es; Calle del Maestro Victoria 2; ⏲10am-1.45pm & 4.30-8pm Mon-Sat; Ⓜ Sol) Wandering around central Madrid, it's easy to imagine that flamenco outfits have been reduced to imitation dresses sold as souvenirs to tourists. That's why places like Maty matter. Here you'll find dresses, shoes and all the accessories that go with the genre, with sizes for children and adults. It also does quality disguises for Carnaval. These are the real deal, with prices to match, but they make brilliant gifts.

ASÍ — CHILDREN

Map p234 (☎91 548 28 28; www.tiendas-asi.com; Gran Vía 47; ⏲10am-8.30pm Mon-Sat; Ⓜ Callao or Santo Domingo) Exquisite handmade children's dolls, all beautifully attired and overflowing from the shop window, are proffered here. Inside it also sells toys and intricate dolls' houses that are works of art; for the last, every single item (furniture, saucepans etc) can be purchased individually. None of it's cheap, but they're once-in-a-lifetime purchases. It also sells some select homewares.

FLIP — FASHION

Map p234 (☎91 366 44 72; www.flipmadrid.com; Calle Mayor 19; ⏲10.30am-9pm Mon-Sat, noon-8pm Sun; Ⓜ Sol) Too cool for its own good, Flip is funky and edgy, with its designer T-shirts, G-Star jeans and brand names like Franklin Marshall, Carhartt, Guess and Diesel, as well as a groovy and often off-beat collection of belts, caps and bags. Staff are as hip as the clothing and always ready with advice. The changing rooms, however, require a contortionist's flexibility.

EL FLAMENCO VIVE — FLAMENCO

Map p234 (www.elflamencovive.es; Calle Conde de Lemos 7; ⏲10.30am-2pm & 5-9pm Mon-Sat; Ⓜ Ópera) This temple to flamenco has it all, from guitars and songbooks to well-priced CDs, polka-dotted dancing costumes, shoes, colourful plastic jewellery and literature about flamenco. It's the sort of place that will appeal as much to curious first timers as to serious students of the art. It also organises classes in flamenco guitar.

SALVADOR BACHILLER — ACCESSORIES

Map p234 (www.salvadorbachiller.com; Gran Vía 65; ⏲10am-9.30pm Mon-Sat, 11am-9pm Sun; Ⓜ Plaza de España, Santo Domingo) The stylish and high-quality leather bags, wallets, suitcases and other accessories of Salvador Bachiller are a staple of Spanish shopping aficionados. This is leather with a typically Spanish twist – the colours are dazzling in bright pinks, yellows and greens. Sound garish? You'll change your mind once you step inside. It also has an **outlet** (Map p254; ☎91 523 30 37; Calle de Gravina 11; ⏲10.30am-9.30pm Mon-Thu, 10.30am-11pm Fri & Sat, noon-9pm Sun; Ⓜ Chueca) in Chueca for superseded stock.

CASA HERNANZ — SHOES

Map p234 (Calle de Toledo 18; ⏲9am-1.30pm & 4.30-8pm Mon-Fri, 10am-2pm Sat; Ⓜ La Latina, Sol) Comfy, rope-soled *alpargatas* (espadrilles), Spain's traditional summer footwear, are worn by everyone from the King of Spain down, and you can buy your own pair at this humble workshop, which has been hand-making the shoes for five generations; you can even get them made to order. Prices range from €5 to €40 and queues form whenever the weather starts to warm up.

FRANSEN ET LAFITE — HOMEWARES, FLOWERS

Map p234 (☎91 142 85 25; www.fransenetlafite.com; Calle del Espejo 5; ⏲10am-8pm Tue-Sat, noon-3pm Sun; Ⓜ Ópera) A stunning collection of flowers from all over Europe is the

FLEA MARKETS OF MADRID

In addition to El Rastro (p66), Madrid has a number of fine, if little-known flea markets, including:

- **Art Market** (Map p234; Plaza del Conde de Barajas; 10am-2pm Sun; Sol) Local art and prints of the greats.
- **Cuesta de Moyano Bookstalls** (p109) Madrid's answer to the bookstalls on Paris' Left Bank.
- **Mercadillo Marqués de Viana** (El Rastrillo; Calle del Marqués de Viana; 9am-2pm Sun; Tetuán) A calmer version of El Rastro in northern Madrid.
- **Mercado de Monedas y Sellos** (Map p234; Plaza Mayor; 9am-2pm Sun; Sol) Old coins and stamps.

main business here, but that's not why we include it. Spread over three floors and with a tranquil outdoor patio, this charming space also has carefully selected homewares, antiques, candles and all manner of decorative pieces. But even more than what they sell, it's the just-rightness of the space that means we'd happily spend time here just for the sheer pleasure of the experience.

CONVENTO DEL CORPUS CRISTI — FOOD

Map p234 (Las Carboneras; 91 548 37 01; Plaza del Conde de Miranda; 9.30am-1pm & 4-6.30pm; Ópera) The cloistered nuns at this convent also happen to be fine pastry chefs. You make your request through a door, then grille on Calle del Codo and the products are delivered through a little revolving door that allows the nuns to remain unseen by the outside world.

LA GRAMOLA — MUSIC

Map p234 (91 559 25 12; Postigo de San Martín 4; 10am-2pm & 5-9pm Mon-Sat; Ópera) In this era of musical downloads, illegal and otherwise, stores like La Gramola are once cause for nostalgia and strangely reassuring. Don't come here looking for something in particular (you could take all day to find it as things are a little all over the shop), but do come to spend a blissful hour thumbing your way through CDs and vinyl just like in the old days.

CHOCOLALABELGA — FOOD

Map p234 (91 843 77 57; www.chocolalabelga.com; Calle de Bonetillo 1; 10am-2pm & 5-8.30pm Mon-Fri; Ópera) Madrid's love affair with chocolate just found another reason to keep rolling on. The chocolates from the Belgian homeland of chocolatier Paul-Hector Bossier are, as you would expect, sinfully delicious, with plenty of modern flavours blended in.

PETRA'S INTERNATIONAL BOOKSHOP — BOOKSHOP

Map p234 (91 541 72 91; www.petrasbookshop.com; Calle de Campomanes 13; 11am-8pm Mon-Sat; Ópera, Santo Domingo) A wonderful little bookshop (with mostly secondhand stock), Petra's has a great selection in all major languages and across most major genres; it's also something of a meeting place for the lively expat community. The friendly owners can point you in the direction of activities in English and other languages. We also like a bookshop with a cat – Pet Ra is its name.

LA LIBRERÍA — BOOKSHOP

Map p234 (91 454 00 18; Calle Mayor 80; 10am-8pm Mon-Fri, 11am-2pm Sat; Ópera, Sol) This bookshop may be small, but it's the place to find books (mostly in Spanish) covering everything to do with Madrid, from coffee-table books to histories of every *barrio* in the capital.

FNAC — DEPARTMENT STORE

Map p234 (91 595 61 00; www.fnac.es; Calle de Preciados 28; 10am-9.30pm Mon-Sat, 11.30-9.30pm Sun; Callao) This four-storey megastore has a terrific range of CDs ranging from flamenco and world music to classical, as well as DVDs, video games, electronic equipment and books (including English-language titles); there's a large children's section on the 4th floor.

La Latina & Lavapiés

Neighbourhood Top Five

❶ Moving from bar to bar ordering wine and tapas along **Calle de la Cava Baja** (p67), one of the world's great culinary streets.

❷ Looking for Goya under one of the largest church domes in the world at the **Basílica de San Francisco El Grande** (p64).

❸ Joining the local crowds on Sunday mornings for **El Rastro** (p66), one of Europe's busiest flea markets, and a Madrid institution.

❹ Getting to the heart of medieval Madrid is the delightfully sloping **Plaza de la Paja** (p65), the gateway to Madrid's Moorish Quarter, La Morería.

❺ Letting flamenco fill your soul with a live performance at **Corral de la Morería** (p73).

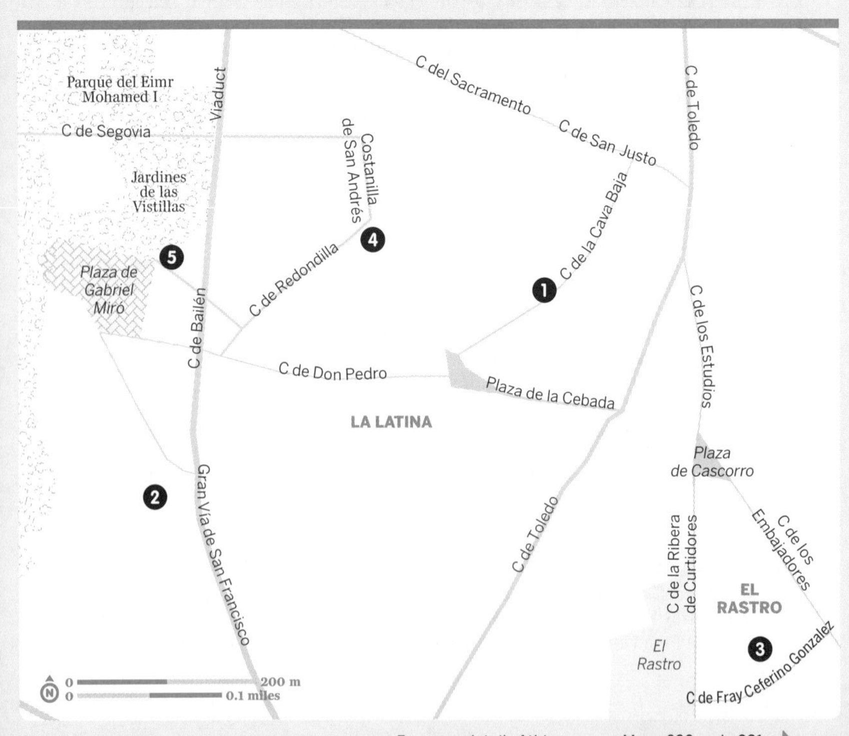

For more detail of this area see Map p232 and p231

Explore: La Latina & Lavapiés

La Latina's proximity to Plaza Mayor and the downtown area make it an easy area to dip into. Need a break nursing a mojito on a warm afternoon? Head for Plaza de la Paja and linger for as much time as you can spare. Eager to understand the buzz surrounding tapas and the local passion for going on a tapas crawl? Most evenings of the week are busy along Calle de la Cava Baja, but early Sunday lunchtime when the El Rastro crowds pour into La Latina is when you'll most appreciate being here.

With few sights to speak of, Lavapiés is a good place for an afternoon stroll or an evening spent catching the sights and sounds of Madrid's most multicultural corner. Access to Lavapiés is either a steep downhill walk from La Latina or an easy stroll along Calle de Argumosa from near the lower end of the Paseo del Prado.

Belonging to and connecting both neighbourhoods is El Rastro which centres on Calle de la Ribera de los Curtidores. Quiet and really rather pretty for six days of the week, it gets overwhelmed on Sundays when market stalls spill out into the surrounding streets. To make the most of your El Rastro experience, get here early to avoid the crowds, but stay long enough to join the post-market dispersal into La Latina's tapas bars.

Local Life

- **Hangout** On Sunday afternoons after El Rastro's clamour has faded and the tapas crowds are thinning, head for the Plaza de la Puerta de Moros for an infectious street party.
- **Secret Service** Visit the recently restored Capilla del Obispo on Plaza de la Paja from Tuesday to Friday at 12.30pm for the beautifully sung church service 'Oficio del Mediodía'.
- **Local Tradition** In Madrid 1pm Sunday is *la hora del vermut* (vermouth hour), a long-standing tradition whereby friends and families head out for a quick aperitif before Sunday lunch. Calle de la Cava Baja is the epicentre of this civilised tradition.

Getting There & Away

- **Metro** Unless you're walking from Plaza Mayor (an easy, agreeable stroll), La Latina metro station (line 5) is the best metro station both for the tapas bars of La Latina and El Rastro; Tirso de Molina station (line 1) is also OK.
- **Metro** If you're only visiting Lavapiés or don't mind a steep uphill climb to La Latina, Lavapiés station (line 3) is your best bet.

Lonely Planet's Top Tip

If you can't stomach an entire meal of *cocido* (meat and chickpea stew), or if you just want to see what all the fuss is about, head to **Malacatín** (p70) where the *degustación de cocido* (taste of *cocido*; €5) at the bar is a great way to try Madrid's favourite dish without going all the way, although locals might say it's a bit like smoking without inhaling.

Best Places to Eat

- Casa Lucio (p68)
- Juana La Loca (p68)
- Almendro 13 (p71)
- Posada de la Villa (p68)
- La Musa Latina (p67)
- Naïa Restaurante (p68)

For reviews, see p67

Best Places to Drink

- Delic (p72)
- Café del Nuncio (p72)
- Gaudeamus Café (p72)
- El Eucalipto (p72)
- Taberna Tempranillo (p72)
- El Viajero (p72)

For reviews, see p71

Best Churches

- Basílica de San Francisco El Grande (p64)
- Iglesia de San Andrés (p65)
- Basílica de Nuestra Señora del Buen Consejo (p66)
- Capilla del Obispo (p65)

TOP SIGHTS
BASILÍCA DE SAN FRANCISCO EL GRANDE

The recently restored Basílica de San Francisco El Grande is a leading candidate for the title of Madrid's favourite church. Its imposing scale, artworks by master painters and the presence of St Francis de Assisi in the story of the church's origins add both a whiff of legend and an unmistakeable sense of gravitas.

The Dome

You could easily spend an hour admiring the basilica's frescoed dome whose eight main panels are devoted to the Virgin Mary. This is the largest-diameter dome in Spain and the fourth largest in the world, with a height of 56m (or 72m above the church's floor) and diameter of 33m.

St Francis & Sabatini

Legend has it that St Francis of Assisi built a chapel on this site in 1217. The current version was designed by Francesco Sabatini in the 18th century. He also designed the Puerta de Alcalá and finished off the Palacio Real, and his unusual floor plan has a circular nave surrounded by chapels.

Goya

Of all the basilica's chapels, most people rush to the Capilla de San Bernardino, where the central fresco was painted by Goya in the early stages of his career. Unusually, Goya has painted himself into the scene (he's the one in the yellow shirt on the right).

Museum Artworks

A series of corridors behind the high altar (accessible only as part of the guided visit) is lined with works of art from the 17th to 19th centuries; highlights include a painting by Francisco Zurbarán.

DON'T MISS...

- The Dome
- St Francis & Sabatini
- Goya
- Museum Artworks

PRACTICALITIES

- Map p232
- Plaza de San Francisco 1
- adult/concession €3/2
- mass 8am-10.30am Mon-Sat, museum 10.30am-12.30pm & 4-6pm Tue-Sun
- M La Latina, Puerta de Toledo

SIGHTS

BASÍLICA DE SAN FRANCISCO EL GRANDE CHURCH
See p64.

IGLESIA DE SAN ANDRÉS & AROUND CHURCH, MUSEUM
Map p232 (Plaza de San Andrés 1; 8am-1pm & 6-8pm Mon-Sat, 8am-1pm Sun; La Latina) This proud church is more imposing than beautiful and what you see today is the result of restoration work completed after the church was gutted during the civil war. Stern, dark columns with gold-leaf capitals against the rear wall lead your eyes up into the dome, all rose, yellow and green, and rich with sculpted floral fantasies and cherubs poking out of every nook and cranny.

Around the back, on the delightful **Plaza de la Paja** (Map p232; Straw Square), is the **Capilla del Obispo**, a hugely important site on the historical map of Madrid. It was here that San Isidro Labrador, patron saint of Madrid, was first buried. When the saint's body was discovered here in the late 13th century, two centuries after his death, decomposition had not yet set in. Thus it was that King Alfonso XI ordered the construction in San Andrés of an ark to hold his remains and a chapel in which to venerate his memory. In 1669 (47 years after the saint was canonised) the last of many chapels was built on the site and that's what you see today. Don't go looking for the saint's remains because San Isidro made his last move to the Basílica de Nuestra Señora del Buen Consejo in the 18th century. From Tuesday to Friday at 12.30pm, stop by for the sung service 'Oficio del Mediodía'.

Down the bottom (north side) of Plaza de la Paja, the walled 18th-century **Jardín del Príncipe Anglona** is a peaceful garden.

FREE **MUSEO DE LOS ORÍGENES** MUSEUM
Map p232 (Casa de San Isidro; 91 366 74 15; www.madrid.es; Plaza de San Andrés 2; 9.30am-8pm Tue-Fri, 10am-2pm Sat & Sun Sep-Jul, 9.30am-2.30pm Tue-Sat Aug; La Latina) Next door to the Iglesia de San Andrés, this engaging museum sits on the spot where San Isidro Labrador is said to have ended his days around 1172. For an overview of Madrid's history, this place is hard to beat, with archaeological finds from the Roman period, including a 4th-century mosaic found on the site of a Roman villa in the *barrio* (district) of Carabanchel, maps, scale models, paintings and photos of Madrid down through the ages. A particular highlight is the large model based on Pedro Teixera's famous 1656 map of Madrid. Of great historical interest (though not much to look at) is the 'miraculous well', where the saint called forth water to slake his master's thirst. In another miracle, the son of the saint's master fell into a well, whereupon Isidro prayed and prayed until the water rose and lifted his son to safety. The museum is housed in a largely new building with a 16th-century Renaissance courtyard and a 17th-century chapel.

LAS VISTILLAS, VIADUCT & CALLE DE SEGOVIA GARDENS
Map p232 (Ópera) The leafy area around and beneath the southern end of the viaduct that crosses Calle de Segovia, is an ideal spot to pause and ponder the curious history of one of Madrid's oldest *barrios*. Probably the best place to do this is just across Calle de Bailén where the *terrazas* (open-air cafes) of **Jardines de las Vistillas** (Las Vistillas) offer one of the best vantage points in Madrid for a drink, with views towards the Sierra de Guadarrama. During the civil war, Las Vistillas was heavily bombarded by Nationalist troops from the Casa de Campo, and they in turn were shelled from a republican bunker here.

The adjacent **viaduct** was built in the 19th century and replaced by a newer version in 1942; the plastic barriers were erected in the late 1990s to prevent suicide jumps. Before the viaduct was built, anyone wanting to cross from one side of the road or river to the other was obliged to make their way down to **Calle de Segovia**

VISITING BASÍLICA DE SAN FRANCISCO EL GRANDE

Entry to the Basílica de San Francisco El Grande is free during morning Mass times, but there is no access to the museum and the lights in the Capilla de San Bernardino won't be on to illuminate the Goya. The same problem applies Friday afternoons or Saturday when there are often weddings. At all other times, visit is by Spanish-language guided tour (included in the admission price).

TOP SIGHTS EL RASTRO

On Sunday mornings this is the place to be, with all of Madrid converging on El Rastro in search of a bargain or simply to soak up the atmosphere. Back in the 17th and 18th centuries, El Rastro was largely dedicated to a meat market (*rastro* means 'stain', in reference to the trail of blood left behind by animals dragged down the hill). The road leading through the market, Calkle de Ribera de los Curtidores, translates as Tanners' Alley. You could easily spend an entire morning inching your way down the hill and the maze of streets that hosts El Rastro. Cheap clothes, luggage, old flamenco records, even older photos of Madrid, faux designer purses, grungy T-shirts, household goods and electronics are the main fare. For every 10 pieces of junk, there's a real gem (a lost masterpiece, an Underwood typewriter) waiting to be found. Antiques are also a major drawcard for traders and treasure hunters alike with a concentration of stores at Nuevas Galerías and Galerías Piquer; Plaza General Vara del Rey also has some curious bric-a-brac. A word of warning: pickpockets love El Rastro as much as everyone else, so keep a tight hold on your belongings and don't keep valuables in easy-to-reach pockets.

DON'T MISS...

- Antiques
- Sense of history
- Treasure hunt

PRACTICALITIES

- Map p231
- Ribera de Curtidores
- ⌚8am-3pm Sun
- Ⓜ La Latina

and back up the other side. If you feel like re-enacting the journey, head down to Calle de Segovia and cross to the southern side. Just east of the viaduct, on a characterless apartment block wall (No 21), is a **coat of arms**, one of the city's oldest. The site once belonged to Madrid's *ayuntamiento* (town hall). A punt would ferry people across what was then a trickling tributary of the Río Manzanares.

You could follow that former trickle's path west, down to the banks of the Manzanares and a nine-arched bridge, the **Puente de Segovia**, which Juan de Herrera built in 1584.

LA MORERÍA NEIGHBOURHOOD

(ⓂLa Latina) The area stretching southeast from the *viaducto* to the Iglesia de San Andrés was the heart of the *morería* (Moorish Quarter). Strain the imagination a little and the maze of winding and hilly lanes even now retains a whiff of the North African medina. This is where the Muslim population of Mayrit was concentrated in the wake of the 11th-century Christian takeover of the town.

IGLESIA DE SAN PEDRO EL VIEJO CHURCH

Map p232 (☎91 365 12 84; Costanilla de San Pedro; ⓂLa Latina) This fine old church is one of the few remaining windows on post-Muslim Madrid, most notably its clearly Mudéjar (a Moorish architectural style) brick bell tower, which dates from the 14th century. The church is generally closed to the public, but it's arguably more impressive from the outside; the Renaissance doorway has stood since 1525. If you can peek inside, the nave dates from the 15th century, although the interior largely owes its appearance to 17th-century renovations. Along with the Iglesia de San Nicolás de los Servitas (p54), the Iglesia de San Pedro El Viejo is one of very few sites where traces of Mudéjar Madrid remain in situ. Otherwise, you need to visit Toledo, 70km south of Madrid, to visualise what Madrid once was like.

BASÍLICA DE NUESTRA SEÑORA DEL BUEN CONSEJO CHURCH

Map p232 (Calle de Toledo 37; ⌚8am-1pm & 6-9pm; ⓂTirso de Molina, La Latina) Towering above the northern end of bustling Calle de Toledo, and visible through the arches from

Plaza Mayor, this imposing church long served as the city's de facto cathedral until Catedral de Nuestra Señora de la Almudena (p51) was completed in 1992.

Still known to locals as the Catedral de San Isidro, the austere baroque basilica was founded in the 17th century as the headquarters for the Jesuits and is today home to the remains of the city's main patron saint, San Isidro (in the third chapel on your left after you walk in). His body, apparently remarkably well preserved, is only removed from here on rare occasions, such as in 1896 and 1947 when he was paraded about town in the hope he would bring rain (he did, at least in 1947). Official opening hours aren't always to be relied upon.

Next door, the Instituto de San Isidro once went by the name of Colegio Imperial and, from the 16th century on, was where many of the country's leading figures were schooled by the Jesuits. You can wander in and look at the elegant courtyard.

PLAZA DE LAVAPIÉS & AROUND SQUARE

Map p231 (MLavapiés) The triangular **Plaza de Lavapiés** is one of the few open spaces in Lavapiés and it's a magnet for all that's good (a thriving cultural life) and bad (drugs and a high police presence) about the *barrio*. It's been cleaned up a little in recent years and the Teatro Valle-Inclán (p74), on the southern edge of the plaza, is a stunning contemporary addition to the eclectic Lavapiés streetscape. To find out what makes this *barrio* tick, consider dropping in to the **Asociación de Vecinos La Corrala** (91 467 05 09; www.lavapiesdiaynoche.org; Calle de Lavapiés 38; MLavapiés), the local neighbours' association just up the hill from the plaza, where staff are happy to highlight all that's good about Lavapiés without dismissing its problems.

In the surrounding streets, one building that catches the community spirit of this lively *barrio* is **La Corrala** (Map p231; cnr Calles de Mesón de Paredes & del Tribulete; Lavapiés), a partial example of an intriguing traditional (if much tidied up) tenement block, with long communal balconies built around a central courtyard; working-class Madrid was once strewn with buildings like this and very few survive. Almost opposite are the **ruins** of an old church, now converted into a library and the stunning Gaudeamus Café (p72).

LA CASA ENCENDIDA CULTURAL CENTRE

(902 430 322; www.lacasaencendida.com; Ronda de Valencia 2; 10am-10pm; MEmbajadores) This cultural centre is utterly unpredictable, if only because of the quantity and scope of its activities – everything from exhibitions, cinema sessions to workshops and more. The focus is often on international artists or environmental themes and, if it has an overarching theme, it's the alternative slant it takes on the world.

EATING

La Latina is Madrid's best *barrio* for tapas, complemented by a fine selection of sit-down restaurants. If you are planning only one tapas crawl while in town, do it here in Calle de la Cava Baja and surrounding streets. Lavapiés is more eclectic and multicultural and, generally speaking, the further down the hill you go, the better it gets, especially along Calle de Argumosa.

TOP CHOICE **LA MUSA LATINA** CONTEMPORARY SPANISH €€

Map p232 (91 354 02 55; www.lamusalatina.com; Costanilla de San Andrés 1; mains €4.50-11.50; MLa Latina) Laid-back La Musa Latina has an ever-popular dining area and food that's designed to bring a smile to your face – the hanging kebabs have achieved something close to legendary status. The outdoor tables are lovely when the weather's warm, while the downstairs bar in the former wine cellar is also charming.

TOP CHOICE **TABERNA MATRITUM** TAPAS €€

Map p232 (91 365 82 37; Calle de la Cava Alta 17; mains €13-18; lunch & dinner Wed-Sun, dinner Mon & Tue; MLa Latina) This little gem is reason enough to detour from the more popular Calle de la Cava Baja next door. The seasonal menu here encompasses terrific tapas, salads and generally creative cooking, and some of the desserts come from the master Catalan chocolatier Oriol Balaguer. The wine list here runs well into the hundreds and it is sophisticated without being pretentious. Highly recommended.

THE ORIGIN OF TAPAS

There are many stories concerning the origins of tapas.

One of the most common explanations derives from the fact that medieval Spain was a land of isolated settlements and people on the move – traders, pilgrims, emigrants and journeymen – who had to cross the lonely high plateau of Spain enroute elsewhere. All along the route, travellers holed up in inns where the keepers, concerned about drunken men on horseback setting out from their village, developed a tradition of putting a 'lid' (*tapa*) of food atop a glass of wine or beer. The purpose was partly to keep the bugs out, but primarily to encourage people not to drink on an empty stomach.

Another story holds that in the 13th century, doctors to King Alfonso X advised him to accompany his small sips of wine between meals with small morsels of food. So enamoured was the monarch with the idea that he passed a law requiring all bars in Castile to follow suit.

In Andalucía in particular, it is also claimed that the name *tapa* attained widespread usage in the early 20th century when King Alfonso XIII stopped at a beachside bar in Cádiz Province. When a strong gust of wind blew sand in the king's direction, a quick-witted waiter rushed to place a slice of *jamón* (ham) atop the king's glass of sherry. The king so much enjoyed the idea (and the *jamón*) that, wind or no wind, he ordered another and the name stuck.

JUANA LA LOCA — TAPAS €€

Map p232 (☎91 364 05 25; Plaza de la Puerta de Moros 4; tapas from €4, mains €8-19; ⊙lunch & dinner Tue-Sun, dinner Mon; Ⓜ La Latina) Juana La Loca does a range of creative tapas with tempting options lined up along the bar, and more on the menu that they prepare to order. But we love it above all for its *tortilla de patatas* (potato and onion omelette; €4), which is distinguished from others of its kind by the caramelised onions – simply wonderful.

TXIRIMIRI — TAPAS €€

Map p232 (☎91 364 11 96; www.txirimiri.es; Calle del Humilladero 6; tapas from €4; ⊙lunch & dinner Mon-Sat, closed Aug; Ⓜ La Latina) This *pintxo* (Basque tapas) bar is a great little discovery just down from the main La Latina tapas circuit. Wonderful wines, gorgeous *pinchos* (tapas; the *tortilla de patatas* is superb) and fine risottos add up to a pretty special combination.

NAÏA RESTAURANTE — FUSION €€

Map p232 (☎91 366 27 83; www.naiarestaurante.com; Plaza de la Paja 3; mains €12-19; ⊙lunch & dinner Tue-Sun; Ⓜ La Latina) On the lovely Plaza de la Paja, Naïa has a real buzz about it, with a cooking laboratory overseen by Carlos López Reyes, modern Spanish cuisine and a chill-out lounge downstairs. The emphasis throughout is on natural ingredients, healthy food and exciting tastes. The asparagus with celery salt and truffled eggs is typical of what to expect. The kitchen stays open until 12.30am on Friday and Saturday nights.

CASA LUCIO — SPANISH €€

Map p232 (☎91 365 32 52; www.casalucio.es; Calle de la Cava Baja 35; mains €12-25; ⊙lunch & dinner Sun-Fri, dinner Sat, closed Aug; Ⓜ La Latina) Lucio has been wowing *madrileños* (people from Madrid) with his light touch, quality ingredients and home-style local cooking for ages – think roasted meats and, a Lucio speciality, eggs in abundance. There's also *rabo de toro* (bull's tail) during the Fiestas de San Isidro Labrador and plenty of *rioja* (red wine) to wash away the mere thought of it. The lunchtime *guisos del día* (stews of the day), including *cocido* (meat and chickpea stew) on Wednesdays, are also popular. Casa Lucio draws an august, always well-dressed crowd, which has included the king of Spain, former US president Bill Clinton and Penélope Cruz.

POSADA DE LA VILLA — MADRILEÑO €€€

Map p232 (☎91 366 18 80; www.posadadelavilla.com; Calle de la Cava Baja 9; mains €20-28; ⊙lunch & dinner Mon-Sat, lunch Sun, closed Aug; Ⓜ La Latina) This wonderfully restored 17th-century *posada* (inn) is something of a local landmark. The atmosphere is formal, the decoration sombre and traditional (heavy timber and brickwork), and the cuisine decidedly local – roast meats, *cocido*, *callos* (tripe) and *sopa de ajo* (garlic soup).

RESTAURANTE JULIÁN DE TOLOSA NAVARRAN €€

Map p232 (☎91 365 82 10; www.casajuliandetolosa.com; Calle de la Cava Baja 18; mains €21.50-29.50; ⊙lunch & dinner Tue-Sun, lunch Mon; MLa Latina) Navarran cuisine is treated with respect at this classy place that's popular with celebrities and well-regarded by food critics. There are only four main dishes to choose from – two fish and two meat – and they haven't changed in years, but it still has a contemporary feel and why change the *chuletón* (T-bone steak) when it's already close to perfection?

ENOTABERNA DEL LEÓN DE ORO SPANISH €€

Map p232 (☎91 119 14 94; www.posadadlleondeoro.com; Calle de la Cava Baja 12; mains €13-15; MLa Latina) The stunning restoration work that brought to life the Posada del León de Oro (p169), also bequeathed to La Latina a fine new bar-restaurant. The emphasis is on matching carefully chosen wines with creative dishes (such as baby squid with potato emulsion and rucula pesto) in a casual atmosphere. It's a winning combination.

LA ANTOÑITA CONTEMPORARY SPANISH €€

Map p232 (☎91 119 14 24; www.posadadeldragon.com; Calle de la Cava Baja 14; tapas €4-13, mains from €12.90; MLa Latina) The restaurants of the stunning new hotel Posada del Dragón, this fine place retains some original features (exposed wooden beams, heavy stonework) of the original inn. It serves tapas at the bar and a range of creative dishes out the back in the sit-down restaurant, such as *secreto ibérico con guacamole* (pork fillet with guacamole).

LA PERIJILA TAPAS €€

Map p232 (☎91 364 28 55; Calle de la Cava Baja 25; tapas from €4.50; ⊙lunch & dinner Mon-Sat, lunch Sun; MLa Latina) This lovely and cosy little place lives and breathes Andalucía, with flamenco decoration and strategically placed flowers. The food is excellent, from summer gazpacho (cold tomato-based soup) to everything from mussels to meatballs.

ENE RESTAURANTE CONTEMPORARY SPANISH €€

Map p232 (☎91 366 25 91; www.enerestaurante.com; Calle del Nuncio 19; mains €11-22, brunch €22; ⊙lunch & dinner daily, brunch 12.30-4.30pm Sat & Sun; MLa Latina) Just across from Iglesia de San Pedro El Viejo, one of Madrid's oldest churches, Ene is anything but old world. The design is cutting edge and awash with reds and purples, while the young and friendly waiters circulate to the tune of lounge music. The food is Spanish-Asian fusion and there are also plenty of *pintxos* to choose from. The chill-out beds downstairs are great for an after-dinner cocktail or even a meal, although they're always reserved well in advance. Its brunch is highly recommended.

LA BUGA DEL LOBO SPANISH €€

Map p231 (☎91 467 61 51; www.labocadellobo.com; Calle de Argumosa 11; mains €8.50-19; ⊙11am-2am Wed-Mon; MLavapiés) La Buga del Lobo has been one of the 'in' places in cool and gritty Lavapiés for years now and it's still hard to get a table. The atmosphere is Bohemian and inclusive, with funky, swirling murals, contemporary art exhibitions and jazz or lounge music. The food's traditional with a few creative detours, with meat and fish dishes for mains and *croquetas* (croquettes), cheeses or salads for entrées, but it's best known for its groovy vibe at any time of day or night.

LAMIAK TAPAS €€

Map p232 (www.lamiak.net; Calle de la Cava Baja 42; raciones €5-9; ⊙lunch & dinner Tue-Sat, lunch Sun; MLa Latina) Another casual La Latina tapas bar, Lamiak is filled to the rafters on Sundays (a sure sign of La Latina

LOCAL KNOWLEDGE

BAR MELO'S

There's no tradition of kebab shops for midnight attacks of the munchies, but there's always **Bar Melo's** (Map p231; ☎91 527 50 54; Calle del Ave María; mains from €7.50; ⊙9pm-2am Tue-Sat, closed Aug; MLavapiés). Bar Melo's is famous across the city for its *zapatillas* – great, spanking *bocadillos* (filled rolls) of *lacón* (cured shoulder of pork) and cheese. They're big, they're greasy and they're damn good. The *croquetas* (croquettes) are also famously good, not to mention epic in scale.

success) and busy at other times, thanks to its contemporary exhibitions, laid-back atmosphere, good wines and tapas dishes such as tomato with goat's cheese and caramelised onion, or red pepper stuffed with seafood.

SANLÚCAR ANDALUCIAN €€

Map p232 (☎91 354 00 52; Calle de San Isidro Labrador 14; mains €12-20; ⌚lunch & dinner Tue-Sat, lunch Sun; Ⓜ La Latina) The seafood-dominated cooking of the Andalucian province of Cádiz is what this place is all about, with every imaginable sea creature (usually lightly fried) sharing the menu with gazpacho served in a tall drinking glass. Quiet at lunchtimes (except on Sundays), it can be hard to find a place in the evenings.

LA CHATA TAPAS €€

Map p232 (☎91 366 14 58; Calle de la Cava Baja 24; mains €8-20; ⌚lunch & dinner Thu-Mon, dinner Wed; Ⓜ La Latina) Behind the lavishly tiled facade, La Chata looks for all the world like a neglected outpost of the past. The decor may be rundown and the bullfighting memorabilia not to everyone's taste, but this is an essential stop on a tapas tour of La Latina. The dishes are mainstays of the local diet (tripe and plenty of seafood), but don't come here without ordering a *cazuela* (stew cooked and served in a ceramic pot, including wild mushrooms with clams).

MALACATÍN MADRILEÑO €€

Map p231 (☎91 365 52 41; www.malacatin.com; Calle de Ruda 5; mains €11-15; ⌚lunch Mon-Wed & Sat, lunch & dinner Thu & Fri; Ⓜ La Latina) If you want to see *madrileños* enjoying their favourite local food, this is one of the best places to do so. The clamour of conversation bounces off the tiled walls of the cramped dining area adorned with bullfighting memorabilia. The speciality is as much *cocido* as you can eat (€19). The *degustación de cocido* (taste of *cocido;* €5) at the bar is a great way to try Madrid's favourite dish.

CASA LUCAS TAPAS €€

Map p232 (☎91 365 08 04; www.casalucas.es; Calle de la Cava Baja 30; tapas/raciones from €5/12; ⌚lunch & dinner Thu-Tue, dinner Wed; Ⓜ La Latina) Receiving plaudits from food critics and ordinary punters alike, Casa Lucas takes a sideways glance at traditional Spanish tapas and heads off in new directions (the foie gras with port and caramelised fruits, for example). There are a range of hot and cold tapas and larger *raciones* (large tapas servings). The menu changes regularly as they come up with new ideas, and they pay particular attention to the wine list.

EL ESTRAGÓN VEGETARIAN €€

Map p232 (☎91 365 89 82; www.elestragonvegetariano.com; Plaza de la Paja 10; mains €8-14; 🖉; Ⓜ La Latina) A delightful spot for crêpes,

WORTH A DETOUR

MADRID RÍO

For decades, nay centuries, Madrid's Río Manzanares (Manzanares River) was a laughing stock. In the 17th century, renowned Madrid playwright Lope de Vega described the beautiful Puente de Segovia over the river to be a little too grand for the 'apprentice river'. He suggested the city buy a bigger river or sell the bridge. Thus it remained until the 21st century when Madrid's town hall decided to bring the river up to scratch.

Planned before the economic crisis swung a wrecking ball through the city's long list of planned infrastructure projects, the Madrid Río development saw the M-30 motorway driven underground and vast areas – up to 500,000 sq metres by some estimates – of abandoned riverside land turned into parkland that one former mayor described as 'a giant green carpet'. A summer beach à la Paris, bike paths, outdoor cafes and children's playgrounds are all part of the mix in this attractive 10km-long stretch of parkland. The three easiest ways to access Madrid Río are:

➡ Walk down the hill from La Latina to the western end of Calle de Segovia.

➡ Catch the metro to the **Estadio Vicente Calderón** (☎91 366 47 07; www.clubatleticodemadrid.com; Paseo de la Virgin del Puerto; Ⓜ Pirámides), the home football stadium of Atlético de Madrid.

➡ Follow the signs from **Matadero Madrid** (☎91 252 52 53; www.mataderomadrid.com; Paseo de la Chopera 14; admission free; Ⓜ Legazpi).

vegie burgers and other vegetarian specialities, El Estragón is undoubtedly one of Madrid's best vegetarian restaurants, although attentive vegans won't appreciate the use of butter. Apart from that, we're yet to hear a bad word about it, and the *menu del día* (daily set menu; from €8) is one of Madrid's best bargains.

ALMENDRO 13 TAPAS €

Map p232 (☎91 365 42 52; Calle del Almendro 13; mains €7-15; ⌚12.30-4pm & 7.30pm-midnight Sun-Thu, 12.30-5pm & 8pm-1am Fri & Sat; Ⓜ La Latina) Almendro 13 is a charming, wildly popular *taberna* (tavern) where you come for traditional Spanish tapas with an emphasis on quality rather than frilly elaborations. Cured meats, cheeses, omelettes and many variations on these themes dominate the menu; it serves both *raciones* and half-sized plates – a full *racion* of the famously good *huevos rotos* (literally, 'broken eggs') served with *jamón* (ham) and thin potato slices is a meal in itself. The only problem is that the wait for a table (low, with wooden stools) requires the patience of a saint, so order a fine wine or *manzanilla* (dry sherry) and soak up the buzz.

TXACOLINA TAPAS €

Map p232 (☎91 366 48 77; Calle de la Cava Baja 26; tapas from €3; ⌚dinner Mon & Wed-Fri, lunch & dinner Sat, lunch Sun; Ⓜ La Latina) Txacolina calls its *pintxos* 'high cuisine in miniature' – the first part is true, but these are some of the biggest *pintxos* (€3 to €5) you'll find and some are a meal in themselves. If ordering tapas makes you nervous because you don't speak Spanish or you're not quite sure how it works, it couldn't be easier here – they're lined up on the bar, Basque style, in all their glory and you can simply point. Whatever you order, wash it down with a *txacoli,* a sharp Basque white.

VIVA LA VIDA VEGETARIAN €

Map p232 (www.vivalavida.com.es; Costanilla de San Andrés 16; buffet 500g plus drink €10; ⌚noon-midnight Mon-Wed, 11am-2am Thu-Sun; ✎; Ⓜ La Latina) The enticing vegetarian buffet with hot and cold food, always filled with flavour, is one of the best deals in town. On the cusp of Plaza de la Paja, this place has a laid-back vibe and is a great place at any time of the day, especially outside normal Spanish eating hours when your stomach's rumbling. It has another **branch** (Map p242; ☎91 369 72 54; Calle de las Huertas 57; ⌚11am-midnight; Ⓜ Antón Martín) in Huertas, although it's more takeaway and food store, with only a handful of stools.

LA CAMARILLA TAPAS

Map p232 (☎91 354 02 07; www.lacamarillarestaurante.com; Calle de la Cava Baja 21; mains €7-21, tapas tasting menu €19.50; ⌚lunch & dinner Thu-Tue; Ⓜ La Latina) With an innovative and frequently changing menu that ranges from sit-down meals to creative tapas, La Camarilla is right at home along Calle de la Cava Baja. Its tapas tasting menu lets you go on a tapas crawl without moving from your bar stool.

TABERNA DE CONSPIRADORES TAPAS €€

Map p232 (☎91 366 58 69; www.conspiradores.com; Calle de la Cava Baja 7; mains €6-18; ⌚noon-midnight; Ⓜ La Latina) This cosy little tapas bar at the northern end of Calle de la Cava Baja is all about the regional cuisine of Extremadura (the *jamón* and other cured meats from there are some of Spain's best), with well-priced wines to wash it down.

DRINKING & NIGHTLIFE

For those whose idea of a night out reaches its limit at the sensible hour of 3am, La Latina and Lavapiés are ideal. Both have memorable cafes and bars that you could spend more than a single night exploring. Most nights (and Sunday afternoons), crowds of happy *madrileños* hop from bar to bar across La Latina. This is a *barrio* beloved by a discerning crowd of 20- and 30-something urban sophisticates, who ensure that there's little room to move in the good places and that the bad ones don't survive long; the scene is a little more diverse on Sundays as crowds fan out from El Rastro. Most of the action takes place along Calle de la Cava Baja, the western end of Calle del Almendro and Plaza de la Paja. Many of these places are better known for their tapas, but they're equally great for a drink. Lavapiés is a completely different kettle of fish altogether – working class and multicultural, with an alternative, often Bohemian crowd and quirky bars brimful of personality. Not everyone loves Lavapiés, but we do.

MADRID'S OLDEST STREET?

There are numerous candidates for the title of Madrid's oldest street. Calle del Arenal stakes a strong claim, although the date when it ceased to be a small river and became a street remains unresolved by historical records. According to the historian Rafael Fraguas, the oldest street in Madrid is Calle de Grafal, which dates back to 1190 when it was called Calle del Santo Grial. But not that you'd notice: in the midst of La Latina's medieval streets, Calle de Grafal is not the *barrio*'s prettiest thoroughfare, with largely modern brick apartment blocks. It runs southwest off Plaza de Segovia Nueva between Calle de Toledo and Calle de la Cava Baja.

GAUDEAMUS CAFÉ CAFE

Map p231 (www.gaudeamuscafe.com; Calle de Tribulete 14, 4th fl; ⏲3pm-midnight Mon-Sat; Ⓜ Lavapiés) What a place! Decoration that's light and airy, with pop-art posters of Audrey Hepburn and James Bond. A large terrace with views over the Lavapiés rooftops. A stunning backdrop of a ruined church atop which the cafe sits. With so much else going for it, it almost seems incidental that it also serves great teas, coffees and snacks (and meals). The only criticism we can think of is that it doesn't stay open later. The terrace is filled to bursting on summer evenings.

DELIC BAR, CAFE

Map p232 (www.delic.es; Costanilla de San Andrés 14; ⏲11am-2am Fri-Sun & Tue-Thu, 7pm-2am Mon; Ⓜ La Latina) We could go on for hours about this long-standing cafe-bar, but we'll reduce it to its most basic elements: nursing an exceptionally good mojito (€8) or three on a warm summer's evening at Delic's outdoor tables on one of Madrid's prettiest plazas is one of life's great pleasures. Bliss. Due to local licensing restrictions, the outdoor tables close two hours before closing time, whereafter the intimate interior is almost as good.

CAFÉ DEL NUNCIO BAR, CAFE

Map p232 (Calle de Segovia 9; ⏲noon-2am Sun-Thu, to 3am Fri & Sat; Ⓜ La Latina) Café del Nuncio straggles down a laneway to Calle de Segovia. You can drink on one of several cosy levels inside or, better still in summer, enjoy the outdoor seating that one local reviewer likened to a slice of Rome. By day it's an old-world cafe, but by night it's one of the best bars in the *barrio*.

TABERNA TEMPRANILLO WINE BAR

Map p232 (Calle de la Cava Baja 38; ⏲1-3.30pm & 8pm-midnight Tue-Sun, 8pm-midnight Mon; Ⓜ La Latina) You could come here for the tapas, but we recommend Taberna Tempranillo primarily for its wines, of which it has a selection that puts many Spanish bars to shame, and many are sold by the glass. It's not a late-night place, but it's always packed in the early evening and on Sundays after El Rastro.

EL EUCALIPTO COCKTAIL BAR

Map p231 (Calle de Argumosa 4; ⏲5pm-2am Sun-Thu, to 3am Fri & Sat; Ⓜ Lavapiés) You'd be mad not to at least pass by this fine little bar with its love of all things Cuban. From the music to the clientele and the Caribbean cocktails (including nonalcoholic), it's a sexy, laid-back place. Not surprisingly, the mojitos are a cut above average, but the juices and daiquiris also have a loyal following.

EL VIAJERO BAR

Map p232 (☎91 366 90 64; www.elviajeromadrid.com; Plaza de la Cebada 11; ⏲1.30pm-2.30am Tue-Sat, noon-8pm Sun; Ⓜ La Latina) The undoubted highlight of this landmark of La Latina nights is the rooftop *terraza* (open-air bar), which boasts fine views down onto the thronging streets. When the weather's warm, it's nigh on impossible to get a table. Our secret? It often closes the *terraza* around 8pm to spruce it up a little; you should be ready to pounce when it reopens and thereafter guard your table with your life.

LA INQUILINA BAR

Map p231 (www.lainquilina.es; Calle del Ave María 39; ⏲7pm-3am Tue-Sat, 1pm-1am Sun; Ⓜ Lavapiés) One of our favourite bars in Lavapiés, La Inquilina has a cool-and-casual vibe and deep roots in the Lavapiés soil. Contemporary artworks by budding local artists adorn the walls and you can either gather around the bar or take a table out the back. It's a small slice of sophistication in a *barrio* not known for such characteristics. They serve tapas for €1 until 10pm if your night is starting early.

BONANNO WINE BAR

Map p232 (☎91 366 68 86; Plaza del Humilladero 4; ⏰noon-2am; Ⓜ La Latina) If much of Madrid's nightlife starts too late for your liking, Bonanno could be for you. It made its name as a cocktail bar, but many people come here for the great wines and it's usually full of young professionals from early evening onwards. Be prepared to snuggle up close to those around you if you want a spot at the bar.

ENTERTAINMENT

CASA PATAS FLAMENCO

Map p231 (☎91 369 04 96; www.casapatas.com; Calle de Cañizares 10; admission €32; ⏰shows 10.30pm Mon-Thu, 9pm & midnight Fri & Sat; Ⓜ Antón Martín, Tirso de Molina) One of the top flamenco stages in Madrid, this *tablao* (flamenco venue) always offers flawless quality that serves as a good introduction to the art. It's not the friendliest place in town, especially if you're only here for the show, and you're likely to be crammed in a little, but no one complains about the standard of the performances.

CORRAL DE LA MORERÍA FLAMENCO

Map p232 (☎91 365 84 46; www.corraldelamoreria.com; Calle de la Morería 17; admission incl drink €42-45; ⏰8.30pm-2.30am, shows 9.30pm & 11.30pm Sun-Fri, 7pm, 10pm & midnight Sat; Ⓜ Ópera) This is one of the most prestigious flamenco stages in Madrid, with 50 years' experience as a leading flamenco venue and top performers most nights. The stage area has a rustic feel, and tables are pushed up close. We'd steer clear of the restaurant, which is overpriced (from €43), but the performances have a far better price-quality ratio. This is where international celebrities (eg Marlene Dietrich, Marlon Brando, Muhammad Ali and Omar Sharif) have all gone for their flamenco fix when in town.

MARULA CAFÉ LIVE MUSIC

Map p232 (☎91 366 15 96; www.marulacafe.com; Calle de Caños Viejos 3; admission free-€10; ⏰11pm-5am Sun-Thu, 11.30pm-6am Fri & Sat; Ⓜ La Latina) An Afro hairstyle would be the perfect look here, where the music (concerts at 11.30pm, DJs until sunrise) is all about funk, soul, jazz, music from the American South, Afrobeat and even a little hip hop. It's a club with attitude and always has a great rhythm. The jazz-soul jam sessions at midnight on Monday are a fine way to start the week. It's a little hard to find – it's almost under the viaduct just down the hill from Calle de la Morería.

CONTRACLUB LIVE MUSIC

Map p232 (☎91 365 55 45; www.contraclub.es; Calle de Bailén 16; admission €6-12; ⏰10pm-6am Wed-Sat; Ⓜ La Latina) ContraClub is a crossover live music venue and nightclub, with live flamenco on Wednesday and an eclectic mix of other live music (jazz, blues, world music and rock) from Thursday to

DISAPPEARED LA LATINA LANDMARKS

The narrow streets of **Calle de la Cava Alta** and **Calle de la Cava Baja** delineate where the second line of medieval Christian city walls ran. They continued north along what is now **Calle de los Cuchilleros** (Knifemakers St) and along the **Calle de la Cava de San Miguel**, and were superseded by the third circuit of walls, which was raised in the 15th century. The *cavas* (caves or cellars) were initially ditches dug in front of the walls, later used as refuse dumps and finally given over to housing when the walls no longer served any defensive purpose.

Just west of La Latina metro station, the busy and bar-strewn corner of Madrid marked by the ill-defined **Plaza de la Cebada** (Barley Square) occupies an important historical space. In the wake of the Christian conquest, the square was, for a time, the site of a Muslim cemetery, and the nearby **Plaza de la Puerta de Moros** (Moors' Gate) underscores that this area was long home to the city's Muslim population. The square later became a popular spot for public executions – until well into the 19th century, the condemned would be paraded along Calle de Toledo, before turning into the square and mounting the gallows. Later the plaza was the site of one of the largest markets in Madrid.

WORTH A DETOUR

MATADERO MADRID

A contemporary arts centre, opened in 2007, Matadero Madrid is a stunning multipurpose space south of the centre. Occupying the converted buildings of the old Arganzuela livestock market and slaughterhouse, Matadero Madrid covers 148,300 sq metres and hosts cutting-edge drama, musical and dance performances as well as exhibitions on architecture, fashion, literature and cinema. It's a dynamic space and its proximity to the newly landscaped riverbank make for a non-touristy alternative to sightseeing in Madrid, not to mention a brilliant opportunity to see the latest avant-garde theatre or exhibitions.

Saturday; after the live acts (which start at 10.30pm), the resident DJs serve up equally eclectic beats (indie, pop, funk and soul) to make sure you don't move elsewhere.

EL JUGLAR — LIVE MUSIC

Map p231 (☎91 528 43 81; www.salajuglar.com; Calle de Lavapiés 37; admission €5-10; ⏰9.30pm-3am Sun-Wed, to 3.30am Thu-Sat; Ⓜ Lavapiés) One of the hottest spots in Lavapiés, this great venue hosts a largely Bohemian crowd who come from all over the city for a flamenco-dominated program leavened with rock and fusion. After the live acts leave the stage around midnight, it's DJ-spun tunes.

EL DESPERTAR — JAZZ

Map p231 (☎91 530 80 95; www.cafeeldespertar.com; Calle de la Torrecilla del Leal 18; admission free-€6; ⏰7.30pm-late Thu-Sun; Ⓜ Antón Martín) El Despertar is all about jazz down to its roots. Everything about this place harks back to the 1920s, with a commitment to old-style jazz and decor to match from its days as a meeting point for the *barrio's* intelligentsia. There are live performances every Friday and Saturday, as well as most Thursdays, Sundays and many other nights. Concerts start between 8.30pm and 11pm; check the website for details.

LA ESCALERA DE JACOB — LIVE MUSIC

Map p231 (www.laescaleradejacob.es; Calle de Lavapiés 11; concerts from €6; ⏰8pm-2am Wed & Thu, 8pm-2.30am Fri, 11am-2.30am Sat, 5pm-1am Sun; Ⓜ Antón Martín, Tirso de Molina) As much a theatre-bar as a live music venue, 'Jacob's Ladder' is one of Madrid's most original stages. Magicians, storytellers, children's theatre (on Saturdays and Sundays at noon), live jazz and other genres are all part of the mix. Behind this intimate venue is a philosophy of crossing boundaries (very Lavapiés). This alternative slant on life makes for some terrific live performances and a crowd of like-minded patrons. And regardless of what's on, it's worth stopping by here for its creative cocktails that you won't find anywhere else – the *fray aguacate* (Frangelico, vodka, honey, avocado and vanilla) should give you an idea of how far they go.

EL RINCÓN DEL ARTE NUEVO — LIVE MUSIC

Map p232 (☎91 365 50 45; www.elrincondelartenuevo.com; Calle de Segovia 17; admission €5-10; ⏰8.30pm-5am, to 6am Fri & Sat; Ⓜ La Latina) With more than 30 years in the business, this small venue knows what its punters like and it serves up a nightly feast of singer-songwriters for an appreciative crowd. The acts are as diverse as the genre itself, with Melendi, Fran Postigo and Diego El Negro among those to have taken the stage here. Concerts start between 9.30pm and 12.30am and sometimes stray into flamenco or pop.

TEATRO CIRCO PRICE — THEATRE

(☎91 528 98 65; www.teatrocircoprice.es; Ronda de Atocha 35; Ⓜ Lavapiés, Embajadores, Atocha) Just south of Lavapiés, this modern theatre does a little bit of everything from concerts and circuses to dance performances. It also hosts the Festival Flamenco Caja Madrid in February.

TEATRO PAVÓN — THEATRE

Map p231 (☎91 528 28 19; teatroclasico.mcu.es; Calle de los Embajadores 9; Ⓜ La Latina, Tirso de Molina) The home of the National Classical Theatre Company, this theatre has a regular calendar of classical shows by Spanish and European playwrights.

TEATRO VALLE-INCLÁN — THEATRE

Map p231 (☎91 505 88 01; http://cdn.mcu.es; Plaza de Lavapiés; tickets €15-18; Ⓜ Lavapiés) The stunning refurbishment of this theatre has brought new life (and quality plays) to this once run-down corner of Lavapiés. Located on the southern end of the Plaza de Lavapiés, it is now the headquarters for the Centro Dramático Nacional (National Drama Centre) and puts on landmark plays by (mostly) Spanish playwrights such as Valle-Inclán and Fernando Arrabal.

SHOPPING

La Latina may be a largely after-dark and weekend affair, but its appeal to a hip, well-to-do urban crowd has drawn small boutiques, especially those specialising in designer jewellery, to the narrow streets. This is also the *barrio* that throngs with Sunday bargain hunters, drawn here by El Rastro (which tumbles down into Lavapiés) and you'll also come across curio shops so specialised that you wonder how they ever keep going.

HELENA ROHNER JEWELLERY

Map p232 (www.helenarohner.com.es; Calle del Almendro 4; ⌚9am-8.30pm Mon-Fri, noon-2.30pm & 3.30-8pm Sat, noon-3pm Sun; Ⓜ La Latina, Tirso de Molina) One of Europe's most creative jewellery designers, Helena Rohner has a spacious boutique in La Latina. Working with silver, stone, porcelain, wood and Murano glass, she makes inventive pieces and her work is a regular feature of Paris fashion shows. In her own words, she seeks to recreate 'the magic of Florence, the vitality of London and the luminosity of Madrid'.

DEL HIERRO CLOTHES, ACCESSORIES

Map p232 (☎91 364 58 91; Calle de la Cava Baja 6; ⌚11am-2.30pm & 5-9pm Mon-Sat, noon-3pm Sun; Ⓜ La Latina, Tirso de Molina) This small boutique has an exceptional selection of handbags from designers such as Iñaki Sampedro, Quique Mestre and Carlos de Caz. The look is sophisticated but colourful.

ALMA DE IBÉRICO FOOD

Map p232 (☎91 366 15 24; www.julianbecerro.com; Calle de la Cava Baja 41; ⌚10am-10pm; Ⓜ La Latina) This purveyor of some of the finest *embutidos* (cured meats) is perfectly at home on this, one of Madrid's culinary streets. The *jamón* comes from the renowned Salamanca region of Castilla y León, with cheeses and other products from around Spain.

CARAMELOS PACO FOOD

Map p232 (☎91 365 42 58; www.caramelospaco.com; Calle de Toledo 53-55; ⌚9.30am-2pm & 5-8.30pm Mon-Fri, 9.30am-2pm Sat, 11am-3pm Sun; Ⓜ La Latina) A sweet shop that needs to be seen to be believed, Caramelos Paco has been indulging children and adults alike since 1934 and it remains unrivalled when it comes to variety. There's almost nothing you can't find here and even the shop window is a work of art.

DE PIEDRA JEWELLERY

Map p232 (☎91 365 96 20; www.depiedracreaciones.com; Calle del Almendro 10; ⌚11am-2pm & 5-8pm Mon-Fri, 11am-7pm Sat, noon-3pm Sun; Ⓜ La Latina) Necklaces, earrings, bracelets and home decorations fill this lovely showroom. Silver and semiprecious stones are the mainstays.

Sol, Santa Ana & Huertas

Neighbourhood Top Five

❶ Discovering the little-known artistic riches of the **Real Academia de Bellas Artes de San Fernando** (p78).

❷ Spending a lazy afternoon watching the world go by from one of the outdoor tables on **Plaza de Santa Ana** (p80).

❸ Stepping back in time at **La Venencia** (p84), an old-style sherry bar that captures the spirit of a Spain that long ago disappeared elsewhere.

❹ Getting into the swing at **Café Central** (p86), an art deco salon that's internationally recognised as one of the world's finest jazz clubs.

❺ Losing yourself in the lanes of the **Barrio de las Letras** (p81) with its echoes of Cervantes and Madrid's literary past.

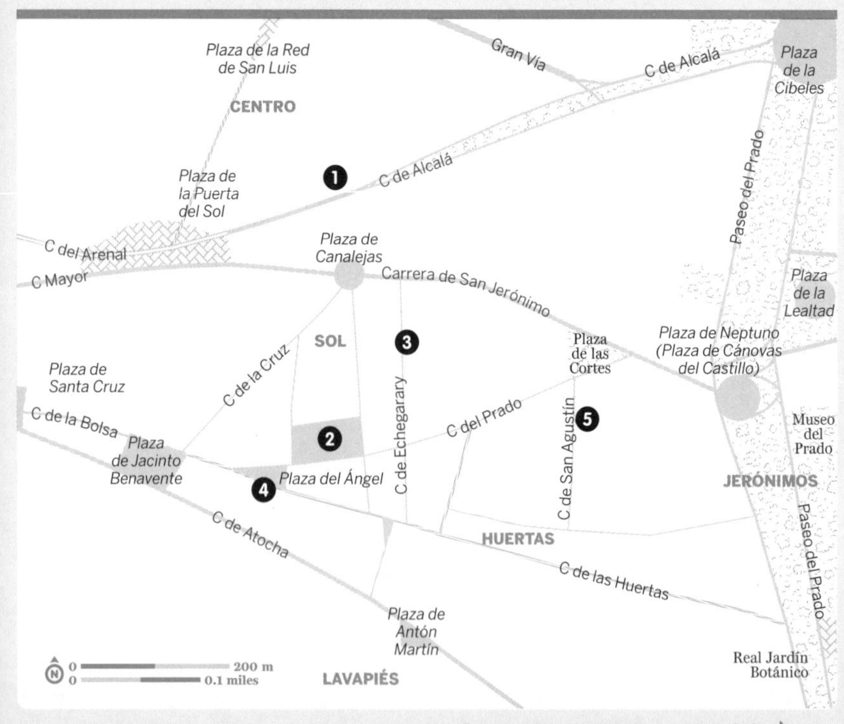

For more detail of this area see Map p242

Explore: Sol, Santa Ana & Huertas

Sol, Santa Ana and Huertas together make up Madrid's most clamorous corner. So many explorations of this neighbourhood begin in the Plaza de la Puerta del Sol, the pulsing heart of downtown Madrid, then move on to nearby Plaza de Santa Ana and the tangle of laneways that tumble down the hillside to the east.

And yet, there are subtle differences between the two squares. Sol is above all a crossroads, a place for people to meet before fanning out across the city. There are reasons to linger, but for the most part a sense of transience is what prevails. And Sol is always busy, no matter the hour.

Plaza de Santa Ana, on the other hand, is a destination in its own right, a stirringly beautiful square that has become emblematic of a city intent on living the good life. It is also a place of many moods. On a sunny weekday afternoon, it can be quiet (by its own rather noisy standards), a place to nurse a wine as you plot your path through the city. This is when the Barrio de las Letras is also at its most accessible, its streets suitably sedate for a *barrio* (district) rich in literary resonance. But come most nights of the week, Sana Ana and the surrounding streets crescendo into life, an explosion of noise and revelry that ripples out across the city.

Local Life

➡ **Hangout** Sunday 1pm is known in Madrid as *la hora del vermut* (vermouth hour). Mostly this resonates in neighbouring La Latina, but Casa Alberto (p81) is arguably the real star of the hour.

➡ **Flamenco** One of the great flamenco venues of Old Madrid, the extravagantly tiled Villa Rosa (p86) has mercifully shed its recent past as a fairly run-of-the-mill nightclub and returned to its roots. It even starred in a Pedro Almodóvar movie.

➡ **Meeting Point** It's a cliché whose time has passed for an in crowd, but meeting at the paving stone that marks Spain's Kilometre Zero on Plaza de la Puerta del Sol (p79) is a time-honoured local tradition.

Getting There & Away

➡ **Metro** Sol metro station is one of the most useful in Madrid, with lines 1, 2 and 3 all passing through.

➡ **Metro** Other useful stations are Sevilla (line 2) and Tirso de Molina and Antón Martín (both line 1).

Lonely Planet's Top Tip

The Real Academia de Bellas Artes de San Fernando may have a collection the envy of many a European gallery but it's free if you come on a Wednesday. And unlike free days at other better-known Madrid art galleries, you'll see no discernible rise in visitor numbers on Wednesday, allowing you to enjoy it both for free and in peace.

Best Places to Eat

➡ Casa Alberto (p81)

➡ La Terraza del Casino (p81)

➡ Casa Labra (p83)

➡ Lhardy (p82)

➡ Vi Cool (p81)

➡ Los Gatos (p82)

For reviews, see p81 

Best Places to Drink

➡ La Venencia (p84)

➡ The Roof (p84)

➡ El Imperfecto (p84)

➡ La Terraza del Urban (p84)

➡ Taberna de Dolores (p85)

➡ Cervecería Alemana (p85)

For reviews, see p84 

Best Literary Landmarks

➡ Calle de Cervantes 2 (p81)

➡ Casa Alberto (p81)

➡ Convento de las Trinitarias (p81)

➡ Casa de Lope de Vega (p79)

TOP SIGHTS
REAL ACADEMIA DE BELLAS ARTES DE SAN FERNANDO

Madrid's 'other' art gallery, the Real Academía de Bellas Artes has for centuries played a pivotal role in the artistic life of the city. As the royal fine arts academy, it has nurtured local talent, thereby complementing the royal penchant for drawing the great international artists of the day into their realm. The pantheon of former alumni reads like a Who's Who of Spanish art, and the collection that now hangs on the academy's walls is a suitably rich one.

DON'T MISS...

- Zurbaran & El Greco
- First Floor Masters
- Picasso, Sorolla & Gris

PRACTICALITIES

- Map p242
- ☎91 524 08 64
- http://rabasf.insde.es
- Calle de Alcalá 13
- adult/child €5/free, free Wed
- 9am-3pm Tue-Sat, to 2.30pm Sun Sep-Jun, hours vary Jul & Aug
- MSol, Sevilla

Bastion of Tradition

In any other city, this gallery would be a stand-out attraction, but in Madrid it often gets forgotten in the rush to the Prado, Thyssen or Reina Sofía. Nonetheless a visit here is a fascinating journey into another age of art; when we tell you that Picasso and Dalí studied at this academy, but found it far too stuffy for their liking, you'll get an idea of what to expect. A centre of excellence since Fernando VI founded the academy in the 18th century, it remains a stunning repository of works by some of the best-loved old masters.

Zurbarán & El Greco

The 1st floor, mainly devoted to 16th- to 19th-century paintings, is the most noteworthy of those in the academic gallery. Among relative unknowns, you come across a hall of works by Zurbarán (especially arresting is the series of full-length portraits of white-cloaked friars) and a *San Jerónimo* by El Greco.

Other First-Floor Masters

At a 'fork' in the exhibition, a sign points right to rooms 11 to 16, the main one showcasing Alonso Cano (1601–67) and José de Ribera (1591–1652). In the others a couple of minor portraits by Velázquez hang alongside the occasional Rubens, Tintoretto and Bellini, which have somehow been smuggled in. Rooms 17 to 22 offer a space full of Bravo Murillo and last, but most captivating, 13 pieces by Goya, including self-portraits, portraits of King Fernando VII and the infamous minister Manuel Godoy, along with one on bullfighting.

Modern Art

The 19th and 20th centuries are the themes upstairs. It's not the most extensive or engaging modern collection, but you'll find drawings by Picasso as well as works by Joaquín Sorolla, Juan Gris, Eduardo Chillida and Ignacio Zuloaga, in most cases with only one or two items each.

SIGHTS

REAL ACADEMIA DE BELLAS ARTES DE SAN FERNANDO MUSEUM

See p78.

PLAZA DE LA PUERTA DEL SOL SQUARE

Map p242 (Plaza de la Puerta del Sol; MSol) The official centrepoint of Spain is a gracious hemisphere of elegant facades and often overwhelming crowds. It is, above all, a crossroads with people forever passing through on their way elsewhere.

In early times, the Puerta del Sol (the Gate of the Sun) was the eastern gate of the city and from here passed a road through the peasant hovels of the outer 'suburbs' en route to Guadalajara, to the northeast. The name of the gate appears to date from the 1520s, when Madrid joined the revolt of the Comuneros against Carlos I and erected a fortress in the east-facing arch in which the sun was depicted. The fort was demolished around 1570.

The main building on the square houses the regional government of the Comunidad de Madrid. The **Casa de Correos**, as it is called, was built as the city's main post office in 1768. The clock was added in 1856 and on New Year's Eve people throng the square to wait impatiently for the clock to strike midnight, and at each gong swallow a grape – not as easy as it sounds! On the footpath outside the Casa de Correos is a plaque marking Spain's **Kilometre Zero**, the point from which Spain's network of roads is measured. The semicircular junction owes its present appearance in part to the Bourbon king Carlos III (r 1759–88), whose equestrian statue (complete with his unmistakable nose) stands in the middle.

Just to the east of Carlos III, the statue of a bear nuzzling a *madroño* (strawberry tree) is the city's symbol.

GRAN VÍA STREET

(Gran Vía; MGran Vía, Callao) It's difficult to imagine Madrid without Gran Vía, the grand boulevard lined with towering belle époque facades that climbs up through the centre of Madrid from Plaza de España then down to Calle de Alcalá. But it has only existed since 1910, when it was bulldozed through what was then a labyrinth of old streets. Plans for the boulevard were first announced in 1862 and so interminable were the delays that a famous *zarzuela* (satirical musical comedy), *La Gran Vía,* first performed in 1886, was penned to mock the city authorities. When finally completed, 14 streets disappeared off the map, as did 311 houses, including one where Goya had once lived.

It may have destroyed whole *barrios,* but Gran Vía is still considered one of the most successful examples of urban planning in central Madrid since the late 19th century.

One eye-catching building, the **Carrión**, on the corner of Gran Vía and Calle de Jacometrezo, was Madrid's first pre-WWI tower-block apartment hotel. Also dominating the skyline about one-third of the way along Gran Vía is the 1920s-era **Telefónica building**, which was for years the highest building in the city. During the civil war, when Madrid was besieged by Franco's forces and the boulevard became known as 'Howitzer Alley' due to the artillery shells that rained down upon it, the Telefónica building was a favoured target.

Among the more interesting buildings is the stunning, French-designed **Edificio Metrópolis** (1905), which marks the southern end of Gran Vía. The winged victory statue atop its dome was added in 1975 and is best seen from Calle de Alcalá or Plaza de la Cibeles. A little up the boulevard is the **Edificio Grassy** (with the Rolex sign), built in 1916. With its circular 'temple' as a crown, and profusion of arcs and slender columns, it's one of the most elegant buildings along Gran Vía.

Otherwise it's home to twice as many businesses (over 1050 at last count) as homes (nearly 600); over 13,000 people work along the street; and up to 55,000 vehicles pass through every day (including almost 185 buses an hour during peak periods). There are over 40 hotels on Gran Vía, but sadly just three of the 15 cinemas for which Gran Vía was famous remain.

FREE **CASA DE LOPE DE VEGA** MUSEUM

Map p242 (91 429 92 16; Calle de Cervantes 11; guided tours every 30min 10am-2pm Tue-Sat; MAntón Martín) Lope de Vega may be little known outside the Spanish-speaking world, but he was one of the greatest playwrights ever to write in Spanish, not to mention one of Madrid's favourite and most colourful literary sons. Scandalously, he shared the house, where he lived and wrote for 25 years until his death in 1635, with a mistress and four children by three different women; Lope de Vega's house was a typical *casa de malicia* (house of ill repute). Today

TOP SIGHTS
PLAZA DE SANTA ANA

The Plaza de Santa Ana is a delightful confluence of elegant architecture and irresistible energy. Situated in the heart of Huertas, it was laid out in 1810 during the controversial reign of Joseph Bonaparte, giving breathing space to what had hitherto been one of Madrid's most claustrophobic *barrios* (districts). The plaza quickly became a focal point for the intellectual life of the day, and the cafes surrounding the plaza thronged with writers, poets and artists engaging in endless *tertulias* (literary and philosophical discussions). Echoes of this literary history survive in the statues of the 17th-century writer Calderón de la Barca and **Federíco García Lorca** (added in 1998 on the 100th anniversary of his birth), and in the **Teatro Español** (formerly the Teatro del Príncipe) at the plaza's eastern end, and continue down into the Barrio de las Letras. Culture of a very different kind – bullfighting – also took centre stage here, with many a (long-since-disappeared) bullfighting bar nearby and the Hotel Reina Victoria (now Me by Melía) the hotel of choice for Spain's best *toreros* (bullfighters). Apart from anything else, the plaza is both the starting point for many long Huertas nights and its outdoor tables are a good place to sit back in the afternoon and ponder the excesses of the night before.

DON'T MISS

- Outdoor Tables
- Lorca Statue
- Teatro Español

PRACTICALITIES

- Map p242
- Plaza de Santa Ana
- MSevilla, Sol, Antón Martín

the house, which was restored in the 1950s, is filled with memorabilia related to his life and times. Out the back is a tranquil garden, a rare haven of birdsong.

ATENEO CIENTÍFICO, LITERARIO Y ARTÍSTICO DE MADRID
CULTURAL BUILDING

Map p242 (91 429 17 50; www.ateneodemadrid.com; Calle del Prado 21; guided visits €2; guided visits 10am-1pm Mon-Fri; MSevilla) Nestled away in the heart of the Barrio de las Letras, this venerable club of learned types was founded in 1821, although the building took on its present form in 1884. Its library and meetings of the great minds prompted Benito Pérez Galdós to describe it as the most important 'intellectual temple' in Madrid and a reference point for the thriving cultural life of the Barrio de las Letras. It's not generally open to the public, but no one seems to mind if you wander into the foyer, which is lined with portraits of terribly serious-looking fellows. They may even let you amble upstairs to the library, a jewel of another age, with dark timber stacks, weighty tomes and creakily quiet reading rooms dimly lit with desk lamps.

FREE CONGRESO DE LOS DIPUTADOS
NOTABLE BUILDING

Map p242 (91 390 65 25; www.congreso.es; Plaza de las Cortes; admission free; guided tours 10.30am-12.30pm Sat; MSevilla) Spain's lower house of parliament was originally a Renaissance building, but it was completely revamped in 1850 and given a facade with a neoclassical portal. The imposing lions watching over the entrance were smelted from cannons used in Spain's African wars during the mid-19th century. On the day that they were mounted outside the parliament building, one irreverent Madrid newspaper wrote 'And what mouths they have! One might imagine them to be parliamentarians!' It was here, on 11 February 1981, that renegade members of Spain's Guardia Civil launched a failed coup attempt. Be sure to bring your passport if you want to visit.

CIRCULO DE BELLAS ARTES
CULTURAL BUILDING

Map p242 (91 360 54 00; www.circulobellasartes.com; Calle de Alcalá 42; admission €1; MBanco de España) The dynamic 'Fine Arts Circle' has just about every kind of artistic expression on show, including exhibitions, concerts, short films and book readings. Overall, it's an elegant space with a program that's anything but staid, allowing it to remain at the forefront of Madrid's cultural life. There's also a fine cafe (p84).

EATING

Sol has something for everyone, but the noise surrounding Huertas nightlife can obscure the fact that the *barrio* is a terrific place to eat out. Its culinary appeal lies in a hotchpotch of styles rather than any overarching personality. There are bastions of traditional cooking with some restaurants serving Basque, Galician, Andalucian and Italian cuisine. When you factor in the *barrio's* fine bars and pulsing nightlife, it's difficult to find a good reason to leave the *barrio* once the sun goes down.

CASA ALBERTO — SPANISH €€

Map p242 (☎91 429 93 56; www.casaalberto.es; Calle de las Huertas 18; mains €16-20; ⌚lunch & dinner Tue-Sat, lunch Sun; Ⓜ Antón Martín) One of the most atmospheric old *tabernas* (taverns) of Madrid, Casa Alberto has been around since 1827 and occupies a building where Cervantes is said to have written one of his books. The secret to its staying power is vermouth on tap, excellent tapas at the bar and fine sit-down meals; Casa Alberto's *rabo de toro* (bull's tail) is famous among aficionados. As the antique wood-panelled decoration will suggest straight away, the *raciones* (large tapas servings) have none of the frilly innovations that have come to characterise Spanish tapas. *Jamón* (ham), Manchego cheese and *croquetas* (croquettes) are recurring themes.

VI COOL — CONTEMPORARY SPANISH €€

Map p242 (☎91 429 49 13; www.vi-cool.com; Calle de las Huertas 12; mains €8-18; Ⓜ Antón Martín) Catalan master chef Sergi Arola is one of the most restless and relentlessly creative culinary talents in the country. Aside from his showpiece Sergi Arola Gastro (p149), he has dabbled in numerous new restaurants around the capital and in Barcelona, but this is one of his most interesting yet – a modern bar-style space with prices that enable your average mortal to sample Arola's formidable gastronomic skills. Dishes are either tapas or larger *raciones,* ranging from his trademark Las Bravas de Arola (a different take on the well-loved Spanish dish consisting of roast potatoes in a spicy tomato sauce) to fried prawns with curry and mint.

LA TERRAZA DEL CASINO — CONTEMPORARY SPANISH €€€

Map p242 (☎91 521 87 00; www.casinodemadrid.es; Calle de Alcalá 15; set menus from €100; ⌚lunch & dinner Mon-Fri, dinner Sat; Ⓜ Sevilla) Perched atop the landmark Casino de Madrid building, this temple of haute cuisine is overseen, albeit from afar, by Ferran Adrià (Spain's premier celebrity chef), but is mostly in the hands of his acolyte Paco Roncero. It's all about culinary

BARRIO DE LAS LETRAS

In medieval Madrid, the Barrio de las Letras – which is bordered by Plaza de Santa Ana (west), Carrera de San Jerónimo (north), Paseo del Prado (east) and Calle de Atocha (south) – was one of Madrid's most important cultural hubs.

At Calle de Cervantes 11, Lope de Vega (1562–1635), arguably Spain's premier playwright, lived and died, and his house is now a museum (p79). But the street on which Lope de Vega's house sits owes its name to an even-more-famous former resident, Miguel de Cervantes Saavedra (1547–1616). Cervantes, the author of *Don Quijote,* spent much of his adult life in Madrid and lived and died at **Calle de Cervantes 2** (Map p242; Calle de Cervantes 2; Ⓜ Antón Martín); a plaque (dating from 1834) sits above the door. Sadly, the original building was torn down in the early 19th century despite a plea from King Fernando VII. When Cervantes died, his body was interred around the corner at the **Convento de las Trinitarias** (Map p242; Calle de Lope de Vega 16; Ⓜ Antón Martín) which is marked by another plaque. Still home to cloistered nuns, the convent is closed to the public, which saves the authorities embarrassment: no one really knows where in the convent the bones of Cervantes lie. A **statue of Cervantes** stands in the Plaza de las Cortes, opposite the parliament building.

experimentation and a menu that changes with each new idea that emerges from the laboratory and into the kitchen. Other celebrity chefs occasionally make an appearance. You may not eat here often, but doing so just once will leave you in raptures.

LHARDY MADRILEÑO €€€

Map p242 (☎91 521 33 85; www.lhardy.com; Carrera de San Jerónimo 8; mains €18.50-39; ⏲lunch & dinner Mon-Sat, lunch Sun, closed Aug; P; MSol, Sevilla) This Madrid landmark (since 1839) is an elegant treasure trove of takeaway gourmet tapas downstairs, while the six upstairs dining areas are the upmarket preserve of traditional Madrid dishes with an occasional hint of French influence. House specialities include *cocido a la madrileña* (€35.50), pheasant and wild duck in an orange perfume. The quality and service are unimpeachable. A favourite haunt of royalty in the 19th century, Lhardy has drawn the great and good of Madrid ever since.

LOS GATOS TAPAS €€

Map p242 (☎91 429 30 67; Calle de Jesús 2; tapas from €3.50; ⏲noon-1am Sun-Thu, to 2am Fri & Sat; MAntón Martín) Tapas you can point to without deciphering the menu and eclectic old-world decor (from bullfighting memorabilia to a fresco of skeletons at the bar) make this a popular choice down the bottom end of Huertas. The most popular orders are the canapés (tapas on toast), which, we have to say, are rather delicious.

THINGS THEY SAID ABOUT... PUERTA DEL SOL

During the first days I could not tear myself away from the square of the Puerta del Sol. I stayed there by the hour, and amused myself so much that I should like to have passed the day there. It is a square worthy of its fame; not so much on account of its size and beauty as for the people, life and variety of spectacle which it presents at every hour of the day. It is not a square like the others; it is a mingling of salon, promenade, theatre, academy, garden, a square of arms, and a market. From daybreak until one o'clock at night, there is an immovable crowd, a crowd that comes and goes through the 10 streets leading into it, and a passing and mingling of carriages which makes one giddy.

Edmondo De Amicis, Spain & the Spaniards (1885)

LA CASA DEL ABUELO TAPAS €€

Map p242 (☎91 000 01 33; www.lacasadelabuelo.es; Calle de la Victoria 12; raciones from €9.50; ⏲8.30am-midnight Sun-Thu, 8am-1am Fri & Sat; MSol) The 'House of the Grandfather' is an ageless, popular place, which recently passed its centenary. The traditional order here is a *chato* (small glass) of the heavy, sweet El Abuelo red wine (made in Toledo province) and the heavenly *gambas a la plancha* (grilled prawns) or *gambas al ajillo* (prawns sizzling in garlic on little ceramic plates). They cook more than 200kg of prawns here on a good day.

SIDRERÍA VASCA ZERAÍN BASQUE €€€

Map p242 (☎91 429 79 09; www.restaurante-vasco-zerain-sidreria.es; Calle Quevedo 3; mains €14-32; ⏲lunch & dinner Mon-Sat, lunch Sun, closed Aug; MAntón Martín) In the heart of the Barrio de las Letras, this sophisticated Basque restaurant is one of the best places in town to sample Basque cuisine. The essential staples include cider, *bacalao* (cod) and wonderful steaks, while there are also a few splashes of creativity thrown in (the secret's in the sauce). We highly recommend the *menú sidrería* (cider-house menu; €38).

LA FINCA DE SUSANA SPANISH €€

Map p242 (www.lafinca-restaurant.com; Calle de Arlabán 4; mains €7-12; MSevilla) It's difficult to find a better combination of price, quality cooking and classy atmosphere anywhere in Huertas. The softly lit dining area is bathed in greenery and the sometimes innovative, sometimes traditional food draws a hip young crowd. The duck confit with plums, turnips and couscous is a fine choice. No reservations.

LA GLORIA DE MONTERA SPANISH €

Map p242 (www.lagloriademontera.com; Calle del Caballero de Gracia 10; mains €7-10; MGran Vía) From the same stable as La Finca de Susana, La Gloria de Montera combines classy decor with eminently reasonable prices. It's not that the food is especially creative, but rather the tastes are fresh and the surroundings sophisticated. You'll get a good initiation into Spanish cooking without paying over the odds. It doesn't take reservations, so turn up early or be prepared to wait.

CASA LABRA TAPAS €

Map p242 (☎91 532 14 05; www.casalabra.es; Calle de Tetuán 11; tapas from €1; ⌚9.30am-3.30pm & 5.30-11pm; Ⓜ Sol) Casa Labra has been going strong since 1860, an era that the decor strongly evokes. Locals love their *bacalao* and ordering it here – either as deep-fried tapas (*una tajada de bacalao* goes for €1.25) or as *una croqueta de bacalao* (€0.80 per croquette) – is a Madrid rite of initiation. As the lunchtime queues attest, they go through more than 700kg of cod every week. This is also a bar with history – it was where the Partido Socialista Obrero Español (PSOE; Spanish Socialist Party) was formed on 2 May 1879. It was a favourite of Lorca, the poet, as well as appearing in Pío Baroja's novel *La Busca*. It's the sort of place that fathers bring their sons, just as their fathers did before them.

MACEIRAS GALICIAN €€

Map p242 (☎91 429 15 84; Calle de las Huertas 66; mains €7-14; Ⓜ Antón Martín) Galician tapas (think octopus, green peppers etc) never tasted so good as in this agreeably rustic bar down the bottom of the Huertas hill, especially when washed down with a crisp white Ribeiro. The simple wooden tables, loyal customers and handy location make this a fine place to rest after (or en route to) the museums along the Paseo del Prado. Galician music plays in the background and the kitchen stays open until 12.45am on Fridays and Saturdays. There's another **branch** (Map p242; Calle de Jesús 7; ⌚lunch & dinner Tue-Sun, dinner Mon) around the corner.

VINOS GONZALEZ TAPAS, DELICATESSEN €

Map p242 (Calle de León 12; tapas from €3.50; ⌚9.30am-midnight Mon-Thu, to 1am Fri & Sat, 11am-6pm Sun; Ⓜ Antón Martín) Ever dreamed of a deli where you could choose a tasty morsel and sit down and eat it right there? Well, here you can. On offer is a tempting array of cheeses, cured meats and other typically Spanish delicacies. The tables are informal, cafe style and it also does takeaway, but we recommend lingering.

LA PIOLA ITALIAN, CAFE €

Map p242 (Calle de León 9; mains from €8; ⌚10am-1am Mon-Thu, 10.30am-2am Fri, 11am-2.30am Sat; Ⓜ Antón Martín) This charming Italian place is part cafe and part bar. The small range of pasta on offer is well priced and filled with subtle flavours. In addition to the rustic tables and bar stools, there's a sofa that has to be the best seat in the house. You're likely to find it full most nights of the week, which has as much to do with the atmosphere as the food.

LA TRUCHA TAPAS, ANDALUCIAN €€

Map p242 (☎91 532 08 90; Calle de Núñez de Arce 6; mains €8.50-13.50; Ⓜ Sol) 'The Trout' is an outpost of Andalucía in central Madrid and is one of Madrid's longest-standing and most popular tapas bars. Beneath Andalucian tile work, the counter is loaded with enticing choices, but the fish cookery – especially the trout and *pescaito frito* (fried fish) – is why most people come here, and the bar staff will have their own idea about what's good to try.

LAS BRAVAS TAPAS €

Map p242 (☎91 522 85 81; Callejón de Álvarez Gato 3; raciones €3.50-10; Ⓜ Sol, Sevilla) Las Bravas has long been the place for a *caña* (small glass of beer) and the best *patatas bravas* (fried potatoes with a spicy tomato sauce; €3.50) in town. In fact, their version of the *bravas* sauce is so famous that they patented it. Other good orders include *calamares* (calamari) and *oreja a la plancha* (grilled pig's ear). The antics of the bar staff are enough to merit a stop, and the distorting mirrors are a minor Madrid landmark. Elbow your way to the bar and be snappy about your orders.

A TASCA DO BACALHAU PORTUGÊS PORTUGUESE €€€

Map p242 (☎91 429 56 75; Calle de Lope de Vega 14; mains from €26.50; ⌚lunch & dinner Tue-Sat, lunch Sun; Ⓜ Antón Martín) One of the few authentic Portuguese restaurants in Madrid, A Tasca do Bacalhau doesn't have a particularly extensive menu, but it's dominated by excellent *bacalhau* (cod) and rice dishes. It claims to have 412 different recipes for cod, although thankfully only a handful of these appear on the menu. If you're not familiar with Portuguese cooking, this is a good place to have your first taste.

RESTAURANTE INTEGRAL ARTEMISA VEGETARIAN €€

Map p242 (☎91 429 50 92; Calle de Ventura de la Vega 4; meals €8.25-15; Ⓜ Sevilla) With a couple of options for meat eaters, this mostly vegetarian restaurant does a brisk trade with its salads, moussaka and rice dishes. The decor is simple, the service is no-nonsense and the salads are what marks this place out as worthy of a visit. Alternatively, try the *plato degustación* (from €24.95) for a range of tastes.

DRINKING & NIGHTLIFE

Huertas comes into its own after dark and stays that way until close to sunrise – this is one of the iconic neighbourhoods of the Madrid night. Bars are everywhere, from Sol down to the Paseo del Prado hinterland, but it's in Plaza de Santa Ana and along Calle de las Huertas that most of the action is concentrated. Huertas is good at any time of the night, but it's in the live jazz (and other music) venues and nightclubs that it really comes into its own.

LA VENENCIA — BAR

Map p242 (Calle de Echegaray 7; ⏲1-3.30pm & 7.30pm-1.30am; MSol) This is how sherry bars should be – old world, drinks poured straight from the dusty wooden barrels and none of the frenetic activity for which Huertas is famous. La Venencia is a *barrio* classic, with fine sherry from Sanlúcar and manzanilla from Jeréz, accompanied by a small selection of tapas with an Andalucian bent. Otherwise, there's no music, no flashy decorations; it's all about you, your *fino* (sherry) and your friends. As one reviewer put it, it's 'a classic among classics'.

EL IMPERFECTO — BAR, LIVE MUSIC

Map p242 (Plaza de Matute 2; ⏲3pm-2am Mon-Thu, to 2.30am Fri & Sat; MAntón Martín) Its name notwithstanding, the 'Imperfect One' is our ideal Huertas bar, with live jazz most Tuesdays at 9pm and a drinks menu as long as a saxophone, ranging from cocktails (€7) and spirits to milkshakes, teas and creative coffees. Its piña colada is one of the best we've tasted and the atmosphere is agreeably buzzy yet chilled.

DRINKING DRESS CODE

Going out for a drink in Madrid is generally a pretty casual affair, but to visit The Roof (p84) or La Terraza del Urban (p84) you should dress well. No running shoes should go without saying, while a button-up shirt for men is close to obligatory. You might get away with jeans depending on the day and who's at the door.

LA TERRAZA DEL URBAN — COCKTAIL BAR

Map p242 (☎91 787 77 70; Carrera de San Jerónimo 34; ⏲8pm-4am; MSevilla) A strong contender with The Roof (p84) and Splash Óscar (p136) in the prize for the best rooftop bar in Madrid, this indulgent terrace sits atop the five-star **Urban Hotel** and has five-star views with five-star prices. Worth every euro, but it's only open while the weather's warm, usually from sometime in May to lateish September. In case you get vertigo, head downstairs to the similarly high-class **Glass Bar** (Map p242; ⏲11pm-3am).

THE ROOF — COCKTAIL BAR

Map p242 (☎91 701 60 20; www.memadrid.com/the-roof; Plaza de Santa Ana 14; admission €25; ⏲9pm-3am Wed & Thu, to 3.30am Fri & Sat; MAntón Martín, Sol) High above the Plaza de Santa Ana, this sybaritic open-air (7th floor) cocktail bar has terrific views over Madrid's rooftops. The high admission price announces straight away that riff-raff are not welcome and it's a place for sophisticates, with chill-out areas strewn with cushions, funky DJs and a dress policy designed to sort out the classy from the wannabes. If you suffer from vertigo, consider the equally classy **Midnight Rose** on the ground floor.

STELLA — CLUB

Map p242 (☎91 531 63 78; www.web-mondo.com; Calle de Arlabán 7; admission €12; ⏲12.30am-6am Thu-Sat; MSevilla) One of the enduring success stories of the Madrid night, Stella is one of Madrid's best nightclubs. If you arrive here after 3am, there simply won't be room and those inside have no intention of leaving until dawn. The DJs here are some of Madrid's best and the great visuals will leave you cross-eyed if you weren't already from the music in this heady place. Thursday and Saturday nights ('Mondo', for electronica) rely on resident and invited DJs, while Friday nights are more house-oriented.

CAFÉ DEL CÍRCULO DE BELLAS ARTES — CAFE

Map p242 (☎91 521 69 42; Calle de Alcalá 42; ⏲9am-1am Sun-Thu, to 3am Fri & Sat; MSevilla)

This wonderful belle époque cafe was designed by Antonio Palacios in 1919 and boasts chandeliers and the charm of a bygone era. Unless you're here between 1.30pm and 4.30pm or after 9pm (when dinners are served), you have to buy a token temporary club membership (€1) to drink here. It does, however, include access to the centre's exhibitions and it's worth every cent, even if the waiters are not averse to looking aggrieved if you put them out. The entrance is on Calle de Marqués de Casa Riera.

LOCAL KNOWLEDGE

HUERTAS HANGOUTS

Huertas nights are the stuff of legend but if you're after a quieter night we rather like beginning at the sedate Café del Círculo de Bellas Artes (p84), then it's on to two of our favourite bars La Venencia (p84) and its chic antithesis The Roof (p84). After that, it just has to be jazz at Café Central (p86) or flamenco at Cardamomo (p87), followed by a lingering piña colada at El Imperfecto (p84).

CERVECERÍA ALEMANA BAR

Map p242 (Plaza de Santa Ana 6; 11am-12.30am Sun-Thu, to 2am Fri & Sat, closed Aug; M Antón Martín, Sol) If you've only got time to stop at one bar on Plaza Santa Ana, let it be this classic *cervecería* (beer bar), renowned for its cold, frothy beers and a wider selection of Spanish beers than is the norm. It's fine inside, but snaffle a table outside in the plaza on a summer's evening and you won't be giving it up without a fight. This was one of Hemingway's haunts, and neither the wood-lined bar nor the bow-tied waiters have changed much since his day.

DOS GARDENIAS BAR

Map p242 (Calle de Santa María 13; 8pm-2.30am Mon-Sat, 5pm-2.30am Sun; M Antón Martín) When Huertas starts to overwhelm, this tranquil little bar is the perfect antidote. The flamenco and chill-out music ensure a relaxed vibe, while sofas, softly lit colours and some of the best mojitos (and exotic teas) in the *barrio* make this the perfect spot to ease yourself into or out of the night.

TABERNA DE DOLORES BAR

Map p242 (91 429 22 43; Plaza de Jesús 4; 11am-1am Sun-Thu, to 2am Fri & Sat; M Antón Martín) Old bottles and beer mugs line the shelves behind the bar at this Madrid institution, known for its blue-and-white tiled exterior and for a 30-something crowd that often includes the odd *famoso* (celebrity) or two. It claims to be 'the most famous bar in Madrid' – that's pushing it, but it's invariably full most nights of the week, so who are we to argue? You get good house wine, great anchovies and what Spaniards like to call 'well-poured beer'.

TABERNA ALHAMBRA BAR

Map p242 (www.tabernaalhambra.es; Calle de la Victoria 9; 11am-1.30am Sun-Wed, to 2am Thu, to 2.30am Fri & Sat; M Sol) There can be a certain sameness about the bars between Sol and Huertas, which is why this fine old *taberna* stands out. The striking facade and exquisite tile work of the interior are quite beautiful; however, this place is anything but stuffy and the feel is cool, casual and busy. It serves tapas and, later at night, there are some fine flamenco tunes.

JAZZ BAR MUSIC BAR

Map p242 (91 429 70 31; www.jazzbar.es; Calle de Moratín 35; 3pm-2.30am; M Antón Martín) Jazz aficionados will love this place for its endless jazz soundtrack and discreet leather booths (at last, a bar that has gone for privacy instead of trying to cram too many people in) and there's plenty of greenery to keep you cheerful. If you want live jazz, head elsewhere, but this place is like a mellow after-party for aficionados in the know.

EL CALLEJÓN MUSIC BAR

Map p242 (91 429 83 97; Calle de Manuel Fernández y González 5; 7.30pm-2.30am Sun-Thu, to 3.30am Fri & Sat; M Sevilla, Antón Martín) Tiny El Callejón lives and breathes flamenco, from the music coming from the sound system to the stars of *cante jondo* (deep flamenco song) who adorn the walls. The clientele includes flamenco stars who recognise authentic flamenco when they hear it. It's a way to sample a more traditional flamenco-in-a-smoky-bar atmosphere than most of the flamenco stages in Madrid, albeit without the live acts.

CAFÉ DEL SOUL CHILL-OUT BAR

Map p242 (91 523 16 06; www.cafedelsoul.es; Calle de Espoz y Mina 14; 4pm-2am Mon-Fri, noon-3am Sat, noon-2am Sun; M Sol) Cocktails (with or without alcohol) for €7 (€4.50 without alcohol) are a big selling point these days in Madrid. If you add chill-out music (that turns to chill-house later in the night) and curious decor that incorporates Moroccan lamps, Café del Soul is more mellow than many in the area.

MALASPINA BAR

Map p242 (91 523 40 24; Calle de Cádiz 9; 11am-2am Sun-Thu, to 2.30am Fri & Sat; ; Sol) Although it serves inviting tapas, we like this cosy bar, with its wooden tables and semirustic decor, as a mellow place for a quiet drink before you head home for an early night. Many of the bars in this area lack character or have sold their soul to the god of tourism. This place is different.

FREE LA NEGRA TOMASA MUSIC BAR

Map p242 (91 523 58 30; www.lanegratomasa.com; Calle de Cádiz 9; 1.30pm-5.30am; Sol) Bar, live music venue, restaurant and magnet for all things Cuban, La Negra Tomasa is a boisterous meeting place for the Havana set, with waitresses dressed in traditional Cuban outfits (definitely pre-Castro) and Cuban musicians playing deep into the night. Groups start at 11.30pm every night of the week, with additional performances at 2.30am on Fridays and Saturdays and 3pm on Sundays. There's even a Tarot card reader tucked away in the corner.

VIVA MADRID BAR

Map p242 (www.barvivamadrid.es; Calle de Manuel Fernández y González 7; 1pm-2am; Antón Martín, Sol) The tiled facade of Viva Madrid is one of Madrid's most recognisable and it's an essential landmark on the Huertas nightlife scene. It's packed to the rafters on weekends and you come here in part for fine mojitos and also for the casual, friendly atmosphere. The recently improved tapas offerings are another reason to pass by.

ENTERTAINMENT

TOP CHOICE CAFÉ CENTRAL JAZZ

Map p242 (91 369 41 43; www.cafecentralmadrid.com; Plaza del Ángel 10; admission €10-15; 1.30pm-2.30am Sun-Thu, to 3.30am Fri & Sat; Antón Martín, Sol) In 2011, the respected jazz magazine *Down Beat* included this art deco bar on the list of the world's best jazz clubs. It's the only place in Spain to earn the prestigious accolade (said by some to be the jazz equivalent of earning a Michelin star) and with well over 9000 gigs under its belt, it rarely misses a beat. Big international names like Chano Domínguez, Tal Farlow and Wynton Marsalis have all played here, and there's everything from Latin jazz and fusion to tango and classical jazz. Performers usually play here for a week and then move on, so getting tickets shouldn't be a problem, except on weekends; shows start at 10pm and tickets go on sale an hour before the set starts.

TOP CHOICE SALA EL SOL LIVE MUSIC

Map p242 (91 532 64 90; www.elsolmad.com; Calle de los Jardines 3; admission €8-25; 11pm-5.30am Tue-Sat Jul-Sep; Gran Vía) Madrid institutions don't come any more beloved than Sala El Sol. It opened in 1979, just in time for *la movida madrileña* (the Madrid scene), and quickly established itself as a leading stage for all the icons of the era, such as Nacha Pop and Alaska y los Pegamoides. *La movida* may have faded into history, but it lives on at El Sol, where the music rocks and rolls and usually resurrects the '70s and '80s, while soul and funk also get a run. It's a terrific venue and although most concerts start at 11pm and despite the official opening hours, some acts take to the stage as early as 10pm. After the show, DJs spin rock, fusion and electronica from the awesome sound system. Check the website (which also allows you to book online) for upcoming acts.

COSTELLO CAFÉ & NITECLUB LIVE MUSIC

Map p242 (www.costelloclub.com; Calle del Caballero de Gracia 10; admission €5-10; 6pm-1am Sun-Wed, to 2.30am Thu-Sat; Gran Vía) Very cool. Costello Café & Niteclub is smooth-as-silk ambience wedded with an innovative mix of pop, rock and fusion in Warholesque surrounds. There's live music at 9.30pm every night of the week except Sundays, with resident and visiting DJs keeping you on your feet until closing time from Thursday to Saturday. Even when there's nothing happening, it's a funky place that draws a sophisticated crowd that usually includes the odd local celebrity. Our only complaint is that they close earlier than we'd like.

VILLA ROSA FLAMENCO

Map p242 (91 521 36 89; Plaza de Santa Ana 15; admission €17; shows 8.30pm & 10.45pm Sun-Thu, 8.30pm, 10.45pm & 12.15am Fri & Sat, 11pm-

6am Mon-Sat; MSol) The extraordinary tiled facade (the 1928 work of Alfonso Romero, who was responsible for the tile work in Madrid's Plaza de Toros) of this longstanding nightclub is a tourist attraction in itself; the club even appeared in the Pedro Almodóvar film *Tacones Lejanos* (High Heels; 1991). It's been going strong since 1914 and has seen many manifestations – it made its name as a flamenco venue and has recently returned to its roots with well-priced shows and meals that won't break the bank.

POPULART JAZZ

Map p242 (91 429 84 07; www.populart.es; Calle de las Huertas 22; admission free; 6pm-2.30am Sun-Thu, to 3.30am Fri & Sat; MAntón Martín, Sol) One of Madrid's classic jazz clubs, this place offers a low-key atmosphere and top-quality music, which is mostly jazz with occasional blues, swing and even flamenco thrown into the mix. Compay Segundo, Sonny Fortune and the Canal Street Jazz Band have all played here. Shows start at 10.45pm but, if you want a seat, get here early.

LA BOCA DEL LOBO LIVE MUSIC

Map p242 (91 429 70 13; www.labocadellobo.com; Calle de Echegaray 11; admission free-€10; 9pm-3.30am; MSol, Sevilla) Known for offering mostly rock and alternative concerts, La Boca del Lobo (The Wolf's Mouth) is as dark as its name suggests and has broadened its horizons to include just about anything – roots, reggae, jazz, soul, ska, flamenco, funk and fusion. Amid all the variety are some mainstays – Wednesdays at 11pm are set aside for a roots and groove jam session, for example. Concerts start between 9.30pm and 11pm (check the website) Wednesday to Saturday and DJs take over until closing time.

CARDAMOMO FLAMENCO

Map p242 (91 369 07 57; www.cardamomo.es; Calle de Echegaray 15; admission incl drink €39, incl meal €72; 10pm-3.30am daily, live shows 9pm Tue-Sun; MSevilla) One of the better flamenco stages in town, Cardamomo draws more tourists than aficionados, but the flamenco is top-notch.

CASA PUEBLO LIVE MUSIC

Map p242 (91 420 20 38; Calle de León 3; 9pm-2am Tue-Sun; MAntón Martín or Banco de España) A storied Huertas bar that prides itself on free live jazz, a bohemian outlook and (according to the owners) political conspiracies, Casa Pueblo is an agreeable bar serving up a winning combination of cakes and cocktails that draws a discerning 30-something crowd.

TEATRO DE LA ZARZUELA THEATRE

Map p242 (91 524 54 00; http://teatrodelazarzuela.mcu.es; Calle de Jovellanos 4; tickets €5-42; box office noon-6pm Mon-Fri, 3-6pm Sat & Sun; MBanco de España) This theatre, built in 1856, is the premier place to see *zarzuela*. It also hosts a smattering of classical music and opera, as well as the cutting edge Compañía Nacional de Danza.

TEATRO ESPAÑOL THEATRE

Map p242 (91 360 14 84; www.teatroespanol.es; Calle del Príncipe 25; MSevilla, Sol, Antón Martín) This theatre, which fronts onto the Plaza de Santa Ana, has been here in one form or another since the 16th century and is still one of the best places to catch mainstream Spanish drama, from the works of Lope de Vega to more recent playwrights.

TEATRO MONUMENTAL THEATRE

Map p242 (91 429 10 55; www.rtve.es/orquesta-coro; Calle de Atocha 65; tickets €10-22; ticket office 11am-2pm & 5-7pm Mon-Fri; MAntón Martín) The main concert season runs from October to March each year, when performances include those of the Banda Sinfónica Municipal Madrid, the Orquesta Sinfónica de RTVE, and occasional operas, ballets or *zarzuelas*. It's a modern theatre with fabulous acoustics.

SHOPPING

The shops in the streets surrounding Sol range from department stores and chain clothing shops to some real gems. Shopping in Huertas is akin to being on a treasure hunt. Small, quirky shops – some run by the same family for generations, others devoted to the most specialised of niches – pop up in the most unlikely places, with especially rich pickings in the tangle of lanes that make up the Barrio de las Letras.

CASA DE DIEGO ACCESSORIES

Map p242 (www.casadediego.com; Plaza de la Puerta del Sol 12; 9.30am-8pm Mon-Sat; MSol) This classic shop has been around since 1858, making, selling and repairing

Spanish fans, shawls, umbrellas and canes. Service is old style and occasionally grumpy, but the fans are works of antique art. They have another **shop and workshop** (Map p242; ☎91 531 02 23; www.casadediego.com; Calle del los Mesoneros Romanos 4; ⏰9.30am-1.30pm & 4.45-8pm Mon-Sat; Ⓜ Callao, Sol) nearby.

GIL — ACCESSORIES

Map p242 (Carrera de San Jerónimo 2; ⏰9.30am-1.30pm & 4.30-8pm Mon-Sat; Ⓜ Sol) You don't see them much these days, but the exquisite fringed and embroidered *mantones* and *mantoncillos* (traditional Spanish shawls worn by women on grand occasions) and delicate *mantillas* (Spanish veils) are stunning and uniquely Spanish gifts. Gil also sells *abanicos* (Spanish fans). Inside this dark shop, dating back to 1880, the sales clerks still wait behind a long counter to attend to you; the service hasn't changed in years and that's no bad thing. Our only complaint? Kitsch tourist souvenirs (T-shirts and the like) have made an appearance here.

JOSÉ RAMÍREZ — MUSIC

Map p242 (☎91 531 42 29; www.guitarrasramirez.com; Calle de la Paz 8; ⏰10am-2pm & 4.30-8pm Mon-Fri, 10.30am-2pm Sat; Ⓜ Sol) José Ramírez is one of Spain's best guitar makers and his guitars have been strummed by a host of flamenco greats and international musicians (even the Beatles). Using Honduran cedar, Cameroonian ebony and Indian or Madagascan rosewood, among other materials, and based on traditions dating back over generations, this is craftsmanship of the highest order. Out the back there's a little museum with guitars dating back to 1830.

JUAN ALVAREZ — MUSIC

(☎91 429 20 33; Calle de San Pedro 7; ⏰5-8pm Mon, 10am-1.30pm & 5-8pm Tue-Fri, 10am-1.30pm Sat; Ⓜ Antón Martín) The shop and workshop (located off Calle de Moratin) may be tiny, but Juan Alvarez is one of the most celebrated guitar makers in Spain. Like his father before him, Juan has been making classical and flamenco guitars for longer than he can remember (the family business dates back to 1945) and former clients include Eric Clapton, Compay Segundo and a host of flamenco greats. Prices start at €150 and don't stop until they reach €12,000.

MARÍA CABELLO — WINE

Map p242 (Calle de Echegaray 19; ⏰9.30am-2.30pm & 5.30-9pm Mon-Fri, 10am-2.30pm & 6.30-9.30pm Sat; Ⓜ Sevilla, Antón Martín) All wine shops should be like this. This family-run corner shop really knows its wines and the decoration has scarcely changed since 1913, with wooden shelves and even a faded ceiling fresco. There are fine wines in abundance (mostly Spanish, and a few foreign bottles), with some 500 labels on show or tucked away out the back.

LOMOGRAPHY — GIFTS

Map p242 (☎91 369 17 99; www.lomography.com; Cuesta de Echegaray 5; ⏰11am-8.30pm Mon-Fri; Ⓜ Sevilla, Sol) Dedicated to the Lomo LC-A, a 1980s-era Russian Kompakt camera that has acquired cult status for its zany colours, fisheye lenses and anticool clunkiness, this eclectic shop sells the cameras (an original will set you back €295) and offbeat design items, from bags and mugs to retro memorabilia loved by adherents of 'lomography'. You can even develop your Lomo photos here. They have another **shop** (Map p254; ☎91 310 44 18; Calle de Argensola 1; ⏰11am-8.30pm Mon-Fri, 11.30am-2.30pm & 5.30-8.30pm Sat; Ⓜ Alonso Martínez, Chueca) in Chueca.

MÉXICO — ANTIQUES

Map p242 (☎91 429 94 76; Calle de las Huertas 20; ⏰9am-2pm & 5-8pm Mon-Fri, 9am-2pm Sat; Ⓜ Antón Martín) A treasure chest of original old maps and drawings, this is a great place to find a unique souvenir of Spain. Some 160 folders hold antique maps of Madrid, Spain and the rest of the world. These are all originals or antique copies, not modern reprints, so prices range from a few hundred to thousands of euros. Just down the road, **México II** (Map p242; ☎91 429 58 12; Calle de las Huertas 17; ⏰9am-2pm & 5-8pm Mon-Fri, 9am-2pm Sat) sells cheaper reprints.

LA VIOLETA — FOOD

Map p242 (☎91 522 55 22; Plaza de Canalejas 6; ⏰10am-2pm & 4.30-8.30pm Mon-Sat Sep-Jul; Ⓜ Sevilla, Antón Martín) In the early 20th century, *violetas* (small violet-coloured sweets and frosted petals from the violet flower) took on an iconic status and remain one of the city's most typical sweets. This tiny shop evokes that era in its decor and they don't serve much else other than the elegantly wrapped sweets.

SANTARRUFINA RELIGIOUS

Map p242 (☎91 522 23 83; www.santarrufina.com; Calle de la Paz 4; ⏰10am-2pm & 4.30-8pm Mon-Fri, 10am-2pm Sat; Ⓜ Sol) This outpost of Spanish Catholicism has to be seen to be believed. Churches, priests and monasteries are some of the patrons of this overwhelming three-storey shop full of everything from simple rosaries to imposing statues of saints and even a litter used to carry the Virgin in processions. Head downstairs for a peek at the extravagant chapel.

EL CORTE INGLÉS DEPARTMENT STORE

Map p242 (☎91 379 80 00; www.elcorteingles.es; Calle de Preciados 3; ⏰10am-10pm Mon-Sat; Ⓜ Sol) In the great tradition of department stores the world over, there's everything you need here, from food and furniture to clothes, appliances, toiletries, electronics, books and music. Although you'll usually pay extra for the convenience of one-stop shopping, the after-sales service is better than most. Branches are scattered throughout the city.

SPORTS & ACTIVITIES

HAMMAM AL-ANDALUS DAY SPA

Map p242 (http://madrid.hammamalandalus.com; Calle de Atocha 14; treatments €24-76.50; ⏰10am-midnight; Ⓜ Sol) Hammam al-Andalus is both an architectural jewel and a sensory indulgence that takes your senses back in time. Housed in the excavated cellars of old Madrid, this imitation traditional Arab bath offers massages and aromatherapy beneath graceful arches and accompanied by the sound of trickling water. Prices are cheapest from 10am to 4pm Monday to Friday (from €24 for the basic bath experience); otherwise, you'll pay from €27.50 up to €76.50 for the full bath and massage experience, depending on the package; there are discounts for students and for those over 65. Reservations are required. There's also a Moroccan-style tea room and restaurant upstairs.

El Retiro & the Art Museums

Neighbourhood Top Five

❶ Take a journey through the richest centuries of Spanish and European art, beginning with Goya and Velázquez, at the **Museo del Prado** (p92).

❷ Marvel at the sheer genius of Picasso as you ponder the many dimensions of *Guernica* at the **Centro de Arte Reina Sofía** (p101).

❸ Tick off just about every European master under one roof at the **Museo Thyssen-Bornemisza** (p97).

❹ Enjoy the peace and beauty of the **Parque del Buen Retiro** (p106), one of the most beautiful city parks in Europe.

❺ Sample all that's innovative about the Spanish food revolution at **Estado Puro** (p109), one of Madrid's premier tapas bars.

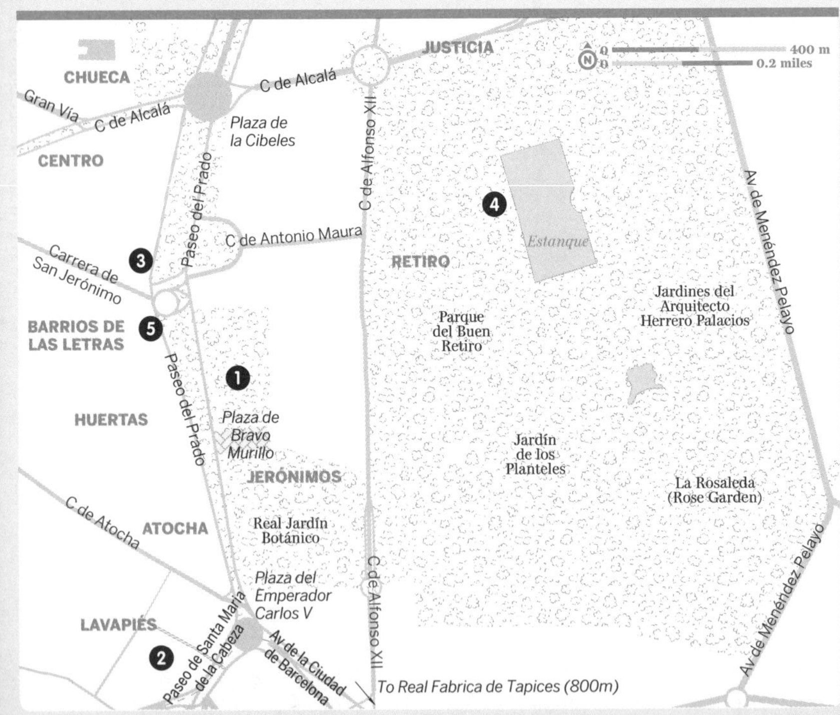

For more detail of this area see Map p246

Explore: El Retiro & the Art Museums

The Paseo del Prado, a former river and now one Europe's grandest boulevards, is all about the fabulous art galleries arrayed along or close to its shores. With other grand monuments and the city's botanical gardens also in residence, its very much a daytime neighbourhood, one that all but shuts down – at least by Madrid standards – after dark. Metro stations sit at either end of the Paseo del Prado with none in between – when walking from one end to the other, take the footpaths under the trees down the centre of the Paseo, not those on the outer extremities. The *barrio* (district) of Huertas climbs up the hill to the west.

Behind the Museo del Prado and Real Jardín Botánico to the east, a gentle rise of tranquil and refined residential streets leads towards the Parque del Buen Retiro. The park is even more of a daytime experience (the gates close soon after sunset), but its moods vary with the days. On weekdays, the park is quiet and sleepy, sprinkled with enough people to feel alive but peaceful in a way that serves as an antidote to the clamour of downtown Madrid nearby. Come Saturday and Sunday, locals stream into the park – when the weather's fine on a Sunday afternoon, it can seem as if the whole city has come here to play.

Local Life

➡ **Meeting Point** A stone's throw from the entrance to the Centro de Arte de Reina Sofía, earthy El Brillante (p109) is a Madrid institution, famous for its *chocolate con churros* (chocolate with deep-fried doughnuts) and *bocadillos de calamares* (rolls stuffed with calamari).

➡ **Retiro Groove** East of the Monument to Alfonso XII in heart of El Retiro park, crowds gather, drumbeats start to roll out across the park and people start to dance as the sun nears the horizon on a Sunday afternoon.

➡ **Madrid's Left Bank** Just off the southern end of the Paseo del Prado, the Cuesta de Claudio Moyano bookstalls (p109) sell secondhand books, drawing the curious as well as serious bibliophiles

Getting There & Away

➡ **Metro** Banco de España metro station (line 2) to the north and Atocha station (line 1) to the south sit at either end of the Paseo del Prado.

➡ **Metro** For the Parque del Buen Retiro, the most convenient station is Retiro (line 2). Ibiza (line 9) also leaves you in a good place, but is less well-connected to the centre.

Lonely Planet's Top Tip

When considering when to visit the Museo del Prado, avoid the free opening hours when crowds can really spoil your visit. First thing in the morning is the best time to come. And if you are paying, and plan to visit the Reina Sofía and Thyssen as well, you'll save €5.40 by purchasing the 'Paseo del Arte' combined ticket – it gets you into all three galleries for €21.60.

Best Places to Eat

➡ Estado Puro (p109)

➡ Viridiana (p107)

➡ El Brillante (p109)

For reviews, see p107 ➡

Best for Art

➡ Museo del Prado (p92)

➡ Centro de Arte de Reina Sofía (p101)

➡ Museo Thyssen-Bornemisza (p97)

➡ Casón del Buen Retiro (p96)

For reviews, see p109 ➡

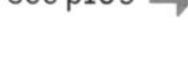

Best for Architecture

➡ Plaza de la Cibeles (p103)

➡ Caixa Forum (p103)

➡ Palacio de Cristal (p106)

➡ Antigua Estación de Atocha (p107)

➡ Iglesia de San Jerónimo El Real (p103)

LAS MENINAS, VELÁZQUEZ. VISIONS OF AMERICA, LLC / ALAMY ©

TOP SIGHTS
MUSEO DEL PRADO

Welcome to one of the world's premier art galleries. The more than 7000 paintings held in the Museo del Prado's collection (although only around 1500 are on display at any one time) are like a window onto the historical vagaries of the Spanish soul, at once grand and imperious in the royal paintings of Velázquez, darkly tumultuous in Goya's *Pinturas Negras* (Black Paintings) and outward-looking with sophisticated works of art from all across Europe.

Goya in the Prado

Goya is sometimes described as the first of the great Spanish masters and his work is found on all three floors of the Prado. Begin at the southern end of the ground or lower level where, in rooms 64 and 65, Goya's *El Dos de Mayo* and *El Tres de Mayo,* rank among Madrid's most emblematic paintings. In the adjacent rooms (66 and 67), his disturbing *Pinturas Negras* (Black Paintings) are so named for the distorted animalesque appearance of their characters. The *Saturno Devorando a Su Hijo* (Saturn Devouring His Son) evokes a writhing mass of tortured humanity, while *La Romería de San Isidro* and *Aquelarre* (El Gran Cabrón) are dominated by the compelling individual faces of the condemned souls. An interesting footnote to *Pinturas Negras* is *El Coloso,* a Goyaesque work hanging next to the Black Paintings that was long considered part of the master's portfolio until the Prado's experts decided otherwise in 2008.

Up on the 1st floor, other masterful works include the intriguing *La Família de Carlos IV,* which portrays the Spanish royal family in 1800; Goya portrayed himself in the background just as Velázquez did in *Las Meninas*. Also present are *La Maja Vestida* (The Young

DON'T MISS...

- Goya
- Velázquez
- Flemish Collection
- *Garden of Earthly Delights*
- El Greco

PRACTICALITIES

- Map p246
- www.museodelprado.es
- Paseo del Prado
- adult/child €12/free, free 6-8pm Mon-Sat & 5-7pm Sun, audioguides €3.50
- 10am-8pm Mon-Sat, 10am-7pm Sun
- M Banco de España

Lady Dressed) and *La Maja Desnuda (The Young Lady Undressed).* These portraits of an unknown woman, commonly believed to be the Duquesa de Alba (who some think may have been Goya's lover), are identical save for the lack of clothing in the latter.

Velázquez

Velázquez's role as court painter means that his works provide a fascinating insight into 17th-century royal life, and the Prado holds the richest collection of his works. Of all the works by Velázquez, *Las Meninas* (The Maids of Honour; Room 12) is what most people come to see. Completed in 1656, it is more properly known as La Família de Felipe IV (The Family of Felipe IV). It depicts Velázquez himself on the left and, in the centre, the infant Margarita. There's more to it than that: the artist in fact portrays himself painting the king and queen, whose images appear, according to some experts, in mirrors behind Velázquez. His mastery of light and colour is never more apparent than here. An interesting detail of the painting, aside from the extraordinary cheek of painting himself in royal company, is the presence of the cross of the Order of Santiago on his vest. The artist was apparently obsessed with being given a noble title. He got it shortly before his death, but in this oil painting he has awarded himself the order years before it would in fact be his!

The rooms surrounding *Las Meninas* (rooms 14 and 15) contain more fine paintings of various members of royalty who seem to spring off the canvas, many of them on horseback. Also nearby is his *La Rendición de Breda* (The Surrender of Breda), while other Spanish painters worth tracking down in the neighbouring rooms include Bartolomé Esteban Murillo, José de Ribera and the stark figures of Francisco de Zurbarán.

The Flemish Collection

The Prado's outstanding collection of Flemish art includes the fulsome figures and bulbous cherubs of Peter Paul Rubens (1577–1640). His signature works are *Las Tres Gracias* and *Adoración de los Reyes Magos.* Other fine works in the vicinity include *The Triumph of Death* by Pieter Bruegel and those by Anton Van Dyck.

Van Der Weyden's 1435 painting *El Descendimiento* is unusual, both for its size and for the recurring crossbow shapes in the painting's upper corners which are echoed in the bodies of Mary and Christ (the painting was commissioned by a Crossbow Manufacturers Brotherhood). Once the central part of a triptych, the painting is filled with drama and luminous colours.

Entrance to the Prado is via the western Puerta de Velázquez or northern Puerta de Goya. Either way tickets must first be purchased from the ticket office at the northern end of the building, opposite the Hotel Ritz and beneath the Puerta de Goya. Once inside, pick up the free plan from the ticket office or information desk just inside the entrance – it lists the location of 50 of the Prado's most famous works and gives room numbers for all major artists; pdf versions are available on the website to help you plan your visit.

PLAN OF ATTACK

Begin on the 1st floor with **Las Meninas** 1 by Velázquez. Although alone worth the entry price, it's a fine introduction to the 17th-century golden age of Spanish art; nearby are more of Velázquez' royal paintings and works by Zurbarán and Murillo. While on the 1st floor, seek out Goya's **La Maja Vestida and La Maja Desnuda** 2 with more of Goya's early works in neighbouring rooms. Downstairs at the southern end of the Prado, Goya's anger is evident in the searing **El Dos de Mayo** and **El Tres de Mayo** 3, and the torment of Goya's later years finds expression in the adjacent rooms with his **Pinturas Negras** 4, or Black Paintings. Also on the lower floor, Hieronymus Bosch's weird-and-wonderful **Garden of Earthly Delights** 5 is one of the Prado's signature masterpieces. Returning to the 1st floor, El Greco's **Adoration of the Shepherds** 6 is an extraordinary work, as is Peter Paul Rubens' **Las Tres Gracias** 7 which forms the centrepiece of the Prado's gathering of Flemish masters. (This painting may have been moved to the 2nd floor.) A detour to the 2nd floor takes in some lesser-known Goyas, but finish in the **Edificio Jerónimos** 8 with a visit to the cloisters and the outstanding bookshop.

ALSO VISIT:

Nearby are Museo Thyssen-Bornemisza and Centro de Arte Reina Sofía. They form an extraordinary trio of galleries.

TOP TIPS

- **Book online** Purchase your ticket online (www.museodelprado.es), save €1 and avoid the queues
- **Best time to visit** As soon after opening time as possible
- **Free tours** The website (www.museodelprado.es/coleccion/que-ver/) has self-guided tours for one- to three-hour visits

Las Tres Gracias (Rubens)
A late Rubens masterpiece, *The Three Graces* is a classical and masterly expression of Rubens' preoccupation with sensuality, here portraying Aglaia, Euphrosyne and Thalia, the daughters of Zeus.

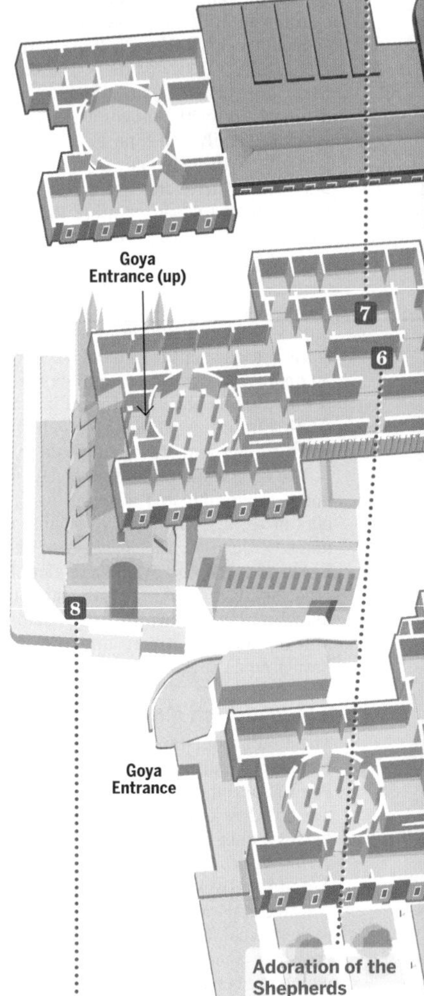

Edificio Jerónimos
Opened in 2007, this state-of-the-art extension has rotating exhibitions of Prado masterpieces held in storage for decades for lack of wall space, and stunning 2nd-floor granite cloisters that date back to 1672.

Adoration of the Shepherds (El Greco)
There's an ecstatic quality to this intense painting. El Greco's distorted rendering of bodily forms came to characterise much of his later work.

RICHARD NEBESKY/GETTY IMAGES ©

Las Meninas (Velázquez)

This masterpiece depicts Velázquez and the Infanta Margarita, with the king and queen whose images appear, according to some experts, in mirrors behind Velázquez.

GIANNI DAGLI ORTI/ALAMY ©

La Maja Vestida & La Maja Desnuda (Goya)

These enigmatic works scandalised early-19th-century Madrid society, fuelling the rumour mill as to the woman's identity and drawing the ire of the Spanish Inquisition. (La Maja Vestida pictured above.)

El Dos de Mayo & El Tres de Mayo (Goya)

Few paintings evoke a city's sense of self quite like Goya's portrayal of Madrid's valiant but ultimately unsuccessful uprising against French rule in 1808. (El Dos de Mayo pictured here.)

RICHARD NEBESKY/ GETTY IMAGES ©

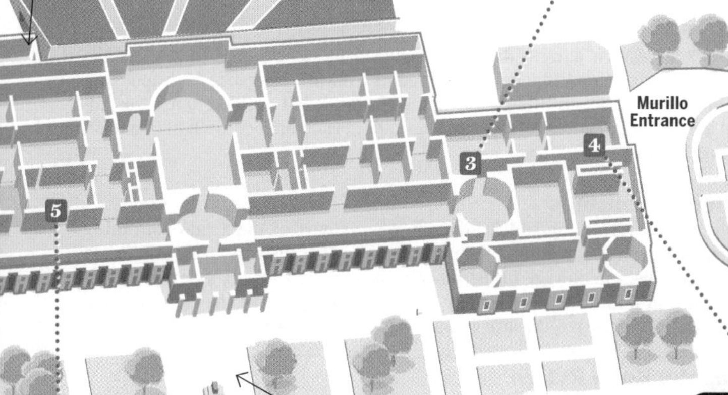

The Garden of Earthly Delights (Bosch)

A fantastical painting in triptych form, this overwhelming work depicts the Garden of Eden and what the Prado describes as 'the lugubrious precincts of Hell' in exquisitely bizarre detail.

Las Pinturas Negras (Goya)

Las Pinturas Negras are Goya's darkest works. *Saturno Devorando a Su Hijo* evokes a writhing mass of tortured humanity, while *La Romería de San Isidro* and *El Akelarre* are profoundly unsettling.

PETER BARRITT/ALAMY ©

On no account miss the weird and wonderful *The Garden of Earthly Delights* (Room 56A) by Hieronymus Bosch (c 1450–1516). No one has yet been able to provide a definitive explanation for this hallucinatory work, although many have tried. The closer you look, the harder it is to escape the feeling that he must have been doing some extraordinary drugs.

Judith at the Banquet of Holofernes, the only painting by Rembrandt in the Prado's collection, was completed in 1634; note the artist's signature and date on the arm of the chair. The painting shows a master at the peak of his powers, with a masterly use of the chiaroscuro style, and the astonishing detail in the subject's clothing and face.

El Greco

This Greek-born artist (hence the name) is considered the finest of the Prado's Spanish Renaissance painters. The vivid, almost surreal works by this 16th-century master and adopted Spaniard, whose figures are characteristically slender and tortured, are perfectly executed. Two of his more than 30 paintings in the collection – *The Annunciation* and *The Flight into Egypt* – were painted in Italy before the artist arrived in Spain, while *The Trinity* and *Knight with His Hand on his Breast* are considered his most important works.

Emperor Carlos V on Horseback (Titian)

Considered one of the finest equestrian and royal portraits in art history, this 16th-century work is said to be the forerunner to similar paintings by Velázquez a century later. One of the great masters of the Renaissance, Titian (1488–1576) was entering his most celebrated period as a painter when he created this, and it is widely recognised as one of his masterpieces.

The Best of the Rest

No matter how long you spend in the Prado, there's always more to discover. Such as the paintings by Dürer, Rafael, Tintoretto, Sorolla, Gainsborough, Fra Angelico, Tiepolo...

Edificio Villanueva

The Prado's western wing (Edificio Villanueva) was completed in 1785 as the neoclassical Palacio de Villanueva. It served as a cavalry barracks for Napoleon's troops between 1808 and 1813. In 1814 King Fernando VII decided to use the palace as a museum. Five years later the Museo del Prado opened with 311 Spanish paintings on display.

Edificio Jerónimos

The Prado's eastern wing (Edificio Jerónimos) is part of the Prado's stunning modern extension. Dedicated to temporary exhibitions (usually to display Prado masterpieces held in storage for decades for lack of wall space), its main attraction is the 2nd-floor cloisters. Built in 1672 with local granite, the cloisters were until recently attached to the adjacent Iglesia de San Jerónimo El Real (p103).

Cason del Buen Retiro

This **building** (Map p246; 90 210 70 77; Calle de Alfonso XII 28; guided visits 11am & 12.30pm Sun; Retiro) overlooking the Parque del Buen Retiro is run as an academic library by the nearby Museo del Prado. The Prado runs guided visits to the stunning Hall of the Ambassadors, which is crowned by the astonishing 1697 ceiling fresco *The Apotheosis of the Spanish Monarchy* by Luca Giordano.

TOP SIGHTS
MUSEO THYSSEN-BORNEMISZA

One of the most extraordinary private collections of predominantly European art in the world, the Museo Thyssen-Bornemisza is a worthy member of Madrid's 'Golden Triangle' of art. Where the Museo del Prado or Centro de Arte Reina Sofía enable you to study the body of work of a particular artist in depth, the Thyssen is a place to immerse yourself in a breathtaking breadth of artistic styles. Not surprisingly, it often ends up being many visitors' favourite Madrid art gallery. The collection's oldest works are on the top floor, with contemporary art on the ground floor: start on the 2nd floor and work your way down.

DON'T MISS...

- Religious art
- El Greco & Tintoretto
- 2nd-Floor European masters
- Dutch & Flemish masters
- Rooms 31 to 35
- The Baroness Collection
- Cubism & surrealism
- Contemporary icons

PRACTICALITIES

- Map p246
- ☎902 760 511
- www.museothyssen.org
- Paseo del Prado 8
- adult/child €9/free
- ⏲10am-7pm Tue-Sun
- MBanco de España

Religious Art

The 2nd floor, which is home to medieval art, includes some real gems hidden among the mostly 13th- and 14th-century and predominantly Italian, German and Flemish religious paintings and triptychs. Much of it is sacred art that won't appeal to everyone, but it somehow captures the essence of medieval Europe.

Rooms 5 to 10

Unless you've a specialist's eye for the paintings that fill the first four rooms, pause for the first time in Room 5 where you'll find one work by Italy's Pierodella Francesca (1410–92) and the instantly recognisable *Portrait of King Henry VIII* by Holbein the Younger (1497–1543). In Room 8 *Jesus Among the Doctors* by Albrecht Dürer, a leading figure in the German Renaissance, is an exceptional, vaguely disturbing work; note Dürer's anagram on the slip of paper emerging from the book in the painting's foreground. Continue on to Room 10 for the evocative 1586 *Massacre of the Innocents* by Lucas Van Valckenborch.

Spain & Venice

Room 11 is dedicated to El Greco (with three pieces) and his Venetian contemporaries Tintoretto and Titian, while Caravaggio and the Spaniard José de Ribera dominate Room 12. A single painting each by Murillo and Zurbarán add further Spanish flavour in the two rooms that follow, while the exceptionally rendered views of Venice by Canaletto (1697–1768) should on no account be missed. Few paintings have come to be the iconic image of a city quite like Canaletto's *View of Piazza San Marco* – the painter's use of line and angle, the intense detail in even the smallest of the painting's figures give a powerful sense of atmosphere and movement.

The Baroness Collection I

Best of all on the top floor is the extension (Rooms A to H) which houses the collection of Carmen Thyssen-Bornemisza; the rest belonged to Baron Thyssen-Bornemisza, a German-Hungarian magnate and her late husband. Room C houses paintings by Canaletto, Constable and Van Gogh, while the stunning Room H includes works by Monet, Sisley, Renoir, Pissarro and Degas.

For decades there was nowhere decent to take a break from all the galleries with a quick and enjoyable snack. That all changed with the opening of Estado Puro (p109), just around the roundabout within sight of the museum entrance, a sophisticated and relentlessly creative tapas bar. If you're still hungry and willing to stray a tiny bit further in search of something a little more earthy and eclectic, Los Gatos (p82) also does tapas but with a more traditional slant. Then again, for a casual sit-down meal it's hard to ignore Maceiras (p83), the purveyors of fine Galician cooking just up the hill in Huertas in the Paseo del Prado hinterland.

Rooms 28 to 35

If all that sounds impressive, the 1st floor is where the Thyssen really shines. There's a Gainsborough in Room 28 and a Goya in Room 31. The latter's *Asensio Julià* is believed to be dedicated to Goya's friend and fellow artist, the eponymous Valencian painter who worked with Goya on the frescoes in the Ermita de San Antonio de la Florida (p146). Art historians also single out this painting's confident brushstrokes as a forerunner to the Romantic movement. Also in Room 31, one of the Thyssen's lesser-known masterpieces, the 19th-century *Dresden Easter Morning* by Caspar David Friedrich, is a haunting study in light and texture by one of the leading figures in the German Romantic movement. The painting is rich in symbolism – the moon and dawn evoke death and resurrection – and the shades of colour portray shifts of extraordinary subtlety.

If you've been skimming the surface, Room 32 is the place to linger over every painting. The astonishing texture of Van Gogh's *Les Vessenots* is a masterpiece, but the same applies to Manet's *Woman in Riding Habit,* Monet's *The Thaw at Véthueil,* Renoir's *Woman with a Parasol in a Garden,* and Pissarro's *Rue Saint-Honoré in the Afternoon.* Simply extraordinary.

There's no time to catch your breath, because Room 33 is similarly something special with Cezanne, Gauguin, Toulouse-Lautrec and Degas all on show. The big names continue in Rooms 34 (Picasso, Matisse and Modigliani) and 35 (Edvard Munch and Egon Schiele).

The Baroness Collection II

In the 1st floor's extension (Rooms I to P), Room K has works by Monet, Pissaro, Sorolla, and Sisley, while Room L is the domain of Gauguin (including his iconic *Mata Mua*), Degas and Toulouse-Lautrec. Rooms M (Munch), N (Kandinsky), O (Matisse and Georges Braque) and P (Picasso, Matisse, Edward Hopper and Juan Gris) round out an outrageously rich journey.

Cubism & Surrealism

Down on the ground floor, in Room 41 you'll see a nice mix of the big three of cubism, Picasso, Georges Braque and Madrid's own Juan Gris, along with several other contemporaries. Kandinsky is the main drawcard in Room 43, while there's an early Salvador Dalí alongside Max Ernst and Paul Klee in Room 44.

MUSEO THYSSEN-BORNEMISZA

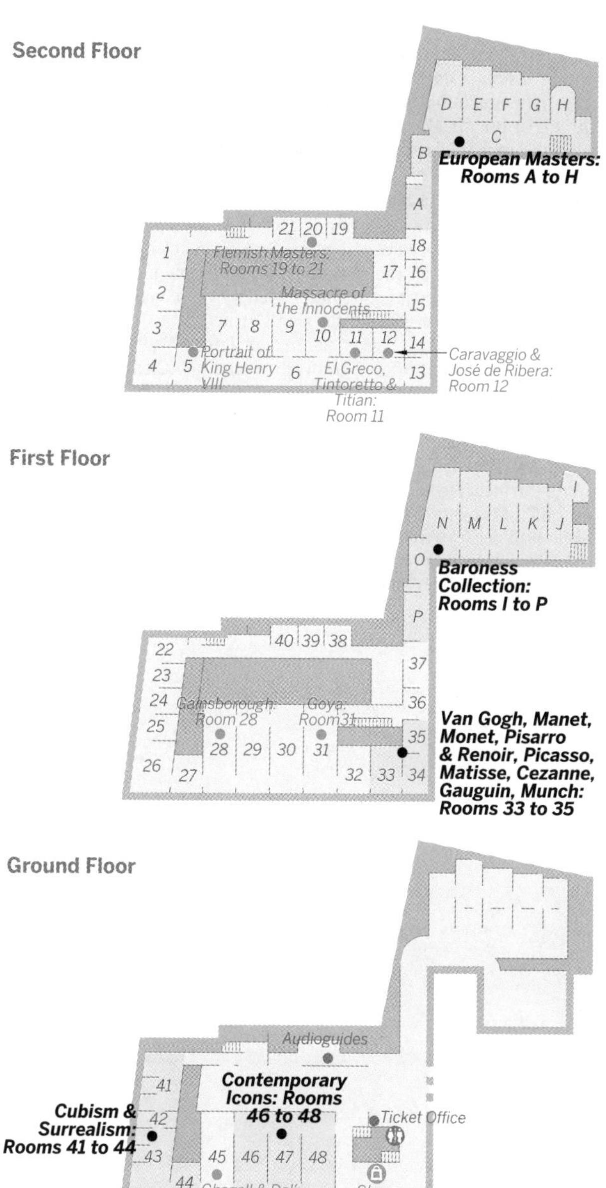

20th-Century Icons

Picasso appears again in Room 45, another one of the gallery's stand-out rooms; it includes works by Marc Chagall and Dalí's hallucinatory *Dream caused by the Flight of a Bee around a Pomegranate, one Second before Waking up.*

There's no let-up as the Thyssen builds to a stirring climax. Room 46 has Joan Miró's *Catalan Peasant with a Guitar,* Jackson Pollock's *Brown and Silver I* and the deceptively simple but strangely pleasing *Untitled (Green on Maroon)* by Mark Rothko. In Rooms 47 and 48, Francis Bacon, Roy Lichtenstein, Henry Moore and Lucian Freud, Sigmund's Berlin-born grandson, are all represented.

The Thyssen-Bornemisza Legend

The story behind the museum's collection is almost as interesting as the paintings themselves. And it is a very Spanish story that has a celebrity love affair at its heart. The paintings held in the museum are the legacy of Baron Thyssen-Bornemisza, a German-Hungarian magnate. Madrid managed to acquire the prestigious collection when the baron married Carmen Tita Cervera, a former Miss España and ex-wife of Lex Barker (of *Tarzan* fame). The deal was sealed when the Spanish government offered to overhaul the neo-Classical Palacio de Villahermosa specifically to house the collection. Although the baron died in 2002, his glamorous wife has shown that she has learned much from the collecting nous of her late husband. In early 2000 the museum acquired two adjoining buildings, which have been joined to the museum to house approximately half of the collection of Carmen Thyssen-Bornemisza. She remains an important figure in the cultural life of the city – when the city authorities threatened in 2006 to tear down some 18th-century trees outside the museum to facilitate the rerouting of the Paseo del Prado, the Baroness threatened to chain herself to one of the trees in protest. The plan was quietly shelved.

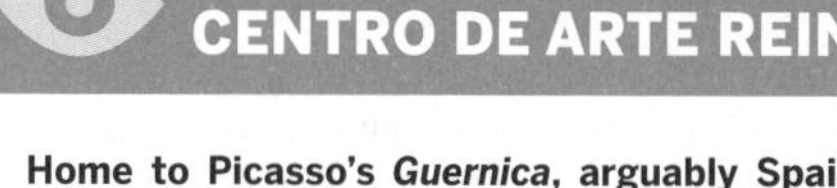

TOP SIGHTS

CENTRO DE ARTE REINA SOFÍA

Home to Picasso's *Guernica*, arguably Spain's single-most famous artwork, and a host of other important Spanish artists, the Centro de Arte Reina Sofía is Madrid's premier collection of contemporary art. In addition to plenty of paintings by Picasso, other major drawcards are works by Salvador Dalí and Joan Miró. The collection spans the 20th century up to the 1980s, and although some non-Spaniard artists make an appearance, most of the collection is strictly peninsular.

Guernica (Picasso)

Claimed by some to be the single-most important artwork of the 20th century, Pablo Picasso's *Guernica* measures 3.5m by 7.8m and is an icon of the cubist style for which Picasso became famous. You could easily spend hours studying the painting, but take the time to both examine the detail of its various constituent elements and step back to get an overview of this extraordinary canvas.

To deepen your understanding of Guernica, don't neglect the sketches that Picasso painted as he prepared to execute his masterpiece. They're in the rooms surrounding Room 206. They offer an intriguing insight into the development of this seminal work.

Guernica was Picasso's response to the bombing of Gernika (Guernica) in the Basque Country by Hitler's Legión Condor, at the request of Franco, on 26 April 1937. At least 200 died in the attack and much of the town was destroyed. The 3.5m by 7.8m painting subsequently migrated to the USA and only returned to Spain in 1981, in keeping with Picasso's wish that the painting return to Spanish

DON'T MISS...

- Picasso's *Guernica*
- Juan Gris & Georges Braque
- Joan Miró
- Salvador Dalí
- Contemporary Spanish art collection
- Edificio Nouvel
- Librería la Central

PRACTICALITIES

- Map p246
- ☎91 774 10 00
- www.museoreinasofia.es
- Calle de Santa Isabel 52
- adult/concession €6/free, free Sun, 7-9pm Mon-Fri & 2.30-9pm Sat
- 10am-9pm Mon-Sat, 10am-2.30pm Sun
- M Atocha

EDIFICIO NOUVEL

Beyond its artwork, the Reina Sofía is an important architectural landmark, adapted from the shell of an 18th-century hospital with eye-catching external glass lifts. The stunning extension (the Edificio Nouvel) that spreads along the western tip of the Plaza del Emperador Carlos V, hosts temporary exhibitions, auditoriums, the bookshop, a cafe and the museum's library.

- The permanent collection is on the 2nd and 4th floors of the museum's main wing, the Edificio Sabatini.
- Guernica's location (Room 206, 2nd floor) never changes.
- The Reina Sofía's paintings are grouped together by theme rather than artist – pick up a copy of the *Planos de Museo* (Museum Flooplans).
- The museum's *Guide to the Collection* (€22), available from the gift shop, takes a closer look at 80 of the museum's signature works.

shores (first to Picasso's preferred choice, the Museo del Prado, then to its current home) once democracy had been restored.

Other Cubist Masters

Picasso may have been the brainchild behind the Cubist form, but he was soon joined by others who saw its potential. Picasso is said to have been influenced by the mask traditions of Africa, and these elements can also be discerned in the work of Madrid-born Juan Gris (1882–1927) or Georges Braque (1882–1963), two of the masters of the genre.

Joan Miró

The work of Joan Miró (1893–1983) is defined by often delightfully bright primary colours. Since his paintings became a symbol of the Barcelona Olympics in 1992, his work has begun to receive the international acclaim it so richly deserves and the museum is a fine place to get a representative sample of his innovative work.

Salvador Dalí

The Reina Sofía is also home to around 20 canvases by Salvador Dalí, of which the most famous is perhaps the surrealist extravaganza *El Gran Masturbador* (1929); at once disturbing and utterly compelling, this is one of the museum's stand-out paintings. Look also for a strange bust of a certain Joelle done by Dalí and his friend Man Ray.

Contemporary Spanish Artists

The Reina Sofía offers a terrific opportunity to learn more about lesser-known 20th-century Spanish artists. Among these are: Miquel Barceló (b 1957); *madrileño* artist José Gutiérrez Solana (1886–1945); the renowned Basque painter Ignazio Zuloaga (1870–1945); and Benjamín Palencia (1894–1980), whose paintings capture the turbulence of Spain in the 1930s. The late Barcelona painter Antoni Tàpies (1923–2012), for years one of Spain's most creative talents, is represented, as is the pop art of Eduardo Arroyo (b 1937), abstract painters such as Eusebio Sempere (1923–85) and members of the Equipo 57 group (founded in 1957 by a group of Spanish artists in exile in Paris), including Pablo Palazuelo (1916–2007).

Sculptures

Of the sculptors, watch for Pablo Gargallo (1881–1934), whose work in bronze includes a bust of Picasso, and the renowned Basque sculptors Jorge Oteiza (1908–2003) and Eduardo Chillida (1924–2002); the latter's forms rendered in rusted wrought-iron are among Spanish art's most intriguing forms.

SIGHTS

MUSEO DEL PRADO — MUSEUM

See p92.

MUSEO THYSSEN-BORNEMISZA — MUSEUM

See p97.

CENTRO DE ARTE REINA SOFÍA — MUSEUM

See p101.

PLAZA DE LA CIBELES — SQUARE

Map p246 (Plaza de la Cibeles; MBanco de España) Of all the grand roundabouts that punctuate the Paseo del Prado, Plaza de la Cibeles most evokes the splendour of imperial Madrid.

The jewel in the crown is the astonishing **Palacio de Comunicaciones**. Built between 1904 and 1917 by Antonio Palacios, Madrid's most prolific architect of the belle époque, it combines elements of the North American monumental style of the period with Gothic and Renaissance touches. It serves as Madrid's *ayuntamiento* (town hall), with the **main post office** occupying the southwestern corner. Other landmark buildings around the plaza's perimeter include the Palacio de Linares and Casa de América (p114), the **Palacio Buenavista** (1769) and the national **Banco de España** (1891). There are fine views east towards the Puerta de Alcalá or, even better, west towards the Edificio Metrópolis.

The spectacular **fountain of the goddess Cybele** at the centre of the plaza is one of Madrid's most beautiful. Ever since it was erected in 1780 by Ventura Rodríguez, it has been a Madrid favourite. Carlos III liked it so much that he tried to have it moved to the royal gardens of the Granja de San Ildefonso, on the road to Segovia, but *madrileños* (people from Madrid) kicked up such a fuss that he let it be.

PUERTA DE ALCALÁ — MONUMENT

Map p246 (Plaza de la Independencia; MRetiro) This imposing triumphal gate was once the main entrance to the city (its name derives from the fact that the road that passed under it led to Alcalá de Henares) and was surrounded by the city's walls. It was here that the city authorities controlled access to the capital and levied customs duties.

The first gate to bear this name was built in 1599, but Carlos III was singularly unimpressed and had it demolished in 1764 to be replaced by another, the one you see today. It's best appreciated from the east for fine views through the arch down towards central Madrid. Our only complaint? It could do with a clean. Twice a year, in autumn and spring, cars abandon the roundabout and are replaced by flocks of sheep being transferred in an age-old ritual from their summer to winter pastures (and vice versa). And the Puerta de Alcalá was immortalised in the cultural lexicon in 1986 when Ana Belén and Victor Manuel's strangely catchy song 'La Puerta de Alcalá' became an unlikely smash hit.

FREE CAIXA FORUM — MUSEUM, ARCHITECTURE

Map p246 (www.fundacio.lacaixa.es; Paseo del Prado 36; ⏲10am-8pm; MAtocha) This extraordinary structure down towards the southern end of the Paseo del Prado, is one of Madrid's most eye-catching architectural innovations. Seeming to hover above the ground, this brick edifice is topped by an intriguing summit of what looks like rusted iron. On an adjacent wall is the *jardín colgante* (hanging garden), a lush vertical wall of greenery almost four storeys high. Inside there are four floors of exhibition and performance space awash in stainless steel and with soaring ceilings. The exhibitions here are always worth checking out and include cover photography, painting and multimedia shows. But the building itself is worth checking out regardless of what's on.

IGLESIA DE SAN JERÓNIMO EL REAL — CHURCH

Map p246 (☎91 420 35 78; Calle de Ruiz de Alarcón; ⏲10am-1pm & 5-8.30pm Mon-Sat Oct-Jun, hrs vary Jul-Sep; MAtocha, Banco de España) Tucked away behind the Museo del Prado, this chapel was traditionally favoured by the Spanish royal family, and King Juan Carlos I was crowned here in 1975 upon the death of Franco. The sometimes-sober, sometimes-splendid mock-Isabelline interior is actually a 19th-century reconstruction that took its cues from the Iglesia de San Juan de los Reyes in Toledo; the original was largely destroyed during the Peninsular War. What remained of the former cloisters has been incorporated into the Museo del Prado.

REAL JARDÍN BOTÁNICO — GARDENS

Map p246 (Royal Botanical Garden; ☎91 420 04 38; www.rjb.csic.es; Plaza de Bravo Murillo 2; adult/child €3/free; ⏲10am-9pm May-Aug, reduced hrs Sep-Apr; MAtocha) Although not as

1

SUPERSTOCK / ALAMY ©

3

2

Masterpieces in Madrid

See the following grand masterpieces of Spanish painting and you've drawn near to greatness. All except *Guernica* are in the Museo del Prado (p92).

El Jardín de las Delicias (Bosch)

1 Amid the Prado's accumulation of dark and sometimes brooding paintings, Hieronymus Bosch's *The Garden of Earthly Delights* seems to spring from an entirely different place. Weird, wonderful and unforgettable, it's a surreal work of art that rewards lengthy inspection.

El Tres de Mayo (Goya)

2 Goya's genius for capturing human drama is nowhere more evident than in *El Tres de Mayo,* with all the intensity and despair of Madrid's failed 1808 rebellion against Napoleon laid bare on canvas.

Guernica (Picasso)

3 Epic in scale, compelling in its original detail, *Guernica* is the spectacular symbol of the Cubist style perfected by Picasso and arguably the most famous painting of the 20th century. It can be found in the Centro de Arte Reina Sofía (p101).

La Rendicíon de Breda (Velázquez)

4 Best known for the intimacy of his royal portraits, Velázquez takes on the drama of a city's surrender in this piece (The Surrender of Breda). In doing so he brings to the canvas his perfect understanding of light, colour and the individuality of human faces.

Las Meninas (Velázquez)

5 This intriguing royal scene (The Maids of Honour) is Velázquez's most recognisable painting, a marriage of a painter at the peak of his powers and a subject matter (royal life) that he made his own.

Clockwise from top left
1 *El Jardín de las Delicias* (Bosch) **2** *El Tres de Mayo* (Goya) **3** *Guernica* (Picasso) © Pablo Picasso/ Succession Picasso. Licensed by Viscopy, 2013

TOP SIGHTS
PARQUE DEL BUEN RETIRO

The glorious gardens of El Retiro are as beautiful as any you'll find in a European city. Littered with marble monuments, landscaped lawns, the occasional elegant building and abundant greenery, it's quiet and contemplative during the week but comes to life on weekends. Put simply, this is one of our favourite places in Madrid.

El Retiro wasn't always so accessible. Laid out in the 17th century by Felipe IV as the preserve of royalty, the park was opened to the public in 1868 and ever since *madrileños* (people from Madrid) gather here to stroll, read the Sunday papers in the shade, take a boat ride or nurse a cool drink at the *terrazas* (open-air cafes). Hidden among the trees south of the lake is the **Palacio de Cristal** (Map p246; ☎91 574 66 14; ⏲11am-8pm Mon-Sat, to 6pm Sun May-Sep, 10am-6pm Mon-Sat, 10am-4pm Sun Oct-Apr), a magnificent metal and glass structure that is arguably El Retiro's most beautiful architectural monument. Weekend buskers, Chinese masseurs and tarot readers ply their trades, while art and photo exhibitions are sometimes held at the various sites around the park. But El Retiro is so big that even on weekends there are plenty of quiet corners away from the crowds.

DON'T MISS

- ➡ El Estanque & Monument to Alfonso XII
- ➡ Palacio de Cristal
- ➡ La Rosaleda
- ➡ El Ángel Caído
- ➡ Boat Ride

PRACTICALITIES

- ➡ Map p246
- ➡ ⏲6am-midnight May-Sep, to 11pm Oct-Apr
- ➡ Ⓜ Retiro, Príncipe de Vergara, Ibiza, Atocha

expansive or as popular as the Parque del Buen Retiro, Madrid's botanical gardens are another leafy oasis in the centre of town. With some 30,000 species crammed into a relatively small 8-hectare area, it's more a place to wander at leisure than laze under a tree, although there are benches dotted throughout the gardens where you can sit.

In the centre stands a statue of Carlos III, who in 1781 moved the gardens here from their original location at El Huerto de Migas Calientes, on the banks of the Río Manzanares. In the **Pabellón Villanueva**, on the eastern flank of the gardens, art exhibitions are frequently staged – the opening hours are the same as for the park and the exhibitions are usually free.

There are Spanish-language **guided visits** to the gardens; reservations by phone are essential.

FREE MUSEO NAVAL — MUSEUM

Map p246 (☎91 523 87 89; www.armada.mde.es/museonaval; Paseo del Prado 5; ⏲10am-7pm Tue-Sun; Ⓜ Banco de España) A block south of Plaza de la Cibeles, this museum will appeal to those who love their ships or who have always wondered what the Spanish Armada really looked like. On display are quite extraordinary models of ships from the earliest days of Spain's maritime history to the 20th century. Lovers of antique maps will also find plenty of interest, especially Juan de la Cosa's parchment map of the known world, put together in 1500. The accuracy of Europe and Africa is astounding, and it's supposedly the first map to show the Americas (albeit with considerably greater fantasy than fact). Also of interest is the wall-sized map showing Spanish maritime journeys of discovery from the 15th to 18th centuries. Littered throughout this pleasant exhibition space are dozens of uniforms, weapons, flags and other naval paraphernalia. Admission is officially free but they do ask for a donation.

MUSEO DE ARTES DECORATIVAS — MUSEUM

Map p246 (☎91 532 64 99; http://mnartesdecorativas.mcu.es; Calle de Montalbán 12; adult/child, student & senior €3/1.50, free Sun; ⏲9.30am-3pm Tue, Wed, Fri & Sat, 9.30am-3pm & 5-8pm Thu, 10am-3pm Sun; Ⓜ Retiro) Those who love sumptuous period furniture, ceramics, carpets, tapestries and the like will find themselves passing a worthwhile hour or two here. There's plenty to catch your eye and the ceramics from around Spain are a definite feature, while the recreations of kitchens from several regions are curiosities. Reconstructions of regal bedrooms, women's drawing rooms and 19th-century salons also help shed light on how the privileged classes of Spain have lived through the centuries.

ANTIGUA ESTACIÓN DE ATOCHA — NOTABLE BUILDING

Map p246 (Plaza del Emperador Carlos V; MAtocha Renfe) In 1992 the northwestern wing of the Antigua Estación de Atocha (Old Atocha train station) was given a stunning overhaul. The structure of this grand iron-and-glass relic from the 19th century was preserved, while its interior was artfully converted into a light-filled tropical garden with more than 500 plant species (and a resident turtle population), in addition to shops, cafes and the Renfe train information offices. The project was the work of architect Rafael Moneo, the man behind the Museo del Prado extension and the Thyssen-Bornemisza Museum, and his landmark achievement was to create a thoroughly modern space that resonates with the stately European train stations of another age.

In the modern northeastern corner of the station, the **11 March 2004 Memorial** (Map p246; 1st fl, Estación de Atocha; admission free; 10am-2pm & 5-8pm daily Apr-Feb, 10am-8pm March; MAtocha Renfe) is a moving monument to the victims of the 2004 terrorist attack at the station. Although partially visible from the Paseo de la Infanta Isabel, the memorial is best viewed from below. A glass panel shows the names of those killed, while the glass-and-perspex dome is inscribed with messages of condolence and solidarity left by well-wishers in a number of languages in the immediate aftermath of the attack. The 12m-high dome is designed so that the sun highlights different messages at different times of the day, while the effect at night is akin to flickering candles.

REAL FÁBRICA DE TAPICES — LANDMARK

Map p246 (91 434 05 50; www.realfabricadetapices.com; Calle de Fuenterrabía 2; admission €4; 10am-2pm Mon-Fri Sep-Jul, guided tours every half-hour; MAtocha Renfe, Menéndez Pelayo) If a wealthy Madrid nobleman wanted to impress, he came here to the Real Fábrica de Tapices (Royal Tapestry Workshop) where royalty commissioned the pieces that adorned their palaces and private residences. The Spanish government, Spanish royalty and the Vatican were the biggest patrons of the tapestry business: Spain alone is said to have collected four million tapestries. With such an exclusive clientele, it was a lucrative business and remains so, 300 years after the factory was founded. Goya began his career here, first as a cartoonist and later as a tapestry designer. Given such an illustrious history, it is, therefore, somewhat surprising that coming here today feels like visiting a carpet shop with small showrooms strewn with fine tapestries. There is a permanent exhibition on show and a sales area. If you're lucky, you'll get to see how they're made.

EATING

In the discreet residential enclave between the Parque del Buen Retiro and the Paseo del Prado you'll find a handful of exclusive restaurants where eating is taken seriously, classic charm is the pervasive atmosphere, and limousines wait outside to ferry the well-heeled back home. On the western shore of the *paseo* is one of Madrid's most exciting tapas bars.

VIRIDIANA — CONTEMPORARY SPANISH €€€

Map p246 (91 523 44 78; www.restauranteviridiana.com; Calle de Juan de Mena 14; mains €27-37; lunch & dinner Mon-Sat; MBanco de España)

LOCAL KNOWLEDGE

FOOTBALL PLAZA CELEBRATIONS

The battle for football supremacy in Madrid is rarely confined to the stadiums. Whenever Real Madrid win a major trophy, crowds head for the Plaza de la Cibeles to celebrate in their hundreds and thousands. To protect the fountain, the city council boards up the statue and surrounds it with police on the eve of important matches. A little further down the Paseo del Prado, Plaza del Neptuno, is where fans of Atlético de Madrid hold equally popular (and every bit as destructive) celebrations.

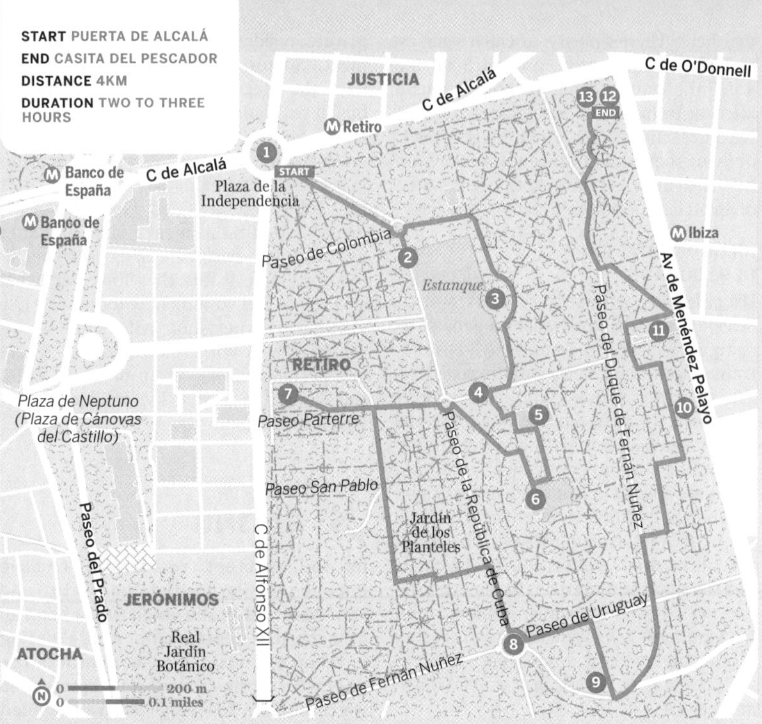

Neighbourhood Walk

Parque del Buen Retiro

This walk takes you from Parque del Buen Retiro's most popular attractions to little-known corners where you'll feel like the park is your own private playground.

Start at the 1 **Puerta de Alcalá**, one of Madrid's grand monumental gates and right next to the northwestern gate of the park. Once inside the park, a gentle climb leads past postcard-pretty flowerbeds to a lovely fountain from where the 2 **estanque (artificial lake)** is visible. Around the lake's eastern shore is the stunning 3 **Monument to Alfonso XII** with its soaring columns and carved lions overlooking the water.

On the lake's southern shore, the 4 **Fuente Egipcia (Egyptian Fountain)**, legend has it, is where Felipe IV buried an enormous fortune in the mid-18th century. Down the hill to the southeast, the brick 5 **Palacio de Velázquez** hosts temporary exhibitions. Even better, among the trees further south is the 6 **Palacio de Cristal**, a magnificent metal and glass structure built in 1887 as a winter garden for exotic flowers and is now used for temporary exhibitions.

Away to the northwest, just inside the Puerta de Felipe IV, stands what is thought to be 7 **Madrid's oldest tree**, a Mexican conifer (*ahuehuete*). Planted in 1633 and with a trunk circumference of 52m, it was used by French soldiers during the Napoleonic Wars in the early 19th century as a cannon mount. Returning southeast, seek out 8 **El Ángel Caído** (the Fallen Angel, aka Lucifer), one of few statues to the devil anywhere in the world. It sits 666m above sea level. Nearby is 9 **La Rosaleda (Rose Garden)** with more than 4000 roses, while a short walk east brings you to the sculpted hedgerows, wandering peacocks and lily ponds of the 10 **Jardines del Arquitecto Herrero Palacios**. Beyond these gardens are the enclosures of the former 11 **Casa de Fieras** (Madrid's zoo until 1972) and the pleasing ruins of the 13th-century 12 **Ermita de San Isidro**, one of the few examples of Romanesque architecture in Madrid. Almost next door is the 13 **Casita del Pescador**, a former royal fishing lodge and now an information office.

The chef here, Abraham García, is a much-celebrated Madrid figure and his larger-than-life personality is reflected in Viridiana's menu. Many influences are brought to bear on the cooking here, among them international innovations and ingredients and well-considered seasonal variations. This place was doing fusion cooking long before it became fashionable and has developed a fiercely loyal clientele as a result. In short, it's one of Madrid's best restaurants.

ESTADO PURO TAPAS €

Map p246 (☎91 330 24 00; www.tapasenestadopuro.com; Plaza de Cánovas del Castillo 4; tapas €5-12.50; ⏲11am-1am Tue-Sat, to 4pm Sun; Ⓜ Banco de España, Atocha) Most places to eat along or around the Paseo del Prado are either tourist traps or upmarket temples to fine dining, but this place bucks the trend. A slick but casual tapas bar attached to the NH Paseo del Prado hotel, Estado Puro serves up fantastic tapas, many of which have their origins in Catalonia's world-famous El Bulli restaurant, such as the *tortilla española siglo XXI* (21st-century Spanish omelette, served in a glass). The kitchen here is overseen by Paco Roncero, the head chef at La Terraza del Casino (p81), who learned his trade with master chef Ferran Adrià. Most of the tapas involve spectacular riffs on traditional Spanish themes. The outdoor tables are often reserved and have higher prices, and the long opening hours are a treat for those whose appetites don't conform to Spanish eating hours. There's another **branch** (Map p242; www.tapasenestadopuro.com; Plaza del Ángel; ⏲lunch & dinner Tue-Sat, lunch Sun; Ⓜ Antón Martín) up the hill just off Plaza de Santa Ana.

EL BRILLANTE SPANISH €

Map p246 (Calle del Doctor Drumén 7; bocadillos €4.50-6.50, raciones €7.50-12; ⏲6.30am-12.30am; Ⓜ Atocha) Just by the Centro de Arte Reina Sofía, this breezy, no-frills bar-eatery is a Madrid institution for its *bocadillos* (filled rolls) – the *bocadillo de calamares* is an old favourite – and no-nonsense *raciones* (large tapas servings). It's also famous for *chocolate con churros* or *porras* (chocolate with deep-fried doughnuts) in the wee hours after a hard night on the tiles. There's another **branch** (Map p238; ☎91 448 19 88; Calle de Eloy Gonzalo 14; ⏲6.30am-12.30am; Quevedo) in Chamberí.

GETTING ACTIVE IN EL RETIRO

Most visitors are content to explore El Retiro on foot, but there are plenty of alternatives on offer.

Renting a **row boat** (Map p246; per boat per 45min €4.65; ⏲10am-8.30pm Apr-Sep, to 5.45pm Oct-Mar) on the lake is a very Madrid thing to do.

Cycling and **rollerblading** are terrific ways to range far and wide across El Retiro; the north–south Paseo del Duque Fernán Nuñez on the park's eastern side is the favoured haunt of rollerbladers. By Bike (p204) rents out both forms of transport (rental fees are the same for both) and is just across the road from El Retiro's eastern edge.

DRINKING & NIGHTLIFE

KAPITAL CLUB

Map p246 (☎91 420 29 06; www.grupo-kapital.com; Calle de Atocha 125; admission from €12; ⏲5.30-10.30pm & midnight-6am Fri & Sat, midnight-6am Thu & Sun; Ⓜ Atocha) One of the most famous megaclubs in Madrid, this seven-storey club has something for everyone: from cocktail bars and dance music to karaoke, salsa, hip hop and more chilled spaces for R&B and soul, as well as an area devoted to 'Made in Spain' music. It's such a big place that a cross-section of Madrid society (VIPs and the Real Madrid set love this place) hangs out here without ever getting in each other's way.

SHOPPING

CUESTA DE CLAUDIO MOYANO BOOKSTALLS BOOKS

Map p246 (Ⓜ Atocha) Madrid's answer to the booksellers that line the Seine in Paris, these secondhand bookstalls are an enduring Madrid landmark. Most titles are in Spanish, but there's a handful of offerings in other languages. Opening hours vary from stall to stall, and some of the stalls close at lunchtime.

Salamanca

For more detail of this area see Map p248

Neighbourhood Top Five

❶ Shopping for Spanish fashions along Calle de Serrano, one of the most prestigious shopping boulevards in Europe, beginning with **Agatha Ruíz de la Prada** (p118)

❷ Gaining an insight into the old-money Salamanca world by visiting the extraordinary art collection at the **Museo Lázaro Galdiano** (p113)

❸ Finding out more about bullfighting by taking a tour at the **Plaza de Toros Monumental de Las Ventas** (p112)

❹ Mingling with celebrities and eating exceptionally well at sophisticated **Sula Madrid** (p115)

❺ Discovering a whole new world of chocolates in the boutique of master chocolatier **Oriol Balaguer** (p118)

Explore: Salamanca

One of the larger *barrios* (districts) that we cover in this book, Salamanca can look daunting on a map, but it's easily navigated for the most part on foot. Calle de Serrano and Calle de José Ortega y Gasset, are the two main shopping strips, and if you're in town to shop then there's very little of interest that's more than a short detour from these two main axes. For the Museo Lázaro Galdiano, it's a stiff uphill climb from the rest of the neighbourhood, while the Plaza de Toros, out in the east of the neighbourhood, is a 30-minute walk from Calle de Serrano, also uphill for much of the way. For both of these major attractions, consider hopping on the metro.

Although you will find bars and nightclubs here, Salamanca is very much a daytime *barrio*. Salamanca's tapas bars and restaurants overflow with a busy lunchtime crowd during the week when eating is often a pitstop on part of a shopping itinerary. We suggest you do likewise to really get under Salamanca's skin. By night, things are much quieter, with many people coming specifically to eat before heading elsewhere in Madrid to continue their night.

Local Life

➡ **Hangout** José Luis (p116), close to the Museo Lázaro Galdiano, is beloved by a wealthy crowd, its outdoor tables invariably inhabited by suits lingering over bottled mineral water.

➡ **Picnic** Mallorca (p117) has some fantastic take-away foods, and it's ideal if you're planning a picnic in the Parque del Buen Retiro which borders Salamanca to the south.

➡ **Slice of Andalucía** At El Rincón de Jerez (p116) at 11pm from Tuesday to Saturday, the room is darkened, candles are lit and everyone sings *La Salve Rociera*, a stirring song with roots in the flamenco and Catholic traditions of the south. Breathtaking.

Getting There & Away

➡ **Metro** Serrano and Velázquez (both line 4) or Nuñez de Balboa (lines 4 and 5) are the most convenient metro stations; the latter means a downhill walk to most of the *barrio*.

➡ **Metro** Gregorio Marañon (lines 7 and 10) is best for the Museo Lázaro Galdiano. Las Ventas (lines 2 and 5) is the station for the Plaza de Toros.

Lonely Planet's Top Tip

María Luisa Banzo, the owner of **La Cocina de María Luisa** (p115), was formerly a prominent figure in the government of conservative Popular Party Prime Minister José María Aznar – keep an eye out for the former PM (also from Castilla y León) and other prominent politicians in her restaurant.

Best Places to Eat

➡ Sula Madrid (p115)

➡ Biotza (p115)

➡ La Colonial de Goya (p116)

➡ La Galette (p116)

➡ La Cocina de María Luisa (p115)

For reviews, see p115 ➡

Best Places to Drink

➡ El Lateral (p116)

➡ The Geographic Club (p117)

➡ Almonte (p117)

For reviews, see p117 ➡

Best Places to Shop

➡ Agatha Ruiz de la Prada (p118)

➡ Manolo Blahnik (p118)

➡ Oriol Balaguer (p118)

➡ Gallery (p118)

➡ Calle de José Ortega y Gasset

BRUCE YUANYUE BI / GETTY IMAGES ©

TOP SIGHTS
PLAZA DE TOROS & MUSEO TAURINO

East of central Madrid, the Plaza de Toros Monumental de Las Ventas (often known simply as Las Ventas) is the heart and soul of Spain's bullfighting tradition and, as such, is the most important and prestigious bullring in the world. A visit here (especially as part of a guided tour) is a good way to gain an insight into this very Spanish tradition, but the architecture will also be of interest to those with no interest in *la corrida* (bullfight).

Architecture
One of the largest rings in the bullfighting world, Las Ventas has a grand Mudéjar (a Moorish architectural style) exterior and a suitably coliseum-like arena surrounding the broad sandy ring. It was opened in 1931 and hosted its first fight three years later; its four storeys can seat 25,000 spectators.

DON'T MISS...
- Architecture
- Puerta de Madrid
- Museo Taurino

PRACTICALITIES
- ☎91 725 18 57
- Calle de Alcalá 237
- admission free, tour adult/child €9/6
- 🕙10am-2pm & 3-7pm Jul-Sep, 10am-6pm Oct-Jun
- Ⓜ Las Ventas

Puerta de Madrid
The grand and decidedly Moorish Puerta de Madrid symbolises the aspiration of all bullfighters and, suitably, it's known colloquially as the 'gate of glory'. Madrid's bullfighting crowd is known as the most demanding in Spain – if they carry a *torero* (bullfighter) out through the gate (usually clutching an ear or a tail0 – other trophies awarded to an elite few), it's because he has performed exceptionally.

Museo Taurino
To gain some insight into the whole subculture that surrounds bullfighting, wander into the Museo Taurino. Here you'll find a curious collection of paraphernalia, costumes (the *traje de luces*, or suit of lights, is one of bullfighting's most recognisable props), photos and other bullfighting memorabilia up on the top floor above one of the two courtyards by the ring.

TOP SIGHTS
MUSEO LÁZARO GALDIANO

This is just the sort of place you expect to find along Calle de Serrano – an imposing early-20th-century Italianate stone mansion set discreetly back from the street. And Don José Lázaro Galdiano (1862–1947), a successful and cultivated businessman, was just the sort of person you'd expect to find in Salamanca. A patron of the arts, he built up an astonishing private collection that he bequeathed to the city upon his death. It was no mean inheritance, with some 13,000 works of art and objets d'art, a quarter of which are on show at any time.

DON'T MISS...

- Old Masters
- Goya Paintings
- Curio Collection
- Frescoes & Textiles

PRACTICALITIES

- Map p248
- 91 561 60 84
- www.flg.es
- Calle de Serrano 122
- adult/concession €6/3, last hr free
- 10am-4.30pm Wed-Sat & Mon, to 3pm Sun
- Gregorio Marañón

Old Masters

It can be difficult to believe the breadth of masterpieces that Señor Lázaro Galdiano gathered during his lifetime, and there's enough here to merit this museum's inclusion among Madrid's best art galleries. The highlights include works by Zurbarán, Claudio Coello, Hieronymus Bosch, Esteban Murillo, El Greco, Lucas Cranach and John Constable, and there's even a painting in room 11 attributed to Velázquez.

Goya

As is often the case, Goya belongs in a class of his own. He dominates room 13, while the ceiling of the adjoining room 14 features a collage from some of Goya's more famous works. Some that are easy to recognise include *La Maja Desnuda*, *La Maja Vestida* and the frescoes of the Ermita de San Antonio de la Florida.

Curio Collection

This remarkable collection ranges beyond paintings to sculptures, bronzes, miniature figures, jewellery, ceramics, furniture, weapons...clearly he was a man of wide interests. The ground floor is largely given over to a display setting the social context in which Galdiano lived, with hundreds of curios from all around the world on show. There are more on the top floor.

Frescoes & Textiles

The lovely 1st floor, which contains many of the Spanish artworks, is arrayed around the centrepiece of the former ballroom and beneath lavishly frescoed ceilings. As you wander from room to room and from floor to floor, seek out the information panels in each room – most include photos of each room as it appeared in Galdiano's prime. And on no account miss the top floor's room 24, which contains some exquisite textiles.

The Man Behind the Collection

Born in Navarra in northeastern Spain, José Lázaro Galdiano moved to Madrid as a young man. He would later become a hugely significant figure in the cultural life of the city. During WWI he was an important supporter of the Museo del Prado and later built his own private collection by buying up Spanish artworks in danger of being sold overseas and bringing home those which had already left. He lived in exile during the Civil War, but continued to collect and upon his return he set up a respected artistic foundation in his former palace that would ultimately house the museum.

SIGHTS

PLAZA DE TOROS & MUSEO TAURINO — STADIUM

See p112.

MUSEO LÁZARO GALDIANO — MUSEUM

See p113.

PALACIO DE LINARES & CASA DE AMÉRICA — NOTABLE BUILDING

Map p248 (☎91 595 48 00; www.casamerica.es; Plaza de la Cibeles 2; adult/child/student & senior €8/free/5; ⏲guided tours 11am, noon & 1pm Sat & Sun Sep-Jul, ticket office 9am-8pm Mon-Fri, 11am-1pm Sat & Sun; Ⓜ Banco de España) So extraordinary is the Palacio de Comunicaciones on Plaza de la Cibeles that many visitors fail to notice this fine 19th-century pleasure dome that stands watch over the northeastern corner of the plaza. Built in 1873, the Palacio de Linares is a worthy member of the line-up of grand facades on the plaza, while its interior is notable for the abundant use of Carrara marble. Tours take an hour and can be reserved on ☎902 221 424 or booked online at www.entradas.com. Alternatively, you can purchase tickets at the ticket office; tickets often sell out in advance, so don't leave it until the last minute. In the palace's grounds is the Casa de América, a modern exhibition centre, which also hosts all sorts of events and concerts.

FREE MUSEO ARQUEOLÓGICO NACIONAL — MUSEUM

Map p248 (http://man.mcu.es; Calle de Serrano 13; ⏲9.30am-8pm Tue-Sat, to 3pm Sun; Ⓜ Serrano) The showpiece Museo Arqueológico Nacional (National Archaeology Museum) contains a sweeping accumulation of artefacts behind its towering facade. The large collection includes stunning mosaics that were taken from Roman villas across Spain, intricate Muslim-era and Mudéjar handiwork, sculpted figures such as the Dama de Ibiza and Dama de Elche, examples of Romanesque and Gothic architectural styles as well as a partial copy of the prehistoric cave paintings of Altamira (Cantabria). At the time of writing, the museum was closed for a major and much-needed overhaul of the building, but it should be open by the time you read this.

FREE BIBLIOTECA NACIONAL & MUSEO DEL LIBRO — LIBRARY, MUSEUM

Map p248 (☎91 580 78 05; www.bne.es; Paseo de los Recoletos 20; admission free; ⏲library 9am-9pm Mon-Fri, 9.30am-2pm Sat, museum 10am-9pm Tue-Sat, to 2pm Sun; Ⓜ Colón) Perhaps the most impressive of the grand edifices that were erected along the Paseo de los Recoletos in the 19th century, the 1892 **Biblioteca Nacional** (National Library) dominates the southern end of Plaza de Colón. The reading rooms are more for use by serious students. Downstairs, and entered through a separate entrance, the fascinating and recently overhauled **museum**, otherwise known as the Museo de la Biblioteca Nacional, is a must-see for bibliophiles, as it contains interactive displays on printing presses and other materials, illuminated manuscripts, the history of the library and literary cafes; although our favourites are the 1626 map of Spain and Picasso's *Mademoiselle Léonie en un Sillón* in the Sala de las Musas. There is not an e-book in sight.

FREE MUSEO AL AIRE LIBRE — SCULPTURE

Map p248 (www.munimadrid.es/museoairelibre; cnr Paseo de la Castellana & Paseo de Eduardo Dato ; ⏲24hr; Ⓜ Rubén Darío) This fascinating open-air collection of 17 abstract sculptures includes works by the renowned Basque artist Eduardo Chillida, the Catalan master Joan Miró, as well as Eusebio Sempere and Alberto Sánchez, one of Spain's foremost sculptors of the 20th century. The sculptures are beneath the overpass where Paseo de Eduardo Dato crosses Paseo de la Castellana, but somehow the hint of traffic grime and pigeon poo only adds to the appeal. All but one are on the eastern side of Paseo de la Castellana.

FREE FUNDACIÓN JUAN MARCH — MUSEUM & CULTURAL CENTRE

Map p248 (www.march.es; Calle de Castelló 77; ⏲11am-8pm Mon-Sat, 10am-2pm Sun & holidays; Ⓜ Núñez de Balboa) This foundation organises some of the better temporary exhibitions in Madrid each year and it's always worth checking its website to see what's on or around the corner. It also stages concerts (p118) across a range of musical genres and other events throughout the year.

EATING

Eating out in Salamanca is, true to *barrio* form, almost always a suave affair and in most places you'll need to dress accordingly. In the same way that the *barrio's* fashion boutiques seem intent on pushing the city in stylish new directions, Salamanca's restaurants invite you to rub shoulders with the young, the beautiful and the very well dressed while celebrity chefs tug the city's most conservative *barrio* in new culinary directions. Gourmet tapas bars are a Salamanca speciality.

TOP CHOICE SULA MADRID
CONTEMPORARY SPANISH €€€

Map p248 (☎91 781 61 97; www.sula.es; Calle de Jorge Juan 33; mains €23.50-27.50, set menus €30-60; ⏲lunch & dinner Mon-Sat; Ⓜ Velázquez) A gastronomic temple that combines stellar cooking with clean-lined sophistication, Sula Madrid – a superstylish tapas bar, top-notch restaurant and ham-and-champagne tasting centre – is one of our favourite top-end restaurants in Madrid and we're not the only one – when master chef Ferran Adrià was asked to nominate his favourite restaurant, he chose Sula. The kitchen, its seasonal menu and the extensive wine list is overseen by wunderkind Quique Dacosta (voted Spain's best chef in 2005) and there's a leaning towards Navarran cuisine, the finest *jamón* (ham) and creative twists on old staples. Design touches added by Amaya Arzuaga help to make this one of Madrid's coolest, black-clad spaces. Despite the clientele, there's nothing snooty about the atmosphere, especially at lunchtime when the menú del día is a great way to sample what all the fuss is about.

BIOTZA
TAPAS, BASQUE €

Map p248 (www.biotzarestaurante.com; Calle de Claudio Coello 27; tapas €2.50-3.50; ⏲9am-midnight Mon-Thu, to 1am Fri & Sat; Ⓜ Serrano) This breezy Basque tapas bar is one of the best places in Madrid to sample the creativity of bite-sized *pintxos* (Basque tapas) as only the Basques can make them. It's the perfect combination of San Sebastián-style tapas and Madrid-style pale-green/red-black decoration and unusual angular benches. The prices quickly add up, but it's highly recommended nonetheless. There's also a more formal Basque restaurant out the back.

LA COCINA DE MARÍA LUISA
CASTILIAN €€

Map p248 (☎91 781 01 80; www.lacocinademarialuisa.es; Calle de Jorge Juan 42; mains €13.90-23.60, tasting menu €54; ⏲lunch & dinner Mon-Sat, closed Aug; Ⓜ Velázquez) The home kitchen of former parliamentarian María Luisa Banzo has one of Salamanca's most loyal followings. The cooking is a carefully charted culinary journey through Castilla y León, accompanied by well-chosen regional wines and rustic decor that add much warmth to this welcoming place. The house specialty comes from María Luisa's mother – pigs' trotters filled with meat and black truffles from Soria.

The chance to choose half-sized versions of most dishes will appeal to many.

SALAMANCA'S DIFFICULT BIRTH

Salamanca, with its expensive boutiques, high-class restaurants and luxury apartments, was born with a silver spoon in its mouth. When Madrid's authorities were looking to expand beyond the newly inadequate confines of the medieval capital, the Marqués de Salamanca, a 19th-century aristocrat and general with enormous political clout, heard the call. He threw everything he had into the promotion of his *barrio* (district) in the 1870s, buying up land cheaply, which he hoped to sell later for a profit. He was ahead of his time: the houses he built contained Madrid's first water closets, the latest in domestic plumbing and water heating for bathrooms and kitchens, while he also inaugurated horse-drawn tramways. In the year of his death, 1883, the streets got electric lighting. Hard as it is now to imagine, there was little enthusiasm for the project and the *marqués* quickly went bankrupt. Towards the end of his life, he wrote 'I have managed to create the most comfortable *barrio* in Madrid and find myself the owner of 50 houses, 13 hotels and 18 million feet of land. And I owe more than 36 million *reales* on all of this. The task is completed but I am ruined.' It was only later that *madrileños* saw the error of their ways.

LOCAL KNOWLEDGE

EL RINCÓN DE JEREZ

Out in the eastern reaches of Salamanca, the Andalucian bar **El Rincón de Jerez** (☎91 355 47 45; Calle de Rufino Blanco 5; raciones €7-13; ⌚lunch & dinner Tue-Sat, lunch Sun, closed Aug; Ⓜ Manuel Bacerra) is utterly unlike anywhere else in Madrid. At 11pm from Tuesday to Saturday, they turn off the lights, light the candles and sing as one *La Salve Rociera*, a near-mythical song with deep roots in the flamenco and Catholic traditions of the south. It will send chills down your spine.

JOSÉ LUIS — SPANISH €€

Map p248 (☎91 562 78 61; Calle de Serrano 89-90; tapas from €5; ⌚lunch & dinner daily ; Ⓜ Gregorio Marañón) With numerous branches around Madrid, José Luis is famous for its fidelity to traditional Spanish recipes. It wins many people's vote for Madrid's best tortilla de patatas (Spanish potato omelette).

LA GALETTE — SPANISH €€

Map p248 (☎91 576 06 41; Calle del Conde de Aranda 11; mains €9.50-19.50; ⌚lunch & dinner Mon-Sat, lunch Sun; 🌶; Ⓜ Retiro) This lovely little restaurant combines an intimate dining area with checked tablecloths and cuisine that the owner describes as 'baroque vegetarian'. The food (both veg and non-veg) is a revelation, blending creative flavours with a strong base in traditional home cooking. The *croquetas de manzana* (apple croquettes) are a house speciality, but the truth is that everything on the extensive menu is good. The only problem here is that the tables are so close together you get the feeling that diners need to breathe in and out at the same time for everyone to fit.

AL-MOUNIA — MOROCCAN €€€

Map p248 (☎91 435 08 28; www.almounia.es; Calle de los Recoletos 5; mains €16-28; ⌚lunch & dinner Mon-Sat, lunch Sun, closed Aug; Ⓜ Recoletos) One of the longest-standing Moroccan restaurants in town, Al-Mounia has a loyal following. The best couscous in Madrid (it bears little relation to packet couscous) is a menu highlight, as are the subtly spiced lamb tagines and the *asado bereber* (Berber roast). The handcrafted traditional decor is breathtaking and greatly complements the cuisine.

LA COLONIAL DE GOYA — TAPAS €

Map p248 (www.restauranterincondegoya.es; Calle de Jorge Juan 34; tapas €3-4.50; ⌚8am-midnight Mon-Fri, noon-1am Sat & Sun; Ⓜ Velázquez) A mere 63 varieties of tapa should be sufficient for most, but they also serve a range of carpaccios, croquettes and main dishes at this engaging little tapas bar. The atmosphere is casual, the all-white decor of wood and exposed brick walls is classy, and some of the dishes (such as the sirloin, brie and quail's eggs) are Spanish nouvelle cuisine at its best.

RESTAURANTE ESTAY — TAPAS €€

Map p248 (www.estayrestaurante.com; Calle de Hermosilla 46; tapas €1.75-5, 6-tapas set menus from €13.80; ⌚8am-12.30am Mon-Sat; Ⓜ Velázquez) Restaurante Estay is partly a standard Spanish bar, where besuited waiters serve *café con leche* (it does breakfasts), and one of the best-loved tapas bars in town. The long list of hot and cold tapas concentrates mostly on Spanish staples, with a selection of more adventurous combinations, such as quail with onion and chocolate. Like this last dish, it all seems rather an odd mix, but it somehow works.

LE CAFÉ — SPANISH €€

Map p248 (www.lecafe.es; Calle de los Recoletos 13; mains €12-19, set menus €11.50-19; ⌚lunch & dinner Mon-Sat; Ⓜ Retiro) It can be almost impossible to get a table here at lunchtime on weekdays, when locals stream in from surrounding offices. The atmosphere is bright and informal and the food is largely traditional Spanish fare (rice dishes are a recurring theme), which is done well; we enjoyed the beef tenderloin hamburger with peanut cream and garlic sprouts.

EL LATERAL — TAPAS €€

Map p248 (www.cadenalateral.es; Calle de Velázquez 57; tapas from €2.3; ⌚noon-midnight Sun-Wed, noon-1am Thu-Sat; Ⓜ Velázquez or Núñez de Balboa) El Lateral does terrific *pinchos* (tapas), which serve as the ideal accompaniment to the fine wines on offer. Tapas are creative without being over the top (wild mushroom croquettes or sirloin with mustard sauce). This being Salamanca, they draw a pretty upmarket crowd, but you'd be surprised how rapidly the ties loosen up after work. Service is restaurant standard, rather than your average tapas-bar brusqueness. They have another

branch (Map p250; ☎91 531 68 77; Calle de Fuencarral 43; ⏰1pm-midnight; Tribunal) in Malasaña, with a further **bar-restaurant** (Map p242; ☎91 420 15 82; www.cadenalateral.es; Plaza de Santa Ana 12; pinchos €3.50; ⏰noon-1am; Ⓜ Antón Martín, Sol) in Huertas.

MALLORCA TAKEAWAY €

Map p248 (☎915771859; www.pasteleria-mallorca.com; Calle de Serrano 6; ⏰9.30am-9pm; Ⓜ Retiro) For fine takeaway food, head to Mallorca, a Madrid institution. Everything here, from gourmet mains to snacks and desserts, is delicious.

DRINKING & NIGHTLIFE

Salamanca is the land of the beautiful people and it's all about gloss and glamour: heels for her and hair gel for him. As you glide through the *pijos* (beautiful people or yuppies), keep your eyes peeled for Real Madrid players and celebrities. Although places do exist in Salamanca's otherwise quiet streets that enable you to spend the whole night here, we're of the view that there are far better *barrios* to get a feel for Madrid's famous nightlife. And many of Salamanca's celebrities would appear to agree – the clubs and cocktail bars of Malasaña, Chueca and elsewhere are where they're more likely to show up. The places we've listed here are only those we think are worth crossing town for.

THE GEOGRAPHIC CLUB BAR

Map p248 (☎91 578 08 62; www.thegeographicclub.com; Calle de Alcalá 141; ⏰1pm-2am Sun-Thu, to 3am Fri & Sat; Ⓜ Goya) With its elaborate stained-glass windows, ethno-chic from all over the world and laid-back atmosphere, The Geographic Club is an excellent choice in Salamanca for an early evening drink. We like the table built around an old hot-air-balloon basket almost as much as the cavernlike pub downstairs.

ALMONTE NIGHTCLUB

Map p248 (☎91 563 25 04; www.almontesalarociera.com; Calle de Juan Bravo 35; ⏰10pm-5am Sun-Fri, to 6am Sat; Ⓜ Núñez de Balboa, Diego de León) If flamenco has captured your soul, but you're keen to do more than watch, head to Almonte, where the whitewashed facade tells you that this is all about Andalucía, the home of flamenco. The young and the beautiful who come here have *sevillanas* (a flamenco dance style) in their soul and in their feet, so head downstairs to see the best dancing. Dance if you dare.

SPANISH WINES

All of Spain's autonomous communities, with the small exceptions of Asturias and Cantabria, are home to recognised wine-growing areas. With so many areas to choose from, and with most Spanish wines labelled primarily according to region or classificatory status rather than grape variety, a little background knowledge can go a long way.

Spanish wine is subject to a complicated system of wine classification with a range of designations marked on the bottle. These range from the straightforward *vino de mesa* (table wine) to *vino de la tierra*, which is a wine from an officially recognised wine-making area. If an area meets certain strict standards for a given period and covers all aspects of planting, cultivating and ageing, it receives Denominación de Origen (DO; Denomination of Origin) status. There are currently over 60 DO-recognised wine-producing areas in Spain.

An outstanding wine region gets the much-coveted Denominación de Origen Calificada (DOC), a controversial classification that some in the industry argue should apply only to specific wines, rather than every wine from within a particular region. At present, the only DOC wines come from La Rioja in northern Spain and the small Priorat area in Catalonia.

Other important indications of quality depend on the length of time a wine has been aged, especially if in oak barrels. The best wines are often, therefore, marked with the designation *crianza* (aged for one year in oak barrels), *reserva* (two years ageing, at least one of which is in oak barrels) and *gran reserva* (two years in oak and three in the bottle).

SERRANO 41 CLUB

Map p248 (☎91 578 18 65; www.serrano41.com; Calle de Serrano 41; admission €12; ⊙11pm-5.30am Wed-Sun; MSerrano) If bullfighters, Real Madrid stars and other A-listers can't drag themselves away from Salamanca, chances are that you'll find them here. Danceable pop and house dominate the most popular Friday and Saturday nights, funk gets a turn on Sunday and it's indie night on Thursday. As you'd imagine, the door policy is stricter than most. Their outdoor terrace opens in late May and is *very* cool until it closes in mid-September.

ENTERTAINMENT

FREE **FUNDACIÓN JUAN MARCH** CONCERT VENUE

Map p248 (www.march.es; Calle de Castelló 77; ⊙Mon, Wed, Sat & Sun; MNúñez de Balboa) A foundation dedicated to promoting music and culture (as well as exhibitions), the Juan March Foundation stages free concerts throughout the year. Performances range from solo recitals to themed concerts dedicated to a single style or composer.

SHOPPING

Salamanca is where you discover that there's so much more to Spanish fashion than Zara and Mango. Fashions range from classically elegant to cool and cutting edge, from both leading and upcoming Spanish designers and the big names in international fashion. As such, the exclusive boutiques of the *barrio* are the ideal place to take the pulse of the Spanish fashion scene and you'll likely find it in rude health. Shopping here is a social event, where people put on their finest and service is often impeccable, if a little stuffy. Throw in a sprinkling of gourmet food shops and you could easily spend days doing little else but shopping.

TOP CHOICE **AGATHA RUIZ DE LA PRADA** FASHION

Map p248 (www.agatharuizdelaprada.com; Calle de Serrano 27; ⊙10am-8.30pm Mon-Sat; MSerrano) This boutique has to be seen to be believed, with pinks, yellows and oranges everywhere you turn. It's fun and exuberant, but not just for kids. It also has serious and highly original fashion; Agatha Ruiz de la Prada is one of the enduring icons of Madrid's 1980s outpouring of creativity known as *la movida madrileña.*

CAMPER SHOES

Map p248 (www.camper.es; Calle de Serrano 24; ⊙10am-9pm Mon-Sat, 11am-8pm Sun; MSerrano) Spanish fashion is not all *haute couture,* and this world-famous cool and quirky shoe brand from Mallorca offers bowling-shoe chic with colourful, fun designs that are all about quality coupled with comfort. There are other outlets throughout the city, including a **shop** (Map p250; ☎91 531 23 47; www.camper.com; Calle de Fuencarral 42; MGran Vía, Tribunal) in Malasaña – check out their website for locations.

GALLERY CLOTHING, ACCESSORIES

Map p248 (www.gallerymadrid.com; Calle de Jorge Juan 38; ⊙10.30am-8.30pm Mon-Sat; MPríncipe de Vergara, Velázquez) This stunning showpiece of men's fashions and accessories (shoes, bags, belts and the like) is the new Madrid in a nutshell – stylish, brand conscious and all about having the right look. There are creams and fragrances to indulge the metrosexual in you, as well as quirkier items such as designer crash helmets. With an interior designed by Tomas Alia, and a growing line in women's fashions, it's one of the city's coolest shops.

MANOLO BLAHNIK

Map p248 (☎91 575 96 48; www.manoloblahnik.com; Calle de Serrano 58; ⊙10am-8.30pm Mon-Sat; MSerrano) Do yo have nothing to wear to the Oscars? Do what many Hollywood celebrities do and head for Manolo Blahnik. The showroom is exclusive and each shoe is displayed like a work of art.

ORIOL BALAGUER FOOD

Map p248 (www.oriolbalaguer.com; Calle de José Ortega y Gasset 44; ⊙9am-9pm Mon-Sat, to 2.30pm Sun; MNuñez de Balboa) Catalan pastry chef Oriol Balaguer has a formidable CV – he worked in the kitchens of Ferran Adrià in Catalonia and won the prize for the World's Best Dessert (the 'Seven Textures of Chocolate') in 2001. His chocolate boutique is presented like a small art gallery, except that it's dedicated to exquisite finely crafted chocolate collections and cakes. You'll never be able to buy ordinary chocolate again.

BOMBONERÍAS SANTA
FOOD, WINE

Map p248 (www.bomboneriassanta.com; Calle de Serrano 56; ⌚10am-8.30pm Mon-Sat Sep-Jun, shorter hours in summer; Ⓜ Serrano) If your style is as refined as your palate, the exquisite chocolates in this tiny shop will satisfy. The packaging is every bit as pretty as the *bombones* within, but they're not cheap – count on paying around €60 per kilo of chocolate.

LAVINIA
WINE

Map p248 (Calle de José Ortega y Gasset 16; ⌚10am-9pm Mon-Sat; Ⓜ Núñez de Balboa) Although we love the intimacy of old-style Spanish wine shops, they can't match the selection of Spanish and international wines available at Lavinia, which has more than 4500 bottles to choose from. It also organises wine courses, wine tastings and excursions to nearby bodegas (wineries).

EKSEPTION & EKS
CLOTHES, ACCESSORIES

Map p248 (www.ekseption.es; Calle de Velázquez 28; ⌚10.30am-2.30pm & 4.30-8.30pm Mon-Sat; Ⓜ Velázquez) This elegant showroom store consistently leads the way with the latest trends, spanning catwalk designs alongside a more informal, though always sophisticated, look. The unifying theme is urban chic and their list of designer brands includes Balenciaga, Prada Sport, Marc Jacobs and Dries van Noten. Next door is the preserve of younger, more casual lines, including a fantastic selection of jeans. Victoria Beckham was a regular customer here in her Madrid days; make of that what you will.

FLAMENCO CHIC
FASHION

Map p248 (☎91 577 48 16; Calle de Ayala 13; ⌚10am-9pm Mon-Sat; Ⓜ Serrano) The name of this vibrant and relentlessly creative clothing store may be slightly misleading, but only up to a point: it has little to do with Spain's best-known musical form other than seeming to capture the spirit and passion that lies at the heart of the genre. Bright colours are the hallmark of its dresses, jackets, tops and other clothing; there's a line in equally colourful children's clothing downstairs. There's another branch in **Chamberí** (Map p238; ☎91 591 30 79; www.flamencochic.com; Calle de Sagasta 25; ⌚10am-9pm Mon-Sat; Ⓜ Alonso Martínez).

TOUS
JEWELLERY

Map p248 (☎91 575 51 71; www.tous.com; Calle de Claudio Coello 65; ⌚10am-2pm & 5-8.30pm Mon-Sat; Ⓜ Serrano) No self-respecting Spanish *pija* (yuppie) could do without the trendy jewellery by Rosa Tous. Some of it is teddy bear–cutesy striving for serious elegance that may seem like an odd combination, but not to Spanish shoppers.

> **TIME TO SHOP**
>
> If you're on a shopping expedition and like to have the shops all to yourself, the best time is between 3pm and 4.30pm when any self-respecting local fashionista is lingering over lunch. Before planning your day, check which Salamanca shops (there are only a few of them) close for lunch, but otherwise there's no better time to explore the *barrio* (district).

CUARTO DE JUEGOS
TOYS

Map p248 (Calle de Jorge Juan 42; ⌚10am-8.30pm Mon-Fri, 10.30am-2pm & 5-8pm Sat; Ⓜ Velázquez or Príncipe de Vergara) We're not sure if it's an official rule, but batteries seem to be outlawed at this traditional toy shop, where all kinds of old-fashioned board games and puzzles are still sold. Yes, there's ludo, Chinese checkers and backgammon, but there's so much more here and it's not just for kids.

MANTEQUERÍA BRAVO
FOOD, WINE

Map p248 (www.bravo1931.com; Calle de Ayala 24; ⌚9.30am-2.30pm & 5.30-8.30pm Mon-Fri, 9.30am-2.30pm Sat; Ⓜ Serrano) Behind this attractive old facade lies a connoisseur's paradise, that is filled with local cheeses, sausages, wines and coffees. The products here are great for a gift, but everything's so good that you won't want to share. Not that long ago, Mantequería Bravo won the prize for Madrid's best gourmet food shop or delicatessen – it's as simple as that.

DE VIAJE
BOOKS

Map p248 (☎91 577 98 99; www.deviaje.com; Calle de Serrano 41; ⌚10am-8.30pm Mon-Fri, 10.30am-2.30pm & 5-8pm Sat; Ⓜ Serrano) Whether you're after a guidebook, a coffee-table tome or travel literature, De Viaje, Madrid's largest travel bookshop, probably has it. Covering every region of the world, it has mostly Spanish titles, but some in English as well. Staff are helpful and there's also a travel agency.

CALLE DE JOSÉ ORTEGA Y GASSET

The world's most prestigious international designers occupy what is known as *la milla del oro* (the golden mile) along Calle de José Ortega y Gasset, close to the corner with Calle de Serrano. All of the following shops are open from 10am to 8.30pm Monday to Saturday unless otherwise stated.

On the south side of the street, there's **Giorgio Armani** (Map p248; ☎91 577 58 07; www.armani.com; Calle de José Ortega y Gasset 16; ⏲10am-8pm Mon-Sat), **Dolce & Gabbana** (Map p248; ☎91 781 09 10; www.dolcegabbana.es; Calle de José Ortega y Gasset 14), **Chanel** (Map p248; ☎91 431 30 36; www.chanel.com; Calle de José Ortega y Gasset 14; ⏲10am-8pm Mon-Sat), **Hermès** (Map p248; ☎91 577 76 09; www.hermes.com; Calle de José Ortega y Gasset 12; ⏲10am-8pm Mon-Sat), **Burberry** (Map p248; ☎91 575 82 99; www.burberry.com; ⏲11am-8pm Mon-Sat) and **Dior** (Map p248; ☎91 781 08 10; www.dior.com). Just across the road is **Louis Vuitton** (Map p248; ☎91 575 13 08; www.louisvuitton.com; Calle de José Ortega y Gasset 17; ⏲10am-8pm Mon-Sat), **Jimmy Choo** (Map p248; ☎91 781 86 08; www.jimmychoo.com; Calle de José Ortega y Gasset 15), **Cartier** (Map p248; ☎91 576 22 81; www.cartier.com; cnr Calles de José Ortega y Gasset & de Serrano; ⏲10am-8.30pm Mon-Fri, 11am-8pm Sat). Also in the vicinity is **Gucci** (Map p248; ☎91 431 17 17; www.gucci.com; cnr Calles de José Ortega y Gasset & de Serrano). What more could you want?

PURIFICACIÓN GARCÍA — FASHION

Map p248 (☎91 435 80 13; www.purificaciongarcia.com; Calle de Serrano 28; ⏲10am-8.30pm Mon-Sat; Ⓜ Serrano) Fashions may come and go but Puri consistently manages to keep ahead of the pack. Her signature style for men and women is elegant and mature designs that are just as at home in the workplace as at a wedding.

SPORTS & ACTIVITIES

LAB ROOM SPA — DAY SPA

Map p248 (☎91 781 14 11; www.thelabroom.com; Calle de Lagasca 63, 1D; ⏲noon-9pm Mon, 10.30am-9pm Tue-Fri, 10am-8pm Sat; Ⓜ Alonso Martínez) An exclusive spa and beauty parlour whose past clients include Penélope Cruz, Jennifer Lopez, Gwyneth Paltrow and Gael García Bernal, the Lab Room is close to the ultimate in pampering for both men and women. It offers a range of make-up sessions, massages and facial and body treatments, although prices can be surprisingly reasonable – manicures start at €25, massages start from €35 and it has a range of well-priced, all-inclusive package deals. There's even a complete 'change of image' which costs €300 – you won't believe the results they promise.

CHI SPA — DAY SPA

Map p248 (☎91 578 13 40; www.thechispa.com; Calle del Conde de Aranda 6; ⏲10am-9pm Mon-Fri, to 6pm Sat; Ⓜ Retiro) Wrap up in a robe and slippers and prepare to be pampered in one of Spain's best day spas. There are separate areas for men and women, and services include a wide range of massages, facials, manicures and pedicures. Now, what was it you were stressed about?

HAMMAM AYALA — DAY SPA

(www.hammamayala.com; Calle de Ayala 126; ⏲10am-8pm Tue & Thu, 1-10pm Wed, Fri, Sat, Sun; Ⓜ Manuel Becerra) Another excellent traditional Arab bath experience, Hammam Ayala offers massages and a range of bath treatments within a faithful re-creation of the Middle East's hammams. All-natural products and the sensory pleasures of exotic oils make this a lovely escape from modern life. The traditional bath ritual costs €50.

Malasaña & Chueca

MALASAÑA | CHUECA

Neighbourhood Top Five

❶ Passing under the fabulous doorway and spending an hour or two delving into Madrid's past at the **Museo de Historia** (p123).

❷ Shopping for retro fashions in the true rebellious spirit of Malasaña at the **Mercado de Fuencarral** (p140).

❸ Taking your pick of restaurants for lunch along one of Madrid's best culinary streets, starting perhaps with **Bazaar** (p129).

❹ Kicking back in true Malasaña style in one of the terrific restaurants along Calle de Manuela Malasaña, such as **La Musa** (p126).

❺ Following the footsteps of Hemingway and other *famosos* (celebrities) by ordering a mojito at the legendary **Museo Chicote** (p136).

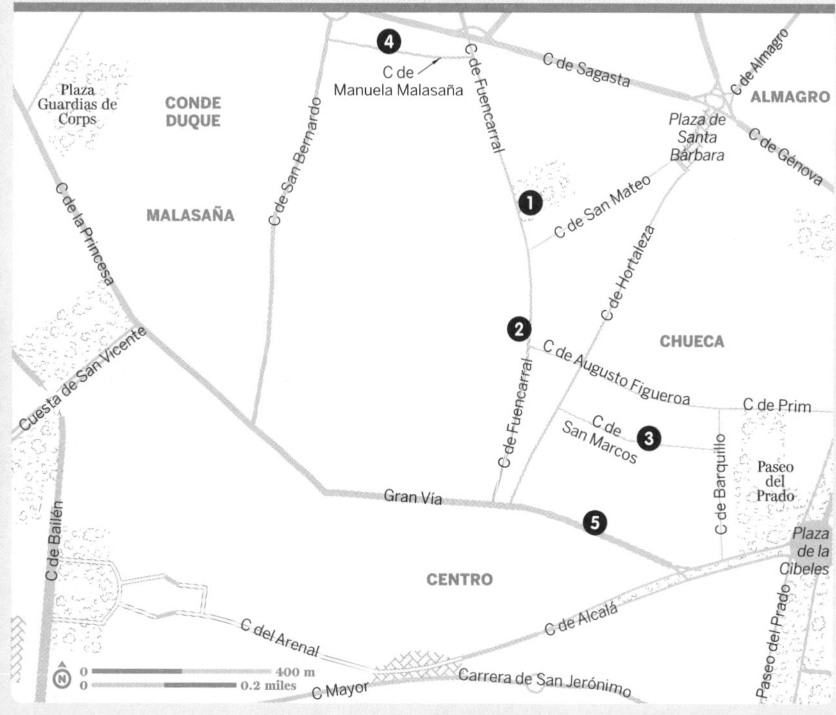

For more detail of this area see Map p250 and p254

Lonely Planet's Top Tip

In order to make the most of their popularity, some restaurants in Malasaña and elsewhere offer two sittings on Friday and Saturday nights, usually around 9pm and 11pm. Unless you can't wait (yes, we know that eating at 11pm and finishing dinner after midnight takes some getting used to), we recommend you reserve a table for the second sitting, otherwise you'll feel that they're hurrying you along.

Best Places to Eat

- Bazaar (p129)
- Albur (p126)
- La Musa (p126)
- Bocaito (p130)
- La Tasquita de Enfrente (p126)

For reviews, see p126

Best Places to Drink

- Museo Chicote (p136)
- Café Comercial (p132)
- Antigua Casa Ángel Sierra (p137)
- El Jardín Secreto (p133)
- Del Diego (p136)
- Café Belén (p136)

For reviews, see p132

Best Architecture

- Sociedad General de Autores y Editores (p123)
- Antiguo Cuartel del Conde Duque (p125)
- Museo de Historia (p123)
- Casa de las Siete Chimeneas (p125)

Explore: Malasaña & Chueca

Malasaña and Chueca are at their best in the evening and into the night – other than a flurry of activity around lunchtime as people hurry to and from their favourite tapas bar or restaurant, these *barrios* (districts) mostly live for the night. That said, the daytime shopping is fantastic in both *barrios*.

Calle de Fuencarral is the dividing line between the two, a narrow but nonetheless major city thoroughfare that has been pedestrianised for much of its length. West of that line in Malasaña, shopfronts announce names like 'True Love Tattoo' and 'Retro City' alongside graffiti and posters of heavy-rocking bands that have become an integral part of its gritty urban charm. Slightly more refined and less clamorous, the sub-*barrio* of Conde Duque, to the west, has the best of Malasaña without quite the same grit and noise.

If Malasaña holds fast to its roots, Chueca, east of Calle de Fuencarral, wears its heart on its sleeve, a *barrio* that the gay and lesbian community has transformed into one of the coolest places in Spain. Sometimes it's in your face, but more often it's what locals like to call 'hetero-friendly'. The further east you go, the more sophisticated Chueca becomes.

Local Life

- **Meeting Point** Café Comercial (p132) is one of Europe's most storied old cafes and it remains a place popular for old men playing chess and pretty young things getting geared up for a long night ahead.
- **Neighbourhood hub** Plaza Dos de Mayo is Malasaña's epicentre, at its best late afternoon when children pour out of nearby schools to play while their parents order beer and wine at adjacent outdoor tables.
- **Hangout** Antigua Casa Ángel Sierra (p137), right on Plaza de Chueca, has seen it all in almost a century of Chueca life and the crowds here stand six or seven deep on a busy Saturday night.

Getting There & Away

- **Metro** Chueca metro station (line 5) sits right in the heart of Chueca, while Tribunal (lines 1 and 10) serves a similar purpose in Malasaña. Noviciado (lines 2 and 10) is good for Conde Duque.
- **Metro** Other convenient metro stations around these neighbourhoods' perimeters include San Bernardo, Bilbao, Alonso Martínez, Gran Vía and Santo Domingo.

SIGHTS

SOCIEDAD GENERAL DE AUTORES Y EDITORES ARCHITECTURE

Map p254 (General Society of Authors & Editors; Calle de Fernando VI 4; MAlonso Martínez) This swirling, melting wedding cake of a building is as close as Madrid comes to the work of Antoni Gaudí, which so illuminates Barcelona. It's a joyously self-indulgent ode to *modernismo* and is virtually one of a kind in Madrid. Casual visitors are actively discouraged, although what you see from the street is impressive enough. The only exceptions are on the first Monday of October, International Architecture Day, and during the **Noche en Blanco** (http://lanocheenblanco.esmadrid.com) festivities. We've had a peek inside and its interior staircase alone is reason enough to come if you're here at one of these times.

MUSEO DEL ROMANTICISMO MUSEUM

Map p254 (91 448 10 45; http://museoromanticismo.mcu.es; Calle de San Mateo 13; adult/child/student €3/free/1.50, free Sat after 2.30pm; 9.30am-8.30pm Tue-Sat & 10am-3pm Sun May-Oct, 9.30am-6.30pm Tue-Sat & 10am-3pm Sun Nov-Apr; MTribunal) This intriguing museum is devoted to the Romantic period of the 19th century. The museum occupies a late-18th-century mansion which was converted into a museum by the Marqués de la Vega-Inclán (who was involved in the creation of the chain of luxury hotels known as the *paradores*) in 1924. It houses a minor treasure trove of mostly 19th-century paintings, furniture, porcelain, books, photos and other bits and bobs from a bygone age and offers an insight into what upper-class houses were like in the 19th century. There's a limit of 100 visitors inside at any one time. The best-known work in the collection is Goya's *San Gregorio Magno, Papa*.

FREE MUSEO DE HISTORIA MUSEUM

Map p250 (www.munimadrid.es/museodehistoria; Calle de Fuencarral 78; 9.30am-8pm Tue-Fri, 10am-2pm Sat & Sun; MTribunal) The fine Museo de Historia (formerly the Museo Municipal) has an elaborate and restored baroque entrance, raised in 1721 by Pedro de Ribera. Behind this facade, a stunning reconstruction of the building has transformed this into one of Madrid's lightest and airiest museums. They were still getting the collection together again and they're due to reopen the various exhibitions throughout 2013, but we've had a sneak preview and we reckon this could be one of Madrid's most rewarding museums. The collection is dominated by paintings and other memorabilia charting the historical evolution of Madrid, of which the highlights are Goya's *Allegory of the City of Madrid* and the expansive models of medieval Madrid.

FREE MUSEO MUNICIPAL DE ARTE CONTEMPORÁNEO MUSEUM

Map p250 (91 588 59 28; www.munimadrid.es/museoartecontemporaneo; Calle del Conde Duque 9-11; MPlaza de España, Ventura Rodríguez, San Bernardo) Spread over two floors, this is a rich collection of modern Spanish art, mostly paintings and graphic art with a smattering of photography, sculpture and drawings. Running throughout much of the gallery are works showcasing creative interpretations of Madrid's cityscape – avant-garde splodges and old-fashioned visions of modern Madrid side by side – and, for many lay visitors, therein lies the museum's greatest appeal. Some examples include Juan Moreno Aquado's *Chamartín* (2000), Luis Mayo's *Cibeles* (1997) and a typically fantastical representation of the Cibeles fountain by one-time icon of *la movida madrileña*, Ouka Lele. The many talented artists represented here include Eduardo Arroyo and Basque sculptor Jorde Oteiza. The museum

TRIBALL – THE NEW MALASAÑA

Although Malasaña is unlikely to shed its carefully cultivated retro image any time soon, a project run by local businesses is seeking to change the way people think about Malasaña. Entitled Triángulo Ballesta (www.triballmadrid.com), it's named after the famously seedy Calle de Ballesta, close to Gran Vía, and includes streets such as Calle del Desengaño (where prostitutes still linger in full view), Calle de Valverde, Calle de la Corredera Baja de San Pablo and surrounds. The project is one of regeneration and involves cleaning up the streets, as well as encouraging new businesses and the avant-garde arts community to make it their *barrio* (district) of choice. They have promised not to stop until they have transformed Malasaña into the new Soho.

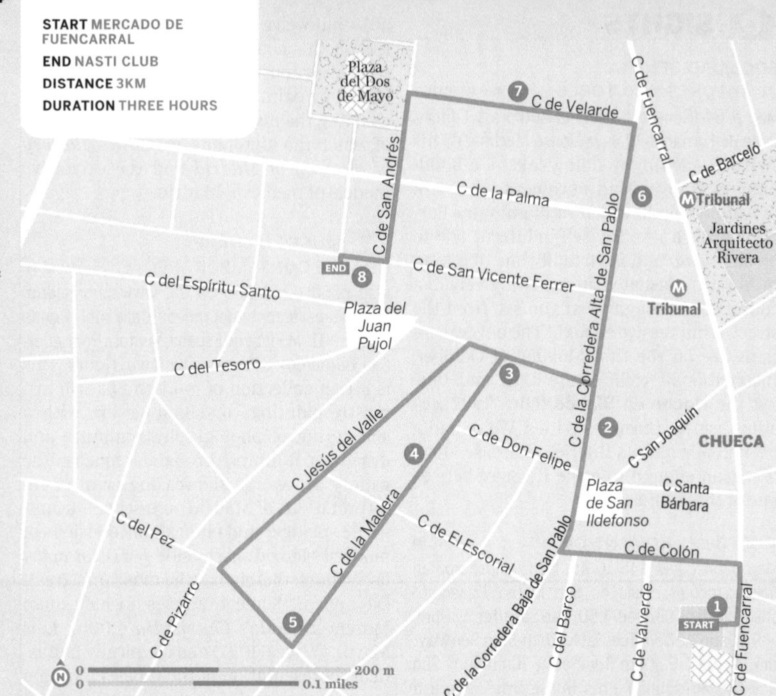

Neighbourhood Walk

Retro Malasaña

Malasaña was the epicentre of *la movida madrileña* in the 1980s and that spirit lives on here. In the retro bars, nightclubs and shops that pay homage to the '70s and '80s, the common theme is an alternative slant on life in a bid to relive or recreate the past.

Begin at Madrid's home of alternative streetwear cool, 1 **Mercado de Fuencarral**. Even if you're not in the market for torn T-shirts, black leather or silver studs, it's always worth a visit to see what excites the neighbourhood's fashionistas. Leave behind Calle de Fuencarral and head down Calle de Corredera Alta de San Pablo where 2 **Retro City** is another offbeat fashion icon of the *barrio* with casual and cast-off fashions.

A short walk down Calle del Espirítu Santo brings you to 3 **Lolina Vintage Café** whose carefully selected retro furnishings and diet of coffee and cocktails play to a Malasaña crowd who likes the idea of the past but without any of its discomforts. A short distance down the hill along Calle de la Madera, 4 **Casa Julio** serves up Madrid's best *croquetas* (croquettes) behind the facade of an otherwise unremarkable old Malasaña *taberna* (tavern).

Onwards down the hill, 5 **Bar Palentino** is the essence of Malasaña's unwillingness to conform to norms taken for granted elsewhere. The utterly unpretentious decor is antistyle in the best Malasaña tradition and young *madrileños* (people from Madrid) love this place.

Time to dance. Back up the hill to the north, 6 **Tuppeware** is kitsch in the finest possible way and infused with the rock-n-roll spirit of Old Malasaña. Its rival as the spiritual home of the Malasaña night is just down the road along Calle de Velarde: 7 **La Vía Láctea** is another bar-nightclub that feels like 1980s Madrid never ended. At the end, up a slight rise on Calle de San Vicente Ferrer, is 8 **Nasti Club**, its presence announced with a wall full of graffiti, its specialty a recurring Malasaña theme of rock and rolling your way towards the dawn.

was closed for major renovations at the time of writing with no scheduled date for reopening.

ANTIGUO CUARTEL DEL CONDE DUQUE NOTABLE BUILDING

Map p250 (Calle del Conde Duque 9; Ⓜ Plaza de España, Ventura Rodríguez, San Bernardo) This grand former barracks dominates Conde Duque on the western fringe of Malasaña with its imposing, recently restored facade stretching 228m down the hill. A recent and massive clean-up of the facade has brought this imposing building back to life in a manner worthy of its local significance. Built in 1717 under the auspices of architect Pedro de Ribera, its highlight is the extravagant 18th-century doorway, which is a masterpiece of the baroque *churrigueresque* style. These days it's home by day to a cultural centre, which hosts government archives, libraries, the Hemeroteca Municipal (the biggest collection of newspapers and magazines in Spain), temporary exhibitions and the Museo Municipal de Arte Contemporáneo (p123). By night, in summer, one of the two large patios becomes an atmospheric concert venue; programs for exhibitions and concerts are posted outside. In the gardens to the northeast of the building, most mornings you'll find old men playing *petanca* (boules) under the trees in a scene from Madrid's village past.

GALERÍA MORIARTY GALLERY

Map p254 (☎91 531 43 65; www.galeriamoriarty.com; Calle de Tamayo y Baus 6; ⏲11am-2pm & 5-8.30pm Tue-Sat; Ⓜ Chueca, Colón) During *la movida madrileña* in the 1980s, Galería Moriarty (then in Calle del Almirante) was one of Madrid's most important meeting places of culture and counterculture, drawing the iconic Agatha Ruiz de la Prada, filmmaker Pedro Almodóvar and photographer García Alix among others to attend its exhibitions and parties. It may have moved a number of times since, but it remains one of the most important small galleries in Madrid, with all manner of interesting contemporary exhibitions.

PALACIO DE LIRIA MANSION

Map p250 (☎91 547 53 02; Calle de la Princesa 20; ⏲guided visit 11am & noon Fri; Ⓜ Ventura Rodríguez) This 18th-century mansion, rebuilt after a fire in 1936, nestles amid the modern architecture just north of Plaza de España as a reminder of the days when Madrid's streets were lined with mansions like these. It holds an impressive collection of art, period furniture and *objets d'art*. To join a guided visit, you need to send a formal request with your personal details to the palace, which is home to the Duke and Duchess of Alba, one of the grandest names in Spanish nobility – ask at the tourist office for details. The waiting list is long and most mere mortals content themselves with staring through the gates into the grounds, but watch this space – we've heard rumours that it might be about to become more accessible.

PALACIO BUENAVISTA NOTABLE BUILDING

Map p254 (Plaza de la Cibeles) Set back amid gardens on the northwest edge of Plaza de la Cibeles stands the Palacio Buenavista, now occupied by the army. It once belonged to the Alba family, and the young Duchess of Alba, Cayetana, who was widely rumoured to have had an affair with the artist Goya in the 18th century, lived here for a time.

CASA DE LAS SIETE CHIMENEAS ARCHITECTURE

Map p254 (Plaza del Rey; Ⓜ Banco de España) A block northwest of Plaza de la Cibeles is the Casa de las Siete Chimeneas, a 16th-century mansion that takes its name from the seven chimneys it still boasts. It's a tantalising glimpse of the sort of residences that once lined the Paseo de la Castellana. They say that the ghost of one of Felipe II's lovers still runs about here in distress on certain evenings. Nowadays, it's home to the Ministry of Education, Culture and Sport.

SMALL PRIVATE GALLERIES

For those with an interest in contemporary art that extends beyond what you'll find at the Centro de Arte Reina Sofía (p101), central Madrid is studded with small galleries showcasing both up-and-coming and longer-established painters, sculptors and photographers. For a near-complete list, check out **Arte Madrid** (www.artemadrid.com); its brochure of the same name, available online in PDF format, contains a map and program of upcoming exhibitions. Many of these galleries are regulars at Madrid's **Arco fair** (www.ifema.es; Feria Internacional de Arte Contemporánea).

MUSEO DE CERA MUSEUM

Map p254 (☎91 319 26 49; www.museoceramadrid.com; Paseo de los Recoletos 41; adult/child €17/12; ⊙10am-2.30pm & 4.30-8.30pm Mon-Fri, 10am-8.30pm Sat & Sun; MColón) If wax museums are your thing, this one with more than 450 characters is a fairly standard version of the genre. With models ranging from the Beatles to Bart Simpson, and from Raúl to Cervantes, Dalí and Picasso, it's a wide collection of international and Spanish figures through the centuries. If you're drawn to the darker side of life, there's everything from the Inquisition to Freddy Krueger, while the **Tren del Terror** is not for the faint hearted. Other attractions include the **Simulador**, which shakes you up a bit as though you were inside a washing machine, and the **Multivisión** journey through Spanish history. It claims to be Madrid's seventh-most-visited museum, although it's hard to see why, unless you've got kids.

EATING

Cool *barrios* (districts). Cool places to eat. Chueca and Malasaña may be radically different, one newly modern, the other firmly rooted in the past, but their restaurants are remarkably similar. Blending old *tabernas* (taverns) with laid-back temples to Spanish nouvelle cuisine, eating here revolves around an agreeable buzz, innovative cooking and casual but stylish surrounds. Some streets stand out, especially Calle de Manuela Malasaña in Malasaña and Calle de la Libertad in Chueca. For cheap but decent international cuisine (eg Asian, Indian, Thai, Persian), head down to Calle de San Bernardino at the lower end of Calle del Conde Duque in Malasaña.

Malasaña

TOP CHOICE ALBUR TAPAS, SPANISH €€

Map p250 (☎91 594 27 33; www.restaurantealbur.com; Calle de Manuela Malasaña 15; mains €13-18; ⊙noon-1am Sun-Thu, to 2am Fri & Sat; MBilbao) One of Malasaña's best deals, this place has a wildly popular tapas bar and a classy but casual restaurant out the back. Albur is known for terrific rice dishes and tapas, and has a well-chosen wine list. The restaurant waiters never seem to lose their cool, and their extremely well-priced rice dishes are the stars of the show, although in truth you could order anything here and leave well satisfied.

LA TASQUITA DE ENFRENTE CONTEMPORARY SPANISH €€€

Map p250 (☎91 532 54 49; www.latasquitadeenfrente.com; Calle de la Ballesta 6; mains €20-32; ⊙lunch & dinner Tue-Sat; MGran Vía) To succeed on the international stage, Spain's celebrity chefs have to take experimentation to new levels, but to succeed at home they usually have to maintain a greater fidelity to traditional bases before heading off in new directions. And therein lies the success of Chef Juanjo López: it's difficult to overstate how popular this place is among people in the know in Madrid's food scene. His seasonal menu never ceases to surprise but also combines simple Spanish staples to stunning effect. His *menu degustación* (tasting menu; €48) and *menú de Juanjo* (€65) would be our choice if this is your first time. Reservations are essential.

LA MUSA SPANISH, FUSION €€

Map p250 (☎91 448 75 58; www.lamusa.com.es; Calle de Manuela Malasaña 18; mains €7-15; ⊙9am-1am Mon-Thu, 9am-2am Fri, 1pm-2am Sat, 1pm-1am Sun; MSan Bernardo) Snug yet loud, a favourite of Madrid's hip young crowd yet utterly unpretentious, La Musa is all about designer decor, lounge music on the sound system and food (breakfast, lunch and dinner) that will live long in the memory and is always fun and filled with flavour. The menu is divided into three types of tapas – hot, cold and BBQ; among the hot varieties is the fantastic *jabalí con ali-oli de miel y sobrasada* (wild boar with honey mayonnaise and *sobrasada* – a soft, mildly spicy sausage from Mallorca). It doesn't take reservations, so sidle up to the bar, add your name to the waiting list and soak up the ambient buzz of Malasaña at its best. If you don't fancy waiting, try the sister restaurant nearby, Ojalá Awareness Club (p134).

CASA PERICO SPANISH €€

Map p250 (☎91 532 81 76; www.casapericomadrid.com; Calle de la Ballesta 18; mains €15-17; ⊙lunch & dinner Mon-Fri, lunch Sat Sep-Jul; MGran Vía) One look at the glowing reviews from the local press plastered across the

GOOD PLACES FOR A SNACK

In the not-too-distant past, the choice for those visitors unaccustomed to eating a big meal at lunchtime (as is the local custom) was limited to grazing on tapas. Although this still represents snacking at its best, there are increasingly places where you can get a sandwich or light meal. These include the following:

➡ **Cacao Sampaka** (p142) A gourmet chocolate shop with a cafe attached, where they serve sandwiches, pastries, cakes and the like.

➡ **Magasand** (Map p254; ☎91 319 68 25; www.magasand.com; Travesía de San Mateo 16; sandwiches €3.80-5, salads €4.20-6.80; ⏰9.30am-10pm Mon-Fri, noon-8pm Sat; Ⓜ Alonso Martínez) Comfy sofas, bar stools, free wi-fi and designer magazines elevate this above your average sandwich bar. They do creative sandwiches and bagels, as well as salads and hot soups.

➡ **Un y 2** (Map p254; ☎91 522 71 92; www.unydos.es; Calle de la Libertad 12; snacks & light mals from €6.50; ⏰9.30am-1.30pm & 3.30-8.30pm; Ⓜ Chueca) Salads, sandwiches and cakes while you enjoy the free wi-fi in a bright, modern space.

➡ **Diurno** (p138) In addition to great coffee throughout the day, they also serve hot and cold *bocadillos* (filled rolls; from €2.30) throughout the day.

➡ **Bar Palentino** (p128) Well-priced *bocadillos* in quintessential Malasaña surrounds.

facade and you'll quickly learn what this place is about: fine traditional cooking at a reasonable price. Going strong since the 1940s, they do everything from legume-based stews to ribs, but their signature dish is *arroz a lo cutre* (literally 'coarse rice', actually a delicious creamy rice dish). When you push open the door, it is not entirely clear you're in a restaurant – the handful of tables covered in checked cloths are huddled behind a mess of wine bottles, crates and who knows what else. Their lunchtime specials include *cocido madrileña* (€20) on Mondays. A great, quirky place to eat.

CASA JULIO — SPANISH €

Map p250 (☎91 522 72 74; Calle de la Madera 37; 6/12 croquetas €5/10; ⏰lunch & dinner Mon-Sat; Ⓜ Tribunal) A city-wide poll for the best *croquetas* in Madrid would see half of those polled voting for Casa Julio and the remainder not doing so only because they haven't been yet. They're that good that celebrities and mere mortals from all over Madrid come here to sit alongside crusty old locals and sample the traditional *jamón* (ham) variety or more creative versions such as spinach with raisins and gorgonzola.

BODEGA DE LA ARDOSA — TAPAS €

Map p250 (☎91 521 49 79; Calle de Colón 13; tapas & raciones €3.50-11; ⏰8.30am-1am; Ⓜ Tribunal) Going strong since 1892, the charming, wood-panelled bar of Bodega de la Ardosa could equally be recommended as a favourite Malasaña drinking hole. Then again, to come here and not try the *salmorejo* (cold tomato soup made with bread, oil, garlic and vinegar), *croquetas, patatas bravas* (potatoes with a spicy tomato sauce) or *tortilla de patatas* (potato and onion omellete) would be a crime. On weekend nights there's scarcely room to move.

LA ISLA DEL TESORO — VEGETARIAN €€

Map p250 (☎91 593 14 40; www.isladeltesoro.net; Calle de Manuela Malasaña 3; mains €12.50-14.50; ⏰lunch & dinner; 🅥; Ⓜ Bilbao) Unlike some vegetarian restaurants that seem to work on the philosophy that basic decor signifies healthy food, the dining area here is like someone's fantasy of a secret garden come to life. The cooking is assured and wide ranging in its influences; the jungle burger is typical in a menu that's full of surprises. The weekday lunchtime *menú del día* (daily set menu) is more varied than most in Madrid, taking a different national cuisine as its base every day.

CRÊPERIE MA BRETAGNE — CREPERIE €

Map p250 (☎91 531 77 74; Calle de San Vicente Ferrer 9; crepes €6-12; ⏰dinner daily; Ⓜ Tribunal) What a wonderful little place this is – dark, candle lit and all about delicious crepes. After eating a main meal of crêpes from the rustic wooden tables, there are more crêpes, this time sweet, for dessert. You'll never want to see a crepe again after overindulging here, but it's a great way to go out.

BAR PALENTINO TAPAS €

Map p250 (☎91 532 30 58; Calle del Pez 8; bocadillos €1.80-2.50; ⏰7am-2pm Mon-Sat; Ⓜ Noviciado) Formica tables, not a single attention to decor detail, and yet… This ageless Malasaña bar is a reminder of an important lesson in eating Spanish style: don't be fooled by appearances. Wildly popular with young and old alike, Bar Palentino has an irresistible charm, thanks in large part to its owners María Dolores (who is there in the morning and early afternoon and claims to be 'the house speciality') and Casto (evenings, and one of few septuagenarians to have his own MySpace profile). And the food? Simple traditional tapas and *bocadillos* (filled rolls) that have acquired city-wide fame, not least for their price.

CONACHE SPANISH €

Map p250 (☎91 522 95 00; www.restaurantecon ache.com; Plaza de San Ildefonso; mains €7.50-14.90; ⏰9.30am-1.30am Mon-Thu, 9.30am-2.30am Fri & Sat; Ⓜ Tribunal) With Asian and African decorations, creative Mediterranean cooking and a noisy Spanish clientele, Conache is a hub of *barrio* life and is as good for breakfast as for dinner. The food is outstanding; the *salmorejo* is among the best we've tasted this far from Córdoba. It's difficult to snaffle a table on the outdoor terrace but worth the wait.

HOME BURGER BAR AMERICAN €

Map p250 (☎91 522 97 28; www.homeburgerbar.com; Calle del Espíritu Santo 12; mains €10-13.50; ⏰lunch & dinner daily; Ⓜ Tribunal) There are times when you just need a burger. One of Madrid's longest and most authentic burger bars, Home Burger Bar is terrific, with an interesting mix of vegetarian, gourmet and classic hamburgers served by friendly waiters in an American-diner-style setting. The meat is 'ecologically sound' and, in the Spanish style, medium-rare (the chef will cook it more if you ask). They have another, larger **restaurant** (Map p250; ☎91 115 12 79; Calle de Silva 25; ⏰lunch & dinner daily; Callao) close to Gran Vía, and another **branch** (Map p254; ☎521 85 31; Calle de San Marcos 26; ⏰lunch & dinner daily) in Chueca.

PEGGY SUE'S AMERICAN DINER AMERICAN €

Map p250 (☎91 521 85 60; www.peggysues.es; Calle de Santa Cruz de Marcenado 13; mains €4.95-6.75; ⏰lunch & dinner daily; Ⓜ San Bernardo) American-style burgers have developed something of a cult following in Madrid in recent years and this place has been at the forefront of the trend. The decor recreates 1950s America and the jukebox belts out Aretha Franklin and Chuck Berry at regular intervals. The burgers are the genuine article and as good as you'll find in town.

BUENAS Y SANTAS FUSION €€

Map p250 (☎91 454 41 72; www.buenasysantas.es; Calle de San Bernardo 85; mains €9-20; ⏰8.30am-11pm Mon-Thu, 8.30am-midnight Fri, 9am-midnight Sat; Ⓜ San Bernardo) An interesting new arrival on the Conde Duque eating scene, Argentinian-run Buenas y Santas has plenty of Argentinian-inspired dishes with terrific salads, quiches, pasta and hamburgers. Some dishes are tasty rather than exciting, but the service is excellent and the decor of minimalist white with no two chairs the same is eclectic and welcoming.

CASA HORTENSIA ASTURIAN €€

Map p250 (☎91 539 00 90; www.casahortensia.com; Calle de la Farmacia 2, 2nd fl; mains €15.50-25; ⏰lunch & dinner Tue-Sat, lunch Sun, closed Aug; Ⓜ Tribunal or Gran Vía) With all the innovations happening elsewhere in Madrid, it's good to know that some things don't change. Casa Hortensia doesn't bother much with decoration, allowing you to concentrate on the Asturian specialities, such as *fabada asturiana* (white-bean stew with pork and blood sausage). *Sidra* (cider) is, of course, obligatory.

LE PAIN QUOTIDIEN BAKERY, CAFE €€

Map p250 (☎91 593 09 39; www.lepainquotidien.com; Calle de Fuencarral 95; mains €9.50-12.50; ⏰8am-midnight Mon-Thu, 8am-1am Fri, 9am-1am Sat, 9am-midnight Sun; Ⓜ Tribunal) From Paris to New York and now in Madrid, this bakery-cum-restaurant has taken the world by storm. Based around a philosophy of homemade bread and ecofriendly principles, it's as good for a loaf of bread and creative breakfasts as for light meals that include Middle Eastern dips and Spanish staples. There are other branches around town.

A DOS VELAS SPANISH, INTERNATIONAL €€

Map p250 (☎91 446 18 63; www.adosvelas.net; Calle de San Vicente Ferrer 16; mains €9.50-18, set menus €10-25; ⏰lunch & dinner Mon-Sat; Ⓜ Tribunal) We're fans of this place where the food is creative with Mediterranean cooking fused with occasional Indian or even Argentine flavours. It has a lovely dining area with soft lighting and exposed brick, and service that's attentive without being intrusive.

COMOMELOCOMO SPANISH, INTERNATIONAL €€

Map p250 (☎91 523 13 23; www.comomelocomo.com; Calle de Andrés Borrego 16; mains €10.50-18; ⏲lunch & dinner daily; Ⓜ Noviciado) Run by the same group that brought you Con Dos Fogones and A Dos Velas (p128), Comomelocomo, down Malasaña's lower end, offers excellent-value traditional Spanish dishes given the odd international twist to suit 21st-century palates. Elsewhere, beautifully presented meals and agreeable surrounds too often mean meagre portions, but not here. The friendly service is another winner.

CON DOS FOGONES SPANISH, INTERNATIONAL €€

Map p250 (☎91 559 63 26; www.condosfogones.com; Calle de San Bernardino 9; mains €10-18; ⏲lunch & dinner daily; Ⓜ Plaza de España) Con Dos Fogones is cool and classy, with bright colours softly lit by designer lamps. The food is everything from salads and hamburgers to great slabs of Argentine beef with plenty of unexpected twists, like brie tempura or cod pâté. The word on the street is that quality has recently taken a downward turn, but we reckon they're still worth a look.

Chueca

TOP CHOICE LE CABRERA TAPAS €€

Map p254 (☎91 319 94 57; www.lecabrera.com; Calle de Bárbara de Braganza 2; tapas €3-22, caviar €85; ⏲lunch & dinner Tue-Sat; Ⓜ Colón, Alonso Martínez) They describe this slick new tapas bar as a 'Cocktail and Gastrobar' and as much thought has gone into the decoration (with mirrors that resemble shattered glass) as the cooking. Perhaps more than other denizens of Spanish nouvelle cuisine, they work overwhelmingly from a traditional base – the emphasis here is on quality rather than experimentation, although some well-known Spanish dishes do head off in all manner of surprising directions. The downstairs cocktail bar (p136) is one of the coolest spots in town.

EL ORIGINAL SPANISH €€

Map p254 (☎91 522 90 69; www.eloriginal.es; Calle de las Infantas 44; mains €8-12, set menus €25-38; ⏲lunch & dinner Mon-Sat; Ⓜ Chueca, Banco de España) With the best products and signature dishes from most Spanish regions, El Original turns out well-priced cooking and instead of messing with some of Spain's favourite dishes, they've gone for creativity in the decor – trees grow throughout the dining area and the decoration is pleasingly contemporary. Dishes include the *suquet de pescado y marisco con patatas nuevas* (fish and shellfish stew with new potatoes).

BAZAAR CONTEMPORARY SPANISH €

Map p254 (www.restaurantbazaar.com; Calle de la Libertad 21; mains €6.50-10; ⏲lunch & dinner; Ⓜ Chueca) Bazaar's popularity among the well heeled and famous shows no sign of abating. Its pristine white interior design, with theatre-style lighting and wall-length windows, may draw a crowd that looks like it stepped out of the pages of *¡Hola* magazine, but the food is extremely well priced and innovative and the atmosphere is casual. For years we've been recommending the *carpaccio de gambas con vinagreta de setas* (prawn carpaccio with mushroom vinaigrette) and see no reason to stop doing so. It doesn't take reservations, so get there early or be prepared to wait, regardless of whether you're famous or not.

BACO Y BETO TAPAS €

Map p254 (☎91 522 84 81; Calle de Pelayo 24; tapas from €4; ⏲dinner Mon-Fri, lunch & dinner Sat; Ⓜ Chueca) Friends of ours in Madrid begged us not to include this place in the guide and we must admit that we were tempted to keep this secret all to ourselves. Some of the tastiest tapas in Madrid are what you find here, either ordered as a *tapa*, such as quail's eggs with *salmorejo*, or *raciones* (larger tapas servings), such as aubergine with parmesan. Their *croquetas* are wonderful and they're not averse to bringing international influences into their dishes. The clientele is predominantly gay, but they, like our friends, can't have it all to themselves.

GASTROMAQUIA TAPAS €

Map p254 (☎91 522 64 13; Calle de Pelayo 8; tapas from €4; ⏲lunch Mon-Thu & Sat, dinner Tue-Sat; Ⓜ Chueca) The exciting reimagining of tapas that would have Hemingway turning in his grave swept through Madrid long ago, but few places have recognised the possibilities of bringing world cuisines (eg couscous) into the mix. The philosophy

COOKING COURSES

There are plenty of places in Madrid to learn Spanish cooking. In most cases, you'll need at least passable Spanish, but some run special classes for English speakers.

- **Alambique** (Map p234; 91 547 42 20; www.alambique.com; Plaza de la Encarnación 2; per person from €50; MÓpera, Santo Domingo) Cooking classes start at around €50, with a handful of English-and French-speaking courses.
- **Apunto – Centro Cultural del Gusto** (Map p254; 91 702 10 41; www.apuntolibreria.com; Calle de Pelayo 60; per person €40-60; MChueca) At this engaging little bookstore whose subtitle translates as 'Cultural Centre of Taste', cooking classes across a range of cuisines start at around €30.
- **Cooking Club** (91 323 29 58; www.club-cooking.com; Calle de Veza 33; MValdeacederas) The regular, respected program of classes encompasses a range of cooking styles.
- **Kitchen Club** (Map p250; 91 522 62 63; www.kitchenclub.es; Calle de Ballesta 8; MGran Vía or Callao) Run by one of Madrid's most celebrated chefs, Andrés Madrigal, Kitchen Club offers a range of courses just off the back of Gran Vía in the city centre. Our pick is the three-and-a-half-hour 'Atelier Madrigal', run by the master chef himself and a bargain at just €90.

behind Gastromaquia (the brainchild of renowned chef Ivan Sánchez) is to encourage Spaniards to relearn the art of eating tapas, taking them on a journey into what he calls 'universal tapas' – try the braised octopus with potato foam to get you rethinking it all. Gastromaquia nonetheless maintains a base in Spanish cooking (helped by its location in an old Chueca *taberna*), but the tastes are always fresh and surprising.

BOCAITO TAPAS €€

Map p254 (91 532 12 19; www.bocaito.com; Calle de la Libertad 4-6; tapas from €3.50, mains €12-20; lunch & dinner Mon-Fri, dinner Sat; MChueca, Banco de España) Film-maker Pedro Almodóvar once described this traditional bar and restaurant as 'the best antidepressant'. Forget about the sit-down restaurant (which is nonetheless well regarded) and jam into the bar, shoulder-to-shoulder with the casual crowd, order a few Andalucian *raciones* off the menu, slosh them down with some gritty red or a *caña* (small glass of beer) and enjoy the theatre in which these busy barmen excel. Specialities include the mussels with bechamel, canapés and fried fish.

MERCADO DE SAN ANTÓN TAPAS €€

Map p254 (www.mercadosananton.com; Calle de Augusto Figueroa 24; meals €10-30; 10am-midnight Mon-Thu, to 1.30am Fri-Sun; MChueca) The renovations to some of Madrid's most important markets has brought a whole new dimension to the city's eating scene. On the 1st floor of this busy Chueca market is a range of fine tapas bars where the cuisine spans Japanese, Italian and Greek with some wonderful Spanish options – stall 23 has some fabulous tapas on display, most of which revolve around foie gras. There's also a wine bar, and a sit-down restaurant with outdoor terrace one floor up.

RIBEIRA DO MIÑO SEAFOOD €€

Map p250 (91 521 98 54; Calle de la Santa Brigida 1; mains €7-14.50; lunch & dinner Tue-Sat; MTribunal) This riotously popular seafood bar and restaurant is where *madrileños* with a love for seafood indulge their fantasy. The *mariscada de la casa* (€31 for two) is a platter of seafood so large that even the hungriest of visitors will be satisfied. Leave your name with the waiter and be prepared to wait up to an hour for a table on weekends.

LA PAELLA DE LA REINA MEDITERRANEAN €€

Map p254 (91 531 18 85; www.lapaelladelareina.com; Calle de la Reina 39; mains €14-25; MBanco de España) Madrid is not renowned for its paella (Valencia is king in that regard), but Valencianos who can't make it home are known to frequent La Paella de la Reina. Like any decent paella restaurant, you need two people to make an order but, that requirement satisfied, you've plenty of choice. The typical Valencia paella is cooked with beans, chicken and rabbit, but there are also plenty of seafood varieties on offer, including *arroz negro* (black rice, whose colour derives from squid ink).

RESTAURANTE MOMO SPANISH €€

Map p254 (☎91 532 73 48; Calle de la Libertad 8; mains €7.50-11, set menus from €12; ⊙lunch & dinner Mon-Sat; ⓂChueca) Momo is a Chueca beacon of reasonably priced home cooking for a casual crowd. It has an artsy vibe and is ideal for those who want a hearty meal without too much elaboration. Unusually, the well-priced three-course set menus spill over into the evening and the famous chocolate *moco* (literally 'snot', but really homemade chocolate pudding) is the tastiest of dessert dishes despite the worrying name. It's a mostly gay crowd, but everyone's welcome.

KIM BU MBU AFRICAN €€

Map p254 (☎91 521 26 81; Calle de Colmenares 7; mains €9-10; ⊙lunch & dinner Mon-Sat, lunch Sun; ⓂChueca or Banco de España) Stepping inside this fine African restaurant, with stunning African decor and a tranquil air, is like entering another world. The *menú de degustación* (€21) is a good way to get acquainted with Cameroonian, Ghanaian, Kenyan and Tanzanian tastes. Then again, the *gambas con mango y batata dulce* (prawns with mango and sweet potato) are pretty self-explanatory and very tasty.

LA MORDIDA MEXICAN €€

Map p254 (☎91 308 20 89; www.lamordida.com; Calle de Belén 13; mains €8-13; ⊙lunch & dinner Sun-Thu, 1.30pm-1am Sat; ⓂChueca) If your idea of Mexican food was born in Taco Bell, La Mordida, owned by singer-songwriter Joaquin Sabina, will show you a whole new world. This is home-style Mexican cooking, the sort of place where most of the names on the menu will need explanation from the waiters. With Mexican cantina-style decor, and Coronitas and margaritas in abundance, this is one of our favourite Mexican restaurants in Madrid.

RESTAURANTE EXTREMADURA EXTREMADURAN €€

Map p254 (☎91 531 88 22; www.restauranteextremadura.com; Calle de la Libertad 13; mains €14-18.50; ⊙lunch Mon, lunch & dinner Tue-Sun; ⓂChueca or Banco de España) Hearty, meat-dominated cooking from the Spanish interior is what you'll find here; *jamón* is a key fixture (some of the best *jamón* comes from Extremadura). The quality of the products is unimpeachable, and the cooks thankfully let the ingredients breathe without too many elaborations.

TEPIC MEXICAN €€

Map p254 (☎91 522 08 50; www.tepic.es; Calle de Pelayo 4; mains €12-18; ⊙lunch & dinner daily; ⓂChueca) Chueca's young professional crowd loves these sorts of places – chic dining rooms, gay-friendly service and international flavours that come with a label, in this case 'Urban Mexican Food'. Tepic's signature dish is the Acapulco Tropical, a cheese taco with meat and pineapple, but it's all good and leaves you with none of that heavy after-dinner feel that spoils the aftermath of so many Mexican meals. Their *menú degustación* (€26) is outstanding, there are lots of Mexican beers to choose from and the margaritas are spectacular.

ALMA LUSA PORTUGUESE €€

Map p254 (☎91 188 84 24; www.almalusa.es; Calle de Colmenares 5; mains €9.50-17; ⊙lunch & dinner daily; ⓂBanco de España) Despite its proximity, Portugal's cuisine remains little-known outside Iberia and this is a good place to get to grips with the national obsession with *bacalao* (cod), which is served in all manner of combinations with potatoes, eggs and the like. The atmosphere is casual, and they've a good *menú del día.*

CHARLOTTE CAFE €

Map p254 (☎91 113 07 31; Calle de Válgame Dios 4; mains from €4.90; ⊙lunch & dinner Mon-Sat; ⓂChueca) Tucked away on a quiet Chueca side street, this attractive little cafe does quiches, crepes and smoothies by day and cocktails in the evening. They've also a well-priced day/night set menu (€9.90/14.90) on weekdays and overall it's a good option when the rest of Chueca starts to overwhelm you with noise.

MAISON BLANCHE CAFE €€

Map p254 (☎91 522 82 17; Calle de Piamonte 10; mains €17-19; ⊙10am-midnight Mon-Sat, noon-6pm Sun; ⓂChueca) If you have a friend from Barcelona who's too cool for Madrid, bring them here and they might just change their mind. A designer clothing store and designer cafe, this has become one of the most fashionable places in town for A-list celebrities; one newspaper called it 'paradise for sybarites'. The food ranges far and wide, but steak tartar is among the most popular choices. This is the new Madrid and it's very cool.

JANATOMO JAPANESE €€

Map p254 (☎91 521 55 66; Calle de la Reina 27; mains €12-18; ⊙lunch & dinner Tue-Sun;

MGran Vía) Restaurateurs Tomoyuki and Eiko Ikenaga arrived in Spain in the 1950s and have watched Spaniards slowly become accustomed to foreign cuisines. Their patience has paid off and now their restaurant, Janatomo, has undergone a style overhaul, adding a Zen ambience to its splendid Japanese cooking. The sight of tour groups from the home country piling in is all the confirmation we need.

WOGABOO FUSION €

Map p254 (91 531 65 67; www.wogaboo.com; Calle de Gravina 18; mains €9.50-13.50; lunch & dinner daily; MChueca) Wogaboo offers cheap and cheerful pasta and noodle dishes in a trendy setting with a clientele to match. They have restaurants across the city.

FRESC CO BUFFET €

Map p254 (www.frescco.com; Calle de Sagasta 30; meals from €9.95; noon-5pm & 8-11.30pm; MAlonso Martínez) If you just can't face deciphering another Spanish menu or are in dire need of a do-it-yourself salad, Fresc Co is a fresh, well-priced and all-you-can-eat antidote. OK, so the atmosphere is cafeteria-style and none too exciting, but the extensive choice of self-service salads, soups, pasta, pizza and other hot dishes more than makes up for it; the price includes a drink and queues often go out the door at lunchtime. There's another **branch** (Map p242; 91 524 06 79; Calle del Caballero de Gracia 8; Gran Vía) just off Gran Vía in the centre.

DRINKING & NIGHTLIFE

Although it's a close-run thing, if you had to choose just one area in Madrid for the complete night out, we'd make it Malasaña and Chueca (Huertas and, to a lesser extent, La Latina are the other prime candidates). Spending a night exploring these two *barrios* is like taking a journey through Madrid's multifaceted past. As close as Madrid came to the intellectual cafes of Paris' Left Bank, the cafes of the Glorieta de Bilbao were in the 1950s and 1960s a centre of coffee-house intellectualism with their *tertulias* (literary discussions) and intrigues. Throughout Malasaña, *rockeros* (rock fans) nostalgic for the hedonistic Madrid of the 1970s and 1980s will find ample bars in which to indulge their memories. At the same time all across the *barrios*, especially in gay Chueca and away to the west in Conde Duque, modern Madrid is very much on show, with chill-out spaces and swanky bars. Small live venues are here, Madrid's best cocktail bars are to be found in Chueca on Calle de la Reina and Gran Vía, and nightclubs that reflect the *barrios'* split personalities keep things moving until dawn. In short, going out at night in Malasaña and Chueca is the stuff of Madrid legend.

Malasaña

TOP CHOICE CAFÉ COMERCIAL CAFE

Map p250 (Glorieta de Bilbao 7; 7.30am-midnight Mon-Thu, 7.30am-2am Fri, 8.30am-2am Sat, 9am-midnight Sun; MBilbao) This glorious old Madrid cafe proudly fights a rearguard action against progress with heavy leather seats, abundant marble and old-style waiters. Café Comercial, which dates back to 1887, is the largest of the *barrio's* old cafes and has changed little since those days, although the clientele has broadened to include just about anyone, from writers on their laptops to old men playing chess.

TOP CHOICE LA REALIDAD BAR

Map p250 (91 532 80 55; Calle de la Corredera Baja de San Pablo 51; 9.30am-1.30am Sun-Thu, to 2.30am Fri & Sat; MTribunal) Great place. Part hip cafe, part funky bar to start your Malasaña night, at once bohemian and yet appealing enough to draw the mainstream punter, La Realidad (The Reality) serves up fine tapas to accompany their equally fine cocktails. They also do brunch, display contemporary art, have weird-and-wonderful furnishings and generally prove that it *is* possible to be all things to all people.

CAFÉ DE MAHÓN CAFE

Map p250 (91 532 47 56; Plaza del Dos de Mayo 4; noon-1.30am Mon-Thu, to 3am Fri-Sun; MBilbao) If we had to choose our favourite slice of Malasaña life, this engaging little cafe, whose outdoor tables watch out over Plaza del Dos de Mayo, would be a prime candidate. It's beloved by *famosos* as much as by the locals catching up for a quiet drink with friends. It has a habit of opening and closing whenever the whim takes it.

CAFÉ MANUELA CAFE

Map p250 (Calle de San Vicente Ferrer 29; ⌚4pm-2am Mon-Fri, noon-3am Sat, noon-2am Sun; Ⓜ Tribunal) Stumbling into this graciously restored throwback to the 1950s along one of Malasaña's grittier streets is akin to discovering hidden treasure. There's a luminous quality to it when you come in out of the night and, like so many Madrid cafes, it's a surprisingly multifaceted space, serving cocktails, delicious milkshakes and offering board games atop the marble tables in the unlikely event that you get bored.

LOLINA VINTAGE CAFÉ CAFE

Map p250 (Calle del Espíritu Santo 9; ⌚9am-2.30am Mon-Fri, 10am-2.30am Sat, 11am-2.30am Sun; Ⓜ Tribunal) Lolina Vintage Café seems to have captured the essence of the *barrio* in one small space. With a studied retro look (comfy old-style chairs and sofas, gilded mirrors and 1970s-era wallpaper), it confirms that the new Malasaña is not unlike the old but is a whole lot more sophisticated. It's low-key, full from the first breakfast to closing time and they cater to every taste with salads and cocktails.

EL JARDÍN SECRETO BAR, CAFE

Map p250 (Calle del Conde Duque 2; ⌚5.30pm-12.30am Sun-Thu & Sun, 6.30pm-2.30am Fri & Sat; Ⓜ Plaza de España) 'The Secret Garden' is intimate and romantic in a *barrio* that's one of Madrid's best-kept secrets. Lit by Spanish designer candles, draped in organza from India and serving up chocolates from the Caribbean, El Jardín Secreto ranks among our favourite drinking corners in Conde Duque. They serve milkshakes, cocktails and everything in between. It's at its best on a summer's evening, but the atmosphere never misses a beat, with a loyal and young professional crowd.

CAFÉ AJENJO CAFE

Map p250 (☎91 447 70 76; Calle de la Galería de Robles 4; ⌚3pm-2am Sun-Thu, to 2.30am Fri & Sat; Ⓜ Bilbao) Malasaña's old cafes don't come any better than this one, with beguiling old-world decor, a vaguely intellectual air and some of the best cakes and coffees in the *barrio*. It's the sort of place to retreat if Malasaña gets too much, although it does get lively here without getting out of hand.

LOCAL KNOWLEDGE

LITERARY CAFES

For a tour of Madrid's grand old literary cafes (a Malasaña specialty), start down on Paseo de los Recoletos at Gran Café de Gijón (p133), followed by Café-Restaurante El Espejo (p133) then Café Comercial (p132). Having ticked off the big three, El Parnasillo (p134) and Café de Ruiz (p134) also capture the spirit of another age. Café Manuela (p133) is another fine old place.

CAFÉ-RESTAURANTE EL ESPEJO CAFE

Map p254 (Paseo de los Recoletos 31; ⌚8am-midnight Sun-Thu, 10am-3am Fri & Sat; Ⓜ Colón) Once a haunt of writers and intellectuals, this architectural gem blends modernista and art deco styles and its interior could well overwhelm you with all the mirrors, chandeliers and bow-tied service of another era. The atmosphere is suitably quiet and refined, although our favourite corner is the elegant glass pavilion out on the Paseo de los Recoletos, where the outdoor tables are hugely popular in summer.

LA VÍA LÁCTEA BAR, CLUB

Map p250 (Calle de Velarde 18; ⌚9pm-3am; Ⓜ Tribunal) A living, breathing and delightfully grungy relic of *la movida*, La Vía Láctea remains a Malasaña favourite for a mixed, informal crowd who seems to live for the 1980s. The music ranges across rock, pop, garage, rockabilly and indie. There are plenty of drinks to choose from and by late Saturday night anything goes. Expect long queues to get in on weekends.

GRAN CAFÉ DE GIJÓN CAFE

Map p254 (www.cafegijon.com; Paseo de los Recoletos 21; ⌚7am-1.30am; Ⓜ Chueca, Banco de España) This graceful old cafe has been serving coffee and meals since 1888 and has long been a favourite with Madrid's literati – *all* of Spain's great literary figures of the 20th century came here for coffee and *tertulias* (literary discussions). You'll find yourself among intellectuals, conservative Franco diehards and young *madrileños* looking for a quiet drink.

CAFÉ PEPE BOTELLA CAFE, BAR

Map p250 (Calle de San Andrés 12; ⌚10am-2am Mon-Thu, 10am-2.30am Fri & Sat, 11am-2am Sun; Ⓜ Bilbao, Tribunal) Pepe Botella has hit on a fine formula for success. As good in the hours around midnight as it is in the afternoon when its wi-fi access draws the laptop-toting crowd, it's a classy bar with green-velvet benches, marble-topped tables, and old photos and mirrors on the walls. The faded elegance gives the place the charm that has made it one of the most enduringly popular drinking holes in the *barrio.*

EL NARANJA BAR

Map p250 (www.elnaranja.info; Calle de San Vicente Ferrer 52; ⌚10am-1am Tue-Thu, 10am-2.30am Fri, 6pm-2.30am Sat, 6pm-midnight Sun; Ⓜ Noviciado) Packed to its orange rafters from Thursday to Saturday, this fine little corner bar (they prefer the epithet of 'cultural space') represents the starting point for Conde Duque if you've come down the hill from the rest of Malasaña. And what a beguiling introduction it is. DJ sessions, concerts and even film nights are regular events, but even without such adornments it's always cool, casual, intelligent fun.

TUPPERWARE BAR, CLUB

Map p250 (☎91 446 42 04; Calle de la Corredera Alta de San Pablo 26; ⌚8pm-3.30am Tue-Sat; Ⓜ Tribunal) A Malasaña stalwart and prime candidate for the bar that best catches the enduring *rockero* spirit of Malasaña, Tupperware draws a 30-something crowd, spins indie rock with a bit of soul and classics from the '60s and '70s, and generally revels in its kitsch (eyeballs stuck to the ceiling, and plastic TVs with action-figure dioramas lined up behind the bar). It can get pretty packed on a weekend after 1am. By the way, locals pronounce it 'Tupper-warry'.

MOLOKO BAR-NIGHTCLUB

Map p250 (Calle de Quiñones 12; ⌚10pm-3.30am Tue-Sat; Ⓜ San Bernardo) Its walls plastered with old concert flyers and the odd art-house movie poster (*A Clockwork Orange,* for example), Moloko remains an excellent late-night option in the Conde Duque area of western Malasaña. The music – indie, rock, soul, garage and '60s – is consistently good, which is why people return here again and again.

CAFÉ DE RUIZ CAFE

Map p250 (☎91 446 12 32; Calle de Ruiz 11; ⌚2.30pm-2.30am Sun-Thu, to 3.30am Fri & Sat; Ⓜ Bilbao) Another of the old Malasaña cafes that so distinguish the northern end of the *barrio,* Café de Ruiz has all-wooden furniture and columns, draws a mature crowd and offers everything from creative teas and coffees to milkshakes and cocktails.

CAFÉ ISADORA CAFE

Map p250 (☎91 445 71 54; Calle del Divino Pastor 14; ⌚4pm-2am Sun-Thu, to 2.30am Fri & Sat; Ⓜ Bilbao or San Bernardo) Echoing the distinguished cafes that once dominated northern Malasaña and tucked away in one of Malasaña's quieter corners, Café Isadora has the old-world signposts of another age, with the memorabilia of high culture adorning its walls and mid-20th-century decor. This being Malasaña, it's as good for a mellow evening coffee as a livelier middle-of-the-night cocktail.

EL PARNASILLO CAFE

Map p250 (☎91 447 00 79; Calle de San Andrés 33; ⌚2.30pm- 3am Sun-Thu, to 3.30am Fri & Sat; Ⓜ Bilbao) Another of the grand old literary cafes to have survived close to the Glorieta de Bilbao, El Parnasillo has seigneurial decor with muted art nouveau frescoes and stained glass adorning the walls, but it's a favourite drinking hole for the diverse crowd drawn to the Malasaña night for reasons other than the heavy rock scene.

OJALÁ AWARENESS CLUB LOUNGE

Map p250 (Calle de San Andrés 1; ⌚8.30am-1am Sun-Wed, to 2am Thu-Sat; Ⓜ Tribunal) From the people who brought you La Musa (p126), Ojalá is every bit as funky and has a lot more space to enjoy. Yes, you eat well here, but we love it first and foremost for a drink (especially a daiquiri) at any time of the day. Its lime-green colour scheme, zany lighting and a hip, cafe-style ambience all make it an extremely cool place to hang out, but the sandy floor and cushions downstairs take chilled to a whole new level.

POLYESTER BAR-NIGHTCLUB

Map p254 (www.polyesterbar.com; Travesía de San Mateo 10; ⌚10pm-3am Thu, to 3.30am Fri & Sat; Ⓜ Tribunal) They've chosen the perfect name for this place, another essential element of the local indie circuit. It attracts a mixed gay-straight crowd and the soundtrack revolves around the likes of Franz Ferdinand and The Smiths.

LA PALMERA BAR

Map p250 (Calle de la Palma 67; ⌚7.30pm-2am Mon-Sat; Ⓜ Noviciado) Tucked away in the quiet-by-day laneways of Conde Duque, this tiny, unprepossessing place is covered in blue and yellow tiles and has an antique bar that looks like a huge bathtub. La Palmera draws an artsy crowd who come to sit at the small wooden tables and nurse a drink or two. The atmosphere is very low-key. In summer the outdoor tables are the place to be.

PICNIC BAR-NIGHTCLUB

Map p250 (Calle de las Minas 1; ⏲5pm-1.30am Sun-Thu, to 2am Fri & Sat, closed Aug; Ⓜ Noviciado) The quieter little brother to the much more-famous Tupperware (p134), Picnic is another diehard bar that gives Malasaña its indie soul. The look is retro, as you'd expect in this Malasaña subculture, and there are concerts most Sundays.

NASTI CLUB CLUB, LIVE MUSIC

Map p250 (☎91 521 76 05; www.nasti.es; Calle de San Vicente Ferrer 33; admission free-€10; ⏲10pm-6am Thu-Sat; Ⓜ Tribunal) It's hard to think of a more off-putting entrance than Nasti Club's graffiti and abandoned-building look. You also won't find the name outside – if you want to come here, you're supposed to know where to find it. Indie rock and post-punk are the mainstays. But it's not as nasty as it sounds and the crowd can span the full range of 1970s throwbacks from a who's who of Madrid's underground to some surprisingly respectable types. Above all it's a place with attitude and, as their own publicity says, they're *not* from Barcelona, they *don't* play electronica, people who come here *are* cool and no one's ever heard of the live acts who appear here until they become famous two years later. Says it all really. Very Malasaña.

BAR EL 2D BAR

Map p250 (☎91 445 88 39; Calle de Velarde 24; ⏲1pm-2am Sun-Thu, to 2.30am Fri & Sat; Ⓜ Tribunal) One of the enduring symbols of *la movida madrileña*, El 2D's fluted columns, 1970s-brown walls and 1980s music suggest that it hasn't quite arrived in the 21st century yet. No one seems to care, mind you.

EL CAFÉ SIN NOMBRE CAFE

Map p250 (☎91 548 09 72; Calle del Conde Duque 10; ⏲9.30am-1.30am Mon-Fri, 8pm-2.30pm Sat; Ⓜ Plaza de España or Ventura Rodríguez) The 'Cafe With No Name' is one of Conde Duque's many well-kept secrets. With its exposed brickwork and wooden beams, it's a classy, casual look and a good place for first drinks.

PACHÁ NIGHTCLUB

Map p254 (☎91 447 01 28; www.pacha-madrid.com; Calle de Barceló 11; admission €12; ⏲midnight-6am Wed-Sat; Ⓜ Tribunal) A mega-club that is a branch of the international chain of clubs that earned its fame in Ibiza, became a major Madrid club during *la movida*. The name still has a certain cachet on the Madrid nightlife scene, so the odd celebrity turns up here and gets all sweaty dancing to house, pop, R&B and other related genres across the three dance floors.

SALA BASH/OHM GAY, CLUB

Map p250 (www.ohmclub.es; Plaza de Callao 4; admission €12; ⏲midnight-6am Thu-Sun; Ⓜ Callao) The DJs who get you waving your hands in the air like you just don't care have made this club, and its sessions that go by the name of Ohm, arguably the No 1 nightspot for Madrid's gay community. The music never strays far from techno-house. Saturdays are slightly more mixed, but it remains a gay icon.

SIROCO NIGHTCLUB

Map p250 (☎91 593 30 70; www.siroco.es; Calle de San Dimas 3; admission €8; ⏲9.30pm-6am Thu-Sat; Ⓜ Noviciado) One of the most popular and eclectic nightclubs in Madrid, Siroco does everything from reggae to drum 'n' bass, funk, soul and danceable disco tunes. It gets a diverse crowd and queues can be long. The one unifying theme is the commitment to Spanish music (there are often upcoming local rock bands at 10pm before the action really kicks off) and it's a good place to hear local music before it becomes too mainstream.

MOROCCO CLUB

Map p250 (☎91 531 51 67; www.morocco-madrid.com; Calle del Marqués de Leganés 7; admission €10; ⏲midnight-6am Fri & Sat; Ⓜ Santo Domingo or Noviciado) Owned by the zany Alaska, the standout musical personality of *la movida*, Morocco has decor that's so kitsch it's cool, and a mix of musical styles that never strays too far from 1980s Spanish and international tunes, with electronica another recurring theme. The bouncers have been known to show a bit of attitude, but then that kind of comes with the profession. We've heard it said that they need to turn the volume up, but we doubt that the neighbours agree.

LAYDOWN REST CLUB LOUNGE, COCKTAIL BAR

Map p250 (☎91 548 79 37; www.laydown.es; Plaza de Mostenses 9; ⏰9pm-3am Tue-Sun; Ⓜ Plaza de España or Noviciado) The name says it all. DJs, cabaret-style shows and cocktails are a fairly familiar Madrid mix, but this is one of few places where you get to enjoy them while reclining on a comfy bed. It's a pretty sophisticated 30-something crowd that's up for a dance when they're not flat-out drinking. It can be difficult to find – from Plaza de Mostenses, head east along Calle del General Mitre then take the first lane on the right.

Chueca

TOP CHOICE **MUSEO CHICOTE** COCKTAIL BAR

Map p254 (www.museo-chicote.com; Gran Vía 12; ⏰6pm-3am Mon-Thu, to 4am Fri & Sat; Ⓜ Gran Vía) The founder of this Madrid landmark is said to have invented more than a hundred cocktails, which the likes of Hemingway, Ava Gardner, Grace Kelly, Sophia Loren and Frank Sinatra all enjoyed at one time or another. It's still frequented by film stars and top socialites, and it's at its best after midnight, when a lounge atmosphere takes over, couples cuddle on the curved benches and some of the city's best DJs do their stuff (CDs are available). The 1930s-era interior only adds to the cachet of this place. We don't say this often, but if you haven't been here, you haven't really been to Madrid – it's that much of an icon.

LE CABRERA COCKTAIL BAR

Map p254 (☎91 319 94 57; www.lecabrera.com; Calle de Bárbara de Braganza 2; ⏰4pm-2.30am Mon-Thu, 4pm-2.30am Fri, 1pm-2.30am Sat; Ⓜ Colón, Alonso Martínez) In the basement below the exciting new tapas bar of the same name, this oh-so-chic cocktail bar is every bit as appealing. The more than 60 different cocktail varieties are the work of Diego Cabrera, the long-standing barman of renowned master chef Sergi Arola and, along with the designer decor, the combination has transformed this into one of the 'in' places in not just the *barrio* but the entire city.

SPLASH ÓSCAR LOUNGE

Map p254 (Plaza de Vázquez de Mella 12; ⏰5pm-2am Mon-Thu, 4pm-3am Fri-Sun; Ⓜ Gran Vía) Another of the stunning rooftop terraces (although this one has a small swimming pool), atop Hotel Óscar (p173), this chilled space with gorgeous skyline views has become something of a retreat among A-list celebrities.

CAFÉ BELÉN BAR

Map p254 (Calle de Belén 5; ⏰3.30pm-3am; Ⓜ Chueca) Café Belén is cool in all the right places – lounge and chill-out music, dim lighting, a great range of drinks (the mojitos are especially good) and a low-key crowd that's the height of casual sophistication. In short, it's one of our favourite Chueca watering holes.

DEL DIEGO COCKTAIL BAR

Map p254 (☎91 523 31 06; Calle de la Reina 12; ⏰7pm-3am Mon-Thu, to 3.30am Fri & Sat; Ⓜ Gran Vía) Calle de la Reina is much loved by *famosos,* especially models, actors and designers, as a place for terrific cocktails in stately surrounds. Del Diego fits this bill perfectly and over its 20 years of existence has become one of the city's most celebrated cocktail bars. The decor blends old-world cafe with New York style, and it's the sort of place where the music rarely drowns out the conversation. Even with around 75 cocktails to choose from, we'd still order the signature 'El Diego' (vodka, advocaat, apricot brandy and lime).

BAR COCK COCKTAIL BAR

Map p254 (☎91 532 28 26; www.barcock.com; Calle de la Reina 16; ⏰8pm-3am; Ⓜ Gran Vía) With a name like this, Bar Cock could go either way, but it's definitely cock as in 'rooster', so the atmosphere is elegant and classic rather than risqué. The decor evokes an old gentlemen's club, but it is beloved by A-list celebrities, A-list wannabes and a refined 30-something crowd who come here for the lively atmosphere and great cocktails. On weekends all the tables seem to be reserved, so be prepared to hover on the fringes of fame.

EL JUNCO JAZZ CLUB JAZZ, CLUB

Map p254 (☎91 319 20 81; www.eljunco.com; Plaza de Santa Bárbara 10; concerts €6-10; ⏰8pm-3.30pm Mon, 8pm-6am Tue-Fri, 11pm-6am Sat & Sun, concerts 11pm Tue-Sun; Ⓜ Alonso Martínez) El Junco has established itself on the Madrid nightlife scene by appealing as much to jazz aficionados as to clubbers. Its secret is high-quality live jazz gigs from

Spain and around the world, followed by DJs spinning funk, soul, nu jazz, blues and innovative groove beats. There are also jam sessions at 11pm in jazz (Tuesday) and blues (Sunday). The emphasis is on music from the American South and the crowd is classy and casual.

MERCADO DE LA REINA GIN CLUB COCKTAIL BAR

Map p254 (☎91 521 31 98; www.mercadodelareina.es; Calle de la Reina 16; ⏲4pm-2am; Ⓜ Gran Vía) In this area of Madrid known for its classy cocktails, this gin club fits right in. But unlike other choices nearby – eg Bar Cock, Del Diego and Museo Chicote – this place has no pretensions to former grandeur; the decor is supermodern and, like the clientele, all dressed in black. With 20 types of gin (€6 to €12 – they're cheaper before 9pm) and DJs at night from Thursday to Saturday, it's a happening place.

AREIA LOUNGE

Map p254 (www.areiachillout.com; Calle de Hortaleza 92; ⏲1pm-3am; Ⓜ Chueca, Alonso Martínez) The ultimate lounge bar by day (cushions, chill-out music and dark secluded corners, where you can hear yourself talk or even snog quietly), this place is equally enjoyable by night. That's when groovy DJs take over (from 11pm Sunday to Wednesday, and from 9pm the rest of the week) with deep and chill house, nu jazz, bossa and electronica. It's cool, funky and low-key all at once.

BRISTOL BAR CAFE, BAR

Map p254 (☎91 522 45 68; www.bristolbar.es; Calle del Almirante 20; ⏲10am-1am Mon-Wed, 10am-2am Thu & Fri, 11am-2am Sat; Ⓜ Chueca) You could come here for the English breakfast (€14) or the brunch (€19.50 to €24.50), but we like this place for its 75 different types of gin. By day, the atmosphere is that of a quiet cafe; after work, a busy gathering place; and, as the evening wears on, a sophisticated gin parlour.

STROMBOLI COCKTAIL BAR

Map p254 (☎91 319 46 28; Calle de Hortaleza 96; ⏲9pm-3am Wed & Thu, to 3.30am Fri & Sat; Ⓜ Chueca, Tribunal) After a number of years as a fairly standard small club, Stromboli has found its niche as a minimalist cocktail bar. In addition to the cocktails – our favourite is 'Bubaloo' (vodka, syrup of bubble gum and sugar, mint, blueberry juice and lemon) – there's also a carefully chosen menu of Champagnes and *cavas* (sparkling wines). There's also a popular dance floor.

GAY CHUECA

If you're eager to tap into the gay networks of Chueca, Mamá Inés is the place to start – apart from being a gay meeting place par excellance, the bar staff have their finger on the pulse. Also outstanding is Librería Berkana (p143), where you'll find the biweekly *Shanguide* (jammed with listings and contact ads), *Shangay Express* (better for articles) and possibly the *Mapa Gaya de Madrid* which lists gay bars, discos and saunas.

MAMÁ INÉS CAFE, GAY

Map p250 (www.mamaines.com; Calle de Hortaleza 22; ⏲10am-2am Sun-Thu, to 3am Fri & Sat; Ⓜ Chueca) A gay meeting place with its low lights and low music, this cafe-bar is never sleazy and has a laid-back ambience by day and a romantic air by night. You can get breakfast, yummy pastries and the word on where that night's hot spot will be. There's a steady stream of people coming and going throughout the day and they turn the lights down low and crank up the music as evening turns into night.

CAFÉ ACUARELA CAFE, GAY

Map p254 (www.cafeacuarela.es; Calle de Gravina 10; ⏲11am-2am Sun-Thu, to 3am Fri & Sat; Ⓜ Chueca) A few steps up the hill from Plaza de Chueca and long a centrepiece of gay Madrid – a huge statue of a nude male angel guards the doorway – this is an agreeable, dimly lit salon decorated with, among other things, religious icons. It's ideal for quiet conversation and catching the weekend buzz as people plan their forays into the more clamorous clubs in the vicinity.

ANTIGUA CASA ÁNGEL SIERRA TAVERNA

Map p254 (☎91 531 01 26; Calle de Gravina 11; ⏲noon-1am; Ⓜ Chueca) This historic old *taberna* is the antithesis of modern Chueca chic – it has hardly changed since it opened in 1917. As Spaniards like to say, the beer on tap is very 'well poured' here, and it also has vermouth on tap. Fronting onto the vibrant Plaza de Chueca, it can get pretty lively of a weekend evening when it spills over onto the plaza. Just don't expect service with a smile.

STOP MADRID BAR

Map p250 (☎91 521 88 87; Calle de Hortaleza 11; ⏰12.30-4pm & 6.30pm-2am; Ⓜ Gran Vía) The name may not be Madrid's most evocative but this terrific old *taberna* is friendly and invariably packed with people and wins the vote of at least one Lonely Planet author for the best sangria in Madrid. The tapas are also outstanding and there's always a buzz here in the evenings.

LA BARDEMCILLA BAR

Map p254 (☎91 521 42 56; www.labardemcilla.com; Calle de Augusto Figueroa 47; ⏰noon-5.30pm & 8pm-2am Mon-Fri, 8pm-2am Sat; Ⓜ Chueca) Run by the family of film heart-throb Javier Bardem, this bar has an agreeable buzz most nights of the week. A comfortable space to relax, a slightly Bohemian air and a loyal following add up to a great package. The clientele includes a regular cast of celebrities, but the atmosphere is resolutely informal, with cinema decor and allusions to the cinematic world through the menu, such as the *croquetas jamón jamón* (named after the film in which Javier Bardem made his name).

BLACK & WHITE GAY, CLUB

Map p254 (www.discoblack-white.net; Calle de la Libertad 34; ⏰10pm-5.30am Sun-Thu, to 6am Fri & Sat; Ⓜ Chueca) People still talk about the opening party of Black & White way back in 1982, and ever since it's been a pioneer of Chueca's gay nights. This place is extravagantly gay with drag acts, male strippers and a refreshingly no-holds-barred approach to life.

WHY NOT? CLUB

Map p254 (www.whynotmadrid.com; Calle de San Bartolomé 7; admission €10; ⏰10.30pm-6am; Ⓜ Chueca) Underground, narrow and packed with bodies, gay-friendly Why Not? is the sort of place where nothing's left to the imagination (the gay and straight crowd who come here are pretty amorous) and it's full nearly every night of the week. Pop and top-40 music are the standard here, and the dancing crowd is mixed and serious about having a good time. We're not huge fans of the bouncers here but, once you get past them, it's all good fun.

DIURNO CAFE

Map p254 (www.diurno.com; Calle de San Marcos 37; ⏰9am-midnight Mon-Thu, 9am-1am Fri, 10am-1am Sat, 10am-midnight Sun; Ⓜ Chueca) One of the most important hubs of *barrio* life in Chueca, this cafe (with DVD store attached) has become to modern Chueca what the grand literary cafes were to another age. It's always full with a fun Chueca crowd relaxing amid the greenery. They also serve well-priced meals and snacks if you can't bear to give up your seat.

LIQUID MADRID GAY, CLUB

Map p254 (www.liquid.es; Calle de Barbieri 7; ⏰9pm-3am Mon-Thu, to 3.30am Fri & Sat; Ⓜ Chueca) An essential stop on any gay itinerary through Chueca, Liquid is a little overwhelming with its multiple video screens and endless movement of people .

CLUB 54 STUDIO CLUB

Map p254 (www.studio54madrid.com; Calle de Barbieri 7; ⏰11.30am-3.30am Wed-Sat; Ⓜ Chueca) Modelled on the famous New York club Studio 54, this nightclub draws a predominantly gay crowd, but its target market is more upmarket than many in the *barrio*. Unlike other Madrid nightclubs where paid dancers up on stage try to get things moving, here they let the punters set the pace.

☆ ENTERTAINMENT

In addition to the places listed here, some of Malasaña's nightclubs begin the night with live music acts, among them Nasti Club (p135) and Siroco (p135).

TOP CHOICE CAFÉ LA PALMA LIVE MUSIC

Map p250 (☎91 522 50 31; www.cafelapalma.com; Calle de la Palma 62; admission free-€12; ⏰4.30pm-3am; Ⓜ Noviciado) It's amazing how much variety Café La Palma has packed into its labyrinth of rooms. Live shows featuring hot local bands are held at the back, while DJs mix it up at the front. Some rooms have a cafe style, while others evoke an Arab tea room, pillows on the floor and all. You might find live music other nights as well, but there are always two shows at 10pm and midnight from Thursday to Saturday. Every night is a little different and the various rooms ensure that you spend the whole night here, simply moving from room to room depending on your mood. Later on, some of Madrid's better DJs take over.

BARCO LIVE MUSIC

Map p250 (☎91 521 24 47; www.barcobar.com; Calle del Barco 34; admission free-€12; ⏰10pm-5.30am Sun-Thu, to 6am Fri & Sat; Ⓜ Tribunal) Just before Malasaña spills over into the seedy backside of Gran Vía, BarCo is an outstanding live venue with jazz, flamenco (Sunday at 9pm), Latin music (Brazilian music is the focus from 11pm Thursday), funk, rock or blues; it's also the headquarters for Madrid's School of Creative Music. Concerts start at 11pm and there's room to dance if the mood takes you. There's a fantastic jazz jam session from 12.30am every second Sunday.

ZANZIBAR LIVE MUSIC

Map p254 (☎91 319 90 64; www.zanzibarmadrid.com; Calle de Regueros 9; admission free-€8; ⏰4pm-3am Wed-Sun; Ⓜ Alonso Martínez or Chueca) This fantastic little venue is styled with African decor – it does indeed have world music, but its repertoire extends to jazz, singer-songwriter, rock, funk, blues, country, soul-rap and even storytelling. Concerts start as early as 8pm or as late as 11.30pm, and there's a lovely cafe-style intimacy about the place.

BOGUI JAZZ JAZZ

Map p254 (☎91 521 15 68; www.boguijazz.com; Calle de Barquillo 29; ⏰10pm-6am Thu-Sat; Ⓜ Chueca) One of Madrid's best-loved jazz clubs has finally reopened its doors after years of being closed (they fell foul of a council crackdown on licensing laws). They've picked up right where they left off, with 10.30pm live jazz shows from Thursday to Saturday, followed by rock DJs until dawn – an intoxicating mix.

EL BÚHO REAL LIVE MUSIC

Map p254 (☎91 319 10 88; www.buhoreal.com; Calle de Regueros 5; admission €5-10; ⏰8pm-3am Sun-Thu, to 3.30am Fri & Sat; Ⓜ Alonso Martínez or Chueca) It looks like your average Madrid *bar de copas* (bar serving spirits and mixed drinks), but El Buho Real (The Royal Owl) is all about acoustic music. It interprets the term pretty widely to include flamenco, rock and singer-songwriter solo acts, and it's been around long enough to have drawn a loyal following. Concerts start at 9.30pm.

LIBERTAD 8 LIVE MUSIC

Map p254 (☎91 532 11 50; www.libertad8cafe.com; Calle de la Libertad 8; admission free-€6; ⏰4pm-2.30am; Ⓜ Chueca) One of the most enduring live venues in Chueca, this small-stage bar attracts storytellers, poets and local and international singer-songwriters and a whole range of other acts; they also often have exhibitions. We like the mix, and it's intimate venues like these that add depth to Madrid nightlife.

TABOÓ LIVE MUSIC

Map p250 (☎91 524 11 89; www.taboo-madrid.com; Calle de San Vicente Ferrer 23; admission €5-10; ⏰10pm-6am Fri & Sat; Ⓜ Tribunal) With everything from pop to hard-core punk and a whole lot of house music in between, Taboó likes to keep its options open. Check out the website to see which way it's leaning, and spend as little time as possible talking to the bouncers while you wait in the queue.

TEATRO ALFIL THEATRE

Map p250 (☎91 521 45 41, 91 521 58 27; www.teatroalfil.es; Calle del Pez 10; Ⓜ Noviciado) Staging a broad range of alternative and experimental Spanish-language theatre, Teatro Alfil is a good place to catch up-and-coming Spanish actors and comedians, and mingle with an eclectic crowd.

SHOPPING

Malasaña is one of Madrid's quirkiest *barrios* in which to shop, home to edgy clothing stores and shops where mainstream designers show off their street credibility. Shop staff here won't look down their noses at you no matter what you wear – they have seen it all before. Chueca, on the other hand, can be zany or elegant and caters as much for gay clubbers as for a refined gay sensibility. Where Chueca eases gently down the hill towards the Paseo de los Recoletos and beyond to Salamanca, especially in Calle de Piamonte, Calle del Conde de Xiquena and Calle del Almirante, niche designers take over with exclusive boutiques and the latest individual fashions. In short, it is Madrid in microcosm and ideal for those style-conscious shoppers who value an alternative look at life.

Malasaña

TOP CHOICE MERCADO DE FUENCARRAL CLOTHING

Map p250 (www.mdf.es; Calle de Fuencarral 45; ⏲11am-9pm Mon-Sat; ⓂTribunal) Madrid's home of alternative club cool is still going strong, revelling in its reverse snobbery. With shops like Fuck, Ugly Shop and Black Kiss, it's funky, grungy and filled to the rafters with torn T-shirts and more black leather and silver studs than you'll ever need. This is a Madrid icon and when it was threatened with closure in 2008, there was nearly an uprising.

NEST GIFTS

Map p250 (☎91 523 10 61; www.nest-boutique.com; Plaza de San Ildefonso 3; ⏲11am-2.30pm & 4-8.30pm Mon-Fri, 11am-8.30pm Sat; ⓂTribunal) Small offerings of lamps, Japanese dolls, wrapping paper, jewellery and so much more fill this intimate little British-run boutique. It's difficult to describe the secret of its success, but it unmistakeably has what Spaniards call *encanto* (charm) and is a welcome recent addition to Malasaña's shopping portfolio. The same deal but for children (books and toys in a gorgeous space with plenty of organised activities) resides at **Baby Nest** (Map p250; ☎91 522 94 67; www.babynestmadrid.com; Plaza Dos de Mayo 3; ⏲11am-2.30pm & 4-8.30pm Mon-Fri, 11am-8.30pm Sat; ⓂTribunal) nearby.

NATIONAL GEOGRAPHIC BOOKS, CLOTHING

Map p250 (☎91 279 84 80; www.ngmadridstore.com/es/madrid; Gran Vía 74; ⏲10am-10pm Mon-Sat, noon-9pm Sun; ⓂPlaza de España) Just about everything you've ever associated with National Geographic (except, strangely, the magazine) can be found at this wonderful large store, with pricey but high-quality clothing, bags, travel acccesories, books and DVDs. They have also a full calendar of events in their comfy basement auditorium. And the upstairs cafe is very cool.

POPLAND GIFTS

Map p250 (☎91 591 21 20; www.popland.es; Calle de Manuela Malasaña 24; ⏲11am-8.30pm Mon-Sat; ⓂSan Bernardo) 'Curiosity' and 'retro' are the buzzwords here and Popland has both by the vinyl-suitcase load. 'Go Eighties' T-shirts, Pink Panther dolls, Elvis card games, candy handcuffs, mirrored disco balls, Space Invaders handbags... If you can't find it here, it simply didn't exist in the world of street pop art.

CURIOSITE GIFTS

Map p250 (www.curiosite.es; Calle de la Corredera Alta de San Pablo 28; ⏲11am-3pm & 4-9pm Mon-Sat; ⓂTribunal) Some of Madrid's more original gifts are on offer in this quirky shop that combines old favourites (eg Star Wars Lego, Voodoo dolls) and a sideways glance at mundane household items. It's fun and modern and retro all at once, which makes it a perfect fit for Malasaña.

KLING FASHION

Map p250 (☎91 522 51 45; www.kling.es; Calle de Ballesta 6; ⏲11am-9pm Mon-Sat; ⓂGran Vía) Like a classy version of Zara but with just a hint of attitude, Kling is housed in a reconceived former sex club (prostitutes still scout for clients outside) and is one of Madrid's best-kept secrets. It's ideal for fashion-conscious women who can't afford Salamanca's prices.

L'HABILLEUR FASHION

Map p254 (☎91 531 32 22; Plaza de Chueca 8; ⏲11am-2pm & 5-9pm Mon-Sat; ⓂChueca) This popular Paris boutique now has a branch on Plaza de Chueca and the deal is the same: designer names at discounted prices, especially downstairs. For women, top names include Forte-Forte, Dr Fango, Marlota and Sofie Doore, while men are served by Hartford, Ganesh and Vintage.

CUSTO BARCELONA FASHION

Map p250 (☎91 360 46 36; www.custo-barcelona.com; Calle de Fuencarral 29; ⏲10am-9pm Mon-Sat, noon-8pm Sun; ⓂGran Vía) The chic shop of Barcelona designer Custo Dalmau wears its Calle de Fuencarral address well, because the now-iconic T-shirts are at once edgy, awash in attitude and artfully displayed. It's not to everyone's taste, but always worth a look.

DIVINA PROVIDENCIA FASHION

Map p250 (☎91 521 10 95; www.divinaprovidencia.com; Calle de Fuencarral 42; ⓂTribunal, Gran Vía) Divina Providencia has moved seamlessly from fresh new face on the Madrid fashion scene to almost mainstream stylish, with fun clothes for women and strong retro and Asian influences.

ADOLFO DOMÍNGUEZ FASHION

Map p250 (☎91 523 39 38; www.adolfodominguez.com; Calle de Fuencarral 5; ⊙10am-9pm Mon-Sat; Ⓜ Gran Vía) The stylish shop of this inventive Spanish designer is where you'll find utterly casual and colourful designs for the consciously cool among us.

COORLEONE'S COMPANY FASHION

Map p254 (☎91 521 47 46; www.coorleonecompany.com; Calle de Hortaleza 37; ⊙11am-9pm Mon-Sat, noon-8pm Sun; Ⓜ Gran Vía or Chueca) This stunning shop has been used to film TV series, advertisements and movies, but you come here primarily for designer clothing, belts and handbags from international designers and a few big local names thrown in, among them Davidelfín and Locking Shocking.

H.A.N.D. CLOTHES & ACCESSORIES FASHION

Map p250 (☎91 521 51 52; www.hand-haveaniceday.es; Calle de Hortaleza 26; ⊙11am-2.30pm & 5-9pm Mon-Sat; Ⓜ Gran Vía or Chueca) Looking for all the world like a small slice of Paris, H.A.N.D. (as in 'Have A Nice Day') is an effortlessly chic little boutique where you find dresses, skirts and other clothing from a range of predominantly French designers such as Les Petites, Manoush and Malene Birger. The look is classy with a fresh and sometimes vaguely vintage feel.

SNAPO CLOTHING, ACCESSORIES

Map p250 (☎91 532 12 23; Calle del Espíritu Santo 5; ⊙11am-2pm & 5-8.30pm Mon-Sat; Ⓜ Tribunal) Snapo is rebellious Malasaña to its core, thumbing its nose at the niceties of fashion respectability – hardly surprising given that one of its lines of clothing is called Fucking Bastardz Inc. It does jeans, caps and jackets, but its T-shirts are the Snapo trademark; there are even kids' T-shirts for *really* cool parents. Down through the years, we've seen everything from a mocked-up cover of 'National Pornographic' to Pope John Paul II with fist raised and 'Vatican 666' emblazoned across the front. Need we say more?

RETRO CITY CLOTHING

Map p250 (Calle de Corredera Alta de San Pablo 4; ⊙11.30am-9pm Mon-Thu, noon-9.30pm Fri & Sat; Ⓜ Tribunal) Malasaña down to its Dr Martens, Retro City lives for the colourful '70s and '80s and proclaims its philosophy to be all about 'vintage for the masses'. Whereas other such stores in the *barrio* have gone for an angry, thumb-your-nose-at-society aesthetic, Retro City just looks back with nostalgia.

EL TEMPLO DE SUSU CLOTHING, ACCESSORIES

Map p250 (☎91 523 31 22; Calle del Espíritu Santo 1; ⊙11am-9pm Mon-Sat; Ⓜ Tribunal) It won't appeal to everyone, but El Templo de Susu's secondhand clothes from the 1960s and 1970s have clearly found a market among Malasaña's too-cool-for-the-latest-fashions types. It's kind of like charity shop meets unreconstructed hippie, which is either truly awful or retro cool, depending on your perspective.

RADIO CITY DISCOS MUSIC

Map p250 (☎91 547 77 67; www.radiocitydiscos.com; Plaza Guardias de Corps 2; ⊙11am-2pm & 5-8.30pm Tue-Sat; Ⓜ Plaza de España or Ventura Rodríguez) In these days of music megastores and internet downloads, it's nice to find small, specialist music shops still going strong. True to Malasaña's roots, Radio City Disco's small collection of CDs and vinyl spans the 1970s, roots, funk, rock and indie, with a small section devoted to Brazil's Tropicalismo. If they don't have it, they promise to track it down for you.

MUJI HOMEWARES

Map p250 (☎91 521 08 47; www.muji.com/es; Calle de Fuencarral 36; ⊙10.30am-8pm Mon-Sat, noon-8pm Sun; Ⓜ Tribunal) From clean-lined notebooks and folders to all manner of homewares small and large, this shop is almost impossible to pass. The look has all the clean lines of Japanese design wedded to functionality – not only do you need everything here, you'll want to display it prominently. They've another **branch** (Map p248; ☎91 576 44 24; Calle de Goya 9; ⊙10.30am-8pm Mon-Sat, noon-8pm Sun; Serrano) in Salamanca.

J&J BOOKS & COFFEE BOOKS

Map p250 (☎91 521 85 76; www.jandjbooksandcoffee.com; Calle del Espíritu Santo 47; ⊙11am-11pm Mon-Thu, to 1.30am Fri, to midnight Sat, 4-10pm Sun; Ⓜ Noviciado) Downstairs from this bar-cafe that serves as a meeting place for Madrid's expats (they have international exchange nights from 8pm on Wednesday and Thursday), this place claims to have more than 20,000 books for sale. Most of these are in English and the bar is the perfect place to flick through those you're considering buying.

UNO DE 50 JEWELLERY

Map p250 (☎91 523 99 75; www.unode50.com; Calle de Fuencarral 25; ⊙10am-8.30pm Mon-Sat; MGran Vía or Tribunal) Close to where in-your-face Malasaña intersects with could-go-either-way Chueca, Uno de 50 offers up silver jewellery that wouldn't look out of place in either *barrio*. It's chunky and loud and not very subtle, but there are some great pieces here and they're as original as the manner in which they're displayed.

Chueca

LOEWE FASHION

Map p254 (☎91 522 68 15; www.loewe.com; Gran Vía 8; ⊙10am-8.30pm Mon-Sat; MGran Vía) Born in 1846 in Madrid, Loewe is arguably Spain's signature line in high-end fashion and its landmark store on Gran Vía is one of the most famous and elegant stores in the capital. Classy handbags and accessories are the mainstays and prices can be jaw-droppingly high, but it's worth stopping by here, even if you don't plan to buy. There's another **branch** (Map p248; ☎91 426 35 88; Calle de Serrano 26 & 34; ⊙10am-8.30pm Mon-Sat; MSerrano) in Salamanca.

LURDES BERGADA FASHION

Map p254 (☎91 531 99 58; www.lurdesbergada.es; Calle del Conde de Xiquena 8; ⊙10am-8.30pm Mon-Sat; MChueca, Colón) Lurdes Bergada and Syngman Cucala, a mother-son designer team from Barcelona, offer classy and original men's and women's fashions using neutral colours and all-natural fibres. They've developed something of a cult following for their clothes that are stylish yet casual in a very Chueca kind of way. It's difficult to leave without finding something that you just have to have. They have another **branch** (Map p250; www.lurdesbergada.es; Calle de Fuencarral 70; ⊙10.30am-8.30pm Mon-Sat; MTribunal) in Malasaña.

PATRIMONIO COMUNAL OLIVARERO FOOD

Map p254 (www.pco.es; Calle de Mejía Lequerica 1; ⊙10am-2pm & 5-8pm Mon-Fri, 10am-2pm Sat; MAlonso Martínez) You could buy your Spanish olive oil at El Corte Inglés, but to catch the real essence of the country's olive-oil varieties (Spain is the world's largest producer), Patrimonio Comunal Olivarero is perfect. With examples of the extra-virgin variety (and nothing else) from all over Spain, you could spend ages agonising over the choices. The staff know their oil and are happy to help out if you speak a little Spanish.

PONCELET FOOD

Map p254 (☎91 308 02 21; www.poncelet.es; Calle de Argensola 27; ⊙10.30am-8.30pm Mon-Sat; MAlonso Martínez) For Spanish and other European cheeses, this fine cheese shop is the best of its kind in Madrid. The variety is outstanding and the staff really know their cheese.

CACAO SAMPAKA FOOD

Map p254 (☎91 319 58 40; www.cacaosampaka.com; Calle de Orellana 4; ⊙10am-9.30pm; MAlonso Martínez) If you thought chocolate was about fruit 'n' nut, think again. This gourmet chocolate shop is a chocoholic's dream come true, with more combinations to go with humble cocoa than you ever imagined possible. If you only come to one chocolate shop in Madrid, make it this one.

RESERVA Y CATA WINE

Map p254 (☎91 319 04 01; www.reservaycata.com; Calle del Conde de Xiquena 13; ⊙11am-2.30pm & 5-9pm Mon-Fri, 11am-2.30pm Sat; MColón or Chueca) This old-style shop stocks an excellent range of local wines, and the knowledgeable staff can help you pick out a great one for your next dinner party or a gift for a friend back home. It specialises in quality Spanish wines that you just don't find in El Corte Inglés and there's often a bottle open so that you can try before you buy.

ISOLÉE FOOD, FASHION

Map p254 (☎902 876 136; www.isolee.com; Calle de las Infantas 19; ⊙11am-9pm Mon-Sat; MGran Vía or Chueca) Multipurpose lifestyle stores were late in coming to Madrid, but they're now all the rage and there's none more stylish than Isolée. It sells a select range of everything from clothes (Andy Warhol to Adidas) and shoes to CDs and food. They have another **branch** (Map p248; Calle de Claudio Coello 55; ⊙11am-8.30pm Mon-Fri, 11am-9pm Sat; MSerrano) in Salamanca.

ELISA BRACCI FASHION

Map p254 (☎91 435 03 05; www.elisabracci.es; Calle de Bárbara de Braganza 2; ⊙10.30am-2.30pm & 5.30-8.30pm Mon-Sat; MAlonso Martínez or Colón) One of the most enduring and respected names of Spanish catwalk fashion and a key figure of the 1980s outpouring of cultural creativity that was *la movida madrileña*, Elisa Bracci is the place to find that evening dress for a special occasion. Just entering this store makes you feel like a celebrity and the mix of colours and unrestrained elegance suggests a confident designer who long ago reached the pinnacle of her profession.

FUTURAMIC VINTAGE

Map p254 (☎91 531 63 57; www.futuramics.com; Calle de Válgame Dios 5; ⏲11.30am-3pm & 5.30-8.30pm Mon-Fri, 11am-2.30pm Sat; Ⓜ Chueca) Looking for that 1960s jukebox? Or a real-life parking meter? Just about anything you can imagine in memorabilia (either original or in replica) from the 1930s to the 1980s is available here. Not everything is for sale (the life-size London phone booth, for example), as many of the items are in demand for movie sets, but much of it is. Ring before you head here as the staff are often out on location.

ALDABA HOMEWARES

Map p254 (☎91 308 38 33; Calle de Belén 4; ⏲10am-8.30pm Mon-Sat; Ⓜ Chueca) You never quite know what you'll find in this packed designer homewares store on a quiet street towards the northern end of Chueca. There's a specialist kitchen section but every corner of your house is catered for, as is your every mood – products range from Alessi to 'ex-lover's voodoo dolls'.

BIBLIOKETA BOOKS

Map p254 (☎91 391 00 99; www.biblioketa.com; Calle de Justiniano 4; ⏲10.30am-2.30pm & 5-8pm Mon-Sat; Ⓜ Alonso Martínez) Biblioketa is perhaps the best multilingual children's bookshop in Madrid, with a range of quality titles in English, Spanish and French. Check out the basement 'cave', where it runs a range of activities offering an 'apprenticeship' in reading with an emphasis on fun.

EL TINTERO CLOTHING

Map p254 (☎91 308 14 18; www.eltintero.es; Calle de Gravina 5; ⏲11am-2pm & 5-9pm Mon-Fri, 11am-2.30pm & 5-9pm Sat; Ⓜ Chueca) Terrific T-shirts are all that El Tintero sells. So if you're looking for a colourful *camiseta* (T-shirt) with Spanish-language slogans that translate as 'I'm maturing – apologies for any inconvenience' or 'Does anyone have an instruction manual?', this is your place. It's all good, clean fun and they also take a similar approach with kids' wear, from newborns to aged 10 years.

LA JUGUETERÍA SEX SHOP

Map p254 (☎91 308 72 69; www.lajugueteria.com; Travesía del San Mateo 12; ⏲11am-3pm & 5-9pm Mon-Sat; Ⓜ Alonso Martínez) We don't normally include sex shops in our guides but this softly lit one tickled our fancy. Home to sultry staff and carefully chosen feathers and erotic toys, there's nothing brown paper bag and men in anoraks about this place; you won't feel guilty entering. It's very Chueca.

MACCHININE CHILDREN

Map p254 (☎91 701 05 18; www.macchinine.es; Calle de Barquillo 7; ⏲10am-2pm & 4.30-8.30pm Mon-Sat; Ⓜ Banco de España) Collectors and children will love this small shop in equal measure, packed as it is with perfectly created replica model cars and wooden and metal figures. There are also games, toys without batteries and all manner of perfectly proportioned knick-knacks.

LIBRERÍA BERKANA BOOKS, GAY

Map p254 (☎91 522 55 99; www.libreriaberkana.com; Calle de Hortaleza 64; ⏲10.30am-9pm Mon-Fri, 11.30am-9pm Sat, noon-2pm & 5-9pm Sun; Ⓜ Chueca) One of the most important gay and lesbian bookshops in Madrid, Librería Berkana stocks gay books, movies, magazines, music, clothing, and a host of free magazines for nightlife and other gay-focused activities in Madrid and around Spain.

Parque del Oeste & Northern Madrid

Neighbourhood Top Five

❶ Visiting the **Ermita de San Antonio de la Florida** (p146), a stunning collection of frescoes that remain exactly where Goya painted them.

❷ Surrounding yourself with paintings infused with the clear light of the Mediterranean at the **Museo Sorolla** (p147)

❸ Propping up the bar and ordering *patatas bravas* (fried potatoes with a spicy tomato sauce) and a vermouth at the ageless **Bodega de la Ardosa** (p150)

❹ Discovering the weird-and-wonderful world of Spanish nouvelle cuisine by dining at **Sergi Arola Gastro** (p149)

❺ Watching Real Madrid play in front of 80,000 passionate fans at the **Estadio Santiago Bernabéu** (p148)

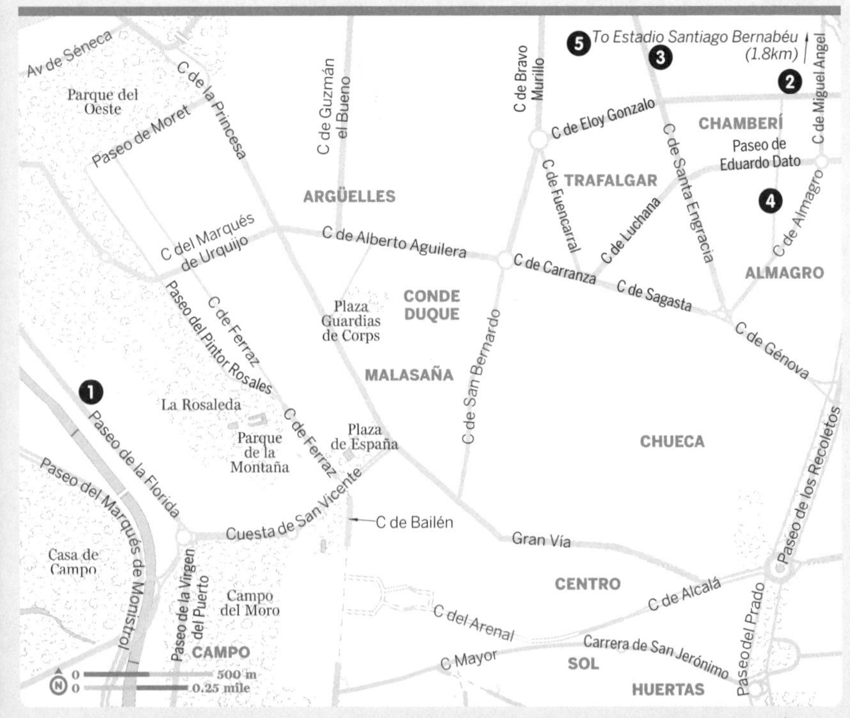

For more detail of this area see Map p238 and p240

Explore: Parque del Oeste & Northern Madrid

Ranged around central Madrid to the north and west, these neighbourhoods cover a vast area and visiting here requires a little planning. Chamberí is worth visiting in its own right, a reasonably self-contained *barrio* (district) with enough sights, shops and restaurants to warrant at least half a day. Chamberí is good at any time of the day or night, but to understand its appeal as one of the more accessible slices of Madrid life away from the tourist crowds, late afternoon is our favourite time of the day.

The rest of the attractions are fairly thinly spread, although you could easily catch the metro to Moncloa metro station, and then follow Parque del Oeste roughly south and then on down to Templo de Debod on the cusp of the city centre. Ermita de San Antonio de la Florida is more of a dedicated (though easily made) excursion – catch the metro to Príncipe Pío and walk to the hermitage, before returning via the same route.

Northern Madrid follows the path of that great Madrid artery, known for much of its length as Paseo de la Castellana. Again, you're more likely to come here as part of a surgical strike on a particular sight or restaurant, but metro connections are good.

Local Life

- **Meeting Point** Plaza de Olavide is the heart and soul of Chamberí, from the old timers watching the world go by from park benches and children in the playgrounds to the outdoor tables that encircle the plaza.
- **Hangout** Bodega de la Ardosa (p150) is one of the best places in Madrid to understand the appeal of the neighbourhood bar – utterly unpretentious, serving great food and drawing a cast of regulars, it's Madrid in microcosm.
- **Traditional Shops** A Chamberí specialty are the shops that have been serving the *barrio* for decades, places such as Calzados Cantero (p153), Antigüedades Hom (p153) and Bazar Matey (p153).

Getting There & Away

- **Metro** The most convenient metro stations for Chamberí are Bilbao (lines 1 and 4), Quevedo (line 2) and Iglesia (line 1).
- **Metro** Other useful stations include Príncipe Pío (lines 6 and 10) for Ermita de San Antonio de la Florida and Moncloa (lines 3 and 6) or Argüelles (lines 3 and 4) for Parque del Oeste. Metro line 10 connects Northern Madrid to the rest of Madrid.

Lonely Planet's Top Tip

From 8am to 1.30pm or 2pm on Sundays, Calle de Fuencarral between Quevedo and Bilbao metro stations is closed to traffic and all the *barrio* comes out to play. Joining them will make you feel like a local as you mingle with kids on bicycles and roller blades, jumping castles and the like. This has been a *barrio* tradition for over four decades, and also occurs on public holidays.

Best Places to Eat

- Sergi Arola Gastro (p149)
- Costa Blanca Arrocería (p150)
- Las Tortillas de Gabino (p149)
- El Pedrusco (p150)
- Sagaretxe (p150)
- Santceloni (p151)

For reviews, see p149

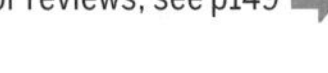

Best Places to Drink

- Bodega de la Ardosa (p150)
- Real Café Bernabéu (p152)
- Honky Tonk (p152)
- Clamores (p152)

For reviews, see p152

Best Museums

- Ermita de San Antonio de la Florida (p146)
- Museo Sorolla (p147)
- Museo de América (p148)
- Templo de Debod (p147)

TOP SIGHTS
ERMITA DE SAN ANTONIO DE LA FLORIDA

This small church ranks alongside Madrid's finest art galleries. Recently restored and also known as the Panteón de Goya, this chapel has frescoed ceilings as painted by Goya in 1798 on the request of Carlos IV. As such, it's one of the few places to see Goya masterworks in their original setting.

The Miracle of St Anthony

Figures on the dome depict the miracle of St Anthony. The saint heard word from his native Lisbon that his father had been unjustly accused of murder. The saint was whisked miraculously to his hometown from northern Italy and Goya's painting depicts the moment in which St Anthony calls on the corpse to rise up and absolve his father.

An 18th-century Madrid Crowd

As interesting as the miracle that forms the fresco's centrepiece, a typical Madrid crowd swarms around the saint. It was customary in such works that angels and cherubs appear in the cupola, above all the terrestrial activity, but Goya, never one to let himself be confined within the mores of the day, places the human above the divine.

Goya's Tomb

The painter is buried in front of the altar. His remains were transferred in 1919 from Bordeaux (France), where he died in self-imposed exile in 1828. Oddly, the skeleton that was exhumed in Bordeaux was missing one important item – the head.

Fiesta de San Antonio

Young women (traditionally seamstresses) flock to the hermitage on 13 June to petition for a partner. Whether spiritually inclined or not, the attitude seems to be 'why take a chance?'

DON'T MISS...

- Miracle of St Anthony
- An 18th-century Madrid crowd
- Goya's Tomb
- Fiesta de San Antonio

PRACTICALITIES

- Map p240
- Glorieta de San Antonio de la Florida 5
- 9.30am-8pm Tue-Fri, 10am-2pm Sat & Sun
- M Príncipe Pío

SIGHTS

ERMITA DE SAN ANTONIO DE LA FLORIDA ART

See p146.

MUSEO SOROLLA GALLERY

Map p238 (www.museosorolla.mcu.es; Paseo del General Martínez Campos 37; adult/child €3/free, free Sun; ⌚9.30am-8pm Tue-Sat, 10am-3pm Sun; Ⓜ Iglesia, Gregorio Marañón) The Valencian artist Joaquín Sorolla immortalised the clear Mediterranean light of the Valencian coast. His Madrid house, a quiet mansion surrounded by lush gardens that he designed himself, was inspired by what he had seen in Andalucía and now contains the most complete collection of the artist's works.

On the ground floor there's a cool *patio cordobés,* an Andalucian courtyard off which is a room containing collections of Sorolla's drawings. The 1st floor, with the main salon and dining areas, was mostly decorated by the artist himself. On the same floor are three separate rooms that Sorolla used as studios. In the second one is a collection of his Valencian beach scenes. The third was where he usually worked. Upstairs, works spanning Sorolla's career are organised across four adjoining rooms.

MUSEO DE CERRALBO MUSEUM

Map p240 (☎91 547 36 46; www.museocerralbo.mcu.es; Calle de Ventura Rodríguez 17; adult/concession €3/free, free Sun, 2-3pm Sat & 5-8pm Thu; ⌚9.30am-3pm Tue, Wed, Fri & Sat, 9.30am-3pm & 5-8pm Thu, 10am-3pm Sun; Ⓜ Ventura Rodríguez) Huddled beneath the modern apartment buildings northwest of Plaza de España, this noble old mansion is a reminder of how wealthy *madrileños* (people from Madrid) once lived. The former home of the 17th Marqués de Cerralbo (1845–1922) – politician, poet and archaeologist – is a study in 19th-century opulence. The upper floor boasts a gala dining hall and a grand ballroom. The mansion is jammed with the fruits of the collector's eclectic meanderings – from Oriental pieces to religious paintings and clocks.

On the main floor are spread suits of armour from around the world, while the Oriental room is full of carpets, Moroccan kilims, tapestries, musical instruments and 18th-century Japanese suits of armour, much of it obtained at auction in Paris in

TOP SIGHTS TEMPLO DE DEBOD

Yes, that *is* an Egyptian temple in downtown Madrid. No matter which way you look at it, there's something incongruous about finding the Templo de Debod in the Parque de la Montaña northwest of Plaza de España. The temple was saved from the rising waters of Lake Nasser in southern Egypt when Egyptian president Gamal Abdel Nasser built the Aswan High Dam. After 1968 it was sent block by block to Spain as a gesture of thanks to Spanish archaeologists in the Unesco team that worked to save the monuments that would otherwise have disappeared forever.

Begun in 2200 BC and completed over many centuries, the temple was dedicated to the god Amon of Thebes, about 20km south of Philae in the Nubian desert of southern Egypt. According to some authors of myth and legend, the goddess Isis gave birth to Horus in this very temple, although obviously not in Madrid.

Rather than treating the temple as a sight on its own, consider a stroll in the surrounding parkland from where the views towards the Palacio Real are some of Madrid's prettiest.

DON'T MISS

- Temple interior
- Parque de la Montaña

PRACTICALITIES

- Map p240
- www.munimadrid.es/templodebod
- Paseo del Pintor Rosales
- ⌚10am-2pm & 6-8pm Tue-Fri, 10am-2pm Sat & Sun Apr-Sep, 9.45am-1.45pm and 4.15-6.15pm Tue-Fri & 10am-2pm Sat & Sun Oct-Mar
- Ⓜ Ventura Rodríguez

TOP SIGHTS ESTADIO SANTIAGO BERNABÉU

Football fans and budding Madridistas (Real Madrid supporters) will want to make a pilgrimage to the Estadio Santiago Bernabéu, a temple to all that's extravagant and successful in football. For a tour of the stadium, buy your ticket at window 10 (next to gate 7). The self-guided tours take you up into the stands for a panoramic view of the stadium, then pass through the presidential box, press room, dressing rooms, players' tunnel and even onto the pitch itself. The tour ends in the extraordinary Exposición de Trofeos (trophy exhibit).

Better still, attend a game alongside 80,000 delirious fans. For bigger games, tickets are difficult to find unless you're willing to take the risk with scalpers. For less important matches, you shouldn't have too many problems. Tickets can be purchased online – click on 'Entradas', by phone (☎902 324 324) or in person from the ticket office at Gate 42 on Calle de Conche de Espina; for the latter, turn up early in the week before a scheduled game (eg a Monday morning for a Sunday game).

The football season runs from September (or the last weekend in August) until May, with a two-week break just before Christmas until early in the New Year.

DON'T MISS

- Guided Tour
- Tienda Real Madrid (p153)
- Exposición de Trofeos

PRACTICALITIES

- ☎91 398 43 00, 902 301 709
- www.realmadrid.com
- Calle Concha Espina 1
- 10am-7.30pm Mon-Sat, 10.30am-6.30pm Sun, except match days
- Ⓜ Santiago Bernabéu

the 1870s. The music room is dominated by a gondola of Murano glass and pieces of Bohemian crystal. The house is also replete with porcelain, including Sèvres, Wedgwood, Meissen and local ceramics. Clearly the *marqués* was a man of diverse tastes and it can all be a little overwhelming, especially once you factor in artworks by Zurbarán, Ribera, van Dyck and El Greco.

CEMENTERIO DE LA FLORIDA CEMETERY

Map p240 (Calle de Francisco Jacinto y Alcantara; ⓂPríncipe Pío) Across the train tracks from the Ermita de San Antonio de la Florida is the cemetery where 43 rebels executed by Napoleon's troops lie buried. They were killed on the nearby Montaña del Príncipe Pío in the predawn of 3 May 1808, after the Dos de Mayo uprising. The event was immortalised by Goya in his *Dos de Mayo* and *Tres de Mayo* paintings, which hang in the Museo del Prado. A plaque was placed here in 1981. The forlorn cemetery, established in 1796, is often closed.

MUSEO DE AMÉRICA MUSEUM

Map p240 (www.museodeamerica.mcu.es; Avenida de los Reyes Católicos 6; adult/concession €3/1.50, free Sun; 9.30am-8.30pm Tue-Sat, 10am-3pm Sun; ⓂMoncloa) Empire may have become a dirty word but it defined how Spain saw itself for centuries. Spanish vessels crossed the Atlantic to the Spanish colonies in Latin America carrying adventurers one way and gold and other looted artefacts from indigenous cultures on the return journey. These latter pieces – at once the heritage of another continent and a fascinating insight into imperial Spain – are the subject of this excellent museum.

The two levels of the museum show off a representative display of ceramics, statuary, jewellery and instruments of hunting, fishing and war, along with some of the paraphernalia of the colonisers. The display is divided into five thematic zones: **El Conocimiento de América** (which traces the discovery and exploration of the Americas), **La Realidad de América** (a big-screen summary of how South America wound up as it has today), and others on society, religion and language, which each explore tribal issues, the clash with the Spanish newcomers and its results. The Colombian gold collection, dating as far back as the 2nd century AD, is particularly eye-catching.

TELEFÉRICO CABLE CAR

Map p240 (☎91 541 11 18; www.teleferico.com; one-way/return €3.85/5.60; ⏲noon-9pm Mon-Fri, to 9.30pm Sat & Sun Jun-Aug, reduced hours Sep-May; Ⓜ Argüelles) One of the world's most horizontal cable cars (it never hangs more than 40m above the ground), the Teleférico putters out from the slopes of La Rosaleda (the rose garden of Parque del Oeste). The 2.5km journey takes you into the depths of the Casa de Campo (p151), Madrid's enormous green open space (in summer more a dry olive hue) to the west of the city centre. Try to time it so you can settle in for a cool lunch or evening tipple on one of the *terrazas* along Paseo del Pintor Rosales.

PARQUE DEL OESTE GARDENS

Map p240 (Avenida del Arco de la Victoria; Ⓜ Moncloa) Sloping down the hill behind Moncloa metro station, Parque del Oeste (Park of the West) is quite beautiful, with plenty of shady corners where you can recline under a tree in the heat of the day and fine views out to the west towards Casa de Campo. It has been a *madrileño* favourite ever since its creation in 1906.

Until a few years ago, the Paseo de Camoens, a main thoroughfare running through the park, was lined with prostitutes by night. To deprive the prostitutes of clients, the city authorities now close the park to wheeled traffic from 11pm on Friday until 6am on Monday.

FREE **ESTACIÓN DE CHAMBERÍ** MUSEUM

Map p238 (Andén 0; www.esmadrid.com/anden0 ; cnr Calles de Santa Engracia & de Luchana; ⏲11am-1pm & 5-7pm Fri-Sun; Ⓜ Iglesia, Bilbao) For years, *madrileños* wondered what happened to the Chamberí metro station – they knew it existed, yet it appeared on no maps and no trains stopped there. The answer was that Chamberí station lay along line 1, between the stops of Bilbao and Iglesia, until 1966 when Madrid's trains were lengthened. Logistical difficulties meant that Chamberí could not be extended and the station was abandoned. In 2008 the station finally reopened to the public, if not for trains, serving as a museum piece that recreates the era of the station's inauguration in 1919 with advertisements from the time (including Madrid's then four-digit phone numbers), ticket offices and other memorabilia almost a century old. It's an engaging journey down memory lane.

METRO LINE 10

Two of the neighbourhood's top sights – the Ermita de San Antonio de la Florida and the Estadio Santiago Bernabéu – may seem far flung but they're actually connected by metro line 10. En route between the two, the line also has stops on Plaza de España and Tribunal, which are handy stations for the rest of the *barrio* (district).

EATING

Chamberí & Argüelles

TOP CHOICE **SERGI AROLA GASTRO** CONTEMPORARY SPANISH €€€

Map p238 (☎91 310 21 69; www.sergiarola.es; Calle de Zurbano 31; mains €43-52, set menus €105-135; ⏲lunch & dinner Mon-Fri, dinner Sat; Ⓜ Alonso Martínez) Sergi Arola, a stellar Catalan acolyte of the world-renowned chef Ferran Adrià, runs this highly personalised temple to all that's innovative in Spanish gastronomy. The menus change with the seasons – a recent sample included smoked beetroot raviolis with celery consommé, or Jerusalem artichoke soft cream, truffled poultry mousse, mascarpone cheese and fine herbs. You pay for the privilege of eating here. But this is culinary indulgence at its finest, the sort of place where creativity, presentation and taste are everything. And oh, what tastes… With just 26 seats, booking well in advance is necessary.

LAS TORTILLAS DE GABINO SPANISH €€

Map p238 (☎91 319 75 05; www.lastortillasdegabino.com; Calle de Rafael Calvo 20; tortillas €9-15.50, mains €12-18; ⏲lunch & dinner Mon-Fri, dinner Sat; Ⓜ Iglesia) It's a brave Spanish chef that fiddles with the iconic *tortilla de patatas* (potato and onion omelette), but the results here are delicious – such as tortilla with octopus, and with all manner of surprising combinations. This place also gets rave reviews for its *croquetas* (croquettes). The service is excellent and the bright yet classy dining area adds to the sense of a most agreeable eating experience. Reservations are highly recommended.

SAGARETXE BASQUE TAPAS €€

Map p238 (☎91 446 25 88; www.sagaretxe.com; Calle de Eloy Gonzalo 26; tapas from €2.50; ⊙noon-5pm & 7pm-1am; MIglesia) One of the best Basque *pintxos* (Basque tapas) bars in Madrid, Sagaretxe takes the stress out of eating tapas, with around 20 varieties lined up along the bar (and up to 150 that can be prepared in the kitchen upon request). Simply point and any of the wonderful selection will be plated up for you. Better still, order the *surtido de 8/12 pintxos* (your own selection of eight/12 tapas) for €14/20. There's a more expensive but equally good Basque restaurant downstairs.

BODEGA DE LA ARDOSA TAPAS €

Map p238 (☎91 446 58 94; Calle de Santa Engracia 70; raciones from €6.50; ⊙9am-3pm & 6-11.30pm Thu-Tue; MIglesia) Tucked away in a fairly modern corner of Chamberí, this fine old relic has an extravagantly tiled facade complete with shrapnel holes dating back to the Spanish Civil War. For decades locals have been coming here for their morning tipple and for some of the best traditional Spanish *patatas bravas* (fried potatoes with a spicy tomato sauce) in town. It also has vermouth on tap.

COSTA BLANCA ARROCERÍA SPANISH €€

Map p238 (☎91 448 58 32; Calle de Bravo Murillo 3; mains €9-18; ⊙lunch & dinner; MQuevedo) Even if you don't have plans to be in Chamberí, it's worth a trip across town to this casual bar-restaurant that offers outstanding rice dishes, including paella. The quality is high and prices are among the cheapest in town. Start with *almejas a la marinera* (baby clams) and follow it up with *paella de marisco* (seafood paella) for the full experience. As always in such places, you'll need two to make up an order.

EL PEDRUSCO SPANISH €€

Map p238 (☎91 446 88 33; www.elpedruscodealdealcorvo.com; Calle de Juan de Austria 27; mains €15-24; ⊙lunch Mon-Thu, lunch & dinner Fri & Sat; MIglesia) If you haven't time to visit one of the *asadores* (restaurants specialising in roasted meats) of Segovia, head to this fine restaurant where the *cochinillo asado* (roast suckling pig) and quarter *lechazo* (roast lamb) are succulent and as good as any in Madrid. It's the sort of place where a salad is a must to counterbalance all that meat and you'll be delighted to see a vegetable.

LA FAVORITA SPANISH €€

Map p238 (☎91 448 38 10; www.restaurante-lafavorita.com; Calle de Covarrubias 25; mains €13-22, menú degustación €70; ⊙lunch & dinner Mon-Fri, dinner Sat; MAlonso Martínez) Set in a delightful old mansion and famous for its opera arias throughout the night sung by professional opera singers masquerading as waiters, La Favorita has an ambience all of its own. The outdoor garden courtyard is delightful on a summer's evening, while the music and food (which leans towards the cuisine of the northeastern Spanish region of Navarra) are top drawer.

IL CASONE ITALIAN €€

Map p238 (☎91 591 62 66; Calle de Trafalgar 25; mains €8-14; ⊙lunch & dinner daily; MQuevedo, Iglesia or Bilbao) With its outdoor tables on the lovely Plaza de Olavide in summer, reasonable prices and fresh and inventive Italian cooking, Il Casone is outstanding. There are flashes of creativity in the pasta, such as *fagottini* with black truffles and cream of foie gras and mushroom, while the salads, carpaccios and grilled provolone are great starters.

CASA MINGO ASTURIAN €

Map p240 (☎91 547 79 18; www.casamingo.es; Paseo de la Florida 34; raciones €3.95-10.30; ⊙lunch & dinner; MPríncipe Pío) Built in 1916 to feed workers building the Príncipe Pío train station, Casa Mingo is a well-known and vaguely cavernous Asturian cider house. It's kept simple here, focusing primarily on the signature dish of *pollo asado* (roast chicken) accompanied by a bottle of cider. Combine with a visit to the neighbouring Ermita de San Antonio de la Florida (p146).

LOCAL KNOWLEDGE

PLAZA DE OLAVIDE

Plaza de Olavide (Map p238) hasn't always had its current form. From 1934, the entire plaza was occupied by a covered, octagonal market. In November 1974, the market was demolished in a spectacular controlled explosion, opening up the plaza as one of Madrid's most agreeable public spaces. To see the plaza's history told in pictures, step into Bar Méntrida at No 3 for a drink and admire the photos on the wall.

WORTH A DETOUR

CASA DE CAMPO

Sometimes called the 'lungs of Madrid', **Casa de Campo** (Map p240; MBatán) is a 17 sq km expanse of greenery stretching west of the Río Manzanares. There are prettier and more central parks in Madrid but it's less manicured and has walking trails, lakeside restaurants and other attractions. And visit the *madrileños* do, nearly half a million of them every weekend.

The **Zoo Aquarium de Madrid** (902 345014; www.zoomadrid.com; Casa de Campo; adult/child €21.35/17.60; 10.30am-8.30pm Jul & Aug, reduced hours Sep-Jun; 37 from Intercambiador de Príncipe Pío, MCasa de Campo) is a standard European city zoo and is home to about 3000 animals. Exhibits range from white Siberian tigers to lions, zebras, giraffes, rhinos, flamingos, koalas and a pair of celebrity pandas. You can also watch dolphins and sea lions get up to their tricks. Arriving by bus is the best option as it leaves you right at the door; if you take the metro to Casa de Campo, you've a 15-minute walk from the station, or you can take bus 37 from the station for one stop.

The **Parque de Atracciones** (91 463 29 00; www.parquedeatracciones.es; Casa de Campo; height >120cm/90-120cm/<90cm €29.90/23.90/free; noon-midnight Sun-Fri, to 1am Sat Jul & Aug, reduced hours Sep-Jun; 37 from Intercambiador de Príncipe Pío, MBatán) has the usual collection of high-adrenaline rides, shows for the kids and kitsch at every turn. In the Zona de Máquinas (the rather ominous sounding Machines Zone) are most of the bigger rides, but there's also a Zona de Tranquilidad (with a gentle Ferris wheel) and a Zona Infantil where younger kids can get their own thrills on less hair-raising rides.

Northern Madrid

The business and well-to-do clientele who eat in the restaurants of northern Madrid know their food and they're happy to pay for it. Often it's a fair metro or taxi ride north of the centre, but well worth it for a touch of class.

TOP CHOICE SANTCELONI — CATALAN €€€

Map p238 (91 210 88 40; www.restaurantesantceloni.com; Paseo de la Castellana 57; mains €43-69, set menus €150-180; lunch & dinner Mon-Fri, dinner Sat; MGregorio Marañón) The Michelin-starred Santceloni is one of Madrid's best restaurants, with luxury decor that's the work of star interior designer Pascual Ortega, and nouvelle cuisine from the kitchen of chef Óscar Velasco, protege of master chef Santi Santamaría, who died suddenly in 2011. Each dish is an exquisite work of art and the menu changes with the seasons, but we'd recommend one of the *menús gastronómicos* to really sample the breadth of surprising tastes on offer. Make no mistake: this is one of Madrid's best restaurants.

ZALACAÍN — BASQUE, NAVARRAN €€€

Map p238 (91 561 48 40; www.restaurantezalacain.com; Calle de Álvarez de Baena 4; mains €28-50, menú degustación €105.60; lunch & dinner Mon-Fri, dinner Sat, closed Aug; MGregorio Marañón) Where most other fine-dining experiences centre on innovation, Zalacaín is a bastion of tradition, with a refined air and a loyal following among Spain's great and good. Everyone who's anyone in Madrid, from the king down, has eaten here since the doors opened in 1973; it was the first restaurant in Spain to receive three Michelin stars. The pig's trotters filled with mushrooms and lamb is a house speciality, as is the lobster salad. The wine list is purported to be one of the best in the city (it stocks an estimated 35,000 bottles with 800 different varieties). You should certainly dress to impress (men will need a tie and a jacket).

PUERTA 57 — SPANISH €€€

(91 457 33 61; Gate 57, Estadio Santiago Bernabéu, Calle de Padre Damián; mains €20-35; lunch & dinner Mon-Sat, lunch Sun; MSantiago Bernabéu) There are many reasons to recommend this place, but the greatest novelty lies in its location – inside the home stadium of Real Madrid; its Salón Madrid (one of a number of dining rooms) looks out over the playing field. Needless to say, you'll need to book a long time in advance for a meal during a game. The cuisine is traditional Spanish with an emphasis on seafood and it gets rave reviews from its predominantly business clientele.

DRINKING & NIGHTLIFE

REAL CAFÉ BERNABÉU BAR

(☎91 458 36 67; www.realcafebernabeu.es; Gate 30, Estadio Santiago Bernabéu, Avenida de Concha Espina; ⌚9pm-1am; Ⓜ Santiago Bernabéu) Overlooking one of the most famous football fields on earth, this trendy cocktail bar will appeal to those who live and breathe football or those who simply enjoy mixing with the beautiful people. Views are exceptional, although it closes two hours before a game and doesn't open until an hour after. There's also a good restaurant.

MACUMBA NIGHTCLUB

(www.fsmgroup.es; Plaza Estación de Chamartín; admission €12; ⌚midnight-6am Fri & Sat, 1pm-midnight Sun; Ⓜ Chamartín) Macumba, on the 2nd floor of the Chamartín train station, may be a fair trip north of the centre (although still well within city limits), but it's one of the most prestigious nightclubs in Madrid. Here you'll find a cast of local and international DJs spinning house and techno over the incredible sound system. For something different, Sunday ('Space of Sound') is for those who can't bear their weekend to end.

ENTERTAINMENT

Chamberí & Argüelles

CLAMORES LIVE MUSIC

Map p238 (☎91 445 79 38; www.clamores.es; Calle de Alburquerque 14; admission €5-15; ⌚6pm-3am; Ⓜ Bilbao) Clamores is a one-time classic jazz cafe that has morphed into one of the most diverse live music stages in Madrid. Jazz is still a staple, but world music, flamenco, soul fusion, singer-songwriter, pop and rock all make regular appearances. Live shows can begin as early as 7pm on weekends but sometimes really only get going after 1am. On the rare nights when there's nothing live, a DJ takes over, spinning pop, indie and funk.

GALILEO GALILEI LIVE MUSIC

Map p238 (☎91 534 75 57; www.salagalileogalilei.com; Calle de Galileo 100; admission free-€15; ⌚6pm-4.30am; Ⓜ Islas Filipinas) There's no telling what will be staged here next, but it's sure to be good, as the list of past performers attests: Jackson Browne, El Cigala, Kiko Veneno, Niña Pastori and Brazilian songstress Cibelle among others. The program changes nightly, with singer-songwriters, jazz, flamenco, folk, fusion, indie, world music and even comedians. Most performances start at 10.30pm.

FREE **HONKY TONK** LIVE MUSIC

Map p238 (☎91 445 61 91; www.clubhonky.com; Calle de Covarrubias 24; admission free; ⌚9pm-5am; Ⓜ Alonso Martínez) Despite the name, this is a great place to see blues or local rock, though many acts have some country, jazz or R&B thrown into the mix, too. It's a fun vibe in a small club that's been around since the '80s and opens 365 days a year. It's a reliable late-night option in a *barrio* of few, and the range of malt whiskies is impressive. Arrive early as it fills up fast.

TEATROS DEL CANAL THEATRE

Map p238 (☎91 308 99 99; www.teatrosdelcanal.org; Calle de Cea Bermúdez 1; Ⓜ Canal) A state-of-the-art theatre complex opened in 2009, Teatros del Canal does major theatre performances, as well as musical and dance concerts.

Northern Madrid

MOBY DICK LIVE MUSIC

(☎91 555 76 71; www.mobydickclub.com; Avenida del Brasil 5; admission free-€20; ⌚9pm-3am Mon-Wed, to 6am Thu-Sat; Ⓜ Santiago Bernabéu) In a corner of Madrid that works hard by day and parties even harder on weekends, Moby Dick is an institution on the live music circuit. It's mostly well-known rock bands who can't quite fill the 25,000-seater venues, and there are plenty of dance bars alongside if the music's not to your liking.

SEGUNDO JAZZ JAZZ

(☎91 554 94 37; www.segundojazz.es; Calle del Comandante Zorita 8; admission free-€10; ⌚7pm-4am; Ⓜ Nuevos Ministerios or Cuatro Caminos) This well-regarded jazz venue focuses on up-and-coming local talents, as well as international acts. It's an agreeable, unpretentious place that's worth the fair hike to get here: the quality is always high and the atmosphere nice and laid-back (the armchairs help). Monday and Tuesday are given over to jam sessions from 11pm, while other concerts start anywhere from 9pm to after midnight.

AUDITORIO NACIONAL DE MÚSICA CLASSICAL MUSIC
(☎91 337 01 40; www.auditorionacional.mcu.es; Calle del Príncipe de Vergara 146; Ⓜ Cruz del Rayo) When it's not playing the Teatro Real, Madrid's Orquesta Sinfonía plays at this modern venue, which also attracts famous conductors from all across the world. It's usually fairly easy to get your hands on tickets at the box office.

SHOPPING

Chamberí & Argüelles

ANTIGÜEDADES HOM ANTIQUES
Map p238 (☎91 594 20 17; Calle de Juan de Austria 31; ⏲5-8pm Mon-Wed, noon-2pm & 5-8pm Thu & Fri; Ⓜ Iglesia) Specialising in antique Spanish fans, this tiny shop is a wonderful place to browse or to find a special gift, especially delicately painted fans and those made with bone. It's open mostly afternoons only because the owner spends the mornings restoring the fans you see for sale. It's also a purveyor of other treasures and bric-a-brac.

CALZADOS CANTERO SHOES
Map p238 (☎91 447 07 35; Plaza de Olavide 12; ⏲10am-2pm & 4.45-8.30pm Mon-Sat; Ⓜ Quevedo, Iglesia, Bilbao) A charming old-world shoe store, Calzados Cantero sells a range of shoes at rock-bottom prices. But it's most famous for its rope-soled *alpargatas* (espadrilles), which start from €6.50. This is a *barrio* classic, the sort of store to which parents bring their children as their own parents did a generation before.

BAZAR MATEY GIFTS
Map p238 (☎91 446 93 11; www.matey.com; Calle de Fuencarral 127; ⏲9.30am-1.30pm & 4.30-8pm Mon-Sat; Ⓜ Bilbao or Quevedo) A wonderful old store, Bazar Matey caters for collectors of model trains, aeroplanes and cars, as well as all sorts of accessories. The items here are the real deal, with near-perfect models of everything from old Renfe trains to aircrafts of obscure international airlines. Prices can be sky high, but that doesn't deter the legions of collectors who stream in from all over Madrid on Saturdays. The kids will love it, too.

PASAJES LIBRERÍA INTERNACIONAL BOOKS
Map p238 (☎91 310 12 45; www.pasajeslibros.com; Calle de Génova 3; ⏲9.30am-9.30pm Mon-Sat; Ⓜ Alonso Martínez) Definitely one of the best bookshops in Madrid, Pasajes has an extensive English section (downstairs at the back), which includes high-quality fiction (if it's a new release, it'll be the first bookshop in town to have it), history, Spanish subject matter and travel, as well as a few literary magazines. There are also French, German, Italian and Portuguese books, children's books and DVDs, and a useful noticeboard.

OCHO Y MEDIO BOOKS
Map p240 (☎91 559 06 28; www.ochoymedio.com; Calle de Martín de los Heros 11; ⏲10am-2pm & 5-8.30pm Mon-Sat; Ⓜ Plaza de España) Close to a number of the best foreign-language cinemas in Madrid, this is a terrific resource for film buffs, with a huge range of books, posters, magazines and other memorabilia. Much of the stock is in Spanish, but there's a smattering of English- and French-language titles and the friendly staff knows its films.

ALTAÏR BOOKS
Map p240 (☎91 543 53 00; www.altair.es; Calle de Gaztambide 31; ⏲10am-2pm & 4.30-8.30pm Mon-Fri, 10.30am-2.30pm Sat; Ⓜ Argüelles) One of the best travel bookshops in Madrid, Altaïr has an exceptional range of books, maps and magazines covering Spain and every other major region of the world. Most are in Spanish, but there are English-language titles scattered throughout, as well as calendars and world-music CDs.

Northern Madrid

TIENDA REAL MADRID SPORTS
(Gate 57, Estadio Santiago Bernabéu, Avenida de Concha Espina 1; ⏲10am-8.30pm; Ⓜ Santiago Bernabéu) The club shop of Real Madrid sells replica shirts, posters, caps and just about everything under the sun to which it could attach a club logo. From the shop window, you can see down onto the stadium itself. There's another branch (Map p242; ☎521 79 50; Calle del Carmen 3; ⏲10am-8.45pm Mon-Sat, 10am-6.45pm Sun; Ⓜ Sol) in the centre of town.

Day Trips from Madrid

San Lorenzo de El Esconial (p155)

One of Spain's grandest monuments, this Unesco World Heritage–listed palace-monastery complex combines a cool mountain setting with the imposing grandeur of imperial Spain.

Toledo (p156)

Toledo is a beautifully sited, architecturally distinguished city with signposts to its glory days as a crossroads of civilisation.

Segovia (p160)

A Roman aqueduct, a castle that inspired Disney and a colour scheme of sandstone and warm terracotta make Segovia one of the most agreeable towns close to Madrid.

Ávila (p162)

Surrounded by the finest medieval walls in Spain, Ávila is an evocative Castilian city that is the spiritual home to the cult of Santa Teresa.

Aranjuez (p164)

A royal getaway down through the centuries, Aranjuez has an extraordinary palace and expansive gardens grafted onto a delightfully small-town canvas.

Chinchón (p164)

Home to one of the prettiest town squares in Spain, Chinchón is a world away from downtown Madrid, with fabulous food thrown in.

TOP SIGHTS
SAN LORENZO DE EL ESCORIAL

Home to the majestic monastery and palace complex of San Lorenzo de El Escorial, this one-time royal getaway rises up from the foothills of the mountains that shelter Madrid from the north and west. The prim little town is overflowing with quaint shops, restaurants and hotels and the fresh, cool air, among other things, has been drawing city dwellers here since the complex was first built on the orders of King Felipe II in the 16th century as both a royal palace and as a mausoleum for Felipe's parents, Carlos I and Isabel.

Patio de los Reyes
At the monastery's main entrance on the west side of the complex, note the statue of St Lawrence holding a symbolic gridiron, the instrument of his martyrdom (he was roasted alive on one). After passing St Lawrence, you'll enter the Patio de los Reyes (Patio of the Kings), which houses statues of the six kings of Judah.

Basílica
Directly ahead of the Patio de los Reyes lies the sombre basilica. Once inside the church proper, turn left to view Benvenuto Cellini's white Carrara marble statue of Christ crucified (1576). Nearby there's an El Greco painting, a far cry from his dream of decorating the whole complex.

DON'T MISS
- Patio de los Reyes
- Basílica
- Museums
- Salas Capitulares
- Jardín del Príncipe

PRACTICALITIES
- ☎91 890 78 18
- www.patrimonionacional.es
- adult/concession €10/5, guide/audio guide €7/4, EU citizens free 5-8pm Wed & Thu
- ⏲10am-8pm Apr-Sep, to 6pm Oct-Mar, closed Mon

Two Museums
As you head downstairs to the complex's northeastern corner you pass the Museo de Arquitectura and the Museo de Pintura. The former tells (in Spanish) the story of how the complex was built, the latter has 16th- and 17th-century Italian, Spanish and Flemish art.

The Crypts
The route through the monastery takes you down into the 17th-century Panteón de los Reyes (Crypt of the Kings), where almost all Spain's monarchs since Carlos I are interred. Nearby is the Panteón de los Infantes (Crypt of the Princesses).

Salas Capitulares
Stairs lead up from the Patio de los Evangelistas (Patio of the Gospels) to the Salas Capitulares (chapterhouses) in the southeastern corner of the monastery. These bright, airy rooms, whose ceilings are richly frescoed, contain a treasure chest of works by El Greco, Titian, Tintoretto, José de Ribera and Hieronymus Bosch.

Jardín del Príncipe
The Prince's Garden, which leads down to the town of El Escorial, is a lovely monumental garden and contains the Casita del Príncipe, a little neo-Classical gem built in 1772 by Juan de Villanueva under Carlos III for his heir, Carlos IV.

Transport
Buses 661 and 664 leave every 15 minutes (€3.55, every half-hour on weekends), from Madrid's Moncloa Intercambiador de Autobuses station. A few dozen Renfe C8 *cercanía* (local train network) trains make the one-hour trip (€3.25) daily from Madrid's Atocha or Chamartín stations to El Escorial.

Toledo

Explore

Toledo's charms, and its proximity to Madrid, mean that it can get choked with tour groups. If you're arriving on the fast train from Madrid, try to make it an early one to arrive before the buses, then try to stay till dusk when the city returns to the locals and the streets take on a moody, other-worldly air.

It's a steep climb up into the old town, but buses 61 and 62 connect the train station with Plaza de Zocodover in the old town, while Bus 5 runs a similar service from the bus station.

The Best

- **Sight** Catedral (p156)
- **Place to Eat** Alfileritos 24 (p157)
- **Place to Drink** Enebro (p159)

Top Tip

If you don't feel like taking the bus up into the old town from down below and feel like walking, the worst of the climb can be avoided by taking the *remonte peatonal* (escalator) which starts near the Puerta de Alfonso VI and ends near the Monasterio de Santo Domingo El Antiguo.

Getting There & Away

Bus The trip from Madrid's Estación Sur (ticket windows 12 and 13) to Toledo takes one hour. Buses run every half-hour. Tickets cost €5.25.

Train Renfe's high-speed AVANT Rail Link is the best way to get to Toledo, with around 11 trains daily. The trip takes 30 minutes.

Need to Know

- **Location** 71km southwest of Madrid
- **Tourist Office City Tourist Office** (☎925 25 40 30; www.t-descubre.com; Plaza del Consistorio 1; ⌚10.30am-6pm) Across from the cathedral.
- **Regional Tourist Office** (☎925 22 08 43; Puerta de Bisagra; ⌚9am-6pm Mon-Fri, 9am-7pm Sat, 9am-3pm Sun)

SIGHTS

The old city and the most important sights are stacked stone upon stone in a crook of the Río Tajo. For a relaxing view of the old city, hop on the Zoco Tren, a small train that does a 45-minute loop up the hill and through Toledo. The train leaves hourly into the early evening and tickets are available from the tourist office.

TOP CHOICE CATEDRAL CATHEDRAL

(Plaza del Ayuntamiento; adult/child €7/free; ⌚10.30am-6.30pm Mon-Sat, 2-6.30pm Sun) Toledo's cathedral reflects the city's historical significance as the heart of Catholic Spain. In the centre of things, the **coro** (choir stall) is a feast of sculpture and carved wooden stalls. The high altar sits in the extravagant **Capilla Mayor**, whose masterpiece is the **retablo** (altarpiece). Behind the main altar lies a mesmerising piece of 18th-century *churrigueresco* (lavish baroque ornamentation), the **Transparente**. The highlight of all, however, is the **sacristía** (sacristy), which contains a gallery with paintings by such masters as El Greco, Zurbarán, Caravaggio, Titian, Rafael and Velázquez.

ALCÁZAR FORTRESS, MUSEUM

(Museo del Ejército; Calle Alféreces Provisionales; adult/child €5/free; ⌚10am-9pm Thu-Tue Jun-Sep, to 7pm Oct-May) At the highest point in the city looms the foreboding Alcázar. Abd ar-Rahman III raised an *al-qasr* (fortress) here in the 10th century, which was thereafter altered by the Christians. The Alcázar was heavily damaged during the siege of the garrison by loyalist militias at the start of the Civil War in 1936. Rebuilt under Franco, it recently reopened as an enormous military museum. The usual displays of uniforms and medals are here, but the best part is the in-depth overview of the nation's history in Spanish and English; the Civil War is skipped over in one paragraph to avoid controversy.

MONASTERIO SAN JUAN DE LOS REYES MONASTERY

(Calle San Juan de los Reyes 2; admission €2.50; ⌚10am-6.45pm) This imposing 15th-century Franciscan monastery and church of San Juan de los Reyes was provocatively founded in the heart of the Jewish quarter by the Catholic Kings Isabel and Fernando to demonstrate the supposed supremacy of their faith. The highlight is the amazing two-level cloister, a harmonious fusion of late ('flamboyant') Gothic downstairs and Mudéjar (a Moorish architectural style) upstairs, with superb statuary, arches, vaulting, elaborate pinnacles and gargoyles surrounding a lush garden with orange trees and roses.

IGLESIA DE SANTO TOMÉ CHURCH

(www.santotome.org; Plaza del Conde; admission €2.50; ⏲10am-6pm, to 7pm summer) This church contains El Greco's masterpiece *El Entierro del Conde de Orgaz* (The Burial of the Count of Orgaz). When the count was buried in 1322, Saints Augustine and Stephen supposedly descended from heaven to attend the count's funeral. El Greco's work depicts the event, complete with miracle guests including himself, his son and Cervantes.

FREE **MUSEO DE SANTA CRUZ** MUSEUM

(Calle Cervantes 3; ⏲10am-6.30pm Mon-Sat, to 2pm Sun) The 16th-century Museo de Santa Cruz is a beguiling combination of Gothic and Plateresque styles. The cloisters and carved wooden ceilings are superb, as is the collection of Spanish ceramics. Also upstairs are a number of El Grecos, a crucifixion attributed to Goya, and the wonderful 15th-century *Tapestry of the Astrolabes*.

SINAGOGA DE SANTA MARÍA LA BLANCA SYNAGOGUE

(Calle de los Reyes Católicos 4; admission €2.50; ⏲10am-6.45pm) This pretty Mudéjar synagogue has five naves divided by rows of horseshoe and multifoil arches. Admire the stucco work and ornate capitals.

MEZQUITA DEL CRISTO DE LA LUZ MOSQUE

(Calle Cristo de la Luz; admission €2.50; ⏲10am-2pm & 3.30-6.45pm Mon-Fri, 10am-6.45pm Sat & Sun) On the northern slopes of town you'll find a modest, yet beautiful, mosque, where architectural traces of Toledo's medieval Muslim conquerors remain. Built around AD 1000, it suffered the usual fate of being converted to a church (hence the religious frescoes), but the original vaulting and arches survived.

MUSEO DEL GRECO MUSEUM, GALLERY

(☎925 22 44 05; http://museodelgreco.mcu.es; Paseo del Tránsito; adult/child €3/1.50, incl Sinagoga del Tránsito €5; ⏲9.30am-8pm Tue-Sat Apr-Sep, to 6.30pm Oct-Mar, 10am-3pm Sun) This museum has a lovely patio and a good selection of paintings, including a set of the apostles by El Greco, a Zurbarán, and works by El Greco's son and various followers. Entry is free on Saturday after 2pm and all day Sunday.

EATING & DRINKING

Of Toledo's specialties, *cuchifritos* (a pot-pourri of lamb, tomato and egg cooked in white wine with saffron) is especially good, while *carcamusa* (a pork dish) is also popular. Otherwise, it's good, hearty Castilian fare.

TOP CHOICE **ALFILERITOS 24** MODERN SPANISH €€

(www.alfileritos24.com; Calle de los Alfileritos 24; mains €15-21, bar food €6-11; ⏲bar food 9.30am-midnight, to 1am Fri & Sat) The 14th-century surroundings of columns, beams and

EL GRECO IN TOLEDO

Few artists are as closely associated with a city as El Greco is with Toledo. Born in Crete in 1541, Domenikos Theotokopoulos (El Greco; the Greek) moved to Venice in 1567 to be schooled as a Renaissance artist. Under the tutelage of masters such as Tintoretto, he learned to express dramatic scenes with few colours, concentrating the observer's interest in the faces of his portraits and leaving the rest in relative obscurity, a characteristic that remained one of his hallmarks.

El Greco came to Spain in 1577 hoping to get a job decorating El Escorial, but Felipe II rejected him as a court artist. In Toledo, the painter managed to cultivate a healthy clientele and command good prices. He had to do without the patronage of the cathedral administrators, who were the first of many clients to haul him to court for his obscenely high fees.

As Toledo's fortunes declined, so did El Greco's personal finances, and although the works of his final years are among his best, he often found himself unable to pay the rent. He died in 1614, leaving his works scattered about the city.

Toledo

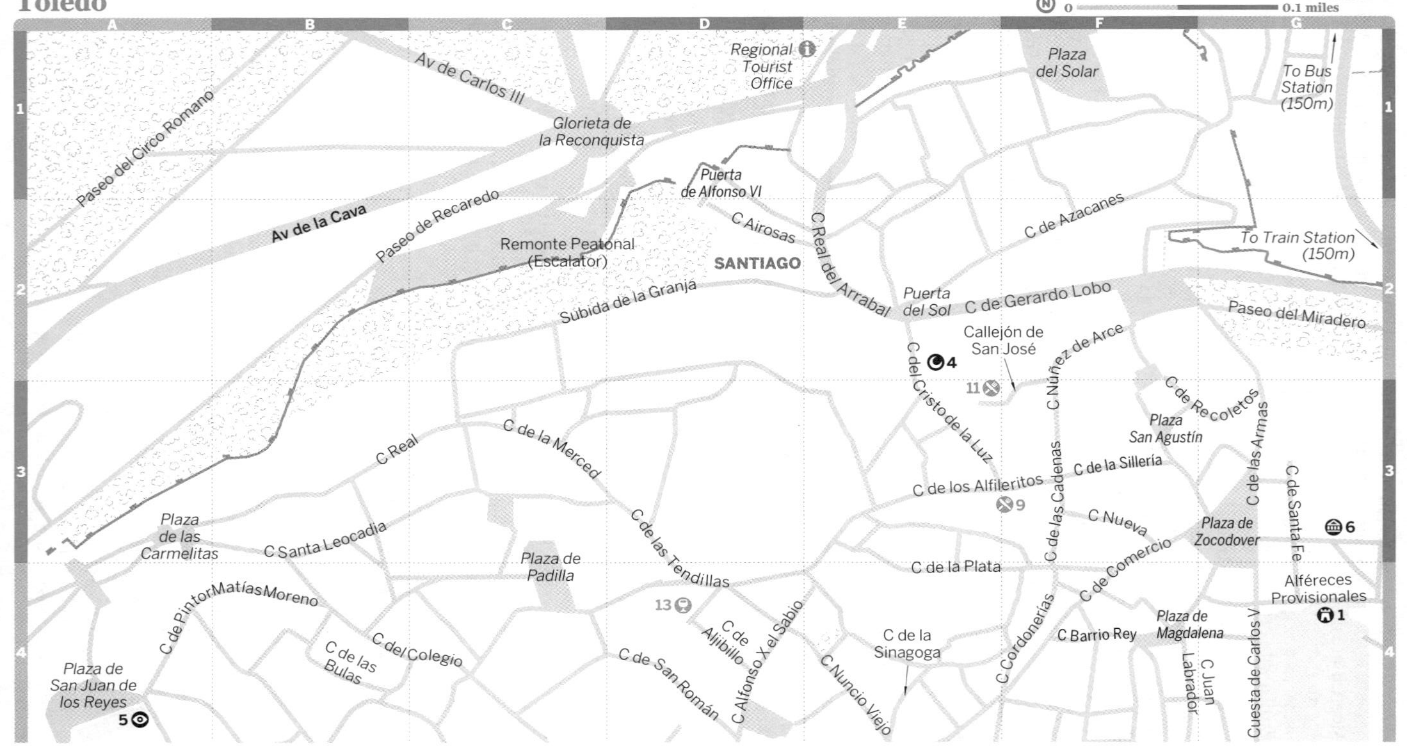
200 m
0.1 miles
Paseo del Circo Romano
Av de Carlos III
Glorieta de la Reconquista
Regional Tourist Office
Plaza del Solar
To Bus Station (150m)
Av de la Cava
Paseo de Recaredo
Puerta de Alfonso VI
C Airosas
C Real del Arrabal
C de Azacanes
To Train Station (150m)
Remonte Peatonal (Escalator)
SANTIAGO
Subida de la Granja
Puerta del Sol
C de Gerardo Lobo
Paseo del Miradero
Callejón de San José
C Núñez de Arce
C del Cristo de la Luz
C de Recoletos
Plaza San Agustín
C de las Armas
C Real
C de la Merced
C de la Sillería
C de los Alfileritos
C de las Cadenas
C de Santa Fe
C Nueva
Plaza de Zocodover
Plaza de las Carmelitas
C Santa Leocadia
Plaza de Padilla
C de las Tendillas
C de la Plata
C de Comercio
Alféreces Provisionales
C de Pintor Matías Moreno
C de Aljibillo
C Alfonso X el Sabio
C de la Sinagoga
C Cordonerías
C Barrio Rey
Plaza de Magdalena
C del Colegio
C de las Bulas
C de San Román
C Nuncio Viejo
C Juan Labrador
Cuesta de Carlos V
Plaza de San Juan de los Reyes

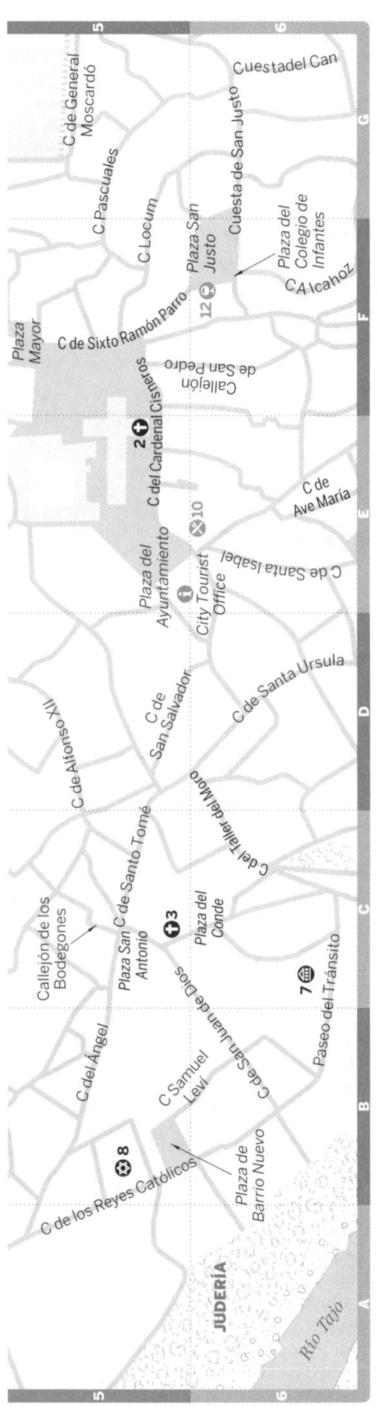

Toledo

Sights

1	Alcázar	G4
2	Catedral	E5
3	Iglesia de Santo Tomé	C5
4	Mezquita del Cristo de la Luz	E2
5	Monasterio San Juan de los Reyes	A4
6	Museo de Santa Cruz	G3
7	Museo del Greco	C6
8	Sinagoga de Santa María La Blanca	B5

Eating

9	Alfileritos 24	F3
10	Casa Aurelio	E6
11	Hierbabuena	E3

Drinking & Nightlife

12	Enebro	F6
13	Lúpulo	D4

barrel-vault ceilings are coupled with modern artwork and bright dining rooms in an atrium space spread over four floors. The menu demonstrates an innovative flourish in the kitchen, with dishes like loins of venison with baked-in-the-bag Reineta apple.

HIERBABUENA SPANISH

(☎925 22 39 24; www.restaurantehierbabuena.com; Callejón de San José 17; meals €35-40; ⊙lunch & dinner Mon-Sat, lunch only Sun) Classy Hierbabuena is a dress-for-dinner restaurant serving food that's a cut above the usual traditional cooking with plenty of steaks, pâté and artichokes stuffed with Catalan sausages and creamed leeks.

CASA AURELIO SPANISH **€€€**

(☎925 22 77 16; www.casa-aurelio.com; Plaza del Ayuntamiento 4; mains €21-24; ⊙lunch & dinner Tue-Sat, lunch Mon) The three restaurants under this name are among the best of Toledo's traditional eateries (the other branches are Calle de la Sinagoga 1 and 6). Game, fresh produce and time-honoured dishes are prepared with panache.

ENEBRO BAR

(www.barenebro.com; Plaza San Justo 9; ⊙8am-midnight Mon-Fri, noon-1am Sat & Sun) Ease into your evening with a drink under the trees in this pretty square, enjoying generous complimentary tapas and Hendrix (or similar) on the sound system.

LÚPULO BAR

(☎925 25 71 36; Calle de Aljibillo 5) Serves more than 50 Spanish and foreign beers, and has a popular spill-over outdoor terrace.

Segovia

Explore

Amid the rolling hills of Castile, Segovia is a year-round, 24-hour destination. In the mornings and afternoons, Segovia goes quietly about its business with a steady stream of visitors animating the city's beautiful (and largely pedestrianised) streets. One time not to miss is the last couple of hours before sunset, best enjoyed from the gardens close to the Alcázar entrance. And if you're here after dark, the winking lights of the old town framed by the aqueduct (sometimes floodlit, sometimes not) are rather lovely.

One other issue of timing to remember is that the city's restaurants are frequently booked out on winter weekends for lunch when people flock from all over the region (including Madrid) in search of *cochinillo asado* (roast suckling pig). If you plan to join them, you'll need a reservation.

The Best

- **Sight** Alcázar (p160)
- **Place to Eat** Casa Duque (p161)
- **Place to Drink** La Tasquina (p161)

Top Tip

Unless you're in a hurry, consider taking the slow train back. From Segovia it climbs up through the villages of the Sierra de Guadarrama foothills, then down to Madrid.

Getting There & Away

Bus Services by **La Sepulvedana** (☎902 119 699; www.lasepulvedana.es) leave every half-hour from Madrid's Intercambiador de Príncipe Pío (platforms 6 and 7) and arrive in Segovia's central bus station 1¼ hours later. Tickets cost €6.70.

Train There are two options by train, both operated by **Renfe** (☎902 240 202; www.renfe.es). Up to nine normal trains run daily from Madrid to Segovia (one way €7.70, two hours), leaving you at the main train station 2.5km from the aqueduct. The faster option is the high-speed AVE (one way €12.20, 28 minutes), which deposits you at the new Segovia-Guiomar station, 5km from the aqueduct.

Need to Know

- **Location** 90km northwest of Madrid
- **Tourist Office** (Centro de Recepción de Visitantes; ☎921 466 720; www.turismodesegovia.com; Plaza del Azoguejo 1; ⌚10am-8pm)
- **Regional Tourist Office** (www.segoviaturismo.es; Plaza Mayor 10; ⌚9am-8pm Sun-Thu, 9am-9pm Fri & Sat)

SIGHTS

ALCÁZAR CASTLE

(www.alcazardesegovia.com; Plaza de la Reina Victoria Eugenia; adult/child €4/3, tower €2, EU citizens free 3rd Tue of month; ⌚10am-7pm Apr-Sep) Rapunzel towers, turrets topped with slate witches hats and a deep moat at its base make the Alcázar a prototype fairy-tale castle, so much so that its design inspired Walt Disney's vision of Sleeping Beauty's castle. Fortified since Roman days, the site takes its name from the Arabic *al-qasr* (fortress) and what you see today is an evocative, over-the-top reconstruction of the original. Highlights include the **Sala de las Piñas**, and the **Sala de Reyes**, featuring a three-dimensional frieze of 52 sculptures of Spanish kings. The views from the summit of the **Torre de Juan II** are truly exceptional.

ACUEDUCTO AQUEDUCT

Segovia's most recognisable symbol is El Acueducto, an 894m-long engineering wonder. First raised here by the Romans in the 1st century AD, the aqueduct was built with not a drop of mortar to hold the more than 20,000 uneven granite blocks together. It's made up of 163 arches and, at its highest point in Plaza del Azoguejo, rises 28m high. It was most probably built around AD 50 as part of a complex system of aqueducts and underground canals that brought water from the mountains more than 15km away. By some accounts, it once reached as far as the Alcázar.

CATEDRAL CATHEDRAL

(Plaza Mayor; adult/concession €3/2; ⌚9.30am-6.30pm) Started in 1525 after its Romanesque predecessor had burned to the ground in the War of the Communities, Segovia's cathedral is a final, powerful expression of Gothic architecture in Spain that took almost 200 years to complete. The austere three-nave interior is anchored by an imposing choir stall and enlivened by 20-odd chapels. One of these, the **Capilla del Cristo del Consuelo**, which leads into the cloister, houses a magnificent Romanesque doorway preserved from the original church. The **Capilla del Cristo Yacente** (with its fine ceiling) and **Capilla del Santísimo Sacramento** are also especially beautiful. The Gothic cloister is lovely.

PLAZA MAYOR SQUARE

(Plaza Mayor) The shady Plaza Mayor is the nerve centre of old Segovia, lined by an eclectic assortment of buildings, arcades and cafes and an open pavilion in its centre. It's also the site of the *catedral* and the tourist office. The road connecting Plaza Mayor and the aqueduct is a pedestrian thoroughfare that locals know simply as Calle Real.

PLAZA DE SAN MARTÍN SQUARE

This is one of the most captivating small plazas in Segovia. The square is presided over by a statue of Juan Bravo, the 14th-century **Torreón de Lozoya** (admission free; ⌚5-9pm Tue-Fri, noon-2pm & 5-9pm Sat & Sun), a tower that now houses exhibitions, and the **Iglesia de San Martín** (Plaza de San Martín; ⌚before & after Mass), a pièce de Romanesque résistance with its Mudéjar tower and arched gallery. The interior boasts a Flemish Gothic chapel.

IGLESIA DE VERA CRUZ CHURCH

(Carretera de Zamarramala; admission €1.75; ⌚10.30am-1.30pm & 4-7pm Tue-Sun, closed Nov) This 12-sided church is the most interesting of Segovia's churches, and one of the best-preserved of its kind in Europe. Built in the early 13th century by the Knights Templar and based on Jerusalem's Church of the Holy Sepulchre, it once housed a piece of the Vera Cruz (True Cross), now in the nearby village church of Zamarramala (on view only at Easter). For fantastic views of the town and the Sierra de Guadarrama, walk uphill behind the church for approximately 1km.

EATING & DRINKING

If you love your meat, you'll love Segovia. People come here from all over Spain for delicious *cochinillo asado* and *asado de cordero* (roasted lamb). Reservations are highly recommended, especially on weekends.

TOP CHOICE **CASA DUQUE** GRILL **€€€**

(☎921 46 24 87; www.restauranteduque.es; Calle de Cervantes 12; set menus €21-40, meals €25-35) *Cochinillo asado* has been served here since the 1890s. For the uninitiated, try the *menú segoviano* (€30), which includes *cochinillo,* or the *menú gastronómico* (€43.50). Downstairs is the informal *cueva* (cave), where you can order tapas and *cazuelas* (stews). Reservations recommended.

TOP CHOICE **RESTAURANTE EL FOGÓN SEFARDÍ** SEPHARDIC **€€€**

(☎921 46 62 50; www.lacasamudejar.com; Calle de Isabel la Católica 8; meals €30-40) This is one of the most original places in town. Sephardic cuisine is served either on the intimate patio or in the splendid dining hall with original 15th-century Mudéjar flourishes. The theme in the bar is equally diverse with dishes from all the continents, and some fabulous set menus. Downstairs, the tapas are similarly creative. Reservations recommended.

MESÓN JOSÉ MARÍA CASTILIAN **€€**

(www.rtejosemaria.com; Calle del Cronista Lecea 11; mains €14-26) Offers great tapas in the bar and its five dining rooms serve exquisite *cochinillo asado* and other local specialities.

MESÓN DE CÁNDIDO GRILL **€€€**

(☎921 42 81 03; www.mesondecandido.es; Plaza del Azoguejo 5; meals €30-40) Set in a delightful 18th-century building in the shadow of the aqueduct, Mesón de Cándido is famous throughout Spain for its *cochinillo asado* and the more unusual roast boar with apple. Reservations recommended.

LA TASQUINA WINE BAR

(Calle de Valdeláguila 3; ⌚9pm-late) This wine bar draws crowds large enough to spill out onto the pavement nursing their good wines, *cavas* (sparkling wines) and cheeses.

Ávila

Explore

You wouldn't come to Ávila for the nightlife, but the view of the floodlit walls is worth waiting around for before catching the train or bus back to Madrid. The eerily quiet, lamplit streets within the walls after dark also speak strongly of magic.

By day, the sense of a somnambulent provincial town is palpable – head outside the walls to Plaza de Santa Teresa for a more animated slice of local life.

Ávila is one of the best places in Castilla y León to watch the solemn processions of Easter, so it's worth planning to be here at this time if you're in the area. It all begins on Holy Thursday and the most evocative event is the early morning Good Friday procession which circles the city wall beginning around 5am.

The Best

➡ **Sight** Murallas (p162)

➡ **Place to Eat** Hostería Las Cancelas (p163)

➡ **Place to Drink** La Bodeguita de San Segundo (p164)

Top Tip

Ávila is one of the coldest and windiest cities in Spain and winter snow is always a possibility. If you're coming in winter, come prepared.

Getting There & Away

Bus Up to nine buses (fewer on weekends) connect Madrid's Estación Sur and Ávila (1½ hours, €8). Contact the **bus station** (☎920 25 65 05; Avenida de Madrid 2) for more information.

Train The company **Renfe** (☎902 240 202; www.renfe.es) runs up to 30 trains to Ávila daily. The trip takes up to two hours (one way from €6.80).

Need to Know

➡ **Location** 101km west of Madrid

➡ **Tourist Office Tourist Office** (Centro de Recepción de Visitantes; ☎920 22 59 69; www.avilaturismo.com; Avenida de Madrid 39; ⏲10am-6pm Nov-Mar, 9am-8pm Apr-Oct)

MURALLAS WALLS

(adult/child €4/2.50; ⏲10am-8pm Tue-Sun) Raised to a height of 12m, Ávila's splendid 12th-century walls (with 88 watchtowers and more than 2500 turrets) stretch for 2.5km atop the remains of earlier Roman and Muslim battlements. Two sections of the walls can be climbed – a 300m stretch that can be accessed from just inside the Puerta del Alcázar, and a longer 1300m stretch that runs the length of the old city's northern perimeter, in the process connecting the two access points at **Puerta de los Leales** and **Puerta del Puente Adaja**. The last tickets are sold at 7.15pm. The regional tourist office runs free guided tours.

CATEDRAL CATHEDRAL

(Plaza de la Catedral; admission €4; ⏲10am-7.30pm Mon-Fri, 10am-8pm Sat, noon-6.30pm Sun) Ávila's 12th-century cathedral is at once a house of worship and an ingenious fortress: its stout granite apse forms the central bulwark in the heavily fortified eastern wall of the old city. The interior boasts an exquisite altar painting and stunning ochre-stained limestone columns and cantilevered ceilings in the side aisles. Off the fine cloisters, a small museum contains a painting by El Greco and a splendid silver monstrance by Juan de Arfe.

EL MONASTERIO DE SANTO TOMÁS MONASTERY

(☎920 22 04 00; Plaza de Granada 1; admission €3; ⏲10am-1pm & 4-8pm) Commissioned by the Reyes Católicos (Catholic Monarchs), Fernando and Isabel, and completed in 1492, this monastery is an exquisite example of Isabelline architecture. Three interconnected cloisters lead up to the church that contains the alabaster tomb of Don Juan, the monarchs' only son. The magnificent choir stalls are accessible from the upper level of the third cloister, the Claustro de los Reyes. It's thought that the Grand Inquisitor Torquemada is buried in the sacristy.

MONASTERIO DE LA ENCARNACIÓN MONASTERY

(Calle de la Encarnación; admission €2; ⏲9.30am-1.30pm & 3.30-6pm Mon-Fri, 10am-1pm & 4-6pm Sat & Sun) North of the city walls, this unadorned Renaissance monastery is where Santa Teresa fully took on the monastic life and lived for 27 years. There are three

IN THE FOOTSTEPS OF SANTA TERESA

Probably the most important woman in the history of the Catholic church in Spain, Santa Teresa spent most of her life in Ávila.

Teresa de Cepeda y Ahumada – a Catholic mystic and reformer – was born in Ávila on 28 March 1515, one of 10 children of a merchant family. Raised by Augustinian nuns after her mother's death, she joined the Carmelite order at age 20. After her early, undistinguished years as a nun, she was shaken by a vision of Hell in 1560, which crystallised her true vocation: she would reform her order.

With the help of many supporters Teresa founded convents of the Carmelitas Descalzas (Shoeless Carmelites) all over Spain. Santa Teresa's writings were first published in 1588 and proved enormously popular, perhaps partly for their earthy style. She died in 1582 in Alba de Tormes, where she is buried. She was canonised by Pope Gregory XV in 1622.

main rooms open to the public. The most interesting is the third (up the stairs where the saint is said to have had a vision of the baby Jesus), where you'll find relics such as the piece of wood used by Teresa as a pillow. To reach here, head north from Plaza de Fuente el Sol, via Calle de la Encarnación, for approximately 500m.

BASÍLICA DE SAN VICENTE CHURCH

(Plaza de San Vicente; admission €2; ⌚10am-6.30pm Mon-Sat, 4-6pm Sun) This graceful church is a masterpiece of Romanesque simplicity: a series of largely Gothic modifications in sober granite contrast with the warm sandstone of the Romanesque original. Work started in the 11th century, supposedly on the site where three martyrs – San Vicente and his sisters – were slaughtered by the Romans in the early 4th century.

FREE CONVENTO DE SANTA TERESA MUSEUM

(⌚8.45am-1.30pm & 3.30-9pm Tue-Sun) Built in 1636 over the saint's birthplace, this is the epicentre of the cult surrounding Santa Teresa. There are three attractions in one here: the church, a relics room and museum. Inside the main church, to the left of the main altar, the room where Teresa was born in 1515 is now a chapel smothered in gold and lorded over by a baroque altar.

IGLESIA DE SANTO TOMÉ EL VIEJO CHURCH, MUSEUM

(Plaza de Italia; incl Museo Provincial €1.20, Sat & Sun free; ⌚10am-2pm & 5-8pm Tue-Sat, 10am-2pm Sun) This church dates from the 13th century, and it was from this pulpit that Santa Teresa was castigated most vehemently for her reforms. It has been restored to house mostly Roman foundation stones and a splendid floor mosaic.

LOS CUATRO POSTES VIEWPOINT

Northwest of the city, on the road to Salamanca, this viewpoint provides the best views of Ávila's walls. It also marks the place where Santa Teresa and her brother were caught by their uncle as they tried to run away from home (they were hoping to achieve martyrdom at the hands of the Muslims). The best views are at night.

EATING & DRINKING

Ávila is famous for its *chuleton de avileño* (T-bone steak) and *judias del barco de Ávila* (white beans, usually with chorizo, in a thick sauce).

TOP CHOICE HOSTERÍA LAS CANCELAS CASTILIAN €€

(☎920 21 22 49; www.lascancelas.com; Calle de la Cruz Vieja 6; mains €16-25; ⌚Feb-Dec) This courtyard restaurant occupies a delightful interior patio dating back to the 15th century; across the road, the summer-only terrace occupies part of a former cathedral courtyard. Traditional meals are prepared here with a salutary attention to detail; the *solomillo con salsa al ron y nueces* (sirloin in a rum and walnut sauce) is a rare deviation from tradition. Reservations recommended.

RESTAURANTE REYES CATÓLICOS CASTILIAN €€

(www.restaurante-reyescatolicos.com; Calle de los Reyes Católicos 6; set menu €16, mains €16-24)

WORTH A DETOUR

ARANJUEZ & CHINCHÓN

Aranjuez was founded as a royal pleasure retreat, away from the riff-raff of Madrid, and it remains a place to escape the rigours of city life. The **Palacio Real** (☎91 891 07 40; www.patrimonionacional.es; palace adult/concession €9/4, guide/audioguide €6/4, EU citizens free 5-8pm Wed & Thu, gardens free; ⊙palace 10am-8pm Tue-Sun Apr-Sep, 10am-6pm Tue-Sun Oct-Mar, gardens 8am-9.30pm mid-Jun–mid-Aug, reduced hours mid-Aug–mid-Jun) started as one of Felipe II's modest summer palaces but took on a life of its own as a succession of royals lavished money upon it. The obligatory guided tour (in Spanish) provides insight into the palace's art and history. In the lush gardens, you'll find the Casa de Marinos, which contains the **Museo de Falúas** (admission €3; ⊙10am-4pm Oct-Mar, to 6.15pm Apr-Sep), a museum of royal pleasure boats from days gone by. The 18th-century neoclassical **Casa del Labrador** (☎91 891 03 05; adult/child, senior or student €5/2.50; ⊙10am-6pm Tue-Sun Apr-Sep, to 5pm Tue-Sun Oct-Mar) is also worth a visit. If you're here for lunch, try the Michelin-starred **Casa José** (☎91 891 14 88; www.casajose.es; Calle de Abastos 32; mains €20-30, set menus €63-74; ⊙lunch & dinner Tue-Sat, lunch Sun). Aranjuez is accessible from Madrid aboard C3 *cercanía* (local trains serving suburbs and nearby towns) that leave every 15 or 20 minutes from Madrid's Atocha station (€3.20).

Another fine day trip is to Chinchón, just 45km from Madrid yet worlds away. Visiting here is like stepping back into a charming, ramshackle past, with most of the appeal concentrated around the glorious **Plaza Mayor**. The pick of the restaurants serving roasted meats surrounding the square is **Café de la Iberia** (☎91 894 08 47; www.cafedelaiberia.com; Plaza Mayor 17; mains €13-22). To get here, the La Veloz bus 337 leaves half-hourly to Chinchón from Avenida del Mediterráneo in Madrid, 100m west of Plaza del Conde de Casal. The 50-minute ride costs €3.35.

Fronted by a popular tapas bar, this place has bright decor and an accomplished kitchen that churns out traditional dishes that benefit from a creative tweak. Its range of set menus includes the stellar *menú degustacion cocina tradicional de Ávila* (tasting menu of traditional Ávila cooking, €12).

POSADA DE LA FRUTA CASTILIAN €

(www.posadadelafruta.com; Plaza de Pedro Dávila 8; bar mains €7.90-12.90, restaurant €10.90-19.80; ⊙bar lunch & dinner daily, restaurant lunch & dinner Wed-Mon) Simple tasty meals can be had in a light-filled, covered courtyard, while the traditional *comedor* (dining room) is typically all about hearty meat dishes offset by simple fresh salads. The unusual international meat dishes that include gazelle, kangaroo and eland are the standout here.

TOP CHOICE LA BODEGUITA DE SAN SEGUNDO WINE BAR

(www.vinoavila.com; Calle de San Segundo 19; ⊙11am-midnight Thu-Tue) Situated in the 16th-century Casa de la Misericordia, this superb wine bar is standing-room only most nights and more tranquil in the quieter afternoon hours. Its wine list is renowned throughout Spain with over 1000 wines to choose from, with tapas servings of cheeses and cured meats the perfect accompaniment.

LA TABERNA AFTER WORK BAR

(Calle del Tostado; ⊙4pm-2am Sun-Wed, to 3am Thu-Sat) A strange mix of underground medieval arches and the ambience of a wood-panelled British pub, this agreeable bar has an especially good range of gins.

Sleeping

Madrid has high-quality accommodation at prices that haven't been seen in the centre of other European capitals in decades. Five-star temples to good taste and a handful of buzzing hostels bookend a fabulous collection of midrange hotels; most of the latter are creative originals, blending high levels of comfort with an often-quirky sense of style.

Hotels

Madrid's accommodation scene has undergone something of a revolution in recent years. Central to this transformation has been the appearance of exciting new hotels all across the city centre, in the process crowding out what had for decades been a rather predictable collection of midrange and top-end places. The best of the old have survived, upgrading their facilities while adhering to old-style values of discretion and hospitality. They have been joined by utterly modern designer hotels that capture the essence of Spain's style revolution.

Many of these newcomers have taken the shells of charming traditional architecture and converted their interiors into chic, high-tech accommodation that blends the casual and the classy, two essential elements in the personality of contemporary Spain. These *hoteles con encanto* (hotels with charm) share the market with monuments to 21st-century fashions that seem to push the boundaries of design in ways that were once the preserve of Barcelona, that eternal rival up the road.

It's in the midrange price category that you'll find the best examples of this revolution. At reasonable prices, hotels in this category enable you to feel pampered without the price tag of a five-star hotel. And if the top end is your end of the market, you'll be able to choose between the grand old dames that are counted among Europe's elite of luxury hotels and newly minted boutique hotels.

Hostales

The Spanish *hostal* is a cross between a cheap hotel and a hostel and usually represents outstanding value. The better ones can be bright and spotless, with full en suite bathroom (*baño completo*), most often with a shower (*ducha*) rather than bathtub, usually a TV and air-conditioning and/or heating. Some are new and slick, but the overwhelming majority are family run, adhering to traditional old-style decor and old-style warmth.

Hostels

At the budget end of the market, Madrid has its share of hostel-style accommodation with multibed (usually bunk) dorms and busy communal areas. They're cheap, usually plugged in to the local nightlife scene and are terrific places to meet other travellers.

APARTMENTS

If you'll be in Madrid for more than a few days and you'd like the comfort and space of your own apartment, there are some options scattered around the city centre. Most of these have, in addition to bedrooms, a kitchen and an independent sitting room. Some are serviced (ie cleaned) daily and operate in much the same way as a hotel (although reception may not necessarily be in the same building).

Where to Stay

Neighbourhood	For	Against
Plaza Mayor & Royal Madrid	Walking distance to most attractions, as well as shopping and restaurants; good metro connections elsewhere	Can be noisy, although generally of night-time revellers rather than traffic
La Latina & Lavapiés	Excellent central location, combining medieval architecture with terrific restaurants and tapas bars	Uphill walk from the art galleries; can be noisy in the evening (less so later at night)
Sol, Santa Ana & Huertas	Close to most attractions and excellent eating, drinking and entertainment options	Possibly Madrid's noisiest neighbourhood with all-night revellers, especially on weekends; steep hills can test weary legs
El Retiro & the Art Museums	You're right next door (or just around the corner) from Madrid's big three art galleries	Traffic noise can be a problem; most restaurants at least a 10-minute walk away
Salamanca	Puts you in the heart of fantastic shopping and close to good eating options; quieter by night than most Madrid neighbourhoods	A decent walk from the rest of the city
Malasaña & Chueca	Lively streets and wonderful places to eat and drink; sense of Madrid beyond the tourist crowds; gay-friendly (Chueca)	Another noisy night-time neighbourhood
Parque del Oeste & Northern Madrid	Removed from clamour of downtown but a short metro ride away; immersion in local Madrid life	Attractions more thinly spread

Lonely Planet's Top Choices

Hotel Meninas (p168) Cool, classy and contemporary and right in the heart of the city.

Posada del Dragón (p169) Stunningly converted old inn along Madrid's best tapas street.

Hotel Puerta América (p174) Landmark hotel with rooms designed by world-famous architects.

Praktik Metropol (p169) New hotel with quirky decor, fine views and high levels of comfort.

Hotel Óscar (p173) Chueca landmark with central location and ultra-modern rooms.

Hotel Abalú (p172) Designer rooms with zany pop-art themes at reasonable prices.

Best Budget

Hostal Madrid (p168)

Chic & Basic Colors (p170)

Hostal Adriano (p170)

Cat's Hostel (p169)

Flat 5 Madrid (p173)

Hostal Luis XV (p170)

Best Midrange

Mario Room Mate (p168)

Antigua Posada del Pez (p172)

Hotel Plaza Mayor (p169)

Hotel El Pasaje (p171)

Petit Palace Posada del Peine (p168)

Best Top End

Hotel Ritz (p172)

Casa de Madrid (p168)

Westin Palace (p172)

Hotel AC Santo Mauro (p174)

Me by Melía (p170)

Best for Contemporary Cool

Hotel Urban (p169)

Me by Melía (p170)

Adler Hotel (p172)

Posada del León de Oro (p169)

Hotel Alicia (p170)

Best Hotel Chains

AC (www.ac-hoteles.com)

Hi Tech (www.hthoteles.com)

NH (www.nh-hotels.com)

Room Mate (www.room-matehoteles.com)

Vincci (www.vinccihoteles.com)

Best Dorms

Cat's Hostel (p169)

Mad Hostel (p169)

Los Amigos Sol Backpackers' Hostel (p168)

Albergue Juvenil (p173)

Best Apartments

Apartamentos Mayor Centro (p168)

Apartasol (p171)

NEED TO KNOW

Price Guide

Throughout this book, accommodation is listed according to *barrio* (district), then by author preference. Rate symbols are for a double room per night:

€ up to €75

€€ €75 to €200

€€€ more than €200

Room Rates & Reservations

Some places have separate prices for *temporada alta* (high season), *temporada media* (midseason) or *temporada baja* (low season), but in Madrid prices are more likely to vary on a daily basis according to occupancy, trade fairs and other major events.

Taxes

All accommodation prices have 10% IVA (value-added tax). When quoted a price, always ask: '*¿Está incluido el IVA?*' ('Is IVA included?').

Terminology

A *habitación doble* (double room) usually indicates a room with two single beds; cuddly couples should request a *cama de matrimonio* (literally, a marriage bed).

Useful Websites

Reserva Madrid (☎91 000 69 19; www.reservamadrid.com) Good for well-priced apartments.

Centro de Turismo de Madrid (www.esmadrid.com) Good overview of accommodation scene.

Lonelyplanet.com (http://hotels.lonelyplanet.com) For more reviews and bookings online.

Plaza Mayor & Royal Madrid

TOP CHOICE HOTEL MENINAS BOUTIQUE HOTEL €€
Map p234 (91 541 28 05; www.hotelmeninas.com; Calle de Campomanes 7; s/d from €99/119; ; MÓpera) This is a classy, cool choice. The colour scheme is black, white and grey, with dark-wood floors and splashes of fuchsia and lime-green. Flat-screen TVs in every room, sleek bathroom fittings and even a laptop in some rooms, round out the clean lines and latest innovations. We love the location as well and the value is extraordinary. We've yet to hear a bad word about this place, and past guests include Viggo Mortensen and Natalie Portman.

HOSTAL MADRID HOSTAL, APARTMENT €
Map p234 (91 522 00 60; www.hostal-madrid.info; Calle de Esparteros 6; s €35-55, d €45-75, d apt per night €55-150, per month €1200-2500; ; MSol) Economic crisis or no economic crisis, the 24 rooms at this well-run *hostal* have been wonderfully renovated with exposed brickwork, brand-new bathrooms and a look that puts many three-star hotels to shame. They also have terrific apartments (some recently renovated and ranging in size from 33 sq metres to 200 sq metres) with fully equipped kitchens, their own sitting area, bathroom and, in the case of the larger ones (room 51 on the 5th floor is one of the best), an expansive terrace with good views over the rooftops of Madrid. It's a favoured haunt of writers (Gunter Grass wrote one of his novels in room 53). Fabulous value all round. The apartments have a separate website – www.apartamentosmayorcentro.com.

CASA DE MADRID HOTEL €€€
Map p234 (91 559 57 91; www.casademadrid.com; 2nd fl, Calle de Arrieta 2; r from €100-340, ste from €370; ; MGran Vía) Refined, extravagantly decorated rooms make Casa de Madrid a luxurious choice overlooking the Teatro Real. The rooms, in an 18th-century building, are awash in antique furnishings and marble busts, with each built around a theme (eg Japan, India etc). It's a little like staying at the Ritz, but more discreet and the service is far more personal.

HOTEL PRECIADOS BUSINESS HOTEL €€
Map p234 (91 454 44 00; www.preciadoshotel.com; Calle de Preciados 37; d from €145; ; MSanto Domingo, Callao) With a classier feel than many of the other business options around town, the Preciados gets rave reviews for its service. Soft lighting, light shades and plentiful glass personalise the rooms and provide an intimate feel.

MARIO ROOM MATE BOUTIQUE HOTEL €€
Map p234 (91 548 85 48; www.room-matehoteles.com; Calle de Campomanes 4; s €80-125, d €100-150; ; MÓpera) Entering this swanky boutique hotel is like crossing the threshold of Madrid's latest nightclub – staff dressed all in black, black walls and swirls of red lighting in the lobby. Rooms can be small but with high ceilings and simple furniture, light tones contrasting smoothly with muted colours and dark surfaces; some rooms are pristine white, others have splashes of colour with zany murals.

HOTEL LAURA BOUTIQUE HOTEL €€
Map p234 (91 701 16 70; www.room-matehoteles.com; Travesía de Trujillos 3; d €90-200, apt €150-280; ; MSol or Ópera) Another fine offering from the Room Mate chain, Hotel Laura combines location with interiors that are the work of the famous interior designer Tomas Alia. It's all very slick, contemporary and colourful behind the somewhat staid facade.

PETIT PALACE POSADA DEL PEINE BOUTIQUE HOTEL €€
Map p234 (91 523 81 51; www.hthoteles.com; Calle de Postas 17; r from €120; ; MSol) This hotel combines a splendid historic building (dating to 1610), brilliant location (just 50m from the Plaza Mayor) and modern hi-tech rooms. The bathrooms sparkle with stunning fittings and hydromassage showers, and the rooms are beautifully appointed; many historical architectural features remain in situ in the public areas. It's just a pity some of the rooms aren't larger.

LOS AMIGOS SOL BACKPACKERS' HOSTEL HOSTEL €
Map p234 (91 559 24 72; www.losamigoshostel.com; 4th fl, Calle de Arenal 26; dm incl breakfast €17-19; @; MÓpera, Sol) If you arrive in Madrid keen for company, this could be the place for you – lots of students stay here, the staff are savvy (and speak English) and there are bright dorm-style rooms (with

free lockers) that sleep from two to four people. There's also a kitchen for guests. A steady stream of repeat visitors is the best recommendation we can give.

La Latina & Lavapiés

TOP CHOICE POSADA DEL DRAGÓN BOUTIQUE HOTEL €€

Map p232 (☎91 119 14 24; www.posadadeldragon.com; Calle de la Cava Baja 14 ; r from €91; ; MLa Latina) At last, a boutique hotel in the heart of La Latina. This restored 19th-century inn sits on one of our favourite streets in Madrid and rooms either look out over the street or over the pretty internal patio. The rooms? Bold, brassy colour schemes and designer everything distract (for the most part) from the fact that some rooms are on the small side. There's a terrific bar-restaurant downstairs.

POSADA DEL LEÓN DE ORO BOUTIQUE HOTEL €€

Map p232 (☎91 119 14 94; www.posadadelleondeoro.com; Calle de la Cava Baja 12; r from €121; ; MLa Latina) Next door to Posada del Dragón and a similarly spectacular place, this rehabilitated inn has muted colour schemes and generally large rooms. There's a *corrala* (traditional internal or communal patio) in its core, and thoroughly modern rooms along one of Madrid's best-loved streets. The downstairs bar is terrific.

CAT'S HOSTEL HOSTEL €

Map p231 (☎91 369 28 07; www.catshostel.com; Calle de Cañizares 6; dm €15-20; @; MAntón Martín) Forming part of a 17th-century palace, the internal courtyard here is one of Madrid's finest – lavish Andalucian tilework, a fountain, a spectacular glass ceiling and stunning Islamic decoration, surrounded on four sides by an open balcony. There's a supercool basement bar with free internet and fiestas, often with live music.

MAD HOSTEL HOSTEL €

Map p231 (☎91 506 48 40; www.madhostel.com; Calle de la Cabeza 24; dm €17-23; @; MAntón Martín) From the people who brought you Cat's Hostel, Mad Hostel is similarly filled with life. The 1st-floor courtyard – with retractable roof – recreates an old Madrid *corrala* and is a wonderful place to chill, while the four- to eight-bed rooms are smallish but clean. There's a small rooftop gym.

HOSTAL HORIZONTE HOSTEL €

Map p231 (☎91 369 09 96; www.hostalhorizonte.com; 2nd fl, Calle de Atocha 28; s with/without bathroom €40/29, d €55/44; ; MAntón Martín) Billing itself as a hostel run by travellers for travellers, Hostal Horizonte is a well-run place. The rooms have far more character than your average hostel, with high ceilings, deliberately old-world furnishings and modern bathrooms. The King Alfonso XII room (€72) is especially well presented.

Sol, Santa Ana & Huertas

TOP CHOICE PRAKTIK METROPOL BOUTIQUE HOTEL €€

Map p242 (☎91 521 29 35; www.hotelpraktikmetropol.com; Calle de la Montera 47; s/d from €65/79; ; MGran Vía) You'd be hard-pressed to find better value anywhere in Europe than here in this recently overhauled hotel. The rooms have a fresh, contemporary look with white wood furnishings and some (especially the corner rooms) have brilliant views down to Gran Vía and out over the city. It's spread over six floors and there's a roof terrace if you don't have a room with a view.

HOTEL URBAN LUXURY HOTEL €€€

Map p242 (☎91 787 77 70; www.derbyhotels.com; Carrera de San Jerónimo 34; r from €225; ; MSevilla) This towering glass edifice is the epitome of art-inspired designer cool. With its clean lines and original artworks from Africa and Asia (there's a small museum dedicated to Egyptian art in the basement), it's a wonderful antidote to the more classic charm of Madrid's five-star hotels of longer standing. Dark-wood floors and dark walls are offset by plenty of light, while the dazzling bathrooms have wonderful designer fittings – the washbasins are sublime. The rooftop swimming pool is one of Madrid's best and the gorgeous terrace is heaven on a candle-lit summer's evening. If money were no object, we would need a good reason to stay anywhere else.

HOTEL PLAZA MAYOR HOTEL €€

Map p242 (☎91 360 06 06; www.h-plazamayor.com; Calle de Atocha 2; s/d from €55/85; ; MSol, Tirso de Molina) We love this place. Sitting just across from the Plaza Mayor, here you'll find stylish decor, charming original elements of this 150-year-old building and helpful staff. The rooms are attractive, some with a light colour scheme and wrought-iron furniture. The attic rooms (doubles from €130) boast dark wood and designer lamps, and have lovely little terraces with wonderful rooftop views of central Madrid.

CHIC & BASIC COLORS HOTEL €

Map p242 (☎91 429 69 35; www.chicandbasic.com; 2nd fl, Calle de las Huertas 14; r €50-75; ; MAntón Martín) At this little hotel/hostel they claim to have Madrid's most colourful rooms. The rooms are white in a minimalist style with flat-screen TVs, dark hardwood floors with a bright colour scheme superimposed on top, with every room a different shade. It's all very comfortable, contemporary and casual. Only three of the rooms look out onto the street, but those on the inside of the building don't feel quite as claustrophobic as in some places. Prices increase on Friday and Saturday and they sometimes require a two-night minimum stay on weekends. It also has some apartments in the same building and the slightly more upmarket hotel **Chic & Basic Atocha** (Map p246; ☎91 369 28 95; Calle de Atocha 113; s/d from €80/100; ; MAntón Martín).

HOTEL ALICIA BOUTIQUE HOTEL €€

Map p242 (☎91 389 60 95; www.room-mate hoteles.com; Calle del Prado 2; d €100-175, ste from €200; ; MSol, Sevilla, Antón Martín) One of the landmark properties of the designer Room Mate chain of hotels, Hotel Alicia overlooks Plaza de Santa Ana with beautiful, spacious rooms. The style (the work of designer Pascua Ortega) is a touch more muted than in other Room Mate hotels, but the supermodern look remains intact, the downstairs bar is oh-so-cool, and the service is young and switched on. Two of the duplex suites have their own terrace with a small private pool.

HOTEL DE LAS LETRAS HOTEL €€

Map p242 (☎91 523 79 80; www.hoteldelasletras.com; Gran Vía 11; d from €100; MGran Vía) If you want to cause a stir in Madrid with a new hotel, make sure it has a rooftop bar overlooking the city. They're all the rage, and Hotel de las Letras started the craze. The bar's wonderful, but the entire hotel is excellent, with individually styled rooms, each with literary quotes from famous writers written on the walls. We don't always get the colour scheme – it may just come down to personal taste. The building dates from 1917 and the public areas retain original features, including mosaic tiles.

HOTEL SENATOR HOTEL €€

Map p242 (☎91 531 41 51; www.playasenator.com; Gran Vía 21; s/d from €95/113; ; MGran Vía) One of central Madrid's prettiest facades conceals some of the most attractive accommodation in the city centre. Unusually, only one room on each floor doesn't face onto the street, and the views down Gran Vía from the corner rooms are brilliant. Rooms are sophisticated and come with armchairs and, wait for it, reclinable beds. Room rates vary from day to day and when they drop they're Madrid's best bargain.

HOSTAL LUIS XV HOSTAL €

Map p242 (☎91 522 10 21; www.hrluisxv.net; Calle de la Montera 47, 8th fl; s/d from €45/59; ; MGran Vía) Everything here – especially the spacious rooms and the attention to detail – makes this family-run place feel pricier than it is. You'll find it hard to tear yourself away from the balconies outside every exterior room, from where the views are superb (especially from the triple in room 820) and you're so high up that noise is rarely a problem. When you come out the door, head left onto Gran Vía, rather than seedy Calle de la Montera. If full, try downstairs at its sister hostel, **Hostal Jerez** (Map p242; ☎91 532 90 73; www.hrjerez.net; 6th fl, Calle de la Montera 47), which has the same prices and similar views.

ME BY MELÍA LUXURY HOTEL €€€

Map p242 (☎91 701 60 00; www.memadrid.com; Plaza de Santa Ana 14; r from €179; ; MSol, Antón Martín) Once the landmark Gran Victoria Hotel, the Madrid home of many a famous bullfighter, this audacious new hotel is a landmark of a different kind. Overlooking the western end of Plaza de Santa Ana, this luxury hotel is decked out in minimalist white with curves and comfort in all the right places. This is one place where it's worth paying extra for the view, quite apart from the additional space that you'll have in the plaza-facing Supreme rooms.

HOSTAL ADRIANO HOSTAL €

Map p242 (☎91 521 13 39; www.hostaladriano.com; 4th fl, Calle de la Cruz 26; s/d €49/60; ; MSol) They don't come any better than this bright and friendly hostel wedged in the streets that mark the boundary between Sol and Huertas. Most rooms are well sized and each has its own colour scheme. Indeed, more thought has gone into the decoration than in your average hostel, from the bed covers to the pictures on the walls. On the same floor, the owners run the **Hostal Adria Santa Ana** (Map p242; www.hostaladriasantaana.com; 4th fl, Calle de la Cruz 26; s/d €59/68; ❄📶), which is a step up in price, style and comfort. Both *hostales* drop their prices in summer.

HOSTAL ACAPULCO HOSTAL €

Map p242 (☎91 531 19 45; www.hostalacapulco.com; 4th fl, Calle de la Salud 13; s/d €55/65; ❄📶; MGran Vía) A cut above many other hostels in Madrid, this immaculate little *hostal* has marble floors, recently renovated bathrooms (with bathtubs), double-glazed windows and comfortable beds. Street-facing rooms have balconies overlooking a sunny plaza and are flooded with natural light. The staff are also friendly and always more than happy to help you plan your day in Madrid. There's also a coffee machine.

CATALONIA LAS CORTES HOTEL €€

Map p242 (☎91 389 60 51; www.hoteles-catalonia.es; Calle del Prado 6; s/d €170/180; ❄📶; MAntón Martín) Occupying an 18th-century palace and renovated in a style faithful to the era, this elegant hotel is a terrific choice right in the heart of Huertas. It's something of an oasis surrounded by the nonstop energy of the *barrio's* streets, and the service is discreet and attentive. It gets plenty of return visitors which is just about the best recommendation we can give.

HOTEL EL PASAJE HOTEL €€

Map p242 (☎91 521 29 95; www.elpasajehs.com; Calle del Pozo 4; r incl breakfast from €85; ❄📶; MSol) If you were to choose your ideal location in Huertas, Hotel El Pasaje would be hard to beat. Set on a quiet lane largely devoid of bars, yet just around the corner from the Plaza de la Puerta del Sol, it combines a central location with a quiet night's sleep, at least by the standards of Huertas. The feel is intimate and modern, with good bathrooms, minibars and enough space to leave your suitcase without tripping over it. The twins have balconies; the doubles are on the inside of the building.

SUITE PRADO HOTEL SUITES €€

Map p242 (☎91 420 23 18; www.suiteprado.com; Calle de Manuel Fernández y González 10; ste €99-180; ❄📶; MSevilla) The spacious modern suites at this centrally located hotel have plenty of space and are semiluxurious. All have sitting rooms, good bathrooms and kitchenettes.

HOTEL MIAU BOUTIQUE HOTEL €€

Map p242 (☎91 369 71 20; www.hotelmiau.com; Calle del Príncipe 26; s incl breakfast €50-85, d €60-105; ❄📶; MSol, Antón Martín) If you want to be close to the nightlife of Huertas or can't tear yourself away from the beautiful Plaza de Santa Ana, then Hotel Miau is your place. Light tones, splashes of colour and modern art adorn the walls of the rooms, which are large and well equipped. It can be noisy, but you chose Huertas...

HOSTAL SARDINERO HOSTAL €

Map p242 (☎91 429 57 56; www.hostalsardinero.com; Calle del Prado 16; d from €63; ❄@; MSol, Antón Martín) The cheerful rooms here have high ceilings, air-conditioning, a safe, hairdryers, comfortable mattresses and renovated bathrooms, and are complemented nicely by the owners who are attentive without being in your face. We especially like the light-filled room 5 (a triple), but all the rooms are well turned out.

APARTASOL APARTMENTS

(☎91 828 95 11; www.apartasol.com; apt per night €50-115) If you'll be in Madrid for more than a few days and you'd like the comfort and space of your own apartment, consider Apartasol. This traveller-friendly agency has well-equipped modern apartments scattered around the vicinity of the Puerta del Sol and Gran Vía. Prices are first-rate and there are discounts available for longer stays.

HOTEL EUROPA HOTEL €€

Map p242 (☎91 521 29 00; www.hoteleuropa.es; Calle del Carmen 4; s/d from €80/100; ❄📶; MSol) Around since 1917 but with tastefully renovated rooms, Hotel Europa combines excellent service with modern midrange comforts just a few steps from Puerta del Sol. Here you'll find all the benefits of the central location (including unrivalled convenience and a sense of Madrid's nonstop energy swirling around you) with few of its drawbacks – windows are double-glazed. You pay more for rooms that overlook the square.

El Retiro & the Art Museums

TOP CHOICE HOTEL RITZ LUXURY HOTEL €€€

Map p246 (☎91 701 67 67; www.ritzmadrid.com; Plaza de la Lealtad 5; d from €324, ste €850-5000; ❄☎; MBanco de España) The grand old lady of Madrid, the Hotel Ritz is the height of exclusivity. One of the most lavish buildings in the city, it has classic style and impeccable service that is second to none. Unsurprisingly it's the favoured hotel of presidents, kings and celebrities. The public areas are palatial and awash with antiques, while the rooms are extravagantly large, opulent and supremely comfortable. In the Royal Suite, the walls are covered with raw silk and there's a personal butler to wait upon you. We challenge you to find a more indulgent hotel experience anywhere in Spain.

WESTIN PALACE LUXURY HOTEL €€€

Map p246 (☎91 360 80 00; www.westinpalacemadrid.com; Plaza de las Cortes 7; d/ste from €289/600; ❄☎; MBanco de España, Antón Martín) An old Madrid classic, this former palace of the Duque de Lerma opened as a hotel in 1911 and was Spain's second luxury hotel. Ever since, it has looked out across Plaza de Neptuno at its rival, the Ritz, like a lover unjustly scorned. Its name may not have the world-famous cachet of the Ritz, but it's not called the Palace for nothing and is extravagant in all the right places. The 1999 renovations cost €144,000 per room... After the snooty Ritz banned actors and other public performers in the early 20th century, the Palace became the hotel of choice for celebrities – Mata Hari lived here during WWI and her ghost reportedly occupies the corridors, while Hemingway, Dalí and Lorca were all regulars in the cocktail bar.

HOTEL MORA HOTEL €

Map p246 (☎91 420 15 69; www.hotelmora.com; Paseo del Prado 32; s €60-71, d €66-74; ❄☎; MAtocha) Alongside the landmark Caixa Forum, close to the main museums and a short (uphill) walk from the city centre, this simple, friendly hotel is a well-located and extremely well-priced option. Rooms are a little sparse and the furnishings a little tired, but they're spacious and clean, and some look out across the Paseo del Prado.

Salamanca

ADLER HOTEL BOUTIQUE HOTEL €€€

Map p248 (☎91 426 32 20; www.adlermadrid.com; Calle de Velázquez 33; d/ste from €220/495; ❄☎; MVelázquez) A five-star boutique hotel at the intersection of two of Salamanca's iconic streets, the Adler combines classy and supremely comfortable rooms with near-faultless service. Room decor subscribes to a vaguely old-world elegance, but is light-filled and never stuffy.

PETIT PALACE ART GALLERY HOTEL €€

Map p248 (☎91 435 54 11; www.hthoteles.com; Calle de Jorge Juan 17; d from €135; ❄☎; MSerrano) Occupying a stately 19th-century Salamanca building, this landmark property of the Petit Palace chain is a lovely designer hotel that combines hi-tech facilities with an artistic aesthetic, with loads of original works dotted around the public spaces and even in some of the rooms. Hydromassage showers, laptop computers and exercise bikes in many rooms are just some of the extras, and the address is ideal for the best of Salamanca.

Malasaña

TOP CHOICE HOTEL ABALÚ BOUTIQUE HOTEL €€

Map p250 (☎91 531 47 44; www.hotelabalu.com; Calle del Pez 19; d/apt from €84/110; ❄☎; MNoviciado) You may love the mean streets of Malasaña, but that doesn't mean you want to sleep rough. Malasaña's very own boutique hotel is an oasis of style amid the *barrio's* timeworn feel. Suitably located on cool Calle del Pez, each room here has its own design drawn from the imagination of Luis Delgado, from retro chintz to Zen, baroque to pure white, and most aesthetics in between. Some of the suites have Jacuzzis and large-screen home cinemas. You're close to Gran Vía, but away from the tourist scrum.

ANTIGUA POSADA DEL PEZ HOTEL €€

Map p250 (☎91 531 42 96; www.antiguaposadadelpez.com; Calle de Pizarro 16; r €60-110; ❄☎; MNoviciado) If only all places to stay were this good. This place inhabits the shell of an historic Malasaña building, but the rooms are slick and contemporary with designer bathrooms. You're also just a few steps up the hill from Calle del Pez, one of Malasaña's most happening streets. It's an exceptionally good deal, even when prices head upwards.

FLAT 5 MADRID HOSTAL €

Map p250 (☎91 127 24 00; www.flat5madrid.com; 5th fl Calle de San Bernardo 55; r €60-100, without bathroom €34-50; ❄📶; Ⓜ Noviciado) Unlike so many other hostels in Madrid where the charm depends on a timeworn air, Flat 5 Madrid has a fresh, clean-lined look with bright colours, flat-screen TVs and flower boxes on the window sills. Even the rooms that face onto a patio have partial views over the rooftops. If the rooms and bathrooms were a little bigger, we'd consider moving in.

PETIT PALACE HOTEL DUCAL HOTEL €€

Map p250 (☎91 521 10 43; www.hthoteles.com; Calle de Hortaleza 3; d from €95; ❄📶; Ⓜ Gran Vía) Fusing elegant old buildings with state-of-the-art rooms and hi-tech facilities is the hallmark here. The rooms boast strong, contrasting colours, polished floorboards, clean lines, comfy beds and armchairs, and plenty of light and mirrors. Each room also has its own computer with free internet. Hydromassage showers are standard.

HOSTAL LA ZONA HOSTAL €

Map p250 (☎91 521 99 04; www.hostallazona.com; 1st fl Calle de Valverde 7; s/d incl breakfast €50/70; ❄📶; Ⓜ Gran Vía) Catering primarily to a gay clientele, the stylish Hostal La Zona has exposed brickwork, subtle colour shades and wooden pillars. We like a place where a sleep-in is encouraged – breakfast is served from 9am to noon, which is exactly the understanding Madrid's nightlife merits. Arnaldo and Vincent are friendly hosts.

HOSTAL AMÉRICA HOSTAL €

Map p250 (☎91 522 64 48; www.hostalamerica.net; Calle de Hortaleza 19, 5th fl; s/d €45/55; ❄📶; Ⓜ Gran Vía) Run by a lovely mother-son team, the América has superclean, spacious and IKEA-dominated rooms. As most rooms face onto the usual interior 'patio' of the building, you should get a good night's sleep despite the busy area. For the rest of the time, there's a roof terrace – quite a luxury for a hostal in downtown Madrid – with tables, chairs and a coffee machine.

ALBERGUE JUVENIL HOSTEL €

Map p254 (☎91 593 96 88; www.ajmadrid.es; Calle de Mejía Lequerica 21; dm incl breakfast €21-27; ❄@📶; Ⓜ Bilbao, Alonso Martínez) If you're looking for dormitory-style accommodation, you'd need a good reason to stay anywhere other than here while you're in Madrid. The Albergue has spotless rooms, no dorm houses more than six beds (each has its own bathroom), and facilities include a pool table, a gymnasium, wheelchair access, free internet, laundry and a TV/DVD room with a choice of movies. All the facilities are modern. Yes, there are places with more character or a more central location, but we'd still rate this as one of Madrid's best hostels for backpackers.

Chueca

TOP CHOICE HOTEL ÓSCAR BOUTIQUE HOTEL €€

Map p254 (☎91 701 11 73; www.room-matehoteles.com; Plaza de Vázquez de Mella 12; d €90-200, ste €150-280; ❄📶🏊; Ⓜ Gran Vía) Outstanding. Hotel Óscar belongs to the highly original Room Mate chain of hotels and the designer rooms ooze style and sophistication. Some have floor-to-ceiling murals, the lighting is always funky, and the colour scheme is asplash with pinks, lime greens, oranges or a more minimalist black and white. Like all Room Mate hotels, this one's themed around an individual personality, in this case Óscar, who describes himself as 'nocturnal, cosmopolitan and ready for anything'. There's a fine street-level tapas bar and a rooftop terrace.

HOSTAL DON JUAN HOSTAL €

Map p250 (☎tel/fax 91 522 31 01; Plaza de Vázquez de Mella 1, 2nd fl; s/d/tr €40/55/75; Ⓜ Gran Vía) Paying cheap rates for your room doesn't mean you can't be treated like a king. This elegant two-storey *hostal* is filled with original artworks and antique furniture that could grace a royal palace, although mostly it's restricted to the public areas. Rooms are large and simple but luminous; most have a street-facing balcony. The location is good, close to where Chueca meets Gran Vía.

HOSTAL SAN LORENZO HOTEL €

Map p254 (☎91 521 30 57; www.hotel-sanlorenzo.com; Calle de Clavel 8; s/d/tr from €40/50/70; ❄📶; Ⓜ Gran Vía) Hostal San Lorenzo is generally an excellent deal: original stone walls and some dark-wood beams from the 19th century in the public areas, and modern, comfortable and bright rooms (some with splashes of old-world charm) that you'll be more than happy to return to at the end of the day. Some of the rooms could be larger.

CASA CHUECA HOSTAL €

Map p254 (☎91 523 81 27; www.casachueca.com; 2nd fl, Calle de San Bartolomé 4; s/d from €45/60; 📶; Ⓜ Gran Vía) If you don't mind lugging your suitcase up to the 2nd floor, Casa Chueca is outstanding. The rooms are modern, colourful and a cut above your average *hostal*; in keeping with the *barrio* that it calls home, Casa Chueca places a premium on style. Add casual, friendly service and you'd be hard pressed to find a better price-to-quality ratio anywhere in central Madrid.

Parque del Oeste & Northern Madrid

TOP CHOICE HOTEL PUERTA AMÉRICA LUXURY HOTEL €€

(☎91 744 54 00; www.hoteles-silken.com; Avenida de América 41; d/ste from €125/250; P ❄ 📶; Ⓜ Cartagena) When the owners of this hotel saw its location – halfway between the city and the airport – they knew they had to do something special to build a self-contained world so innovative and luxurious that you'd never want to leave. Their idea? Give 22 of world architecture's most creative names (eg Zaha Hadid, Sir Norman Foster, Ron Arad, David Chipperfield, Jean Nouvel) a floor each to design. The result? An extravagant pastiche of styles, from zany montages of 1980s chic to bright-red bathrooms that feel like a movie star's dressing room. Even the bar ('a temple to the liturgy of pleasure'), restaurant, facade, gardens, public lighting and car park had their own architects. It's an extraordinary, astonishing place.

HOTEL AC SANTO MAURO HOTEL €€€

Map p238 (☎91 319 69 00; www.ac-hotels.com; Calle de Zurbano 36; d/ste from €225/450; ❄ 📶 🏊; Ⓜ Alonso Martínez) Everything about this recently renovated place oozes exclusivity and class, from the address – one of the elite patches of Madrid real estate – to the 19th-century mansion that's the finest in a *barrio* of many. It's a place of discreet elegance and warm service, and rooms are suitably lavish, with a predominantly modern aesthetic in some rooms and a more old-world look (with Persian carpets on the floor) in others; the Arabian-styled indoor pool isn't bad either. David Beckham, Madonna and Richard Gere have been guests here.

Understand Madrid

Madrid Today

In these times of dire economic forecasts, Madrid has become the epicentre of the deepest economic crisis in half a century, rocked to its core having gone from boom to spectacular bust in a few short years. Protest movements against austerity measures and disenchantment with the ruling political class have become the norm in a city that was, until recently, riding a wave of optimism. Daily life continues in all its customary Madrid vibrancy, but there's little doubt that the city's confidence has been shaken.

Best on Film

Pepi, Luci, Bom y Otras Chicas del Montón (1980) Early Almodóvar film showcasing 1980s Madrid.

La Colmena (1982) Faithful rendering of Camilo José Cela's Madrid during the grim 1950s.

La Comunidad (2000) Cheerfully off-the-wall tale of greed in a Madrid apartment block.

Los Fantasmas de Goya (2006) Goya, the Spanish Inquisition and the painter's many scandals.

Volver (2006) Heart-warming Almodóvar film starring Penélope Cruz in outer Madrid.

Best in Print

A Heart So White (Javier Marías) A tale of subtle family intrigue by one of Spain's most respected writers.

Madrid: A Cultural and Literary History (Elizabeth Nash) Joyfully written account of the city's past and present.

Winter in Madrid (CJ Sansom) Easy-to-read spy thriller set in post-Civil War Madrid.

Historias del Kronen (José Ángel Mañas) Cult novel about alienated urban Madrid youth.

A Load of Bull: An Englishman's Adventures in Madrid (Tim Parfitt) Humorous love letter to Madrid in the 1980s and beyond.

Boom to Bust

It can be difficult to remember now, but Spain was, not so long ago, the envy of Europe. Its economy was booming and the whole country seemed brimful of optimism. Then things fell apart. In 2008 unemployment stood at around 6%. Four years later, one out of every four Spaniards (over 5.5 million people) can't find work. Old-timers you speak to can't remember a time this bad, with businesses closing their doors forever, including many that weathered civil war and dictatorship down through the decades.

Madrid is doing slightly better than the rest of the country (in the second quarter of 2012, the capital's unemployment rate stood at 18.86%, compared with 24.6% country-wide. But with one in five *madrileños* (people from Madrid) looking for work, no one is celebrating.

National elections in November 2011 replaced a left-of-centre government that waited painfully long to recognise that a crisis was looming with a right-of-centre one promoting a deep austerity drive that threatens the generous welfare state on which Spaniards have come to depend. Opinions are divided – strangling the life out of the economy, say some; taking much-needed remedial action to correct years of spending beyond our means, counter others. Where did it all go wrong? Spain's (and to a large extent Madrid's) economy was heavily reliant on construction and tourism, two industries that are exceptionally susceptible to economic downturns. Spain's property market also spiralled out of control for far too long – prices rose exponentially, prompting banks to hand out money to those who simply couldn't afford to pay it back. What began in 2008 shows no signs of abating, and it's almost impossible these days to have a conversation in Spain that doesn't make reference to *la crisis*.

Young People

If Spain's economic numbers make for depressing reading, those relating to the country's younger generation can seem catastrophic. Almost one out of every two young Spaniards is out of work, and there is talk of an entire generation being lost to the economic downturn. The disparity between salaries – the *mileuristas* (those earning no more than €1000 a month) became a cause célèbre in the Spanish media – and high house prices means that Spaniards are taking ever longer to move out of home. And for the first time in decades, younger Spaniards are leaving the country in search of opportunity in greater numbers than there are immigrants wanting to come to Spain.

Striking Back

And yet, many of Spain's young and restless have refused to play the role of victims. On 15 May 2011, the *indignados* (those who are indignant) took over the Plaza de la Puerta del Sol in the centre of Madrid in a peaceful sit-in protest. Their popularity maintained by social media networks, they stayed for months, the forerunner to numerous such movements around the world, including Occupy Wall Street and its offshoots. The protests, which drew Spaniards from all walks of life, were driven by a dissatisfaction with mainstream politics, and a desire to overturn some of the more unfair aspects of Spanish economic life; among these is the requirement that homeowners whose homes are repossessed by banks must continue to pay their mortgage (ie the bank gets the house and the money).

While it was business as usual during the elections in November 2011, which swept the conservative Popular Party to power, the *indignados*' public meetings and prominent media presence continue, prompting many to hope that a new kind of politics may have been born. With the economy in freefall and with Spain's government forced to seek a massive bailout for its banking industry from the EU, protesters returned to the streets of Madrid and other Spanish cities in growing numbers in 2012. By the middle of the year, deep budget cuts prompted large and almost daily protests, including a march on the capital by miners from Asturias. Heavy government crackdowns on protesters only served to heighten the sense of crisis.

if Madrid were 100 people

84 would be Spanish
3 would be Ecuadorian
1 would be Bolivian
1 would be Colombian
1 would be Peruvian
10 would be Other

belief systems
(% of population)

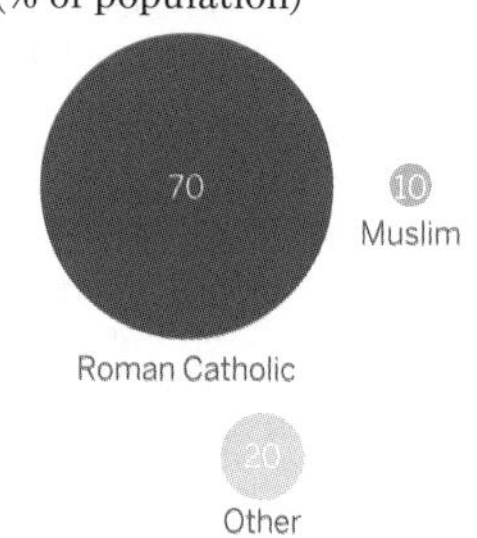

population per sq km

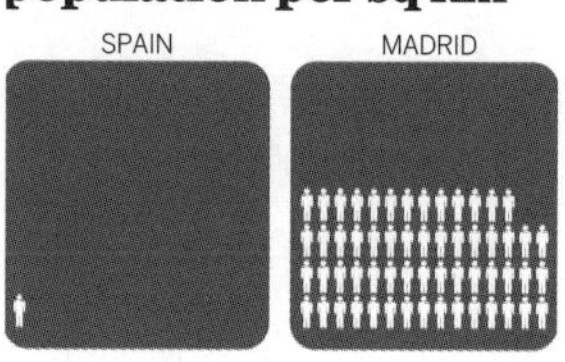

≈ 95 people

History

Founded as a Muslim garrison town in the 9th century and a squalid settlement for centuries thereafter, Madrid suddenly took centre stage in 1561 when it was unexpectedly chosen as Spain's capital. As the centre of a global empire and as the seat of the Spanish royal court, Madrid was transformed from a cultural backwater into the most important city in Spain. In the centuries that followed, the city grew into its role as capital, accumulating prestige, people from all across Spain and beyond, and the trappings of power and wealth. The end result is the most Spanish of all Spain's major cities.

MUSLIM MAYRIT

When the Muslim army of Tariq ibn Ziyad crossed the Straits of Gibraltar in the 8th century, it sparked an upheaval that would convulse the Iberian Peninsula for more than 700 years. In 756 the emirate of Córdoba was established in the south in what the Muslims called Al-Andalus and its soldiers and administrators would occupy much of the peninsula until the beginning of the 9th century.

As Iberia's Christians began the Reconquista (Reconquest) – the centuries-long campaign by Christian forces to reclaim the peninsula – the Muslims of Al-Andalus constructed a chain of fortified positions through the heart of Iberia. One of these forts was built by Muhammad I, emir of Córdoba, in 854, on the site of what would become Madrid. They called the new settlement Mayrit (or Magerit), which comes from the Arabic word *majira,* meaning water channel. As the Reconquista gathered strength, forts such as Mayrit grew in significance as part of a defensive line against Christian incursion. Recognising that Mayrit lacked natural fortifications to the east, Muhammad I constructed a defensive wall within whose boundaries only Muslims could live; Mayrit's small Christian community lived outside, near what is now the Iglesia de San Andrés. The last remaining fragment of the Muralla Árabe sits below the modern Catedral de Nuestra Señora de la Almudena.

Mayrit's strategic location in the centre of the peninsula drew an increasing number of soldiers and traders. To accommodate the many

TIMELINE

1st–5th centuries AD

The Roman Empire subdues the Celtiberian tribes. The Roman road that connects Mérida with Toledo (Toletum), Segovia, Alcalá de Henares and Zaragoza (Cesaraugusta) runs close to Madrid.

854

Muhammad I, emir of Córdoba, establishes the fortress of Mayrit, one of many across the so-called Middle March, a frontier land connecting Al-Andalus with the small Christian kingdoms of the north.

End 9th century

Muhammad I orders the construction of a wall along the ridgeline, enclosing the current Catedral de Nuestra Señora de la Almudena and what is now the Plaza de Oriente.

BEAR NECESSITIES

Madrid's emblem – a bear nuzzling a *madroño*, or strawberry tree (so named because its fruit looks like strawberries), framed by seven five-point stars and topped by a crown – is one of the most photographed corners of the Plaza de la Puerta del Sol. When Alfonso VI accepted Mayrit from the Muslims in 1083, it was seen as an example of things to come for Christian forces hoping to sweep across Spain from the north. Taking the theme further, a group of seven stars that lies close to the North Star in the northern hemisphere forms a shape known as the Ursa Minor, or small she-bear. Thus the bear (once a common sight in the El Pardo area north of the city) and seven stars came to symbolise Madrid. The five points of the stars later came to represent the five provinces that surround Madrid (Segovia, Ávila, Toledo, Cuenca and Guadalajara).

newcomers, Mayrit grew into a town. The main mosque was built on what is now the corner of Calle Mayor and Calle de Bailén, although only the smallest fragment remains. Even so, Mayrit was dispensable to its far-off Muslim rulers. As the armies of Muslim and Christian Spain battled for supremacy elsewhere, Mayrit was not considered one of the great prizes and ultimately passed into Christian hands without a fight. In 1083 Toledo's ruler gave Mayrit to King Alfonso VI of Castile during a period of rare Muslim-Christian entente.

A MEDIEVAL CHRISTIAN OUTPOST

Madrid never again passed into Muslim hands, although the city was often besieged by Muslim forces. As the frontline gradually pushed south, Christian veterans from the Reconquista and clerics and their orders flooded into Madrid and forever changed the city's character. A small Muslim community remained and to this day the warren of streets around Vistillas, where they lived, is known as the *morería* – the Moorish quarter. Nearby, the Plaza de la Paja was the site of the city's main market. By the end of the 13th century, a new city wall, bordered by what are now Calle Arenal, Cava de San Miguel, Calle de la Cava Baja, Plaza de la Puerta de Moros and Calle de Bailén, was built. Where the Plaza Mayor, Plaza de España and the Plaza de la Puerta del Sol all stand then lay beyond the walls.

Madrid may have been growing, but its power was negligible and the city existed in the shadow of the more established cities of Segovia and Toledo. Left largely to their own devices, a small number of local families set about governing themselves, forming Madrid's first town council, the Consejo de Madrid. The travelling Cortes (royal court and

The remains of Roman villas and inns have been found in the Madrid region. The small Roman outpost known as Miacum, close to modern Madrid, was an obscure waystation on the important Roman road that crossed the Iberian Peninsula.

Around 1070

Madrid's patron saint, San Isidro Labrador, is born among the small community of Christians clustered around the Iglesia de San Andrés (where he was buried in 1130) in Muslim Mayrit.

1083

Mayrit passes into the hands of King Alfonso VI of Castile without a fight, ending Muslim rule over Mayrit, in return for the king's assistance in capturing Valencia.

1110

Almoravid Muslims attack Madrid in an attempt to wrest the city back from Christian rule. They succeed in destroying Madrid's walls but are unable to seize the *alcázar* (fortress).

1222

Madrid's emblem of seven stars and a bear nuzzling a *madroño* (strawberry tree) appears for the first time in historical records. A statue of it now stands in the Plaza de la Puerta del Sol.

parliament) sat in Madrid for the first time in 1309. This first sign of royal favour was followed by others – Madrid was an increasingly popular residence with the Castilian monarchs, particularly Enrique IV (r 1454–74). They found it a relaxing base from which to set off on hunting expeditions, especially for bears in the El Pardo district.

Despite growing evidence of royal attention, medieval Madrid remained dirt-poor and small-scale. In 1348 the horrors of the Black Death struck, devastating the population, and a handful of local families ran a feudal system of government, lording it over the peasants who worked the surrounding *tierra* (land). As one 15th-century writer observed, 'in Madrid there is nothing except what you bring with you'. It simply bore no comparison with other major Spanish, let alone European, cities.

For medieval travellers to Madrid, the lasting impression was of streets 'which would be beautiful if it were not for the mud and filth'. The houses were 'bad and ugly and almost all made of mud'. Rubbish and human excrement were thrown from the balconies, 'a thing which afterwards creates an insupportable odour'.

A TALE OF TWO CITIES

When Carlos I's son and successor, Felipe II, ascended the Spanish throne in 1556, Madrid was surrounded by walls that boasted 130 towers and six stone gates. Although it sounds impressive, these fortifications were largely built of mud and were designed more to impress than provide any meaningful defence of the city. Such modest claims to significance notwithstanding, Madrid was chosen by Felipe II as the capital of Spain in 1561.

Felipe II was more concerned with the business of empire and building his monastic retreat at San Lorenzo de El Escorial than in developing Madrid. Despite a handful of elegant churches, the imposing *alcázar* and a smattering of noble residences, Madrid consisted, for the most part, of precarious, whitewashed houses that were little more than mud huts. They lined chaotic, ill-defined and largely unpaved lanes and alleys. The monumental Paseo del Prado, which now provides Madrid with so much of its grandeur, was nothing more than a small creek. Even so, Madrid went from having just 2000 homes in 1563 to more than 7000 just 40 years later as opportunists, impoverished rural migrants, would-be princes and fortune-seekers flocked to the city hoping for a share of the glamour and wealth that came from being close to royalty.

The sumptuous Palacio del Buen Retiro was completed in 1630 and replaced the *alcázar* as the prime royal residence (the former Museo del Ejército building and Casón del Buen Retiro), are all that remain. Countless grand churches, convents and mansions were also built and, thanks to royal patronage, this was the golden age of art in Spain: Velázquez, El Greco, José de Ribera, Zurbarán, Murillo and Coello were all active in Madrid in the 17th century. For the first time, Madrid began to take on the aspect of a city.

1309

The Cortes sits for the first time in Madrid and the royals declare war on Granada; the Reconquista's demands ensure that the royal court often travels throughout Spain.

1348

The Black Death sweeps across Spain, killing King Alfonso XI and many of his compatriots. Estimates suggest that the plague kills anywhere between 20% and 50% of Madrid's population.

1426

In the midst of a devastating drought, devout *madrileños* (people from Madrid) take the body of San Isidro, Madrid's patron saint, out onto the streets, whereupon it begins to rain.

San Isidro

A CAPITAL CHOICE

When Felipe II decided to make Madrid Spain's capital in 1561, you could almost hear the collective gasp of disbelief from Spain's great and good, few of whom lived in Madrid. Madrid was home to just 30,000 people, whereas Toledo and Seville each boasted more than 80,000. Even Valladolid, the capital of choice for Isabel and Fernando, had 50,000 inhabitants. What's more, in the 250 years since 1309, Madrid had hosted Spain's travelling road show of royalty just 10 times, far fewer than Spain's other large cities.

Madrid's apparent obscurity may, however, explain precisely why Felipe II chose it as his capital. Valladolid was considered to be of questionable loyalty. Toledo, which like Madrid stands close to the geographical heart of Spain, was known for its opinionated nobles and powerful clergy who had shown an annoying tendency to oppose the king's whims and wishes. In contrast, more than one king had described Madrid as 'very noble and very loyal'. By choosing Madrid Felipe II was choosing the path of least resistance. Felipe II also wanted the capital to be 'a city fulfilling the function of a heart located in the middle of the body'.

In 1601 Felipe III, tired of Madrid, moved the court to Valladolid. Within five years, the population of Madrid halved. The move was so unpopular, however, that the king, realising the error of his ways, returned to Madrid. *'Sólo Madrid es corte'* (roughly, 'Only Madrid can be home to the court') became the catch cry and thus it has been ever since.

By the middle of the 17th century Madrid had completely outgrown its capacity to cope: it was home to 175,000 people, making it the fifth-largest city in Europe. But if you took away the court, the city amounted to nothing and when Pedro Texeiro drew the first map of the city in 1656, the place was still largely a cesspit of narrow, squalid lanes.

THE BOURBONS LEAVE THEIR MARK

After King Carlos II died in 1700 without leaving an heir, the 12-year War of the Spanish Succession convulsed Europe. While Europe squabbled over the Spanish colonial carcass, Felipe V (grandson of Louis XIV of France and Maria Teresa, a daughter of Felipe IV) ascended the throne in 1702 as the first member of the Bourbon dynasty which remains at the head of the Spanish state today. Felipe's centralisation of state control and attempts at land reform are viewed by some historians as the first steps in making Spain a modern European nation, and the former clearly cemented Madrid's claims to being Spain's pre-eminent city. He preferred to live outside the noisy and filthy capital, but when

1479–81

Isabel, Queen of Castile, marries Fernando, King of Aragón. An edict by Madrid's authorities forces Muslims to wear signs identifying their religion.

1492

The last Muslim rulers of Al-Andalus are defeated by Christian armies in Granada, uniting the peninsula for the first time in seven centuries. Jews are expelled from the peninsula.

1520

Madrid joins Toledo in the rebellion of the Comuneros against Carlos I, a disastrous decision that prompts the victorious king to rein in Madrid's growing independence.

1561

Against all the odds, Felipe II establishes his permanent court at Madrid, which was, in Felipe II's words, 'a city fulfilling the function of a heart located in the middle of the body'.

in 1734 the *alcázar* was destroyed in a fire, the king laid down plans for a magnificent new Palacio Real (Royal Palace) to take its place.

His immediate successors, especially Carlos III (r 1759–88), also gave Madrid and Spain a period of comparatively commonsense governance. Carlos (his equestrian statue dominates the Puerta del Sol) came to be known as the best 'mayor' Madrid had ever had. By introducing Madrid's first program of sanitation and public hygiene, he cleaned up a city that was, by all accounts, the filthiest in Europe. He was so successful that, near the end of Carlos III's reign, France's ambassador in Madrid described the city as one of the cleanest capitals in Europe. Mindful of his legacy, Carlos III also completed the Palacio Real, inaugurated the Real Jardín Botánico (Royal Botanical Gardens) and carried out numerous other public works. His stamp upon Madrid's essential character was also evident in his sponsorship of local and foreign artists, among them Goya and Tiepolo. Carlos III also embarked on a major road-building program.

When, in the 17th century, all home owners were ordered to reserve the second storey of their homes for government bureaucrats and clergy newly arrived in the city, *madrileños* instead built homes with just a single-storey facade at street level, building additional storeys out the back, away from prying government eyes.

NAPOLEON & EL DOS DE MAYO

Within a year of Carlos III's death Europe was again in uproar, this time as the French Revolution threatened to sweep away the old order of privileged royals and inherited nobility. Through the machinations of Carlos IV, the successor to Carlos III, and his self-serving minister, Manuel Godoy, Spain incurred the wrath of both the French and the British. The consequences were devastating. First, Nelson crushed the Spanish fleet in the Battle of Trafalgar in 1805. Next, Napoleon convinced a gullible Godoy to let French troops enter Spain on the pretext of a joint attack on Portugal, whereby General Murat's French detachment took control of Madrid. By 1808 the French presence had become an occupation and Napoleon's brother, Joseph Bonaparte, was crowned king of Spain.

Madrid did not take kindly to foreign rule and, on the morning of 2 May 1808 *madrileños* (people from Madrid), showing more courage than their leaders, attacked French troops around the Palacio Real and what is now Plaza del Dos de Mayo in Malasaña. Murat moved quickly and by the end of the day the rebels were defeated. Goya's masterpieces, *El Dos de Mayo* and *El Tres de Mayo,* on display in the Museo del Prado, poignantly evoke the hope and anguish of the ill-fated rebellion.

Although reviled by much of Madrid's population, Joseph Bonaparte's contribution to Madrid in five short years should not be underestimated. Working hard to win popular support, Bonaparte staged numerous free *espectáculos* – bullfights, festivals of food and drink,

1601

In the last serious challenge to Madrid's position as capital, Felipe III moves Spain's capital to Valladolid, but popular discontent convinces him to return the royal court to Madrid.

1622

Seville-born Diego Rodríguez de Silva Velázquez moves to Madrid, takes up a position as a painter in the royal court and becomes synonymous with the golden age of Spanish art.

Mid-17th century

Madrid's population swells to 175,000 people, up from just 30,000 a century before. Only London, Paris, Constantinople and Naples can boast larger populations in Europe.

1702

Felipe V is crowned king, beginning the Bourbon dynasty that still rules Spain and, save for four decades of the 20th century, has done so from Madrid.

and religious processions. He also transformed Madrid with a host of measures necessary in a city that had grown up without any discernible sense of town planning. These measures included the destruction of various churches and convents to create public squares (such as the Plaza de Oriente, Plaza de Santa Ana, Plaza de San Miguel, Plaza de Santa Bárbara, Plaza de Tirso de Molina and Plaza de Callao) and widening streets. He also conceived the viaduct that still spans Calle de Segovia. Under Bonaparte sanitation was also improved and cemeteries were moved to the outskirts of the city.

The French were finally evicted from Spanish territory in 1813 as a result of the Guerra de la Independencia (War of Independence, or Peninsular War). But when the autocratic King Fernando VII returned in 1814, Spain was in disarray. Though far from Spain's most distinguished ruler, Fernando was responsible for opening to the public the Parque del Buen Retiro, which had been largely destroyed during the war, and founded an art gallery in the Prado.

Madrileños never forgave Bonaparte his foreign origins and the brutality with which he suppressed uprisings against his rule, mocking his yearning for legitimacy by calling him names that included the Cucumber King, Pepe Botella and King of the Small Squares.

PEPE BOTELLA

CAPITAL OF A COUNTRY DIVIDED

For much of the 19th century, Spain and Madrid were in turmoil, with no less than three civil wars (the Carlist Wars between liberals and conservatives as the royal family squabbled over the spoils of succession) and a series of coups and counter coups. At the heart of it all, Madrid was incredibly backward, although the *desmortización* (disentailment) of Church property in 1837, the emergence of a middle class and growing entrepreneurial activity finally enabled Madrid's ordinary inhabitants to emerge from the shadow of royalty and powerful clergy.

In 1851 the city's first railway line, operating between Madrid and Aranjuez, opened. Seven years later the Canal de Isabel II, which still supplies the city with water from the Sierra de Guadarrama, was inaugurated. Street paving, the sewage system and rubbish collection were improved and gas lighting was introduced. More importantly, foreign (mostly French) capital was beginning to fill the investment vacuum. In the years that followed, a national road network radiating from the capital was built and public works, ranging from the reorganisation of the Puerta del Sol to the building of the Teatro Real, Biblioteca Nacional and Congreso de los Diputados (lower house of parliament), were carried out. In the 1860s the first timid moves to create an Ensanche, or extension of the city, were undertaken. The initial spurt of building took place around Calle de Serrano, where the enterprising Marqués de Salamanca bought up land and built high-class housing.

1734

Medieval Madrid's most enduring symbol, the *alcázar*, is destroyed by fire. Plans begin almost immediately for a lavish royal palace to take its place.

1759–88

Carlos III, King of Spain and patron of Madrid, cleans up the city, lays out the Parque del Buen Retiro and sponsors Goya, transforming Madrid into a sophisticated European capital.

1808

Napoleon's troops under General Murat march into Madrid and Joseph Bonaparte, Napoleon's brother, is crowned king of Spain, and citizens rise up to protest against foreign rule.

1812

Thirty thousand *madrileños* die from hunger caused by fighting against the French in the lead-up to the War of Independence. The French were expelled a year later.

In 1873 Spain was declared a republic, but the army soon intervened to restore the Bourbon monarchy. Alfonso XII, Isabel's son, assumed power. In the period of relative tranquillity that ensued, the expansion of the Ensanche gathered momentum, the city's big train stations were constructed and the foundation stones of a cathedral were laid. Another kind of 'cathedral', the Banco de España, was completed and opened its doors in 1891. By 1898 the first city tramlines were electrified and in 1910 work began on the Gran Vía. Nine years later the first metro line started operation.

The 1920s were a period of frenzied activity, not just in urban construction but in intellectual life. As many as 20 newspapers circulated on the streets of Madrid, and writers and artists (including Lorca, Dalí and Buñuel) converged on the capital, which hopped to the sounds of American jazz and whose grand cafes resounded with the clamour of lively *tertulias* (literary discussions). The '20s roared as much in Madrid as elsewhere in Europe.

At the height of the siege of Madrid, the Francoist general Emilio Mola assured a British journalist that he would soon take Madrid with his four columns of soldiers massed on the city's outskirts and with the help of his 'fifth column', a phrase that has since remained in the popular lexicon and referred to Franco's right-wing sympathisers in Madrid.

FIFTH COLUMN

IN THE EYE OF THE STORM

In 1923 the captain-general of Catalonia and soon-to-be dictator, General Miguel Primo de Rivera, seized power and held it until Alfonso XIII had him removed in 1930. Madrid erupted in joyful celebration, but it would prove to be a false dawn. By now, the Spanish capital, home to more than one million people, had become the seething centre of Spain's increasingly radical politics, and the rise of the socialists in Madrid, as well as anarchists in Barcelona and Andalucía, sharpened tensions throughout the country.

Municipal elections in Madrid in April 1931 brought a coalition of republicans and socialists to power. Three days later a second republic was proclaimed and Alfonso XIII fled. The republican government opened up the Casa de Campo – until then serving as a private royal playground – to the public and passed numerous reformist laws, but divisions within the government enabled a right-wing coalition to assume power in 1933. Again the pendulum swung and in February 1936 the left-wing Frente Popular (Popular Front) barely defeated the right's Frente Nacional (National Front) to power. General Francisco Franco was exiled, supposedly out of harm's way, to the Canary Islands, but with the army supporting the right-wing parties and the extreme left clamouring for revolution, the stage was set for a showdown. In July 1936 garrisons in North Africa revolted, quickly followed by others on the mainland. The Spanish Civil War had begun.

1819

Fernando VII opens the Museo del Prado. Originally conceived as a storehouse for royal art accumulated down through the centuries, it later becomes one of the most important art galleries in Europe.

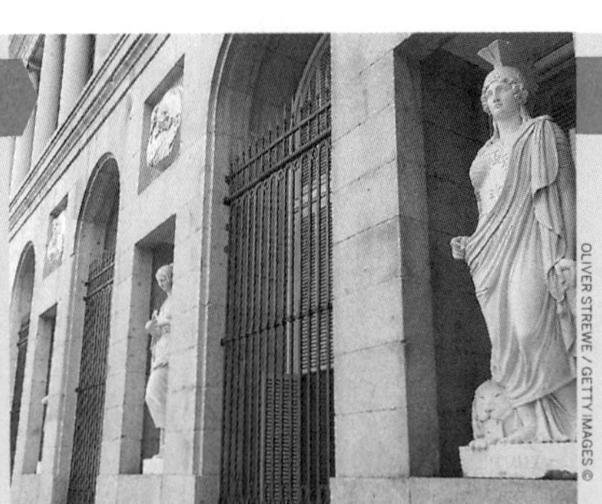

OLIVER STREWE / GETTY IMAGES ©

Museo del Prado (p92)

1833

King Fernando VII dies, leaving three-year-old Isabel II as heir-apparent. Her mother, María Cristina rules as regent and Spain descends into the Carlist civil wars, devastating Madrid.

Having stopped Franco's nationalist troops advancing from the north, Madrid found itself in the sights of Franco's forces moving up from the south. Take Madrid, Franco reasoned, and Spain would be his. By early November 1936 Franco was in the Casa de Campo. The republican government escaped to Valencia, but the resolve of the city's defenders, a mix of hastily assembled and poorly trained recruits, sympathisers from the ranks of the army and air force, the International Brigades and Soviet advisers, held firm. Madrid became an international cause célèbre, drawing luminaries as diverse as Ernest Hemingway and Willy Brandt in defence of the city. For all the fame of the brigades, the fact remains, however, that of the 40,000 soldiers and irregulars defending Madrid, more than 90% were Spaniards.

Madrid's defenders held off a fierce nationalist assault in November 1936, with the fighting heaviest in the northwest of the city, around Argüelles and the Ciudad Universitaria. Soldiers loyal to Franco inside Madrid were overpowered by local militias and 20,000 Franco supporters sought protection inside the walls of foreign embassies. Faced with republican intransigence – symbolised by the catchphrase *'¡No pasarán'* ('They shall not pass!') coined by the Communist leader Dolores Ibarruri – Franco besieged Madrid, bombarded the city from the air and waited for the capital to surrender. It didn't.

The grandiose folly of Franco's Valle de los Caídos monument northwest of Madrid was largely constructed through the forced labour of Republican prisoners of war.

German bombers strafed Madrid, one of the first such campaigns of its kind in the history of warfare, although the Salamanca district was spared, allegedly because it was home to a high proportion of Franco supporters. The Museo del Prado was not so fortunate and most of its paintings were evacuated to Valencia. As many as 10,000 people died in the Battle of Madrid; Franco's approach was summed up by his promise 'I will destroy Madrid rather than leave it to the Marxists'.

By 1938 Madrid was in a state of near famine, with food, clothes and ammunition in short supply. As republican strongholds fell elsewhere across Spain, Madrid's republican defenders were divided over whether to continue the resistance. After a brief internal power struggle, those favouring negotiations won. On 28 March 1939 an exhausted Madrid finally surrendered.

FRANCO'S MADRID

Mindful that he was occupying a city that had hardly welcomed him with open arms, Franco considered shifting the capital south to the more amenable Seville. As if to punish Madrid for its resistance, he opted instead to remake Madrid in his own image and transform the city into a capital worthy of its new master. Franco and his right-wing

1873

Spain's first short-lived republic is declared in February, although the Bourbon monarchy returns to power in Madrid's Palacio Real with help from the army in December of the following year.

1881

The Partido Socialista Obrero Español (PSOE; Spanish Socialist Workers' Party) is founded in a backroom of Casa Labra, still one of Madrid's most prestigious tapas bars.

1898

Spain loses its remaining colonies of Cuba, Puerto Rico and the Philippines to the USA, setting off a period of national angst. In the same year, Madrid's tramlines are electrified.

1919

Madrid's first metro line starts running, crossing the city from north to south, with eight stations and a total length of 3.5km from Puerta del Sol to Cuatro Caminos.

Falangist Party maintained a heavy-handed repression, and Madrid in the early 1940s was impoverished and battle scarred, a 'city of a million cadavers', according to one observer.

In the Francoist propaganda of the day, the 1940s and 1950s were the years of *autarquía* (economic self-reliance), a policy that owed more to Spain's international isolation post-WWII due to its perceived support for Hitler than any principled philosophy. For most Spaniards, however, these were the *años de hambre* (the years of hunger). Throughout the 1940s, tens of thousands of suspected republican sympathisers were harassed, imprisoned, tortured and shot. Thousands of political prisoners were shipped off to Nazi concentration camps. Many who remained were put to work in deplorable conditions.

Books on Madrid History

- *A Traveller's Companion to Madrid (Hugh Thomas)*
- *The New Spaniards (John Hooper)*
- *Hidden Madrid: A Walking Guide (Mark and Peter Besas)*
- *Historia de la Villa de Madrid (José Antonio Vizcaíno)*
- *Illustrated Atlas of the History of Madrid (Pedro López Carcelén)*

The dire state of the Spanish economy forced hundreds of thousands of starving *campesinos* (peasants) to flock to Madrid, increasing the already enormous pressure for housing. Most contented themselves with erecting *chabolas* (shanty towns) in the increasingly ugly satellite suburbs that began to ring the city.

By the early 1960s, the so-called *años de desarollo* (years of development), industry was taking off in and around Madrid. Foreign investment poured in and the services and banking sector blossomed. Factories of the American Chrysler motor company were Madrid's single biggest employers in the 1960s. In 1960 fewer than 70,000 cars were on the road in Madrid; 10 years later more than half a million clogged the capital's streets.

For all the signs of development in Madrid, Franco was never popular in his own capital and an increased standard of living did little to diminish *madrileños'* disdain for a man who held the capital in an iron grip. In the Basque Country the terrorist group Euskadi Ta Askatasuna (ETA; Basque Homeland and Freedom) began to fight for Basque independence. Their first important action outside the Basque Country was the assassination in Madrid in 1973 of Admiral Carrero Blanco, Franco's prime minister and designated successor.

Franco fell ill in 1974 and died on 20 November 1975.

THE TRANSITION TO DEMOCRACY

After the death of Franco, Spaniards began to reclaim their country and Madrid took centre stage.

King Juan Carlos I, of the Bourbon family that had left the Spanish political stage with the flight of Alfonso XIII in 1931, had been groomed as head of state by Franco. But the king confounded the sceptics by entrusting Adolfo Suárez, a former moderate Francoist with whom he

1920s

Madrid has a cultural revival with Salvador Dalí, Federico García Lorca and Luis Buñuel who bring both high culture and mayhem to a city in love with jazz and *tertulias* (literary discussions).

1931

After a period of right-wing dictatorship, Spain's Second Republic is proclaimed and King Alfonso XIII flees, leaving Spain in political turmoil and planting the seeds for civil war.

1936–39

The Spanish Civil War breaks out. Nationalist forces bombard Madrid from the air and with artillery, besieging it for three years, before the exhausted city surrenders on 28 March 1939.

1960s

After two decades of extreme economic hardship, the decade becomes known as the *años de desarollo* (years of development) with investment and rural immigrants flooding into Madrid.

had long been in secret contact, with government in July 1976. With the king's approval Suárez quickly rammed a raft of changes through parliament while Franco loyalists and generals, suddenly rudderless without their leader, struggled to regroup.

Suárez and his centre-right coalition won elections in 1977 and set about writing a new constitution in collaboration with the now-legal opposition. It provided for a parliamentary monarchy with no state religion and guaranteed a large degree of devolution to the 17 regions (including the Comunidad de Madrid) into which the country was now divided.

Spaniards got the fright of their lives in February 1981 when a pistol-brandishing, low-ranking Guardia Civil (Civil Guard) officer, Antonio Tejero Molina, marched into the Cortes in Madrid with an armed detachment and held parliament captive for 24 hours. Throughout a day of high drama the country held its breath as Spaniards waited to see whether Spain would be thrust back into the dark days of dictatorship or whether the fledgling democracy would prevail. With the nation glued to their TV sets, King Juan Carlos I made a live broadcast denouncing Tejero and calling on the soldiers to return to their barracks. The coup fizzled out.

A year later Felipe González' PSOE won national elections. Spain's economic problems were legion – incomes were on a par with those of Iraq, ETA terrorism was claiming dozens of lives every year and unemployment was above 20%. But one thing that Spaniards had in abundance was optimism and when, in 1986, Spain joined the European Community (EC), as it was then called, the country had well and truly returned to the fold of modern European nations.

THE TUNNELATOR

Madrid's first democratically elected conservative mayor, José María Álvarez del Manzano of the PP, ruled from 1991 until 2003 and became known as 'The Tunnelator' for beginning the ongoing mania of Madrid governments for semipermanent roadworks and large-scale infrastructure projects.

LA MOVIDA MADRILEÑA

Madrid's spirits could not be dampened and, with grand events taking place on the national stage, the city had become one of the most exciting places on earth. What London was to the swinging '60s and Paris to 1968, Madrid was to the 1980s. After the long, dark years of dictatorship and conservative Catholicism, Spaniards, especially *madrileños,* emerged onto the streets with all the zeal of ex-convent schoolgirls. Nothing was taboo in a phenomenon known as *'la movida madrileña'* (the Madrid scene) as young *madrileños* discovered the '60s, '70s and early '80s all at once. Drinking, drugs and sex suddenly were OK. All-night partying was the norm, drug taking in public was not a criminal offence (that changed in 1992) and the city howled. All across the city, summer terraces roared to the chattering, drinking, carousing crowds and young people from all over Europe flocked here to take part in the revelry.

1973	1975–78	1980s	1986
Admiral Carrero Blanco, Franco's prime minister and designated successor, is assassinated by ETA in a car-bomb in Salamanca after he left Mass at Iglesia de San Francisco de Borga.	Franco dies in Madrid on 20 November 1975, after 39 years in power. Without an obvious successor to Franco, Spain returns to democratic rule three years later.	*La movida madrileña* (the Madrid scene) takes over the city, and becomes a byword for hedonism. The era produces such talents as Pedro Almodóvar, Agatha Ruiz de la Prada and Alaska.	Spain joins the European Community (EC), later the European Union (EU). EU subsidies and other assistance will later be credited with building the foundations of the Spanish economy.

What was remarkable about *la movida* is that it was presided over by Enrique Tierno Galván, an ageing former university professor who had been a leading opposition figure under Franco and was affectionately known throughout Spain as 'the old teacher'. A Socialist, he became mayor in 1979 and, for many, launched *la movida* by telling a public gathering *'a colocarse y ponerse al loro',* which loosely translates as 'get stoned and do what's cool'. Unsurprisingly he was Madrid's most popular mayor ever and when he died in 1986 a million *madrileños* turned out for his funeral.

But *la movida* was not just about rediscovering the Spanish art of *salir de copas* (going out for a drink). It was also accompanied by an explosion of creativity among the country's musicians, designers and film-makers keen to shake off the shackles of the repressive Franco years. The most famous of these was film director Pedro Almodóvar. Still one of Europe's most creative directors, his riotously colourful films captured the spirit of *la movida,* featuring larger-than-life characters who pushed the limits of sex and drugs. Although his later films became internationally renowned, his first films, *Pepi, Luci, Bom y Otras Chicas del Montón* (Pepi, Luci, Bom and the Other Girls; 1980) and *Laberinto de Pasiones* (Labyrinth of Passion; 1982) are where the spirit of the movement really comes alive. When he wasn't making films, Almodóvar immersed himself in the spirit of *la movida,* doing drag acts in smoky bars that people-in-the-know would frequent.

So what happened to *la movida*? Many say that it died in 1991 with the election of the conservative Popular Party's José María Álvarez del Manzano as mayor. In the following years rolling spliffs in public became increasingly dangerous and creeping clamps (ie closing hours) were imposed on the almost-lawless bars. Pedro Almodóvar was even heard to say that Madrid had become 'as boring as Oslo'. Things have indeed quietened down a little, but you'll only notice if you were here during the 1980s. If only all cities were this 'boring'.

ESPERANZA AGUIRRE

The Popular Party's Esperanza Aguirre became the country's first-ever woman regional president in close-run elections for the Comunidad de Madrid in October 2003, and easily extended her majority in 2007 and 2011.

MADRID SOBERS UP

With the election of a conservative government in 1991 after 12 years of Socialist rule, and with the conservatives taking power at a national level, Madrid's political landscape fundamentally changed. From 1996 until 2004, the three levels of government in Madrid (local, regional and national) remained the preserve of the Partido Popular (PP; Popular Party), a dominance that prompted observers from other regions to claim that the PP overtly favoured development of the capital at the expense of Spain's other regions. Whatever the truth of such accusations, the city

1991

Madrid elects a conservative mayor, José María Álvarez del Manzano of the Partido Popular (PP; Popular Party), for the first time, bringing an end to *la movida*.

1992

In the same year that Barcelona hosts the Summer Olympics, Madrid is designated a European Capital of Culture. Drug taking in public is finally outlawed in the capital.

2004

On 11 March terrorist bombings on four Madrid commuter trains kill 191 people and injure 1755. Three million take to the streets in protest. The PSOE wins national elections on 14 March.

2007

The PP's Alberto Ruiz-Gallardón, who first won election in 2003, wins an absolute majority in municipal elections, cementing the conservatives hold over Madrid's Ayuntamiento.

A CITY OF IMMIGRANTS

In a country where regional nationalisms abound – even Barcelona, that most European of cities, is fiercely and parochially Catalan – Madrid is notable for its absence of regional sentiment. If you quiz *madrileños* as to why this is so, they often reply, 'but we're *all* from somewhere else'. It has always been thus in Madrid. In the century after the city became the national capital in 1561, the population swelled by more than 500%, from 30,000 to 175,000. Most were Spaniards (peasants and would-be nobles) who left behind the impoverished countryside and were drawn by the opportunities that existed on the periphery of the royal court.

During the first three decades of the 20th century Madrid's population doubled from half a million to almost one million; in 1930 a study found that less than 40% of the capital's population was from Madrid. The process continued in the aftermath of the civil war, and in the 1950s alone more than 600,000 arrived from elsewhere in Spain. In the late 20th century the process of immigration took on a new form, as Spain became the EU's largest annual recipient of immigrants. Between 15% and 20% of Madrid's population are foreigners, more than double the national average.

Unsurprisingly, true *madrileños* are something of a rare breed. Those who can claim four grandparents born in the city are dignified with the name *gatos* (cats). The term dates from when one of Alfonso VI's soldiers artfully scaled Muslim Mayrit's formidable walls in 1083. 'Look,' cried his comrades, 'he moves like a cat!'

moved ahead in leaps and bounds, and as the national economy took off in the late 1990s, Madrid reaped the benefits. Extraordinary expansion programs for the metro, highways, airport, outer suburbs and for innercity renewal are unmistakable signs of confidence. By one reckoning, up to 75% of inward foreign investment into Spain was directed at the capital.

On 11 March 2004, just three days before the country was due to vote in national elections, Madrid was rocked by 10 bombs on four rush-hour commuter trains heading into the capital's Atocha station. When the dust cleared, 191 people had died and 1755 were wounded, many of them seriously. It was the biggest such terror attack in the nation's history. Madrid was in shock and, for 24 hours at least, this most clamorous of cities fell silent. Then, some 36 hours after the attacks, more than three million *madrileños* streamed onto the streets to protest against the bombings, making it the largest demonstration in Madrid's history. A further eight million marched in solidarity in cities across Spain. Although deeply traumatised, the mass act of defiance and pride began the process of healing.

Madrid was a candidate for the 2012 and 2016 Olympics, coming third and second respectively. Third time lucky?

2007

Twenty-one people are convicted of involvement in the 11 March 2004 terrorist attacks, although the trial finds no evidence of al-Qaeda involvement in the bombings.

KRZYSZTOF DYDYNSKI / GETTY IMAGES ©

Memorial to 11 March 2004 victims, Parque del Buen Retiro (p106)

2011

The PP win municipal and national elections. Mayor Gallardón is drafted into the national government as Justice Minister. Ana Botella is the new mayor.

City of Painters

Spanish kings down through the centuries were a pretty vain and decadent lot, and liked nothing better than to pose for portraits or to compete with other European royals for the fleeting prestige that came from lavishing money on the great artists of the day. This combination of royal money and personal patronage transformed Madrid into one of the richest producers and storehouses of paintings anywhere in the world. From the early 20th century onwards, Madrid's role as the seat of Spain's finest artistic academies has also drawn Spain's most creative talents.

THE EARLY DAYS

With royal patronage of the arts kicking off in the 16th century, it was difficult for local artists to get a look in. Felipe II – the monarch who made Madrid the permanent seat of the royal court – preferred the work of Italian artists such as Titian (Tiziano in Spanish) ahead of home-grown talent. Even some foreign artists who would later become masters were given short shrift. One of these was the Cretan-born Domenikos Theotokopoulos (1541–1614), known as El Greco (the Greek), who was perhaps the most extraordinary and temperamental 'Spanish' artist of the 16th century, but whom Felipe II rejected as a court artist. The Museo del Prado is the place to see both works by both artists.

VELÁZQUEZ & THE GOLDEN AGE

As Spain's monarchs sought refuge from the creeping national malaise of the 17th century by promoting the arts, they fostered an artist who would rise above all others: Diego Rodríguez de Silva Velázquez (1599–1660). Born in Seville, Velázquez later moved to Madrid as court painter and stayed to make the city his own. He composed scenes (landscapes, royal portraits, religious subjects, snapshots of everyday life) that owe their vitality not only to his photographic eye for light and contrast but also to a compulsive interest in the humanity of his subjects who seem to breathe on the canvas. His masterpieces include *Las Meninas* (The Maids of Honour) and *La Rendición de Breda* (The Surrender of Breda), both on view in the Museo del Prado.

Francisco de Zurbarán (1598–1664), a friend and contemporary of Velázquez, ended his life in poverty in Madrid; it was only after his death that he received the acclaim that his masterpieces deserved. He is best remembered for the startling clarity and light in his portraits of monks, a series of which hangs in the Real Academia de Bellas Artes de San Fernando.

Other masters of the era whose works hang in the Prado, though their connection to Madrid was limited, include José (Jusepe) de Ribera (1591–1652), who was influenced by Caravaggio and produced fine *chiaroscuro* works, and Bartolomé Esteban Murillo (1618–82).

THE 20TH CENTURY & BEYOND

The 17th century may have been Spain's golden age, but the 20th century was easily its rival.

Sorolla & Solana

Valencian native Joaquín Sorolla (1863–1923) flew in the face of the French Impressionist style, preferring the blinding sunlight of the Mediterranean coast to the muted tones favoured in Paris. He lived and worked in Madrid and his work can be studied in Madrid's Museo Sorolla, where he once lived.

Leading the way into the 20th century was Madrid-born José Gutiérrez Solana (1886–1945), whose disturbing, avant-garde approach to painting revels in low lighting, sombre colours and deathly pale figures. His work is emblematic of what historians now refer to as *España negra* (black Spain). A selection of his canvases is on display in the Centro de Arte Reina Sofía.

Picasso, Dalí & Juan Gris

Málaga-born Pablo Ruiz Picasso (1881–1973) is one of the greatest and most original Spanish painters of all time. Although he spent much of his working life in Paris, he arrived in Madrid from Barcelona in 1897 at the behest of his father for a year's study at the Escuela de Bellas Artes de San Fernando. Never one to allow himself to be confined within formal structures, the precocious Picasso instead took himself to the Prado to learn from the masters, and to the streets to depict life as he saw it. Picasso went on to become the master of cubism, which was inspired by his fascination with primitivism, primarily African masks and early Iberian sculpture. This highly complex form reached its high point in *Guernica*, which hangs in the Centro de Arte Reina Sofía.

Picasso was not the only artist who found the Escuela de Bellas Artes de San Fernando too traditional for his liking. In 1922 Salvador Dalí (1904–89) arrived in Madrid from Catalonia, but decided that the eminent professors of the renowned fine-arts school were not fit to judge him. He spent four years living in the 'Resi', the renowned students' residence (which still functions today) where he met poet Federico García Lorca and future film director Luis Buñuel. The three self-styled anarchists and bohemians romped through the cafes and music halls of 1920s Madrid, frequenting brothels, engaging in pranks, immersing themselves in jazz and taking part in endless *tertulias* (literary discussions). Dalí, a true original and master of the surrealist form, was finally expelled from art school and left Madrid, never to return. The only remaining link with Madrid is a handful of his hallucinatory works in the Centro de Arte Reina Sofía.

In the same gallery is a fine selection of the cubist creations of Madrid's Juan Gris (1887–1927), who was turning out his best work in Paris while Dalí and his cohorts were up to no good in Madrid. Along with Picasso and Georges Braque, he was a principal exponent of the cubist style and his paintings can be seen in the Museo Thyssen-Bornemisza and Real Academia de Bellas Artes de San Fernando.

Contemporary Art

The death of Franco in 1975 unleashed a frenzy of activity and artistic creativity that was central to *la movida madrileña* (the Madrid scene). The Galería Moriarty became a focal point of exuberantly artistic reference. A parade of artists marched through the gallery, including

GOYA – A CLASS OF HIS OWN

Francisco José de Goya y Lucientes (1746–1828), who was born in the village of Fuendetodos in Aragón, started his career as a cartoonist in the Real Fábrica de Tapices (Royal Tapestry Workshop) in Madrid. In 1776 Goya began designing for the tapestry factory, but illness in 1792 left him deaf; many critics speculate that his condition was largely responsible for his wild, often merciless style that would become increasingly unshackled from convention. By 1799 Goya was appointed Carlos IV's court painter.

Several distinct series and individual paintings mark his progress. In the last years of the 18th century he painted enigmatic masterpieces, such as *La Maja Vestida* (The Young Lady Dressed) and *La Maja Desnuda* (The Young Lady Undressed), identical portraits but for the lack of clothes in the latter. The rumour mill suggests the subject was none other than the Duchess of Alba, with whom he allegedly had an affair. Whatever the truth of Goya's sex life, the Inquisition was not amused by the artworks, which it covered up. Nowadays all is bared in the Prado.

At about the same time as his enigmatic *Majas*, the prolific Goya executed the playful frescoes in Madrid's Ermita de San Antonio de la Florida, which have recently been restored to stunning effect. He also produced *Los Caprichos* (The Caprices), a biting series of 80 etchings lambasting the follies of court life and ignorant clergy.

The arrival of the French and war in 1808 had a profound impact on Goya and inspired his unforgiving portrayals of the brutality of war: *El Dos de Mayo* (The Second of May) and, more dramatically, *El Tres de Mayo* (The Third of May). The latter depicts the execution of Madrid rebels by French troops.

After he retired to the Quinta del Sordo (Deaf Man's House) west of the Río Manzanares in Madrid, he created his nightmarish *Pinturas Negras* (Black Paintings). Executed on the walls of the house, they were later removed and now hang in the Prado.

Goya spent the last years of his life in voluntary exile in France, where he continued to paint until his death.

leading *movida* lights such as Ceesepe (b 1958; real name Carlos Sánchez Pérez), who captures the spirit of 1980s Madrid with his eight short films and busy paintings full of people and activity (but recently veers towards surrealism). Another Moriarty protégé was Ouka Lele (b 1957, whose real name is Bárbara Allende), a self-taught photographer whose sometimes weird works stand out for her tangy treatment of colour. Her photos can be seen at the Centro de Arte Reina Sofía, Museo de Historia and, when it reopens, the Museo Municipal de Arte Contemporáneo. Another *movida* photographer who still exhibits around town is Alberto García-Alix (b 1956).

The rebellious, effervescent activity in the 1980s tends to cloud the fact that the visual arts in the Franco years were far from dead, although many artists spent years in exile. The art of Eduardo Arroyo (b 1937) in particular is steeped in the radical spirit that kept him in exile for 15 years from 1962. His paintings tend in part towards pop art, brimming with ironic sociopolitical comment. Of the other exiles, one of Spain's greatest 20th-century sculptors, Toledo-born Alberto Sánchez (1895–1962), who can be seen at the open-air Museo al Aire Libre, lived his last years in Moscow. The work of Benjamín Palencia (1894–1980) shows striking similarities with some of Sánchez' sculptures. The inheritors of their legacy, often called the *Escuela de Madrid,* include Francisco Arias, Gregorio del Olmo, Álvaro Delgado, Andrés Conejo and Agustín Redondela. Carlos Franco (b 1951) painted the frescoes on the Real Casa de la Panadería on Plaza Mayor. Apart from Sánchez, all of these artists are on display at the Museo Municipal de Arte Contemporáneo.

Antonio López García (b 1936) takes a photographer's eye to his hyper-realistic paintings. Settings as simple as *Lavabo y Espejo* (Wash

Basin and Mirror, 1967) convert the most banal everyday objects into scenes of extraordinary depth and the same applies to his Madrid street scenes, which are equally loaded with detail, light play and subtle colour, especially *La Gran Vía* (1981) and *Vallecas* (1980). He won the coveted Premio Príncipe de Asturias for art in 1985 and a couple of his works are in the Centro de Arte Reina Sofía. His contemporary, Alfredo Alcain (b 1936), whose textured paintings could at times be mistaken for aerial shots of patchwork fields, won the Premio Príncipe de Asturias in 2004.

For paintings whose subject matter is Madrid (although she also paints other cities), Málaga-born Paula Varona (www.paulavarona.com) has few peers. The Madrid section of her website (which also lists upcoming exhibitions) has a stunning overview of her work.

Architecture

Madrid's architecture spans the centuries and tells the broad sweep of Spain's historical story: the grandeur of Spain's imperial past sits alongside *barroco madrileño* (Madrid baroque), belle époque buildings and innovative contemporary architecture. It all comes together in the grand historical buildings which have been transformed by stunning modern projects of regeneration.

MADRID TO THE 16TH CENTURY

Madrid's origins as a Muslim garrison town yielded few architectural treasures, or at least few that remain. The only reminder of the Muslim presence is a modest stretch of the town wall, known as the Muralla Árabe (Arab Wall) below the Catedral de Nuestra Señora de la Almudena. The bell towers of the Iglesia de San Pedro El Viejo and Iglesia de San Nicolás de los Servitas are the only modest representatives of the rich Mudéjar style (developed by the Moors who remained behind in reconquered Christian territory) that once adorned Madrid.

MADRID BAROQUE & BEYOND

Architect Juan de Herrera (1530–97) was perhaps the greatest figure of the Spanish Renaissance and he bequeathed to the city an architectural style all of its own. Herrera's trademark was to fuse the sternness of the Renaissance style with a timid approach to its successor, the more voluptuous, ornamental baroque. The result was an architectural style known as *barroco madrileño* (Madrid baroque). Herrera's austere masterpiece was the palace-monastery complex of San Lorenzo de El Escorial, but the nine-arched Puente de Segovia, down the southern end of Calle de Segovia, is also his.

Notable Old Buildings

- *Palacio Real*
- *Plaza de la Villa*
- *Real Casa de la Panadería*
- *Palacio de Comunicaciones*
- *Sociedad General de Autores y Editores*
- *Plaza de Toros Monumental de Las Ventas*
- *Edificio Metrópolis*

The most successful proponent of this style was Juan Gómez de Mora (1586–1648), who was responsible for laying out the Plaza Mayor, as well as the Convento de la Encarnación and the Palacio de Santa Cruz. Gómez de Mora's uncle, Francisco de Mora (1560–1610), added to an impressive family portfolio with the Palacio del Duque de Uceda. Other exceptional examples of the style are the Real Casa de la Panadería on Plaza Mayor and the main entrance of what is now the Museo de Historia.

Ventura Rodríguez (1717–85) dominated the architectural scene in 18th-century Madrid. He redesigned the interior of the Convento de la Encarnación. He also sidelined in spectacular fountains, and it is Rodríguez whom we have to thank for the goddess Cybele in the Plaza de la Cibeles and the Fuente de las Conchas in the Campo del Moro.

Where Ventura Rodríguz leaned towards a neoclassical style, Juan de Villanueva (1739–1811) embraced it wholeheartedly, most notably in the Palacio de Villanueva that would eventually house the Museo del Prado. Villanueva also oversaw the rebuilding of the Plaza Mayor after it was destroyed by fire in 1790 and designed numerous outbuildings of the royal residences, such as San Lorenzo de El Escorial.

BELLE ÉPOQUE

As Madrid emerged from the chaos of the first half of the 19th century, a building boom began. The use of iron and glass, a revolution in building aesthetics that symbolised modernity, became all the rage. The Palacio de Cristal in the Parque del Buen Retiro was built at this time.

By the dawn of the 20th century, known to many as the belle époque, Madrid was abuzz with construction. Headed by the prolific Antonio Palacios (1874–1945), architects from all over Spain began to transform Madrid into the city you see today. Many looked to the past for their inspiration. Neo-Mudéjar was especially favoured for bullrings. The ring at Las Ventas, finished in 1934, is a classic example of the neo-Mudéjar style. A more bombastic interpretation of the belle-époque style is Palacios' Palacio de Comunicaciones with its plethora of pinnacles and prancing ornaments, which was finished in 1917.

By the early 20th century architecture in Madrid had come to be known as the 'eclectic' style, a hybrid form of competing influences as architects mixed and matched. Among the joyous and eye-catching examples – Gran Vía is jammed with them – are the 1916 Edificio Grassy and the 1905 Edificio Metrópolis.

Notable New or Fusion Buildings

- *Centro De Arte Reina Sofía*
- *Caixa Forum*
- *Museo del Prado*
- *Antigua Estación de Atocha*
- *Terminal 4, Barajas International Airport*

CONTEMPORARY ARCHITECTURE

Madrid's contribution to the revolution in Spanish architecture circles has been muted, although there are some standout buildings.

Designed by Richard Rogers, Terminal Four (T4) of Madrid's Barajas International Airport is a stunning, curvaceous work of art, which deservedly won Rogers the prestigious Stirling Prize in October 2006.

Madrid's skyline has been transformed with four skyscrapers rising above the Paseo de la Castellana in northern Madrid. Of these, the Torre Caja Madrid (250m, designed by Sir Norman Foster) is Spain's tallest building, just passing its neighbour, the Torre de Cristal (249.5m, designed by César Pelli). The Torre de Espacio (236m, designed by Henry Cobb) has also won plaudits for its use of glass.

Of the architectural innovations that travellers to Madrid are more likely to experience up close and at greater depth, the most exciting is perhaps the extension of the Museo del Prado, which opened in October 2007. The work of one of Spain's premier architects, the Madrid-based, Pritzker-prize-winning Rafael Moneo, the extension links the main gallery with what remains of the cloisters of the Iglesia de San Jerónimo el Real. Moneo won plaudits for his use of traditional building materials such as granite and oak, while the Prado's director, Miguel Zugzaga, lauded the final effect as being 'like placing a still life by Juan Gris next to one by Zurbarán...discreet, elegant and profoundly modern'. Moneo met two other major Madrid challenges with his remodelling of the Antigua Estación de Atocha and his conversion of the Palacio de Villahermosa into the Museo Thyssen-Bornemisza.

Another landmark project in recent years has been the extension of the Centro de Arte Reina Sofía by the French architect Jean Nouvel. It's a stunning red glass-and-steel complement to the old-world Antigua Estación de Atocha across the Plaza del Emperador Carlos V and the austerity of the remainder of the museum's 18th-century structure.

Between the Reina Sofía and the Prado, the Caixa Forum is one of Madrid's most striking buildings. Designed by Swiss architects Jacques Herzog and Pierre de Meuron, its aesthetic seems to owe more to the world of sculpture than of architecture with its unusual iron-and-brick form. It's a worthy addition to the Paseo del Prado's grandeur.

And one final thing for those who love architecture: while in Madrid you really must stay at the Hotel Puerta América, where each floor has been custom designed by a world-renowned architect.

Madrid's Movie-Makers

The Spanish film industry, with Madrid as its uncontested capital, exists on two radically different levels. First there are the exceptional individual talents, such as Pedro Almodóvar, Penélope Cruz, Antonio Banderas and Javier Bardem, who have become international stars. At the same time the local film-making industry turns out work of real quality but struggles for both funding and international success – in these times of deep economic crisis in Spain, ever-deeper funding cuts, increased ticket prices and the fact that less than 20% of Spanish box office takings are for Spanish films have only deepened the uncertainty surrounding the industry. Hollywood and the home-grown industry come together for the annual Goya awards (Spain's Oscars) in Madrid in February.

DIRECTORS

The still-young Alejandro Amenábar (b 1973) is already one of Spain's most respected directors. He was born in Chile but his family moved to Madrid when he was a child. He announced his arrival with *Tesis* (1996), but it was with *Abre Los Ojos* (Open Your Eyes; 1997), which was later adapted for Hollywood as *Vanilla Sky*, that his name became known internationally. His first English-language film was *The Others* (2001), which received plaudits from critics, but nothing like the clamour that surrounded *Mar Adentro* (The Sea Inside; 2004), his stunning portrayal of a Galician fisherman's desire to die with dignity, which starred Javier Bardem. His 2009 *Ágora* was a stunning follow-up and, with a budget of US$50 million, is the most expensive Spanish film ever made. Not content with directing, Amenábar also writes his own films.

Madrid-born Fernando Trueba (b 1955) has created some fine Spanish films, the best of which was his 1992 release *Belle Epoque*. It portrays gentle romps and bed-hopping on a country estate in Spain in 1931 as four sisters pursue a slightly ingenuous young chap against a background of growing political turbulence. *Belle Epoque* took an Oscar for Best Foreign Language Film in 1993. His more recent works include *El Baile de la Victoria* (2009) and *El Artista y La Modelo* (2012). Trueba is equally well known for his documentary *Calle 54* (2000), which did for Latin jazz what the *Buena Vista Social Club* (1999) did for ageing Cuban musicians. Trueba was a leading personality in the craziness that was *la movida madrileña* in the 1980s.

ACTORS

Of Spain's best-loved actors, few are enjoying international popularity quite like the Oscar-winning heart-throb Javier Bardem, one of the best-known faces in Spanish cinema. Having made his name alongside Penélope Cruz in *Jamón Jamón* (1992), his best-loved roles include those

PEDRO ALMODÓVAR

When Pedro Almodóvar (b 1951) won an Oscar in 2000 for his 1999 hit, *Todo Sobre Mi Madre* (All About My Mother), the world suddenly discovered what Spaniards had known for decades – that Almodóvar was one of world cinema's most creative directors.

Born in a small, impoverished village in Castilla La Mancha, Almodóvar once remarked that in such conservative rural surrounds, 'I felt as if I'd fallen from another planet'. After he moved to Madrid in 1969 he found his spiritual home and began his career making underground Super 8 movies and making a living by selling second-hand goods at El Rastro flea market. He soon became a symbol of Madrid's counterculture, but it was after Franco's death in 1975 that Almodóvar became a nationally renowned cult figure. His early films *Pepi, Luci, Bom y Otras Chicas del Montón* (Pepi, Luci, Bom and the Other Girls; 1980) and *Laberinto de Pasiones* (Labyrinth of Passion; 1982) – the film that brought a young Antonio Banderas to attention – announced him as the icon of *la movida madrileña*, the explosion of hedonism and creativity in the early years of post-Franco Spain. Almodóvar had both in bucketloads; he peppered his films with candy-bright colours and characters leading lives where sex and drugs were the norm. By night Almodóvar performed in Madrid's most famous *movida* bars as part of a drag act called 'Almodóvar & McNamara'. He even appears in this latter role in *Laberinto de Pasiones*.

By the mid-1980s *madrileños* (people from Madrid) had adopted him as one of the city's most famous sons and he went on to broaden his fan base with such quirkily comic looks at modern Spain, generally set in the capital, as *Mujeres al Borde de un Ataque de Nervios* (Women on the Verge of a Nervous Breakdown; 1988) and *Átame* (Tie Me Up, Tie Me Down; 1990). *Todo Sobre Mi Madre* (All About My Mother; 1999) is also notable for the coming of age of the Madrid-born actress Penélope Cruz, who had starred in a number of Almodóvar films and was considered part of a select group of the director's leading ladies long before she became a Hollywood star. Other outstanding movies in a formidable portfolio include *Hable Con Ella* (Talk to Her; 2002), for which he won a Best Original Screenplay Oscar; *La Mala Educación* (Bad Education; 2004), a twisted story of a drag queen, his brother, an abusive priest and a school-friend-turned-filmmaker; and *Volver* (2006), which reunited Almodóvar with Penélope Cruz to popular and critical acclaim.

Pedro Almodóvar's Madrid

- **Plaza Mayor** *La Flor de mi Secreto* (The Flower of My Secret; 1995)
- **El Rastro** *Laberinto de Pasiones* (Labyrinth of Passion; 1982)
- **Villa Rosa** *Tacones Lejanos* (High Heels; 1991)
- **Café del Circulo de Bellas Artes** *Kika* (1993)
- **Viaducto de Segovia** *Matador* (1986)
- **Museo del Jamón** *Carne Trémula* (Live Flesh; 1997)

in *Before Night Falls* (2000), *Mar Adentro* (The Sea Inside; 2004), *Love in the Time of Cholera* (2007) and *No Country for Old Men* (2007); remarkably his Oscar for Best Supporting Actor in 2008 was a first for Spanish actors. Like so many of Spain's best actors, Bardem has passed through the finishing school that are Pedro Almodóvar's movies, appearing in *Carne Trémula* (Live Flesh; 1997). He also comes from one of Spain's most distinguished film-making families: his uncle, Juan Antonio Bardem (1922–2002), is often considered Madrid's senior cinematic bard. Although from Spain's Canary Islands, the Bardems are Madrid identities and run a trendy tapas bar, La Bardemcilla, in the inner-city *barrio* (district) of Chueca.

Penélope Cruz is another Hollywood actress with roots in Madrid (where she was born in 1974). In the late 1990s Penélope Cruz took a leap of faith and headed for Hollywood where she has had success in such films as *Captain Corelli's Mandolin* (2001) and *Vanilla Sky* (2001), but recognition of her acting abilities has come most powerfully for her roles in the Almodóvar classics, *Carne Trémula* (Live Flesh; 1997), *Todo Sobre Mi Madre* (All About My Mother; 1999) and *Volver* (2006); the latter was described by one critic as 'a raging love letter' to Cruz and earned her a Best Actress Oscar nomination, a remarkable achievement for a foreign-language film. She finally won an Oscar for Best Supporting Actress in 2009 for her role in Woody Allen's *Vicky Cristina Barcelona*.

Although not born in Madrid, Málaga-born Antonio Banderas moved to Madrid in 1981 at the age of 19 to launch his career and soon became caught up in the maelstrom of *la movida madrileña*, where he made the acquaintance of Almodóvar. After an early role in *Laberinto de Pasiones* (Labyrinth of Passion; 1982), Banderas would return to the Almodóvar stable with *Mujeres al Borde de un Ataque de Nervios* (Women on the Verge of a Nervous Breakdown; 1988) as his glittering Hollywood career was taking off.

Flamenco

Flamenco seems to capture in musical form all the passion of this most passionate of countries. The power of flamenco is clear to anyone who has heard its melancholy strains in the background of a crowded Spanish bar, and taking in a live performance can be a highlight of any visit to Madrid.

FLAMENCO'S ROOTS

Flamenco's origins have been lost to time. Some have suggested that flamenco derives form Byzantine chants used in Visigothic churches. But most musical historians speculate that it probably dates back to a fusion of songs brought to Spain by the *gitanos* (Roma people) with music and verses from North Africa crossing into medieval Muslim Andalucía. Flamenco as we now know it first took recognisable form in the 18th and early 19th centuries among *gitanos* in the lower Guadalquivir valley in western Andalucía.

Flamenco Resources

A good website for all things flamenco is www.deflamenco.com.

To learn more you could also pass by El Flamenco Vive (p60), which has a wide range of flamenco books and CDs.

FLAMENCO IN MADRID

Madrid claims to be Spain's capital of flamenco, which is true, but only to an extent. The Cádiz-Jerez-Seville axis in Andalucía remains the genre's spiritual home and it remains the area with the most authentic flamenco venues. But Madrid is undoubtedly flamenco's biggest stage, the place where the best performers of flamenco always turn up at one time or another. And therein lies the essence of Madrid's contribution to the development of flamenco: it has always been a stage, often a prestigious one, that has brought flamenco to a wider audience. Most Madrid venues may lack the intimate atmosphere and gritty authenticity that is an essential element of the flamenco experience, but the quality is unimpeachable.

At first the *gitanos* and Andalucians were concentrated in the area around Calle de Toledo. The novelist Benito Pérez Galdós found no fewer than 88 Andalucian taverns along that street towards the end of the 19th century. The scene shifted in the early 20th century to the streets around Plaza de Santa Ana. As flamenco's appeal widened and became a tourist attraction, more *tablaos* (flamenco venues) sprang up throughout Madrid.

Madrid Flamenco Venues

Villa Rosa (p86)

Casa Patas (p73)

Las Tablas (p59)

Corral de la Morería (p73)

Las Carboneras (p59)

FLAMENCO STARS

Two names loom large over the world of flamenco – Paco de Lucía and El Camarón de la Isla – who were responsible for flamenco's revival in the second half of the 20th century. Theirs is the standard by which all other flamenco artists are measured.

Paco de Lucía (b 1947) is the doyen of flamenco guitarists with a virtuosity few can match. For many in the flamenco world, he is the personification of *duende,* that indefinable capacity to transmit the power and passion of flamenco. Other guitar maestros include members of the

FLAMENCO – THE ESSENTIAL ELEMENTS

A flamenco singer is known as a *cantaor* (male) or *cantaora* (female); a dancer is a *bailaor/a*. Most of the songs and dances are performed to a blood-rush of guitar from the *tocaor/a* (male or female flamenco guitarist). Percussion is provided by tapping feet, clapping hands and sometimes castanets. Flamenco *coplas* (songs) come in many different types, from the anguished *soleá* or the intensely despairing *siguiriya* to the livelier *alegría* or the upbeat *bulería*. The first flamenco was *cante jondo* (deep song), an anguished instrument of expression for a group on the margins of society. *Jondura* (depth) is still the essence of pure flamenco.

Montoya family (some of whom are better known by the sobriquet of Los Habichuela), especially Juan (b 1933) and Pepe (b 1944).

In 1968 Paco de Lucía began flamenco's most exciting partnership with his friend El Camarón de la Isla (1950–92); together they recorded nine classic albums. Until his premature death, El Camarón was the leading light of contemporary *cante jondo* and it's impossible to overstate his influence on the art; his introduction of electric bass into his songs, for example, paved the way for a generation of artists to take flamenco in hitherto unimagined directions. Although born in San Fernando in Andalucía's far south, El Camarón was the artist in residence at Madrid's Tablao Torres Bermejas for 12 years, and it was during this period that his collaboration with Paco de Lucía was at its best. In his later years El Camarón teamed up with Tomatito, one of Paco de Lucía's protégés, and the results were similarly ground-breaking. When El Camarón died in 1992 an estimated 100,000 people attended his funeral.

Another artist who reached the level of cult figure was Enrique Morente (1942–2010), whose sudden death sent shockwaves through the flamenco world. Referred to by one Madrid paper as 'the last bohemian', Morente was careful not to alienate flamenco purists but through his numerous collaborations across genres he helped lay the foundations for Nuevo Flamenco and Fusion. His daughter, *cantaora* Estrella Morente (b 1980) is considered one of the genre's most exciting talents.

One of the most venerable *cantaoras* is Carmen Linares (b 1951), who has spent much of her working life in Madrid. Leading contemporary figures include the flighty, adventurous Joaquín Cortés (b 1969), and Antonio Canales (b 1962), who is more of a flamenco purist.

Top Flamenco Albums

- *Paco de Lucía Antología (1995)*
- *Una Leyenda Flamenca – El Camarón de la Isla (1993)*
- *Blues de la Frontera – Pata Negra (1986)*
- *Cositas Buenas – Paco de Lucía (2004)*
- *Lágrimas Negras – Bebo Valdés and Diego El Cigala (2003)*
- *Sueña La Alhambra – Enrique Morente (2005)*
- *Flamenco Chill – Chambao (2002)*

NUEVO FLAMENCO & FUSION

Two of the earliest groups to fuse flamenco with rock back in the 1980s were Ketama and Pata Negra, whose music is labelled by some as Gypsy rock. In the early 1990s, Radio Tarifa emerged with a mesmerising mix of flamenco, North African and medieval sounds. A more traditional flamenco performer, Juan Peña Lebrijano, better known as El Lebrijano, has created some equally appealing combinations with classical Moroccan music. Diego El Cigala, one of modern flamenco's finest voices, relaunched his career with an exceptional collaboration with Cuban virtuoso Bebo Valdés (*Lágrimas Negras;* 2004) and has released three critically acclaimed albums in the years since.

Chambao is the most popular of the Nuevo Flamenco bands doing the rounds at the moment, while Barcelona group Ojos de Brujo has won acclaim for their gritty sound. Also popular is Diego Amador (b 1973), a self-taught pianist. The piano is not a classic instrument of flamenco but Amador makes it work. All of these artists perform in Madrid from time to time.

Survival Guide

Transport

GETTING TO MADRID

Madrid's Barajas Airport is one of Europe's busiest and is served by almost 100 airlines. Direct flights – whether with low-cost carriers or other airlines – connect the city with destinations across Europe. A smaller but nonetheless significant number of airlines also fly into Madrid direct from the Americas, Asia and Africa, and plenty of domestic flights to Madrid from other Spanish cities. Flight times include less than one hour to Lisbon and around two hours to London, Paris and some Moroccan cities.

Within Spain, Madrid is the hub of the country's outstanding bus and train network. Bus routes radiate into and out from the Spanish capital to all four corners of the country with long-haul cross-border services fanning out across Europe with some also going to Morocco. The ongoing expansion of Spain's high-speed rail network has dramatically cut travel times between Madrid and the rest of the country. The rail link to Barcelona in particular has also brought Madrid that much closer to the rest of Europe and there are plans for a high-speed rail link between Paris and Madrid.

Flights, tours and rail tickets can be booked online at www.lonelyplanet.com/travel_services.

Aeropuerto de Barajas

Madrid's **Barajas airport** (☎902 404 704; www.aena.es; Ⓜ Aeropuerto T1, T2 & T3; Aeropuerto T4) lies 15km northeast of the city, and it's Europe's fifth-busiest hub with almost 50 million passengers passing through here every year.

Barajas has four terminals. Terminal 4 (T4) deals mainly with flights of Iberia and its partners (eg British Airways, American Airlines and Vueling), while the remainder leave from the conjoined T1, T2 and (rarely) T3. To match your airline with a terminal, visit the Madrid-Barajas section of www.aena.es and click on 'Airlines'.

Although all airlines conduct check-in *(facturación)* at the airport's departure areas, some also allow check-in at the Nuevos Ministerios metro stop and transport interchange in Madrid itself – ask your airline.

There are car rental services, ATMs, money exchange bureaus, pharmacies, tourist offices, left luggage offices, and parking services at T1, T2 and T4.

Metro

The easiest way into town from the airport is line 8 of the metro to the Nuevos Ministerios transport interchange, which connects with lines 10 and 6 and the local overground *cercanías* (local trains serving suburbs and nearby towns). It operates from 6.05am to 2am. A single ticket costs €4.50 including the €3 airport supplement. If you're buying a 10-ride Metrobús ticket (€12.20), you'll need to top it up with the €3 supplement if you're travelling to/from the airport. The journey to Nuevos Ministerios takes around 15 minutes, or around 25 minutes from T4.

Bus

The Exprés Aeropuerto (Airport Express; Bus No.203; www.emtmadrid.es; €5, 40 minutes; 24hr) runs between Puerta de Atocha train station and the airport. From 11.30pm until 6am, departures are from the Plaza de Cibeles, not the train station. Departures take place every 13 to 25 minutes from the station or at night-time every 35 minutes from Plaza de Cibeles.

Alternatively from T1, T2 and T3 take bus 200 to/from the Intercambiador de Avenida de América (transport interchange on Avenida de América). The same ticket prices apply as for the metro. The first departures from the airport are at 5.10am (T1, T2 and T3). The last scheduled service from the airport is 11.30pm; buses leave every 12 to 20 minutes. There's also a free bus service connecting all four terminals.

CLIMATE CHANGE & TRAVEL

Every form of transport that relies on carbon-based fuel generates CO_2, the main cause of human-induced climate change. Modern travel is dependent on aeroplanes, which might use less fuel per person than most cars but travel much greater distances. The altitude at which aircraft emit gases (including CO_2) and particles also contributes to their climate change impact. Many websites offer 'carbon calculators' that allow people to estimate the carbon emissions generated by their journey and, for those who wish to do so, to offset the impact of the greenhouse gases emitted with contributions to portfolios of climate-friendly initiatives throughout the world. Lonely Planet offsets the carbon footprint of all staff and author travel.

Minibus

Aero City (☎91 747 75 70; www.aerocity.com; per person from €20, express service from €35 per minibus) is a private minibus service that takes you door-to-door between central Madrid and the airport (T1 in front of Arrivals Gate 2, T2 between gates 5 and 6, and T4 arrivals hall). It operates 24 hours and you can book by phone or online. You can reserve a seat or the entire minibus; the latter operates like a taxi.

Taxi

A taxi to the centre (around 30 minutes, depending on traffic, 35 to 40 minutes from T4) costs €23 to €35.

Estación de Atocha

Madrid's main train station, the **Estación de Atocha** sits at the southern end of the Paseo del Prado at the southern edge of the city centre. This is where most international, national and local *cercanías* trains arrive, including many high-speed AVE services.

Downstairs in the station there are ATMs, car rental offices and a left luggage service.

Metro

The **Atocha Renfe metro station** (Line 1; (one-way/10-trip ticket €1.50/12.20; 6.05am-2am; line 1), not to be confused with the nearby Atocha station, is inside the Renfe train station. From Atocha Renfe it's 10 to 15 minutes to Sol station, with connections elsewhere via lines 2 and 3. Buy tickets from machines at the station.

Taxi

Taxis leave from the top floor of the station. A taxi to the centre (five to 10 minutes, depending on traffic) costs around €5 to €7, plus a €3 train station supplement.

Bus

Less easy to decipher than the Metro, numerous bus routes (one-way/10-trip ticket €1.50/12.20; 6.30am-11.30pm; line 1) nonetheless pass close to the station. Check the **Empresa Municipal de Transportes de Madrid** (EMT; ☎902 507 850; www.emtmadrid.es) for route maps.

Estación de Chamartín

North of the city centre, **Estación de Chamartín** (Ⓜ Chamartín) has numerous long-distance rail services, especially those to/from northern Spain.This is also where long-haul international trains arrive from Paris and Lisbon.

Metro

Chamartín station has its own metro station (one-way/10-trip ticket €1.50/12.20; 6.05am-2am, lines 1 and 10). From Chamartín station to Sol takes from 15 to 20 minutes with connections elsewhere via lines 2 and 3. Buy tickets from machines at the station.

Taxi

A taxi to the centre (around 15 minutes, depending on traffic) costs around €10 plus a €3 train station supplement.

Bus

Numerous bus routes (one-way/10-trip ticket €1.50/12.20; 6.30am-11.30pm; line 1) pass close to the station. Check the **Empresa Municipal de Transportes de Madrid** (EMT; ☎902 507 850; www.emtmadrid.es) for route maps.

Estación Sur de Autobuses

Estación Sur de Autobuses (☎91 468 42 00; www.estaciondeautobuses.com; Calle de Méndez Álvaro 83; Ⓜ Méndez Álvaro), just south of the M-30 ring road, is the city's principal bus station. It serves most destinations to the south and many in other parts of the country. Most bus companies have a ticket office here, even if their buses depart from elsewhere.

Metro

The nearest metro station is **Méndez Álvaro station** (one-way/10-trip ticket

€1.50/12.20; 6.05am-2am, line 6). To get to the central Sol station, take line 6 to Legazpi station and change to line 2. Buy tickets from machines at the station.

Taxi

A taxi to the centre (around 20 to 30 minutes, depending on traffic) costs around €10 to €15 plus a €3 bus station supplement.

GETTING AROUND MADRID

Madrid has an excellent public transport network. The most convenient way of getting around is via the metro whose 11 lines criss-cross the city; no matter where you find yourself you're never far from a metro station. The bus network is equally extensive and operates under the same ticketing system, although the sheer number of routes (around 200!) make it more difficult for first-time visitors to master. Taxis in Madrid are plentiful and relatively cheap by European standards. Although there are some excellent places to cycle, using a bicycle as a means of transport can be nerve-wracking unless you're used to Spanish roads.

Bicycle

Lots of people zip around town on *motos* (mopeds), but little has been done to encourage cyclists in Madrid and bike lanes are almost as rare as drivers who keep an eye out for cyclists.

You can transport your bicycle on the metro from 10am to 12.30pm and after 9pm Mondays to Fridays and all day on weekends and holidays. You can also take your bike aboard *cercanías* from 10am onwards Monday to Friday and all day on weekends.

Hire

Bike Spain (Map p234; ☎91 559 06 53; www.bikespain.info; Calle del Codo; bike rental half/full day €12/17, tours from €31; ⏰10am-2pm & 4-7pm Mon-Fri, 10am-2pm Sat & Sun; Ⓜ Ópera) Bicycle hire plus English-language guided city tours by bicycle, by day or (Friday) night, as well as longer expeditions.

By Bike (☎91 154 61 08; www.bybike.info; Avenida de Menédez Pelayo 35; per hr/day from €4/30; ⏰10am-9pm Mon-Fri & 9.30am-9.30pm Sat & Sun Jun-Sep, 10am-3pm & 5-9pm Mon-Fri, 9am-9pm Sat & Sun Oct-May; 👪; Ⓜ Ibiza) Ideally placed for the Parque del Buen Retiro and with child seats/trailers, roller blades and electric bikes for hire. Prices vary depending on the length of hire and number of people.

Urban Movil (☎91 542 77 71; www.urbanmovil.com; Plaza de Santiago 2; per hr/half-/full day incl helmet €4.50/14/19) Another rental outfit located in the city centre.

Bus

Buses operated by Empresa Municipal de Transportes de Madrid travel along most city routes regularly between about 6.30am and 11.30pm. Twenty-six night-bus *búhos* (owls) routes operate from 11.45pm to 5.30am, with all routes originating in Plaza de la Cibeles.

Fares for day and night trips are the same as for the metro: €1.50 for a single trip, €12.20 for a 10-trip Metrobús ticket. Single-trip tickets can be purchased on board.

Metro & Cercanías

Madrid's modern **metro** (www.metromadrid.es), Europe's second-largest, is a fast, efficient and safe way to navigate Madrid, and generally easier than getting to grips with bus routes. There are 11 colour-coded lines in central Madrid, in addition to the modern southern suburban MetroSur system as well as lines heading east to the major population centres of Pozuelo and Boadilla del Monte. Colour maps showing the metro system are available from any metro station or online. The metro operates from 6.05am to 2am.

The short-range *cercanías* regional trains operated by **Renfe** (☎902 320 320; www.renfe.es/cercanias/madrid) are handy for making a quick, north–south hop between Chamartín and Atocha train stations (with stops at Nuevos Ministerios and Sol), or for the trip out to San Lorenzo de El Escorial.

Tickets

Unless you're only passing through en route elsewhere, you should buy a Metrobús ticket valid for 10 rides (bus and metro) for €12.20; single-journey tickets cost €1.50. Tickets can be purchased at stations from manned booths or machines in the metro stations, as well as most *estancos* (tobacconists) and newspaper kiosks. Metrobús tickets are not valid on *cercanías* services. Children under four travel free.

Monthly or season passes *(abonos)* only make sense if you're staying long term and use local transport frequently. You'll need to get a *carnet* (ID card) from metro stations or tobacconists – take a passport-sized photo and your passport.

An **Abono Transporte Turístico** (Tourist Ticket; per 1/2/7 days €8/13.40/33.40) is also possible.

The fine for being caught without a ticket on public transport is €50 – in addition to the price of the ticket, of course.

Taxi

You can pick up a taxi at ranks throughout town or simply flag one down. Flag fall is €2.15 from 6am to 10pm daily, €2.20 from 10pm to 6am Sunday to Friday and €3.10 from 10pm Saturday to 6am Sunday. You pay between €1 and €1.20 per kilometre depending on the time of day. Several supplementary charges, usually posted inside the taxi, apply; these include €5.50 to/from the airport; €3 from taxi ranks at train and bus stations, €3 to/from Parque Ferial Juan Carlos I; and €6.70 on New Year's Eve and Christmas Eve from 10pm to 6am. There's no charge for luggage.

Among the 24-hour taxi services are **Tele-Taxi** (☎91 371 21 31; www.tele-taxi.es) and **Radio-Teléfono Taxi** (☎91 547 82 00; www.radiotelefono-taxi.com).

A green light on the roof means the taxi is *libre* (available). Usually a sign to this effect is also placed in the lower passenger side of the windscreen.

Tipping taxi drivers is not common practice, although most travellers round fares up to the nearest euro or two.

TOURS

The following offer tours around the city and some outlying sights. See also Bike Spain (p204) under the Bicycle Hire section in this chapter.

Insider's Madrid (☎91 447 38 66; www.insidersmadrid.com; tours from €60) An impressive range of tailor-made tours that include walking, tapas, flamenco and bullfighting tours.

Letango Tours (Map p231; ☎91 369 47 52; www.letangospaintours.com; Plaza Tirso de Molina 12, 1ºD; Mon-Fri €95, Sat & Sun €135; Ⓜ Tirso de Molina) Walking tours through Madrid with additional excursions to San Lorenzo El Escorial, Segovia and Toledo.

Madrid Bike Tours (☎680 581 782; www.madridbiketours.com; 4hr tours €55) Londoner Mike Chandler offers a guided two-wheel tour of Madrid as well as tours further afield.

Madrid City Tour (☎902 02 47 58; www.esmadrid.com/en/tourist-bus; 1-day ticket adult €21, child free-€9; ⏲9am-10pm Mar-Oct, 10am-6pm Nov-Feb) Hop-on, hop-off open-topped buses that run every 10 to 20 minutes along two routes: Historical Madrid and Modern Madrid. Information, including maps, is available at tourist offices, most travel agencies and some hotels, or you can get tickets on the bus.

Madrid Original (☎91 521 04 49; www.madridoriginal.com; €110-150) Privately run tours (for up to six people) in English, Spanish or French by professional guides. Tours include the major museums, historical eras, Gran Vía, the Parque del Buen Retiro and tailor-made itineraries.

Madrid Segway Tours (☎659 824 499; www.madsegs.com; 3hr tour per person €65, plus €15 refundable deposit) Most of these Segway tours start in Plaza de España

Madrid en Bicicleta (☎91 355 39 12; www.mtb-spain.com) Mountain-bike tours in the mountains surrounding Madrid. It also runs the two-day Guadarrama tour (€185). Bookings can be made through Bike Spain.

Spanish Tapas Madrid (www.spanishtapasmadrid.com; adult lunch/dinner tour €35/45) Local boy Luis Ortega takes you through some iconic Madrid tapas bars.

Urban Movil (Map p234; ☎91 542 77 71, 687 535 443; www.urbanmovil.com; Plaza de Santiago 2; 1-/2hr Segway tours €40/65; ⏲10am-8pm) Segway tours around Madrid. Prices include 10-minutes worth of training before you set out and it also organises bike tours.

Visitas Guiadas Oficiales (Official Guided Tours; Map p234; ☎902 221 424; www.esmadrid.com; Plaza Mayor 27; adult/child €3.90/free; Ⓜ Sol) Twenty highly recommended guided tours conducted in Spanish and English. Organised by the **Centro de Turismo de Madrid** (☎91 588 16 36; www.esmadrid.com; Plaza Mayor 27; ⏲9.30am-8.30pm; Ⓜ Sol).

Wellington Society (☎609 143203; www.wellsoc.org; tours €50-85) A handful of quirky historical tours laced with anecdotes and led by the inimitable Stephen Drake-Jones. Possibilities include Bullfights, Hemingway's Madrid, Goya's Madrid, Curiosities and Anecdotes of Old Madrid.

Directory A–Z

Business Hours

Reviews throughout this guide won't list opening hours unless they vary from the following standards:

- **Banks** 8.30am to 2pm Mon-Fri; some also open 4pm to 7pm Thu, and 9am to 1pm Sat
- **Central Post Offices** 8.30am to 9.30pm Monday to Friday, 8.30am to 2pm Saturday
- **Nightclubs** midnight or 1am to 5am or 6am
- **Restaurants** lunch 1pm to 4pm, dinner 8.30pm to midnight or later
- **Shops** 10am to 2pm & 4.30pm to 7.30pm or 5pm to 8pm Monday to Saturday; some bigger shops don't close for lunch and many shops open on some Sundays, usually from 11pm or midday to 7pm or 8pm

PRACTICALITIES

- **Currency** euro
- **Weights & Measures** Metric
- **Electric Current** 220V, 50Hz
- **Plugs** European-style, two-pin
- **Major newspapers** centre-left **El País** (www.elpais.com); centre-right **El Mundo** (www.elmundo.es); right-wing **ABC** (www.abc.es). The widely available *International Herald Tribune* includes an eight-page supplement of articles from *El País* translated into English (www.elpais.com/misc/herald/herald.pdf).
- **Radio** Radio Nacional de España (RNE): Radio 1, with general interest and current affairs programs; Radio 5, with sport and entertainment; and Radio 3 ('Radio d'Espop'). Stations covering current affairs include the left-leaning Cadena Ser, or the right-wing COPE. The most popular commercial pop and rock stations are 40 Principales, Kiss FM; Cadena 100 and Onda Cero.
- **TV** Spain's state-run Televisión Española (TVE1 and La 2) or the independent commercial stations (Antena 3, Tele 5, Cuatro and La Sexta). The regional government also runs Telemadrid. Cable and satellite TV is widespread.

Customs Regulations

People entering Spain from outside the EU are allowed to bring in duty-free one bottle of spirits, one bottle of wine, 50mL of perfume and 200 cigarettes. There are no duty-free allowances for travel between EU countries. For duty-paid items bought at normal shops in one EU country and taken into another, the allowances are 90L of wine, 10L of spirits, unlimited quantities of perfume and 800 cigarettes.

Discount Cards

- The International Student Identity Card (ISIC; see www.isic.org), the Euro<26 card (www.euro26.org) and (sometimes) university student cards entitle you to discounts of up to 50% at many sights.
- If you're over 65, you may be eligible for an admission discount to some attractions. Some attractions limit discounts to those with a Seniors Card issued by an EU country or other country with which Spanish citizens enjoy reciprocal rights.
- If you plan to visit the Museo del Prado, Museo Thyssen-Bornemisza and Centro de Arte Reina Sofía while in Madrid, the Paseo del Arte ticket covers them all in a combined ticket for €21.60 and is valid for one visit to

each gallery during a 12-month period; buying separate tickets would cost €27.

Madrid Card (☎91 360 47 72; www.madridcard.com; 1/2/3 days adult €39/49/59, child age 6-12 €20/28/34) If you intend to do some intensive sightseeing and travelling on public transport, it might be worth looking at the Madrid Card. It includes free entry to more than 50 museums in and around Madrid (some of these are already free, but it does include the Museo del Prado, Museo Thyssen-Bornemisza, Centro de Arte Reina Sofía, Estadio Santiago Bernabéu and Palacio Real), free walking tours and discounts in a number of restaurants, shops, bars and car rental.The Madrid Card can be bought online (slightly cheaper), or in person at the tourist offices on Plaza Mayor or Terminal 4 in Barajas Airport, the Metro de Madrid ticket office in Terminal 2 of the airport, the Museo Thyssen-Bornemisza and in some tobacconists and hotels; a list of sales outlets appears on the website.

Electricity

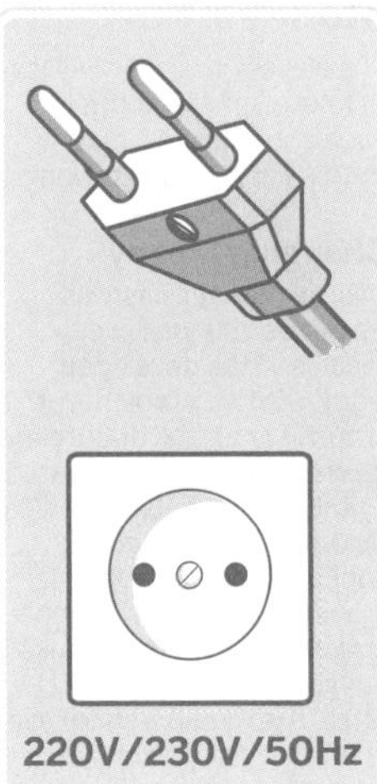

The electric current in Madrid is 220/230V, 50Hz, as in the rest of continental Europe. Several countries outside Europe (such as the USA and Canada) use 110V, 60Hz, which means that it's safest to use a transformer. Plugs have two round pins, as in the rest of continental Europe.

Emergency

To report thefts or other crime-related matters, your best bet is the **Servicio de Atención al Turista Extranjero** (Foreign Tourist Assistance Service; ☎902 102112, 91 548 85 37, 91 548 80 08; www.esmadrid.com/satemadrid; Calle de Leganitos 19; ⏲9am-10pm; Ⓜ Plaza de España, Santo Domingo), which is housed in the central police station or *comisaría* of the National Police. Here you'll find specially trained officers working alongside representatives from the tourism ministry. They can also assist in cancelling credit cards, as well as contacting your embassy or your family. There's also a **general number** (☎902 102 112; 24-hour English and Spanish, 8am to midnight other languages) for reporting crimes.

Ambulance (☎061)

EU Standard Emergency Number (☎112)

Fire Brigade (Bomberos; ☎080)

Local Police (Policía Municipal; ☎092)

Military Police (Guardia Civil; ☎062)

Policía Nacional (☎091)

Teléfono de la Víctima (☎902 180 995) Hotline for victims of racial or sexual violence.

Gay & Lesbian Travellers

Madrid has always been one of Europe's most gay-friendly cities. The city's gay community is credited with reinvigorating the once down-at-heel inner-city *barrio* (district) of Chueca, where Madrid didn't just come out of the closet, it ripped the doors off in the process. Today the *barrio* is one of Madrid's most vibrant and it's very much the heart and soul of gay Madrid with cafes, bars, hotels, shops and nightclubs clearly oriented to a gay clientele abound. But there's nothing ghetto-like about Chueca. Its extravagantly gay-and-lesbian personality is anything but exclusive and the crowd is almost always mixed gay-straight. As gay and lesbian residents like to say, Chueca isn't gay-friendly, it's hetero-friendly. The best time of all to be in town if you're gay or lesbian is around the last Saturday in June for Madrid's gay and lesbian pride march.

Websites

➡ **Chueca** (www.chueca.com)

➡ **Gay Iberia** (Guía Gay de España; www.gayiberia.com)

➡ **Gay Madrid 4 U** (www.gaymadrid4u.com)

➡ **Guía Gay de España** (http://guia.universogay.com)

➡ **LesboNet** (www.lesbonet.org)

➡ **Night Tours.com** (www.nighttours.com)

➡ **Shangay** (www.shangay.com)

Organisations

➡ **Colectivo de Gais y Lesbianas de Madrid** (Cogam; ☎91 522 45 17, 5-9pm Mon-Fri 91 525 00 70; www.cogam.es; Calle de la Puebla 9; Ⓜ Callao or Gran Vía) Offers activities, has an information office and social centre, and runs an **information line** (☎91 523 00 70; ⏲5-9pm Mon-Fri).

➡ **Federación Estatal de Lesbianas, Gays, Transexuales & Bisexuales** (☎902 280 669; www.felgt.org; 1st fl,

Calle de las Infantas 40) A national advocacy group that played a leading role in lobbying for the legalisation of gay marriages.

➡ **Fundación Triángulo** (☎91 593 05 40; www.fundaciontriangulo.es; 1st fl, Calle de Melendez Valdés 52; Ⓜ Iglesia) Another source of information on gay issues; it has a separate information line, **Información LesGai** (☎91 44 66 394).

Internet Access

Internet Cafes

Most of Madrid's better internet cafes have fallen by the wayside. You'll find plenty of small *locutorios* (small shops selling phone cards and cheap phone calls) all over the city and many have a few computers out the back, but we don't list these as they come and go with monotonous regularity. In the downtown area, your best option is the Ayuntamiento's Centro de Turismo de Madrid on Plaza Mayor which offers free internet for up to 15 minutes; its quieter branch beneath Plaza de Colón offers free and unlimited access. Otherwise, your best bet is **Café Comercial** (Glorieta de Bilbao 7; per 50min €1; ⏲7.30am-midnight Mon, 7.30am-1am Tue-Thu, 7.30am-2am Fri, 8.30am-2am Sat, 9am-midnight Sun; Ⓜ Bilbao), one of Madrid's grandest old cafes with internet upstairs.

Medical Services

All foreigners have the same right as Spaniards to emergency medical treatment in a public hospital. European Union (EU) citizens are entitled to the full range of health-care services in public hospitals free of charge, but you'll need to present your European Health Insurance Card (EHIC); inquire at your national health service before leaving home. Even if you have no insurance, you'll be treated in an emergency, with costs in the public system ranging from free to €120 for a basic consultation. Non-EU citizens have to pay for anything other than emergency treatment – one good reason among many to have a travel-insurance policy. If you have a specific health complaint, obtain the necessary information and referrals for treatment before leaving home.

Hospital General Gregorio Marañón (☎91 586 80 00; www.hggm.es; Calle del Doctor Esquerdo 46; Ⓜ Sáinz de Baranda, O'Donnell, Ibiza) One of the city's main (and more central) hospitals.

Unidad Medica (Anglo American; ☎91 435 18 23; www.unidadmedica.com; Calle del Conde de Aranda 1; ⏲9am-8pm Mon-Fri, 10am-1pm Sat; Ⓜ Retiro) A private clinic with a wide range of specialisations, where all doctors speak Spanish and English, with some also speaking French and German. Each consultation costs around €125.

Pharmacies

For minor health problems, try your local *farmacia* (pharmacy), where pharmaceuticals are sold more freely without prescription than in other countries, such as the US, Australia or the UK.

At least one pharmacy is open 24 hours per day in each district of Madrid. They mostly operate on a rota and details appear daily in *El País* and other papers. Otherwise call ☎010. Most pharmacies have a list in their windows indicating the location of nearby after-hours pharmacies – if it says 'Dia y noche', it's open 24 hours. Pharmacies that always remain open include:

Farmacia Mayor (☎91 366 46 16; Calle Mayor 13; ⏲24hr; Ⓜ Sol)

Farmacia Velázquez 70 (☎91 575 60 28; Calle de Velázquez 70; ⏲24hr; Ⓜ Velázquez)

Money

The easiest way to travel is to take a small amount of cash and withdraw money from ATMs as you go along.

Changing Money

You can change cash or travellers cheques in currencies of the developed world without problems at virtually any bank or bureau de change (usually indicated by the word *cambio*). Central Madrid also abounds with banks – most have ATMs.

Exchange offices are open for longer hours than banks but generally offer poorer rates. Also, keep a sharp eye open for commissions at bureaux de change.

WIFI ACCESS

Most midrange and top-end hotels have either wi-fi or cable ADSL in-room connections; even some of the better hotels can run out of cables for the latter so ask for one as soon as you arrive. For everyone else, there are plenty of internet cafes around town.

Chueca Wifi (www.chuecawifi.com) is a *barrio* initiative aimed at transforming Chueca into one big wi-fi hotspot and dozens of businesses have signed up; check out its website for more details. Otherwise, check out www.madridmemata.es/madrid-wifi/ for a reasonable list of wi-fi hotspots.

Credit Cards & ATMs

Major cards, such as Visa, MasterCard, Maestro, Cirrus and, to a lesser extent, Amex, are accepted throughout Spain. They can be used in many hotels, restaurants and shops; in doing so you'll need to show some form of photo ID (eg passport) or, increasingly, you'll be asked to key in your PIN. Credit cards can also be used in ATMs displaying the appropriate sign (if there's no sign, don't risk it), or, if you have no PIN, you can obtain cash advances over the counter in many banks. Check charges with your bank.

If your card is lost, stolen or swallowed by an ATM, you can call the following numbers toll-free to have an immediate stop put on its use:

Amex (902 375 637)

Diners Club (91 211 43 00)

MasterCard (900 971 231)

Visa (900 991 216, 900 991 124)

Post

Correos (902 197 197; www.correos.es), the national postal service, has its **main office** (91 523 06 94; Paseo del Prado 1; 8.30am-9.30pm Mon-Fri, 8.30am-2pm Sat; Banco de España) in the ornate Palacio de Comunicaciones.

Sellos (stamps) are sold at most *estancos* (tobacconists' shops with *Tabacos* in yellow letters on a maroon background), as well as post offices.

For a full list of postage prices, go to www.correos.es (in Spanish) and click on 'Calculador de Tarifas'.

Delivery times are erratic but ordinary mail to other Western European countries can take up to a week; to North America up to 10 days; and to Australia or New Zealand anywhere between one and three weeks.

Public Holidays

Madrid's 14 public holidays are as follows:

Año Nuevo (New Year's Day) 1 January.

Reyes (Epiphany or Three Kings' Day) 6 January.

Jueves Santo (Holy Thursday) March/April.

Viernes Santo (Good Friday) March/April.

Labour Day (Fiesta del Trabajo) 1 May.

Fiesta de la Comunidad de Madrid 2 May.

Fiestas de San Isidro Labrador 15 May.

La Asunción (Feast of the Assumption) 15 August.

Día de la Hispanidad (Spanish National Day) 12 October – a fairly sober occasion with a military parade along the Paseo de la Castellana.

Todos los Santos (All Saints' Day) 1 November.

Día de la Virgen de la Almudena 9 November.

Día de la Constitución (Constitution Day) 6 December.

La Inmaculada Concepción (Feast of the Immaculate Conception) 8 December.

Navidad (Christmas) 25 December.

Safe Travel

Madrid is a generally city, although you should, as in most European cities, be wary of pickpockets on transport and around major tourist sights. Although you should be careful, don't be paranoid; remember that the overwhelming majority of travellers to Madrid rarely encounter any problems.

You're most likely to fall foul of pickpockets in the most heavily touristed parts of town, notably the Plaza Mayor and surrounding streets, the Puerta del Sol, El Rastro and around the Museo del Prado. Tricks abound. They usually involve a team of two or more (sometimes one of them an attractive woman to distract male victims). While one attracts your attention, the other empties your pockets. Be wary of jostling on crowded buses and the metro and, as a general rule, dark, empty streets are to be avoided; luckily, Madrid's most lively nocturnal areas are generally busy with crowds having a good time.

Telephone

Mobile (cell) phone numbers start with 6. Numbers starting with 900 are national toll-free numbers, while those starting 901 to 905 come with varying conditions. A common one is 902, which is a national standard rate number, but which can only be dialled from within Spain. In a similar category are numbers starting with 800, 803, 806 and 807.

Mobile Phones

You can buy SIM cards and prepaid time in Spain for your mobile phone (provided you own a GSM, dual- or tri-band cellular phone). This only works if your national phone hasn't been code-blocked; check before leaving home. Only consider a full contract unless you plan to live in Spain for a while.

All the Spanish mobile phone companies (Telefónica's MoviStar, Orange, Vodafone and Amena) offer *prepagado* (prepaid) accounts for mobiles. The SIM card costs from €50, which includes some prepaid phone time. Phone outlets are scattered across the city. You can then top up in their shops or by buying cards in outlets, such as *estancos* (tobacconists) and newsstands.

You can rent a mobile phone through the Madrid-based **OnSpanishTime.com** (www.onspanishtime.com/web). Delivery and pick-up start from US$5. The basic service costs US$6/32/99 per day/week/month for the phone. You pay a US$100 deposit and the whole operation is done over the internet.

Phonecards

Blue payphones are easy to use to make international and domestic phone calls. They accept coins, *tarjetas telefónicas* (phonecards) that are issued by the national phone company Telefónica and, in some cases, credit cards. Phones that are in hotel rooms are more expensive than street payphones. The Telefónica phonecards are best to use for domestic calls.

For international calls you have two cut-price options. Most internet cafes are Skype enabled, allowing you to call (with your Skype user ID and password) for no more than the cost of your internet time. The other option is an international phonecard, which can be bought from *estancos*, some small convenience stores and news-stands in central Madrid. Most outlets display the call rates for each card. For calls to Australia, the US or Western Europe, Euro Hours has a phonecard costing €6, for more than 600 minutes of call time (plus the cost of the local call) or more than 200 minutes calling a toll-free local number.

Phone Codes

International access code (☎00)

Spain country code (☎34)

Useful Numbers

International directory inquiries (☎11825)

International operator & reverse charges (collect) Europe (☎1008)

International operator & reverse charges (collect) Rest of world (☎1005)

Time

Like most of Western Europe, Madrid is one hour ahead of Greenwich Mean Time/Coordinated Universal Time (GMT/UTC) during winter, two hours during the daylight-saving period from the last Sunday in March to the last Sunday in October. Spaniards use the 24-hour clock for official business (timetables etc), but often in daily conversation switch to the 12-hour version.

Toilets

Public toilets are almost nonexistent in Madrid and it's not really the done thing to go into a bar or cafe solely to use the toilet; ordering a quick coffee is a small price to pay for relieving the problem. Otherwise you can usually get away with it in a larger, crowded place where they can't really keep track of who's coming and going. Another option is the department stores of El Corte Inglés that are dotted around the city.

Tourist Information

Ayuntamiento de Madrid

The Madrid government's **Centro de Turismo** (☎91 588 16 36; www.esmadrid.com; Plaza Mayor 27; ⌚9.30am-8.30pm; Ⓜ Sol) is terrific. Housed in the Real Casa de Panadería on the north side of the Plaza Mayor, it allows free access to its outstanding website and city database, and offers free downloads of the metro map to your mobile; staff are helpful. It also runs a useful general information line (☎010; Spanish only) dealing with anything from transport to shows in Madrid (call ☎91 540 40 10 from elsewhere in Spain, or ☎91 529 82 10 from outside Spain). There's a smaller **tourist office** (Plaza de Colón; ⌚9.30am-8.30pm; Ⓜ Colón), which is accessible via the underground stairs on the corner of Calle de Goya and the Paseo de la Castellana and offices in airport Terminals 2 and 4, while smaller, bright orange Tourist Information Points can be found at the following:

(Plaza de la Cibeles; ⌚9.30am-8.30pm; Ⓜ Banco de España)

(Plaza del Callao; ⌚9am-midnight; Ⓜ Callao)

(cnr Calle de Santa Isabel & Plaza del Emperador Carlos V; ⌚9.30am-8.30pm; Ⓜ Atocha)

Comunidad de Madrid

The website run by the regional **Comunidad de Madrid government** (www.turismomadrid.es; Banco de España) covers the city and surrounding region.

Travellers with Disabilities

Although things are slowly changing, Madrid remains something of an obstacle course for travellers with a disability. Your first stop for more information on accessibility for travellers should be the Madrid tourist office website section known as **Accessible Madrid** (www.esmadrid.com/en/access-madrid), where you can download a list of wheelchair-accessible hotels, and a pdf called 'Lugares Accesibles', a list of wheelchair-friendly restaurants, shopping centres and museums; among the latter are the Museo del Prado, Museo Thyssen-Bornemisza and the Centro de Arte Reina Sofía, although few museums have guides in Braille or allow visually impaired people to touch objects.

The Ayuntamiento's program of **guided tours** (www.esmadrid.com/guidedtours/portal.do) includes tours for blind, deaf and wheelchair-bound travellers, as well as travellers with an intellectual disability; click on 'Rutas Accesibles'.

Audio loops for the hearing impaired in cinemas are almost nonexistent, although most Spanish TV channels allow you to turn on subtitles.

When it comes to transport, metro lines built (or upgraded) since the late 1990s generally have elevators for wheelchair access, but the older lines are generally ill equipped; the updated metro maps available from any metro station (or at www.metromadrid.es) show stations with wheelchair access. On board the metro the name of the next station is usually announced (if the broadcast system is working...). The single-deck *piso bajo* (low floor) buses have no steps inside and in some cases have ramps that can be used by people in wheelchairs. In the long term, there are plans to make at least 50 of the buses on all routes accessible to people with a disability. **Radio-Teléfono Taxi** (☎91 547 82 00; www.radiotelefono-taxi.com) runs taxis for people with a disability in addition to standard taxis. Generally, if you call any taxi company and ask for a 'eurotaxi' you should be sent one adapted for wheelchair users.

One attraction specifically for visually impaired travellers and Spaniards is the **Museo Tifológico** (Museum for the Blind; ☎91 589 42 19; http://museo.once.es/; Calle de la Coruña 18; admission free; ⏲10am-2pm & 5-8pm Tue-Fri, 10am-2pm Sat; Ⓜ Estrecho). Run by the National Organisation for the Blind (ONCE), its exhibits (all of which may be touched) include paintings, sculptures and tapestries, as well as more than 40 scale models of world monuments, including Madrid's Palacio Real and Cibeles fountain, as well as La Alhambra in Granada and the aqueduct in Segovia. It also provides leaflets in Braille and audio guides to the museum.

Further Information

The Spanish association for the blind, **ONCE** (Organización Nacional de Ciegos Españoles; ☎91 577 37 56, 91 532 50 00; www.once.es; Calle de Prim 3, Madrid; Ⓜ Chueca or Colón) occasionally publishes guides to Madrid in Braille.

Hearing-impaired travellers can contact the Comunidad de Madrid's Federation for the Deaf, **Fesorcam** (Federación de Personas Sordas de la Comunidad de Madrid; ☎91 725 37 57; www.fesorcam.org; Calle de Ferrer del Rio 33; Ⓜ Diego de León).

Travellers with an intellectual disability may wish to contact **FEAPS Madrid** (Federación de Organizaciones en Favor de Personas con Discapacidad Intelectual; ☎91 501 83 35; www.feapsmadrid.org; Avenida de la Ciudad de Barcelona 108; Ⓜ Menéndez Pelayo).

Outside Spain, **Accessible Travel & Leisure** (www.accessibletravel.co.uk), which claims to be the biggest UK travel agent dealing with travel for people with a disability and encourages independent travel, might be able to offer Madrid-specific advice.

Visas

Spain is one of 26 member countries of the Schengen Convention, under which EU member countries (except the UK and Ireland) plus Switzerland, Iceland and Norway have abolished checks at common borders. Legal residents of one Schengen country do not require a visa for another Schengen country. Citizens of the UK and Ireland are also exempt. Nationals of many other countries, including Australia, Canada, Israel, Japan, New Zealand and the US, do not require visas for tourist visits of up to 90 days. All non-EU nationals entering Spain for any reason other than tourism (such as study or work) should contact a Spanish consulate, as they may need a specific visa.

If you're a citizen of a non-Schengen country, check with a Spanish consulate about whether you need a visa. The standard tourist visa issued by Spanish consulates (and usually valid for all Schengen countries unless conditions are attached) is valid for up to 90 days and is not renewable inside Spain.

Language

Spanish *(español)* – or Castilian *(castellano)*, as it's also called – belongs to the Romance language family, with Portuguese, Italian and French as its close relatives. It has more than 390 million speakers worldwide.

Most Spanish sounds are pronounced the same as their English counterparts. If you read our coloured pronunciation guides as if they were English, you won't have problems being understood. Note that the kh is a guttural sound (like the 'ch' in the Scottish *loch*), r is strongly rolled, ly is pronounced as the 'lli' in 'million' and ny as the 'ni' in 'onion'. In our pronunciation guides, the stressed syllables are in italics.

Where necessary in this chapter, masculine and feminine forms are marked as 'm/f', while polite and informal options are indicated by the abbreviations 'pol' and 'inf'.

BASICS

Hello.	*Hola.*	o·la
Goodbye.	*Adiós.*	a·*dyos*
How are you?	*¿Qué tal?*	ke tal
Fine, thanks.	*Bien, gracias.*	byen *gra*·thyas
Excuse me.	*Perdón.*	per·*don*
Sorry.	*Lo siento.*	lo *syen*·to
Yes./No.	*Sí./No.*	see/no
Please.	*Por favor.*	por fa·*vor*
Thank you.	*Gracias.*	*gra*·thyas
You're welcome.	*De nada.*	de *na*·da

WANT MORE?

For in-depth language information and handy phrases, check out Lonely Planet's *Spanish phrasebook*. You'll find it at **shop.lonelyplanet.com**, or you can buy Lonely Planet's iPhone phrasebooks at the Apple App Store.

My name is ...
Me llamo ... — me *lya*·mo ...

What's your name?
¿Cómo se llama Usted? — ko·mo se *lya*·ma oo·*ste* (pol)
¿Cómo te llamas? — ko·mo te *lya*·mas (inf)

Do you speak English?
¿Habla inglés? — a·bla een·*gles* (pol)
¿Hablas inglés? — a·blas een·*gles* (inf)

I don't understand.
No entiendo. — no en·*tyen*·do

ACCOMMODATION

guesthouse	*pensión*	pen·*syon*
hotel	*hotel*	o·*tel*
youth hostel	*albergue juvenil*	al·*ber*·ge khoo·ve·*neel*
I'd like a ... room.	*Quisiera una habitación ...*	kee·*sye*·ra *oo*·na a·bee·ta·*thyon* ...
double	*doble*	*do*·ble
single	*individual*	een·dee·vee·*dwal*
air-con	*aire acondicionado*	*ai*·re a·kon·dee·thyo·*na*·do
bathroom	*baño*	*ba*·nyo
bed	*cama*	*ka*·ma
window	*ventana*	ven·*ta*·na

How much is it per night/person?
¿Cuánto cuesta por noche/persona? — *kwan*·to *kwes*·ta por *no*·che/per·*so*·na

Does it include breakfast?
¿Incluye el desayuno? — een·*kloo*·ye el de·sa·*yoo*·no

DIRECTIONS

Where's ...?
¿Dónde está ...? — *don*·de es·*ta* ...

What's the address?
¿Cuál es la dirección? — kwal es la dee·rek·*thyon*

Can you please write it down?
¿Puede escribirlo, por favor? pwe·de es·kree·*beer*·lo por fa·*vor*

Can you show me (on the map)?
¿Me lo puede indicar (en el mapa)? me lo *pwe*·de een·dee·*kar* (en el *ma*·pa)

at the corner	*en la esquina*	en la es·*kee*·na
at the traffic lights	*en el semáforo*	en el se·*ma*·fo·ro
behind ...	*detrás de ...*	de·*tras* de ...
far away	*lejos*	*le*·khos
in front of ...	*enfrente de ...*	en·*fren*·te de ...
left	*izquierda*	eeth·*kyer*·da
near	*cerca*	*ther*·ka
next to ...	*al lado de ...*	al *la*·do de ...
opposite ...	*frente a ...*	*fren*·te a ...
right	*derecha*	de·*re*·cha
straight ahead	*todo recto*	*to*·do *rek*·to

EATING & DRINKING

What would you recommend?
¿Qué recomienda? ke re·ko·*myen*·da

What's in that dish?
¿Que lleva ese plato? ke *lye*·va *e*·se *pla*·to

I don't eat ...
No como ... no *ko*·mo ...

Cheers!
¡Salud! sa·*loo*

That was delicious!
¡Estaba buenísimo! es·*ta*·ba bwe·*nee*·see·mo

Please bring us the bill.
Por favor, nos trae la cuenta. por fa·*vor* nos *tra*·e la *kwen*·ta

I'd like to book a table for ...	*Quisiera reservar una mesa para ...*	kee·*sye*·ra re·ser·*var* *oo*·na *me*·sa *pa*·ra ...
(eight) o'clock	*las (ocho)*	las (*o*·cho)
(two) people	*(dos) personas*	(dos) per·*so*·nas

KEY PATTERNS

To get by in Spanish, mix and match these simple patterns with words of your choice:

When's (the next flight)?
¿Cuándo sale (el próximo vuelo)? *kwan*·do *sa*·le (el *prok*·see·mo *vwe*·lo)

Where's (the station)?
¿Dónde está (la estación)? *don*·de es·*ta* (la es·ta·*thyon*)

Where can I (buy a ticket)?
¿Dónde puedo (comprar un billete)? *don*·de *pwe*·do (kom·*prar* oon bee·*lye*·te)

Do you have (a map)?
¿Tiene (un mapa)? *tye*·ne (oon *ma*·pa)

Is there (a toilet)?
¿Hay (servicios)? ai (ser·*vee*·thyos)

I'd like (a coffee).
Quisiera (un café). kee·*sye*·ra (oon ka·*fe*)

I'd like (to hire a car).
Quisiera (alquilar un coche). kee·*sye*·ra (al·kee·*lar* oon *ko*·che)

Can I (enter)?
¿Se puede (entrar)? se *pwe*·de (en·*trar*)

Can you please (help me)?
¿Puede (ayudarme), por favor? *pwe*·de (a·yoo·*dar*·me) por fa·*vor*

Do I have to (get a visa)?
¿Necesito (obtener un visado)? ne·the·*see*·to (ob·te·*ner* oon vee·*sa*·do)

Key Words

appetisers	*aperitivos*	a·pe·ree·*tee*·vos
bar	*bar*	bar
bottle	*botella*	bo·*te*·lya
bowl	*bol*	bol
breakfast	*desayuno*	de·sa·*yoo*·no
cafe	*café*	ka·*fe*
(too) cold	*(muy) frío*	(mooy) *free*·o
dinner	*cena*	*the*·na
food	*comida*	ko·*mee*·da
fork	*tenedor*	te·ne·*dor*
glass	*vaso*	*va*·so
highchair	*trona*	*tro*·na
hot (warm)	*caliente*	ka·*lyen*·te
knife	*cuchillo*	koo·*chee*·lyo
lunch	*comida*	ko·*mee*·da
main course	*segundo plato*	se·*goon*·do *pla*·to
market	*mercado*	mer·*ka*·do
(children's) menu	*menú (infantil)*	me·*noo* (een·fan·*teel*)
plate	*plato*	*pla*·to
restaurant	*restaurante*	res·tow·*ran*·te
spoon	*cuchara*	koo·*cha*·ra
supermarket	*supermercado*	soo·per·mer·*ka*·do
vegetarian food	*comida vegetariana*	ko·*mee*·da ve·khe·ta·*rya*·na
with/without	*con/sin*	kon/sin

Meat & Fish

beef	*carne de vaca*	*kar*·ne de *va*·ka
chicken	*pollo*	*po*·lyo
cod	*bacalao*	ba·ka·*la*·o
duck	*pato*	*pa*·to
lamb	*cordero*	kor·*de*·ro
lobster	*langosta*	lan·*gos*·ta
pork	*cerdo*	*ther*·do
prawns	*camarones*	ka·ma·*ro*·nes
salmon	*salmón*	sal·*mon*
tuna	*atún*	a·*toon*
turkey	*pavo*	*pa*·vo
veal	*ternera*	ter·*ne*·ra

Fruit & Vegetables

apple	*manzana*	man·*tha*·na
apricot	*albaricoque*	al·ba·ree·*ko*·ke
artichoke	*alcachofa*	al·ka·*cho*·fa
asparagus	*espárragos*	es·*pa*·ra·gos
banana	*plátano*	*pla*·ta·no
beans	*judías*	khoo·*dee*·as
beetroot	*remolacha*	re·mo·*la*·cha
cabbage	*col*	kol
(red/green) capsicum	*pimiento (rojo/verde)*	pee·*myen*·to (*ro*·kho/*ver*·de)
carrot	*zanahoria*	tha·na·o·rya
celery	*apio*	*a*·pyo
cherry	*cereza*	the·*re*·tha
corn	*maíz*	ma·*eeth*
cucumber	*pepino*	pe·*pee*·no
fruit	*fruta*	*froo*·ta
grape	*uvas*	*oo*·vas
lemon	*limón*	lee·*mon*
lentils	*lentejas*	len·*te*·khas
lettuce	*lechuga*	le·*choo*·ga
mushroom	*champiñón*	cham·pee·*nyon*
nuts	*nueces*	*nwe*·thes
onion	*cebolla*	the·*bo*·lya
orange	*naranja*	na·*ran*·kha
peach	*melocotón*	me·lo·ko·*ton*
peas	*guisantes*	gee·*san*·tes
pineapple	*piña*	*pee*·nya
plum	*ciruela*	theer·*we*·la
potato	*patata*	pa·*ta*·ta
pumpkin	*calabaza*	ka·la·*ba*·sa
spinach	*espinacas*	es·pee·*na*·kas
strawberry	*fresa*	*fre*·sa
tomato	*tomate*	to·*ma*·te
vegetable	*verdura*	ver·*doo*·ra
watermelon	*sandía*	san·*dee*·a

Other

bread	*pan*	pan
butter	*mantequilla*	man·te·*kee*·lya
cheese	*queso*	*ke*·so
egg	*huevo*	*we*·vo
honey	*miel*	myel
jam	*mermelada*	mer·me·*la*·da
oil	*aceite*	a·*they*·te
pepper	*pimienta*	pee·*myen*·ta
rice	*arroz*	a·*roth*
salt	*sal*	sal
sugar	*azúcar*	a·*thoo*·kar
vinegar	*vinagre*	vee·*na*·gre

Drinks

beer	*cerveza*	ther·*ve*·tha
coffee	*café*	ka·*fe*
(orange) juice	*zumo (de naranja)*	*thoo*·mo (de na·*ran*·kha)
milk	*leche*	*le*·che
red wine	*vino tinto*	*vee*·no *teen*·to
sparkling wine	*vino espumoso*	*vee*·no es·poo·*mo*·so
tea	*té*	te
(mineral) water	*agua (mineral)*	*a*·gwa (mee·ne·*ral*)
white wine	*vino blanco*	*vee*·no *blan*·ko

EMERGENCIES

Help!	*¡Socorro!*	so·*ko*·ro
Go away!	*¡Vete!*	*ve*·te

Signs

Abierto	Open
Cerrado	Closed
Entrada	Entrance
Hombres	Men
Mujeres	Women
Prohibido	Prohibited
Salida	Exit
Servicios/Aseos	Toilets

Call ...!	*¡Llame a ...!*	*lya*·me a ...
a doctor	*un médico*	oon *me*·dee·ko
the police	*la policía*	la po·lee·*thee*·a

I'm lost.
Estoy perdido/a. es·*toy* per·*dee*·do/a (m/f)

I'm ill.
Estoy enfermo/a. es·*toy* en·*fer*·mo/a (m/f)

It hurts here.
Me duele aquí. me *dwe*·le a·*kee*

I'm allergic to (antibiotics).
Soy alérgico/a a (los antibióticos). soy a·*ler*·khee·ko/a a (los an·tee·*byo*·tee·kos) (m/f)

Where are the toilets?
¿Dónde están los servicios? *don*·de es·*tan* los ser·*vee*·thyos

SHOPPING & SERVICES

I'd like to buy ...
Quisiera comprar ... kee·*sye*·ra kom·*prar* ...

I'm just looking.
Sólo estoy mirando. *so*·lo es·*toy* mee·*ran*·do

Can I look at it?
¿Puedo verlo? *pwe*·do *ver*·lo

I don't like it.
No me gusta. no me *goos*·ta

How much is it?
¿Cuánto cuesta? *kwan*·to *kwes*·ta

That's too expensive.
Es muy caro. es mooy *ka*·ro

Can you lower the price?
¿Podría bajar un poco el precio? po·*dree*·a ba·*khar* oon *po*·ko el *pre*·thyo

There's a mistake in the bill.
Hay un error en la cuenta. ai oon e·*ror* en la *kwen*·ta

ATM	*cajero automático*	ka·*khe*·ro ow·to·*ma*·tee·ko
credit card	*tarjeta de crédito*	tar·*khe*·ta de *kre*·dee·to
internet cafe	*cibercafé*	thee·ber·ka·*fe*
post office	*correos*	ko·*re*·os
tourist office	*oficina de turismo*	o·fee·*thee*·na de too·*rees*·mo

Question Words

How?	*¿Cómo?*	*ko*·mo
What?	*¿Qué?*	ke
When?	*¿Cuándo?*	*kwan*·do
Where?	*¿Dónde?*	*don*·de
Who?	*¿Quién?*	kyen
Why?	*¿Por qué?*	por ke

TIME & DATES

What time is it?
¿Qué hora es? ke *o*·ra es

It's (10) o'clock.
Son (las diez). son (las dyeth)

Half past (one).
Es (la una) y media. es (la *oo*·na) ee *me*·dya

At what time?
¿A qué hora? a ke *o*·ra

At (five) o'clock.
A las (cinco). a las (*theen*·ko)

morning	*mañana*	ma·*nya*·na
afternoon	*tarde*	*tar*·de
evening	*noche*	*no*·che
yesterday	*ayer*	a·*yer*
today	*hoy*	oy
tomorrow	*mañana*	ma·*nya*·na
Monday	*lunes*	*loo*·nes
Tuesday	*martes*	*mar*·tes
Wednesday	*miércoles*	*myer*·ko·les
Thursday	*jueves*	*khwe*·bes
Friday	*viernes*	*vyer*·nes
Saturday	*sábado*	*sa*·ba·do
Sunday	*domingo*	do·*meen*·go
January	*enero*	e·*ne*·ro
February	*febrero*	fe·*bre*·ro
March	*marzo*	*mar*·tho
April	*abril*	a·*breel*
May	*mayo*	*ma*·yo
June	*junio*	*khoo*·nyo
July	*julio*	*khoo*·lyo
August	*agosto*	a·*gos*·to
September	*septiembre*	sep·*tyem*·bre
October	*octubre*	ok·*too*·bre
November	*noviembre*	no·*vyem*·bre
December	*diciembre*	dee·*thyem*·bre

TRANSPORT

Public Transport

boat	*barco*	*bar*·ko
bus	*autobús*	ow·to·*boos*
plane	*avión*	a·*vyon*
train	*tren*	tren
tram	*tranvía*	tran·*vee*·a

Numbers

1	*uno*	oo·no
2	*dos*	dos
3	*tres*	tres
4	*cuatro*	*kwa*·tro
5	*cinco*	*theen*·ko
6	*seis*	seys
7	*siete*	*sye*·te
8	*ocho*	o·cho
9	*nueve*	*nwe*·ve
10	*diez*	dyeth
20	*veinte*	*veyn*·te
30	*treinta*	*treyn*·ta
40	*cuarenta*	kwa·*ren*·ta
50	*cincuenta*	theen·*kwen*·ta
60	*sesenta*	se·*sen*·ta
70	*setenta*	se·*ten*·ta
80	*ochenta*	o·*chen*·ta
90	*noventa*	no·*ven*·ta
100	*cien*	thyen
1000	*mil*	meel

first	*primer*	pree·*mer*
last	*último*	*ool*·tee·mo
next	*próximo*	*prok*·see·mo

I want to go to ...
Quisiera ir a ... kee·*sye*·ra eer a ...

At what time does it arrive/leave?
¿A qué hora llega/sale? a ke o·ra *lye*·ga/*sa*·le

Is it a direct route?
¿Es un viaje directo? es oon *vya*·khe dee·*rek*·to

Does it stop at ...?
¿Para en ...? *pa*·ra en ...

Which stop is this?
¿Cuál es esta parada? kwal es *es*·ta pa·*ra*·da

Please tell me when we get to ...
¿Puede avisarme cuando lleguemos a ...? *pwe*·de a·vee·*sar*·me *kwan*·do lye·*ge*·mos a ...

I want to get off here.
Quiero bajarme aquí. *kye*·ro ba·*khar*·me a·*kee*

a ... ticket	*un billete de ...*	oon bee·*lye*·te de ...
1st-class	*primera clase*	pree·*me*·ra *kla*·se
2nd-class	*segunda clase*	se·*goon*·da *kla*·se
one-way	*ida*	*ee*·da
return	*ida y vuelta*	ee·da ee *vwel*·ta
aisle/window seat	*asiento de pasillo/ ventana*	a·*syen*·to de pa·*see*·lyo/ ven·*ta*·na
bus/train station	*estación de autobuses/ trenes*	es·ta·*thyon* de ow·to·*boo*·ses/ *tre*·nes
cancelled	*cancelado*	kan·the·*la*·do
delayed	*retrasado*	re·tra·*sa*·do
platform	*plataforma*	pla·ta·*for*·ma
ticket office	*taquilla*	ta·*kee*·lya
timetable	*horario*	o·*ra*·ryo

Driving & Cycling

I'd like to hire a ...	*Quisiera alquilar ...*	kee·*sye*·ra al·*kee*·lar ...
4WD	*un todo-terreno*	oon *to*·do·te·*re*·no
bicycle	*una bicicleta*	*oo*·na bee·thee·*kle*·ta
car	*un coche*	oon *ko*·che
motorcycle	*una moto*	oo·na *mo*·to

child seat	*asiento de seguridad para niños*	a·*syen*·to de se·goo·ree·*da* *pa*·ra *nee*·nyos
diesel	*gasóleo*	ga·*so*·le·o
helmet	*casco*	*kas*·ko
mechanic	*mecánico*	me·*ka*·nee·ko
petrol	*gasolina*	ga·so·*lee*·na
service station	*gasolinera*	ga·so·lee·*ne*·ra

How much is it per day/hour?
¿Cuánto cuesta por día/hora? *kwan*·to *kwes*·ta por dee·a/*o*·ra

Is this the road to ...?
¿Se va a ... por esta carretera? se va a ... por *es*·ta ka·re·*te*·ra

(How long) Can I park here?
¿(Por cuánto tiempo) Puedo aparcar aquí? (por *kwan*·to *tyem*·po) *pwe*·do a·par·*kar* a·*kee*

The car has broken down (at ...).
El coche se ha averiado (en ...). el *ko*·che se a a·ve·*rya*·do (en ...)

I have a flat tyre.
Tengo un pinchazo. *ten*·go oon peen·*cha*·tho

I've run out of petrol.
Me he quedado sin gasolina. me e ke·*da*·do seen ga·so·*lee*·na

Are there cycling paths?
¿Hay carril bicicleta? ai ka·*reel* bee·thee·*kle*·ta

Is there bicycle parking?
¿Hay aparcamiento de bicicletas? ai a·par·ka·*myen*·to de bee·thee·*kle*·tas

GLOSSARY

abono – season pass

albergue juvenil – youth hostel; not to be confused with *hostal*

alcázar – Muslim-era fortress

Almoravid – Islamic Berbers who founded an empire in North Africa that spread over much of Spain in the 11th century and laid siege to Madrid in 1110

Ayuntamiento – city or town hall; city or town council

asador – restaurant specialising in roasted meats

baño completo – full bathroom, with a toilet, shower and/or bath and washbasin

barrio – district, quarter (of a town or city)

biblioteca – library

bodega – literally, 'cellar' (especially a wine cellar); also means a winery or a traditional wine bar likely to serve wine from the barrel

bomberos – fire brigade

calle – street

callejón – lane

cama – bed

cantaor/cantaora – flamenco singer (male/female)

capilla – chapel

Carnaval – carnival; a period of fancy-dress parades and merrymaking, usually ending on the Tuesday 47 days before Easter Sunday

carnet – identity card or driving licence

carretera – highway

castizo – literally 'pure'; refers to people and things distinctly from Madrid

catedral – cathedral

centro de salud – health centre

cercanías – local trains serving big cities, suburbs and nearby towns; local train network

cerrado – closed

cervecería – bar where the focus is on beer

chato – glass

churrigueresque – ornate style of baroque architecture named after the brothers Alberto and José Churriguera

comedor – dining room

Comunidad de Madrid – Madrid province

consejo – council

coro – choir stall

correos – post office

corrida (de toros) – bullfight

Cortes – national parliament

cuesta – lane (usually on a hill)

cutre – basic or rough-and-ready

discoteca – nightclub

ducha – shower

duende – an indefinable word that captures the passionate essence of flamenco

entrada – entrance; ticket for a performance

estanco – tobacconist shop

farmacia – pharmacy

feria – fair; can refer to trade fairs as well as city, town or village fairs, bullfights or festivals lasting days or weeks

ferrocarril – railway

fiesta – festival, public holiday or party

fin de semana – weekend

flamenco – traditional Spanish musical form involving any or all of guitarist, singer and dancer and sometimes accompanying musicians

gasolina – petrol (a *gasolinera* is a petrol station)

gatos – literally 'cats'; colloquial name for *madrileños*

gitanos – the Roma people (formerly known as the Gypsies)

glorieta – big roundabout

guiri – foreigner

habitación doble – twin room

hostal – hostel; not to be confused with *albergue juvenil*

iglesia – church

IVA – impuesto sobre el valor añadido (value-added tax)

judería – Jewish quarter

lavabo – washbasin; a polite term for toilet

lavandería – laundrette

librería – bookshop

locutorio – telephone centre

madrileño – a person from Madrid

marcha – action, life, 'the scene'

marisquería – seafood eatery

media raciones – a serving of tapas, somewhere between the size of tapas and *raciones*

menú del día – fixed-price meal available at lunchtime, sometimes evening, too; often just called a *menú*

mercado – market

meseta – the high tableland of central Spain

mezquita – mosque

monasterio – monastery

morería – former Islamic quarter in town

moro – 'Moor' or Muslim, usually in medieval context

moto – moped or motorcycle

movida madrileña – the halcyon days of the post-Franco years when the city plunged into an excess of nightlife, drugs and cultural expression

mozarab – Christians who lived in Muslim-ruled Spain; also style of architecture

Mudéjar – Muslim living under Christian rule in medieval Spain, also refers to their style of architecture

muralla – city wall

museo – museum

oficina de turismo – tourist office

panteón – pantheon (monument to a famous dead person)

parador – state-owned hotel in a historic building

pensión – guesthouse

pijo/pija – yuppie, snob, beautiful people (male/female)

plaza mayor – main plaza or square

puente – bridge

puerta – door or gate

ración – meal-sized serve of tapas

rastro – flea market, car-boot (trunk) sale; El Rastro is Madrid's (and Europe's) largest flea market

ronda – ring road

Semana Santa – Holy Week; the week leading up to Easter Sunday

servicio – toilet

sierra – mountain range

taberna – tavern

tapas – bar snacks traditionally served on a saucer or lid ('tapa' literally means a lid)

taquilla – ticket window/office

tasca – tapas bar

temporada alta/media/baja – high, mid- or low season

terraza – terrace; usually means outdoor tables of a cafe, bar or restaurant; can also mean rooftop open-air place

torero – bullfighter or matador

toro – bull

torreón – tower

turismo – means both tourism and saloon car

zarzuela – form of Spanish dance and music, usually satirical

MENU DECODER

a la parrilla – grilled

aceite de oliva – olive oil

aceite de oliva virgen extra – extra virgin olive oil

aceitunas – olives

adobo – marinade

aguacate –avocado

ajo – garlic

albóndigas – meat balls

alcachofas – artichokes

al horno – baked in the oven

almejas – clams

anchoas – anchovies

arroz – rice

asado – roasted

bacalao – dried and salted cod

bebida – drink

berenjena – aubergine, eggplant

bistec – steak

bocadillo – bread roll with filling

bonito – tuna

boquerones – anchovies marinated in wine vinegar

boquerones en vinagre – fresh anchovies marinated in white vinegar and garlic

boquerones fritos – fried fresh anchovies

butifarra – Catalan sausage

cabrito – kid, baby goat

calamares – calamari

calamares a la Romana – deep-fried calamari rings

caldo – broth, stock

callos – tripe

camarón – small prawn, shrimp

caracol – snail

carne – meat

cebolla – onion

cerdo – pork

champiñones – mushrooms

chipirones – baby squid

chipirones en su tinta – baby squid in their own ink

chorizo – cured pork sausage, sometimes spicy

chuleta – chop, cutlet

churro – long, deep-fried doughnut

cochinillo – suckling pig

cocido a la madrileña – meat, chickpea and broth stew

codorniz – quail

coliflor – cauliflower

conejo – rabbit

confitura – jam

cordero – lamb

cordero asado de lechal – roast spring lamb

croquetas – croquettes

de lata – from a can or tin

dorada – bream

empanadillas – small pie, either savoury or sweet

ensalada – salad

ensalada rusa – Russian salad

ensalada mixta – mixed salad

escabeche – pickle, marinade

espárragos – asparagus

estofado – stew

frito – fried

galleta – biscuit

gambas – prawns, either done *al ajillo*, with garlic, or *a la plancha*, grilled
garbanzos – chickpeas
garbanzos con espinacas – chickpeas and spinach
gazpacho – cold, tomato-based soup
granada – pomegranate
guarnición – side order
helado – ice cream
jamón – cured Spanish ham
judias – beans
langosta – lobster
langostino – king prawn
leche – milk
lechuga – lettuce
lenguado – sole
lentejas – lentils
lomo – loin (pork unless specified otherwise)
maíz – corn
mantequilla – butter
manzana – apple
marisco – seafood or shellfish
mejillones – mussels
merluza – hake
miel – honey
morcilla – black pudding, blood sausage
naranja – orange
ostra – oyster
pan – bread
pastel – cake
patatas bravas – roasted potato chunks bathed in spicy tomato sauce
patatas con huevos fritos – baked potatoes with eggs, also known as *huevos rotos*
patatas fritas – French fries
pato – duck
pavo – turkey
pescado – fish
pescaíto frito – fried fish
pil pil – garlic sauce spiked with chilli
pimentón –paprika
pimiento – pepper, capsicum
pimientos de Padrón – little green peppers from Galicia – some are hot and some not
plátano – banana
plato combinado – combination (or all-in-one) plate, usually with meat and vegetables on the same plate
pollo – chicken
postre – dessert
pulpo a la gallega – boiled octopus served with paprika, Galician style
queso – cheese
queso azul – blue cheese
rabo de toro – bull's tail
raciones – large tapas serving
rebozado – in bread crumbs
relleno – stuffing
repollo – cabbage
revuelto – scrambled eggs
riñón – kidney
rodaballo – turbot
salchichón – salami-like sausage
salmorejo – cold, tomato-based soup
salsa – sauce
sandía – watermelon
sardinas – sardines
sepia – squid
sesos – brains
seta – wild mushroom
solomillo – sirloin (usually of pork)
sopa – soup
sopa de ajo – garlic soup
tarta – cake
ternasco – lamb ribs
ternera – beef or veal
tortilla de patatas – potato and (sometimos) onion omelette
tostada – buttered toast
trucha – trout
verduras a la plancha – grilled vegetables
vinagre – vinegar

Behind the Scenes

SEND US YOUR FEEDBACK

We love to hear from travellers – your comments keep us on our toes and help make our books better. Our well-travelled team reads every word on what you loved or loathed about this book. Although we cannot reply individually to postal submissions, we always guarantee that your feedback goes straight to the appropriate authors, in time for the next edition. Each person who sends us information is thanked in the next edition – the most useful submissions are rewarded with a selection of digital PDF chapters.

Visit **lonelyplanet.com/contact** to submit your updates and suggestions or to ask for help. Our award-winning website also features inspirational travel stories, news and discussions.

Note: We may edit, reproduce and incorporate your comments in Lonely Planet products such as guidebooks, websites and digital products, so let us know if you don't want your comments reproduced or your name acknowledged. For a copy of our privacy policy visit lonelyplanet.com/privacy.

OUR READERS

Many thanks to the travellers who used the last edition and wrote to us with helpful hints, useful advice and interesting anecdotes: Maite Araque Blazquez, Suzanne Brazier, Christian Cantos, José Carreras, Filippo Corvi, Dominic Cullen, Bec Deacon, Clotilde Farah, Gregory Kavadias, Christian Shanti Mohammad, Chris Oates, Maurits Pino, Pablo Sanchez, Tanny (Catherine) Weisgram

AUTHOR THANKS

Anthony Ham

During a decade of living in Madrid, I have been welcomed and assisted by many people whose lives and stories have become a treasured part of the fabric of my own. A huge thank you to the wise Dora Whitaker at Lonely Planet. It was my great fortune a week after arriving in Madrid to meet my wife and soulmate, Marina, who has made this city a true place of the heart. And to my daughters, Carlota and Valentina: truly you are Madrid's greatest gifts of all.

ACKNOWLEDGMENTS

Madrid Metro Map © Diseño Raro S.L. 2010
Illustration p94 by Javier Zarracina.
Cover photograph: buildings in old Madrid, Rudy Sulgan / Corbis ©

THIS BOOK

This 7th edition of Lonely Planet's Madrid guidebook was researched and written by Anthony Ham. The previous three editions were also written by Anthony. This guidebook was commissioned in Lonely Planet's London office, and produced by the following:

Commissioning Editor Dora Whitaker
Coordinating Editor Alison Ridgway
Coordinating Cartographer Jeff Cameron
Coordinating Layout Designer Adrian Blackburn
Managing Editors Sasha Baskett, Barbara Delissen
Managing Cartographers Anita Banh, Anthony Phelan
Managing Layout Designer Jane Hart
Assisting Editors Kate Daly, Carly Hall
Assisting Cartographers Corey Hutchison, Alex Leung
Cover Research Naomi Parker
Internal Image Research Claire Gibson & Rebecca Skinner
Illustrator Javier Zarracina
Language Content Branislava Vladisavljevic

Thanks to Shahara Ahmed, Dan Austin, Ryan Evans, Larissa Frost, Tobias Gattineau, Jouve India, Asha Ioculari, Alison Lyall, Sophie Marozeau, Katie O'Connell, Trent Paton, Raphael Richards, Averil Robertson, Silvia Rosas, Amanda Sierp, Fiona Siseman, Kerrianne Southway, Gerard Walker, Danny Williams

See also separate subindexes for:
- EATING P224
- DRINKING & NIGHTLIFE P225
- ENTERTAINMENT P226
- SHOPPING P226
- SPORTS & ACTIVITIES P227
- SLEEPING P227

Index

Sights 000
Map Pages **000**
Photo Pages **000**

EATING

DRINKING & NIGHTLIFE

ENTERTAINMENT

Sights 000
Map Pages **000**
Photo Pages **000**

SHOPPING

SPORTS & ACTIVITIES

SLEEPING

Madrid Maps

Map Legend

Sights
- Beach
- Buddhist
- Castle
- Christian
- Hindu
- Islamic
- Jewish
- Monument
- Museum/Gallery
- Ruin
- Winery/Vineyard
- Zoo
- Other Sight

Eating
- Eating

Drinking & Nightlife
- Drinking & Nightlife
- Cafe

Entertainment
- Entertainment

Shopping
- Shopping

Sleeping
- Sleeping
- Camping

Sports & Activities
- Diving/Snorkelling
- Canoeing/Kayaking
- Skiing
- Surfing
- Swimming/Pool
- Walking
- Windsurfing
- Other Sports & Activities

Information
- Post Office
- Tourist Information

Transport
- Airport
- Border Crossing
- Bus
- Cable Car/Funicular
- Cycling
- Ferry
- Monorail
- Parking
- S-Bahn
- Taxi
- Train/Railway
- Tram
- Tube Station
- U-Bahn
- Underground Train Station
- Other Transport

Routes
- Tollway
- Freeway
- Primary
- Secondary
- Tertiary
- Lane
- Unsealed Road
- Plaza/Mall
- Steps
- Tunnel
- Pedestrian Overpass
- Walking Tour
- Walking Tour Detour
- Path

Boundaries
- International
- State/Province
- Disputed
- Regional/Suburb
- Marine Park
- Cliff
- Wall

Geographic
- Hut/Shelter
- Lighthouse
- Lookout
- Mountain/Volcano
- Oasis
- Park
- Pass
- Picnic Area
- Waterfall

Hydrography
- River/Creek
- Intermittent River
- Swamp/Mangrove
- Reef
- Canal
- Water
- Dry/Salt/ Intermittent Lake
- Glacier

Areas
- Beach/Desert
- Cemetery (Christian)
- Cemetery (Other)
- Park/Forest
- Sportsground
- Sight (Building)
- Top Sight (Building)

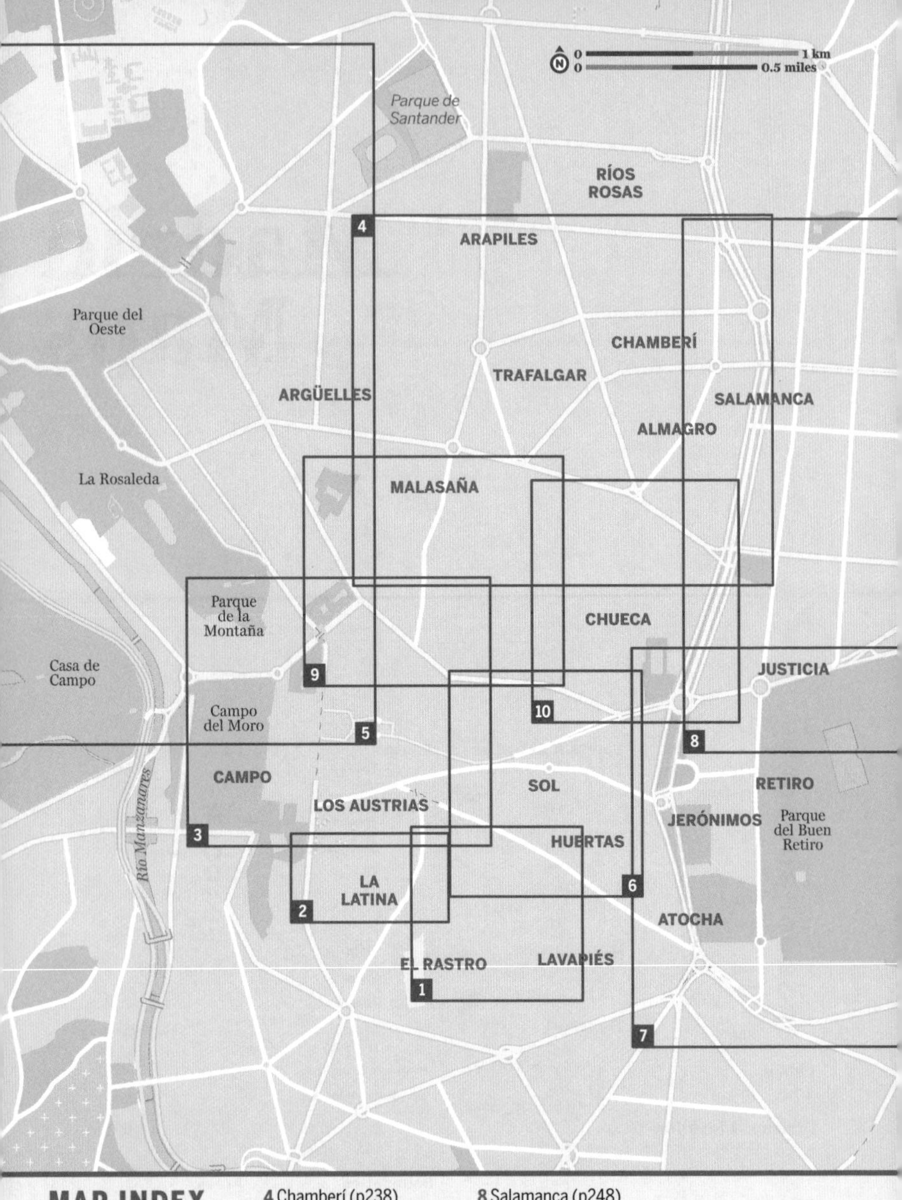
0
0
1 km
0.5 miles
Parque de Santander
RÍOS ROSAS
ARAPILES
Parque del Oeste
CHAMBERÍ
TRAFALGAR
ARGÜELLES
SALAMANCA
ALMAGRO
La Rosaleda
MALASAÑA
Parque de la Montaña
CHUECA
Casa de Campo
JUSTICIA
Campo del Moro
CAMPO
SOL
RETIRO
LOS AUSTRIAS
JERÓNIMOS
Parque del Buen Retiro
HUERTAS
Río Manzanares
LA LATINA
ATOCHA
EL RASTRO
LAVAPIÉS
1
2
3
4
5
6
7
8
9
10

MAP INDEX

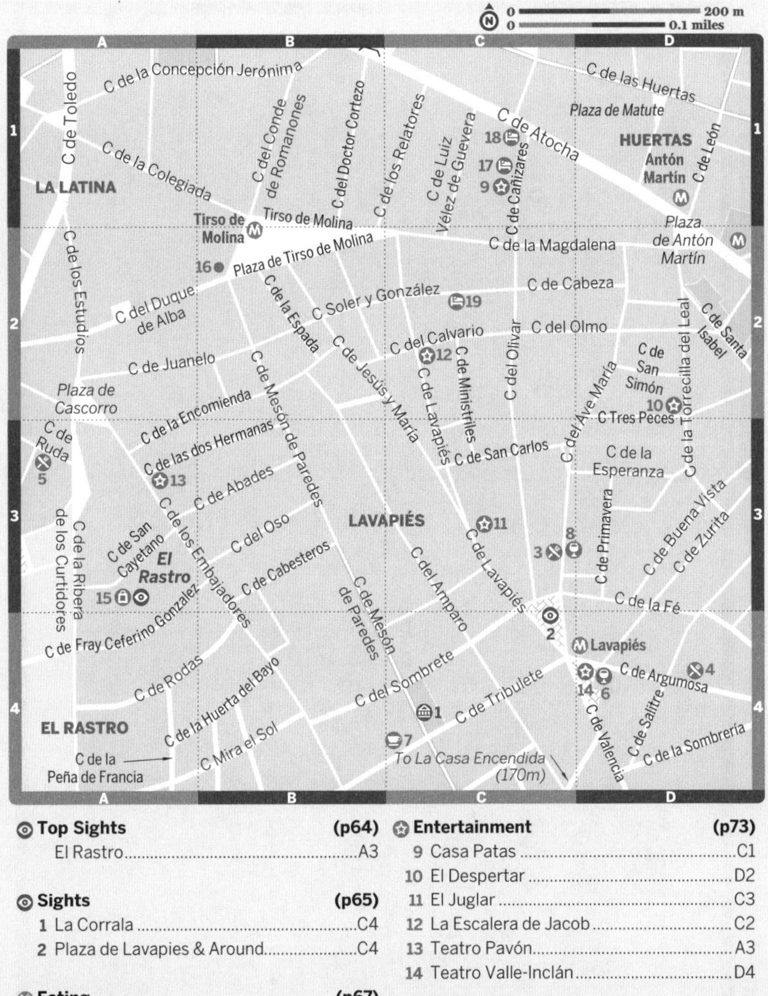

Top Sights (p64)
El Rastro ... A3

Sights (p65)
1 La Corrala ... C4
2 Plaza de Lavapies & Around ... C4

Eating (p67)
3 Bar Melo's ... C3
4 La Buga del Lobo ... D4
5 Malacatín ... A3

Drinking & Nightlife (p71)
6 El Eucalipto ... D4
7 Gaudeamus Café ... C4
8 La Inquilina ... C3

Entertainment (p73)
9 Casa Patas ... C1
10 El Despertar ... D2
11 El Juglar ... C3
12 La Escalera de Jacob ... C2
13 Teatro Pavón ... A3
14 Teatro Valle-Inclán ... D4

Shopping (p75)
15 El Rastro ... A3

Sports & Activities (p205)
16 Letango Tours ... B2

Sleeping (p169)
17 Cat's Hostel ... C1
18 Hostal Horizonte ... C1
19 Mad Hostel ... C2

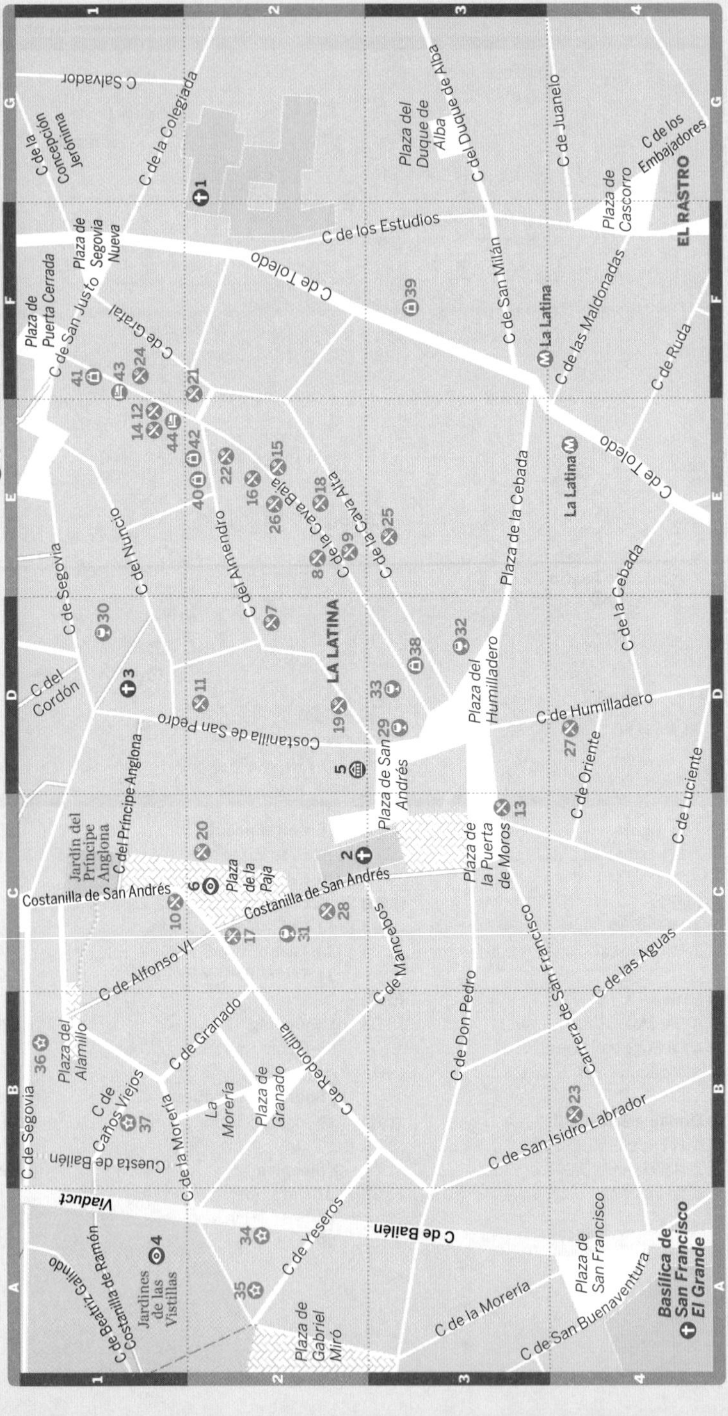

LA LATINA

0 200 m
0 0.1 miles

A B C D E F G
1 2 3 4

C de Segovia
36
Plaza del Alamillo
Costanilla de San Andrés
Jardín del Príncipe Anglona
C del Príncipe Anglona
C del Cordón
C de Segovia
30
3
C del Nuncio
Plaza de Puerta Cerrada
C de San Justo
41
43
14 12
24
44
C de Grafal
Plaza de Segovia Nueva
C de la Concepción Jerónima
C Salvador
C de la Colegiada
1
C de Beatriz Galindo
Costanilla de Ramón
Viaduct
Cuesta de Bailén
C de Caños Viejos
37
Jardines de las Vistillas
4
C de la Morería
C de Alfonso VI
10
6
20
Costanilla de San Pedro
11
40
42
21
La Morería
C de Granado
17
Plaza de la Paja
C del Almendro
22
16
35
34
Plaza de Granado
26
15
7
Plaza de Gabriel Miró
C de Yeseros
C de Redondilla
31
Costanilla de San Andrés
8
C de la Cava Baja
18
28
2
5
19
LA LATINA
C de la Cava Alta
9
C de Toledo
C de los Estudios
C de Mancebos
Plaza de San Andrés
29
33
25
C de Bailén
38
39
Plaza del Duque de Alba
C de la Morería
C de Don Pedro
Plaza de la Puerta de Moros
32
Plaza del Humilladero
C del Duque de Alba
C de San Isidro Labrador
13
Plaza de la Cebada
C de San Milán
Carrera de San Francisco
La Latina
C de San Buenaventura
23
27
C de Humilladero
La Latina
C de Juanelo
Plaza de San Francisco
C de Oriente
C de las Maldonadas
C de las Aguas
C de la Cebada
Plaza de Cascorro
C de Toledo
Basílica de San Francisco El Grande
C de Luciente
C de Ruda
EL RASTRO
C de los Embajadores

LA LATINA

Top Sights **(p64)**
Basílica de San Francisco El Grande A4

Sights **(p65)**
1 Basílica de Nuestra Señora del Buen Consejo G2
2 Iglesia de San Andrés & Around C2
3 Iglesia de San Pedro El Viejo D1
4 Las Vistillas, Viaduct & Calle de Segovia A1
5 Museo de Los Orígenes D2
6 Plaza de la Paja C2

Eating **(p67)**
7 Almendro 13 .... D2
8 Casa Lucas E2
9 Casa Lucio E2
10 El Estragón C1
11 Ene Restaurante D2
12 Enotaberna del León de Oro E1
13 Juana La Loca C3
14 La Antoñita E1
15 La Camarilla E2
16 La Chata E2
17 La Musa Latina C2
18 La Perijila E2
19 Lamiak D2
20 Naïa Restaurante C2
21 Posada de la Villa F2
22 Restaurante Julián de Tolosa E2
23 Sanlúcar B4
24 Taberna de Conspiradores F1
25 Taberna Matritum E3
26 Txacolina E2
27 Txirimiri D4
28 Viva La Vida C2

Drinking & Nightlife **(p71)**
29 Bonanno D3
30 Café del Nuncio D1
31 Delic C2
32 El Viajero D3
33 Taberna Tempranillo D3

Entertainment **(p73)**
34 ContraClub A2
35 Corral de la Morería A2
36 El Rincón del Arte Nuevo B1
37 Marula Café B1

Shopping **(p75)**
38 Alma de Ibérico D3
39 Caramelos Paco F3
40 De Piedra E2
41 Del Hierro F1
42 Helena Rohner E2

Sleeping **(p169)**
43 Posada del Dragón F1
44 Posada del León de Oro E1

Key on p236

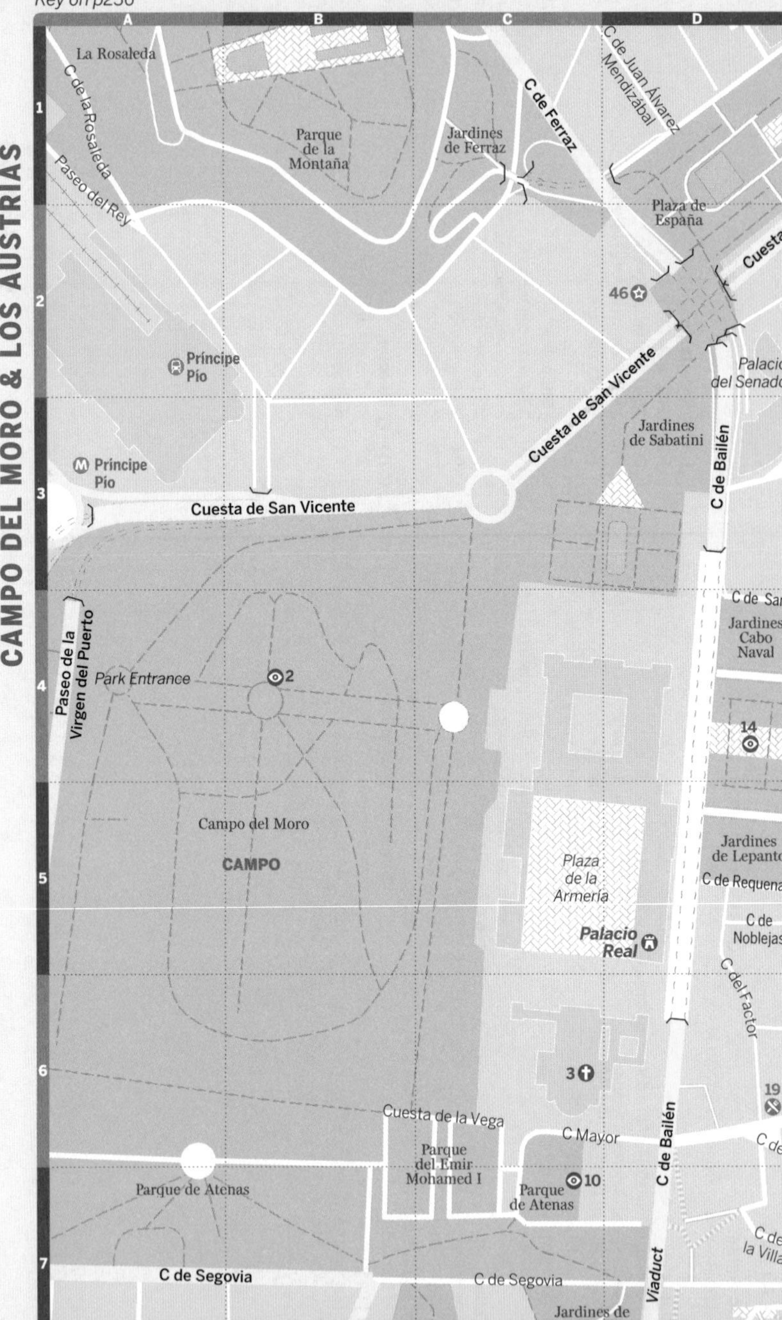
A
B
C
D
1
2
3
4
5
6
7
La Rosaleda
C de la Rosaleda
Paseo del Rey
Parque de la Montaña
Jardines de Ferraz
C de Ferraz
C de Juan Álvarez Mendizábal
Plaza de España
Cuesta
46
Príncipe Pío
Palacio del Senado
Cuesta de San Vicente
Jardines de Sabatini
C de Bailén
Príncipe Pío
Cuesta de San Vicente
C de San
Jardines Cabo Naval
Paseo de la Virgen del Puerto
Park Entrance
2
14
Campo del Moro
CAMPO
Jardines de Lepanto
Plaza de la Armería
C de Requena
C de Noblejas
Palacio Real
C del Factor
3
19
Cuesta de la Vega
C Mayor
C del
Parque del Emir Mohamed I
10
C de Bailén
Parque de Atenas
Parque de Atenas
C de la Villa
C de Segovia
C de Segovia
Viaduct
Jardines de las Vistillas

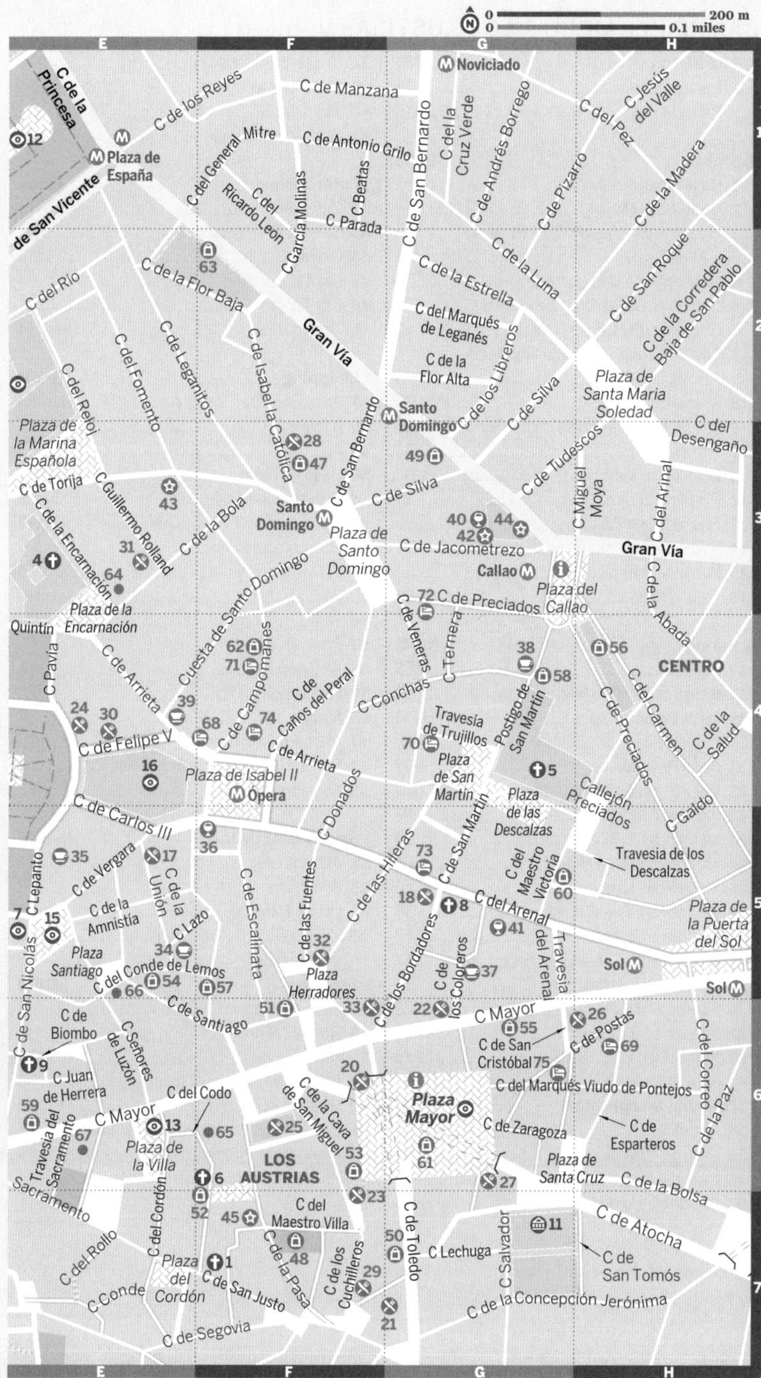

CAMPO DEL MORO & LOS AUSTRIAS
0 200 m
0 0.1 miles
Noviciado
Plaza de España
C de Manzana
C de Antonio Grilo
C de San Bernardo
Gran Vía
Santo Domingo
Plaza de Santo Domingo
C de Jacometrezo
Callao
Plaza del Callao
C de Preciados
CENTRO
Plaza de Isabel II
Ópera
C de Carlos III
C del Arenal
Plaza de la Puerta del Sol
Sol
C Mayor
Plaza Mayor
Plaza de la Villa
LOS AUSTRIAS
Plaza de Santa Cruz
C de Atocha
C de Toledo
C de Segovia
C de la Concepción Jerónima

CAMPO DEL MORO & LOS AUSTRIAS *Map on p234*

CHAMBERÍ *Map on p238*

Map on p238

Sights **(p147)**

1 Estación de Chamberí......E4
2 Museo Sorolla......G2
3 Plaza de Olavide......D3

Eating **(p149)**

4 Bodega de la Ardosa......E2
5 Costa Blanca Arrocería......C3
6 El Brillante......D3
7 El Pedrusco......D3
8 Il Casone......D3
9 La Favorita......E4
10 Las Tortillas de Gabino......G3
11 Sagaretxe......D3
12 Santceloni......G1
13 Sergi Arola Gastro......G4
14 Zalacaín......H1

Entertainment **(p152)**

15 Clamores......D4
16 Galileo Galilei......A1
17 Honky Tonk......E5
18 Teatros del Canal......C1

Shopping **(p153)**

19 Antigüedades Hom......D3
20 Bazar Matey......C4
21 Calzados Cantero......D3
22 Flamenco Chic......E5
23 Pasajes Librería Internacional......F6

Sleeping **(p174)**

24 Hotel AC Santo Mauro......G4

Key on p237

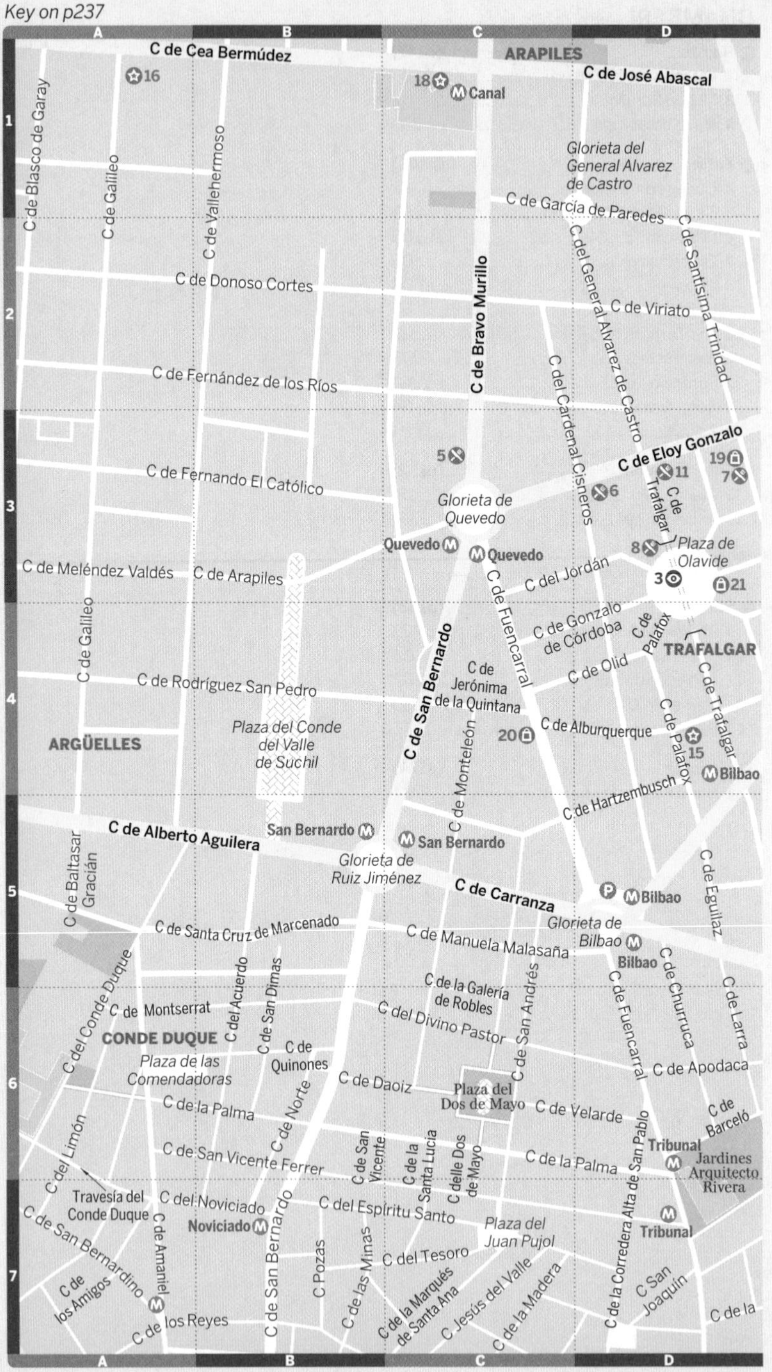
C de Cea Bermúdez
ARAPILES
C de José Abascal
16
18
Canal
C de Blasco de Garay
C de Galileo
C de Vallehermoso
Glorieta del General Alvarez de Castro
C de García de Paredes
C de Santísima Trinidad
C del General Alvarez de Castro
C de Donoso Cortes
C de Bravo Murillo
C de Viriato
C del Cardenal Cisneros
C de Fernández de los Ríos
C de Eloy Gonzalo
5
19
11
7
6
C de Fernando El Católico
Glorieta de Quevedo
C de Trafalgar
Quevedo
Quevedo
8
Plaza de Olavide
C de Meléndez Valdés
C de Arapiles
C del Jordán
3
21
C de Fuencarral
C de Gonzalo de Córdoba
C de Palafox
TRAFALGAR
C de San Bernardo
C de Olid
C de Jerónima de la Quintana
C de Trafalgar
C de Rodríguez San Pedro
C de Alburquerque
C de Palafox
20
15
ARGÜELLES
Plaza del Conde del Valle de Suchil
C de Monteleón
Bilbao
C de Hartzembusch
C de Alberto Aguilera
San Bernardo
San Bernardo
C de Baltasar Gracián
Glorieta de Ruiz Jiménez
C de Carranza
Bilbao
C de Eguilaz
C de Santa Cruz de Marcenado
C de Manuela Malasaña
Glorieta de Bilbao
Bilbao
C del Conde Duque
C del Acuerdo
C de San Dimas
C de la Galería de Robles
C de San Andrés
C de Fuencarral
C de Churruca
C de Larra
C de Montserrat
C del Divino Pastor
CONDE DUQUE
C de Quinones
Plaza de las Comendadoras
C de Daoiz
Plaza del Dos de Mayo
C de Apodaca
C de la Palma
C de Norte
C de Velarde
C de Barceló
C del Limón
C de San Vicente Ferrer
C de San Vicente
C de la Santa Lucía
C delle Dos de Mayo
C de la Palma
Tribunal
C Alta de San Pablo
Jardines Arquitecto Rivera
Travesía del Conde Duque
C del Noviciado
C del Espíritu Santo
C de Amaniel
Noviciado
C de San Bernardino
Plaza del Juan Pujol
Tribunal
C de San Bernardo
C Pozas
C de las Minas
C del Tesoro
C de los Amigos
C de la Marqués de Santa Ana
C Jesús del Valle
C de la Madera
C de la Corredera Alta de San Pablo
C San Joaquín
C de la
C de los Reyes

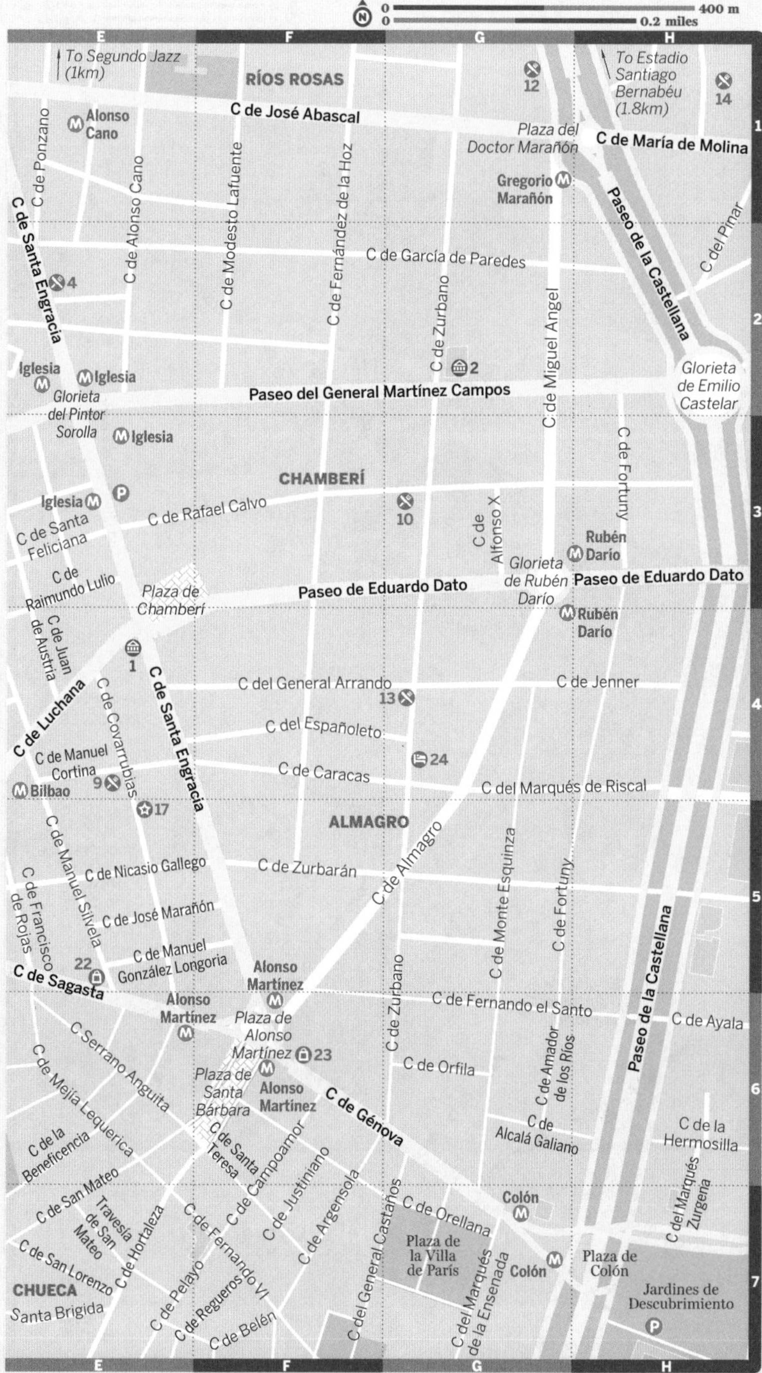
CHAMBERÍ
0 400 m
0 0.2 miles
To Segundo Jazz (1km)
To Estadio Santiago Bernabéu (1.8km)
RÍOS ROSAS
C de José Abascal
Alonso Cano
C de Ponzano
C de Santa Engracia
C de Alonso Cano
C de Modesto Lafuente
C de Fernández de la Hoz
Plaza del Doctor Marañón
C de María de Molina
Gregorio Marañón
Paseo de la Castellana
C del Pinar
C de García de Paredes
C de Zurbano
C de Miguel Angel
Iglesia
Glorieta del Pintor Sorolla
Paseo del General Martínez Campos
Glorieta de Emilio Castelar
C de Fortuny
CHAMBERÍ
C de Rafael Calvo
C de Santa Feliciana
C de Raimundo Lulio
C de Alfonso X
Rubén Darío
Glorieta de Rubén Darío
Plaza de Chamberí
Paseo de Eduardo Dato
C de Juan de Austria
C de Luchana
C de Covarrubias
C del General Arrando
C de Jenner
C del Españoleto
C de Manuel Cortina
C de Caracas
C del Marqués de Riscal
Bilbao
ALMAGRO
C de Manuel Silvela
C de Nicasio Gallego
C de Zurbarán
C de Almagro
C de Monte Esquinza
C de Francisco de Rojas
C de José Marañón
C de Manuel González Longoria
C de Sagasta
Alonso Martínez
Plaza de Alonso Martínez
C de Fernando el Santo
C de Ayala
C Serrano Anguita
C de Orfila
C de Amador de los Ríos
Plaza de Santa Bárbara
C de Génova
C de Mejía Lequerica
C de la Beneficencia
C de Santa Teresa
C de Campoamor
C de Justiniano
C de Argensola
C de Alcalá Galiano
C de la Hermosilla
C del Marqués Zurgena
C de San Mateo
Travesía de San Mateo
C de Hortaleza
C de Fernando VI
C del General Castaños
C de Orellana
Colón
Plaza de la Villa de París
C del Marqués de la Ensenada
Plaza de Colón
C de San Lorenzo
CHUECA
Santa Brigida
C de Pelayo
C de Regueros
C de Belén
Jardines de Descubrimiento

PARQUE DEL OESTE

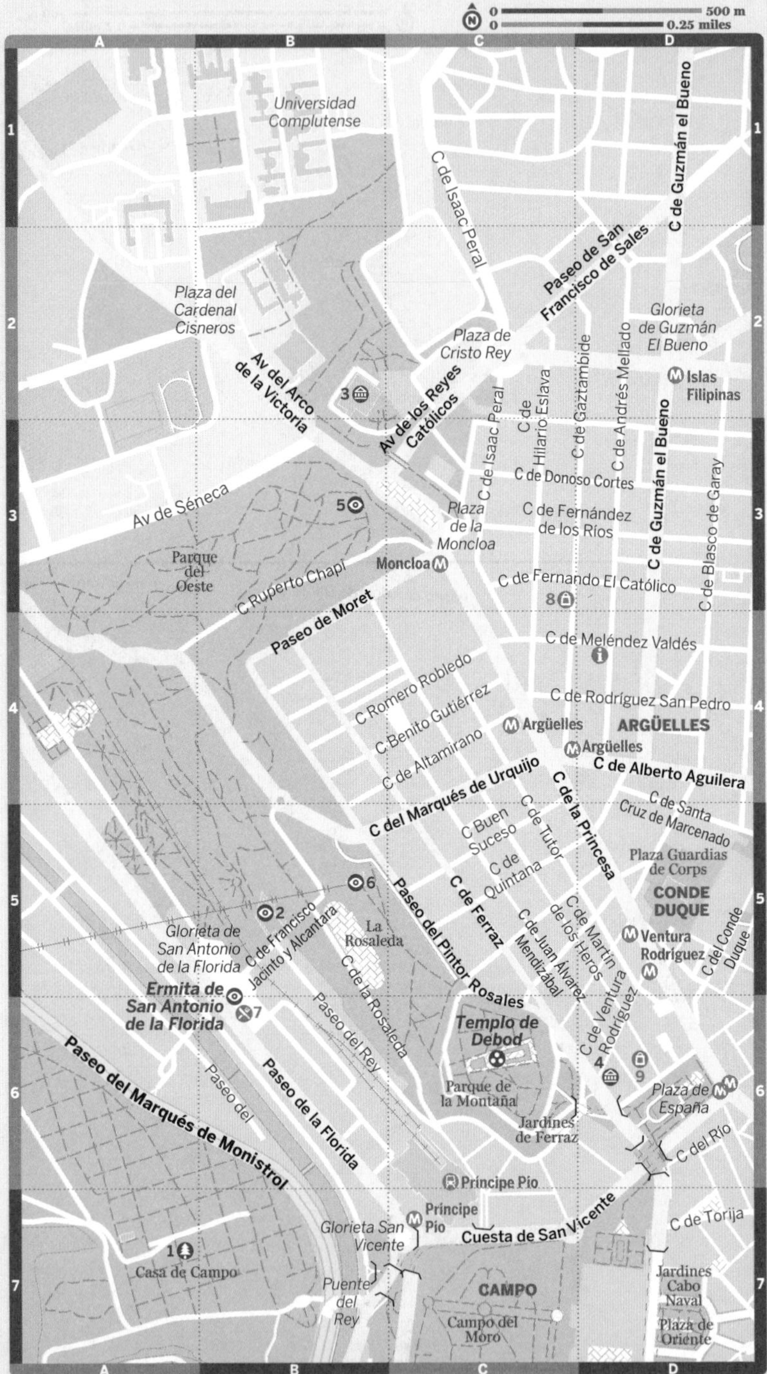

PARQUE DEL OESTE

SOL, HUERTAS & THE CENTRE

Key on p244

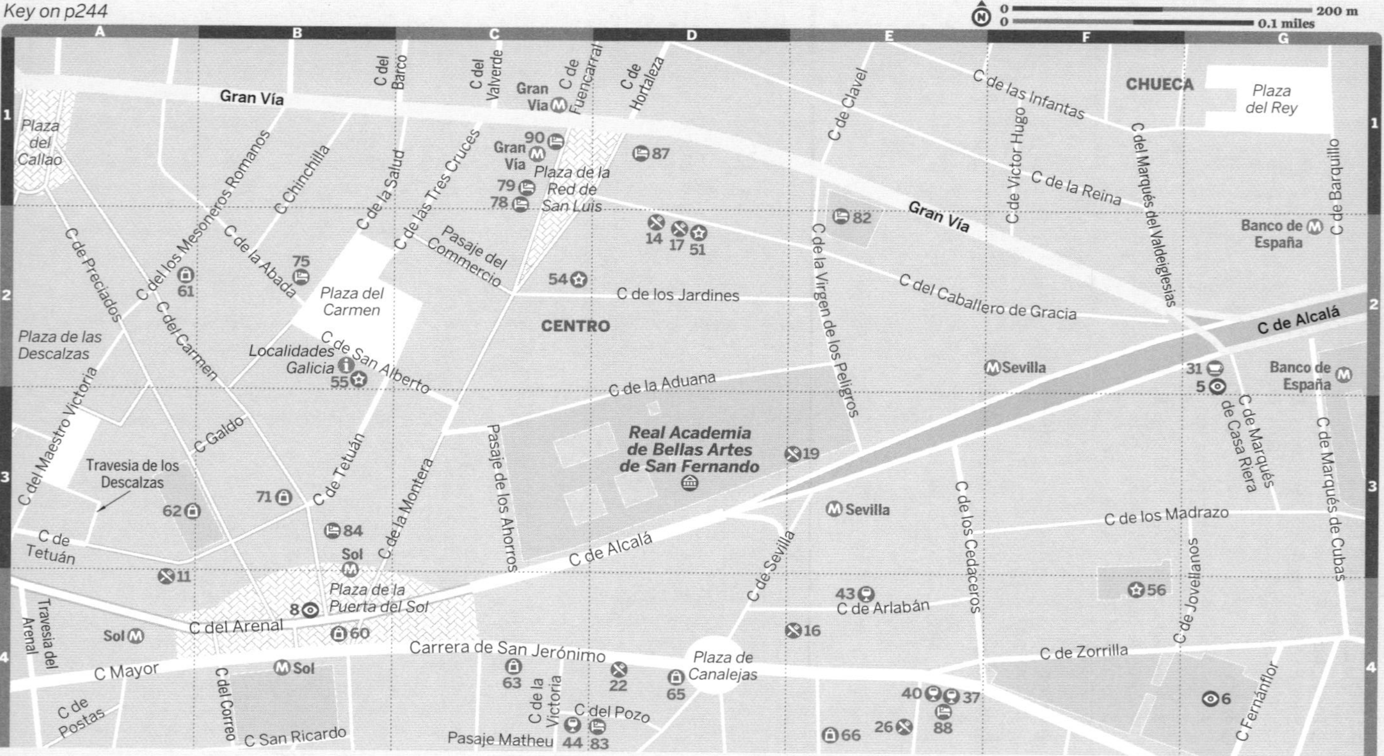

SOL, HUERTAS & THE CENTRE

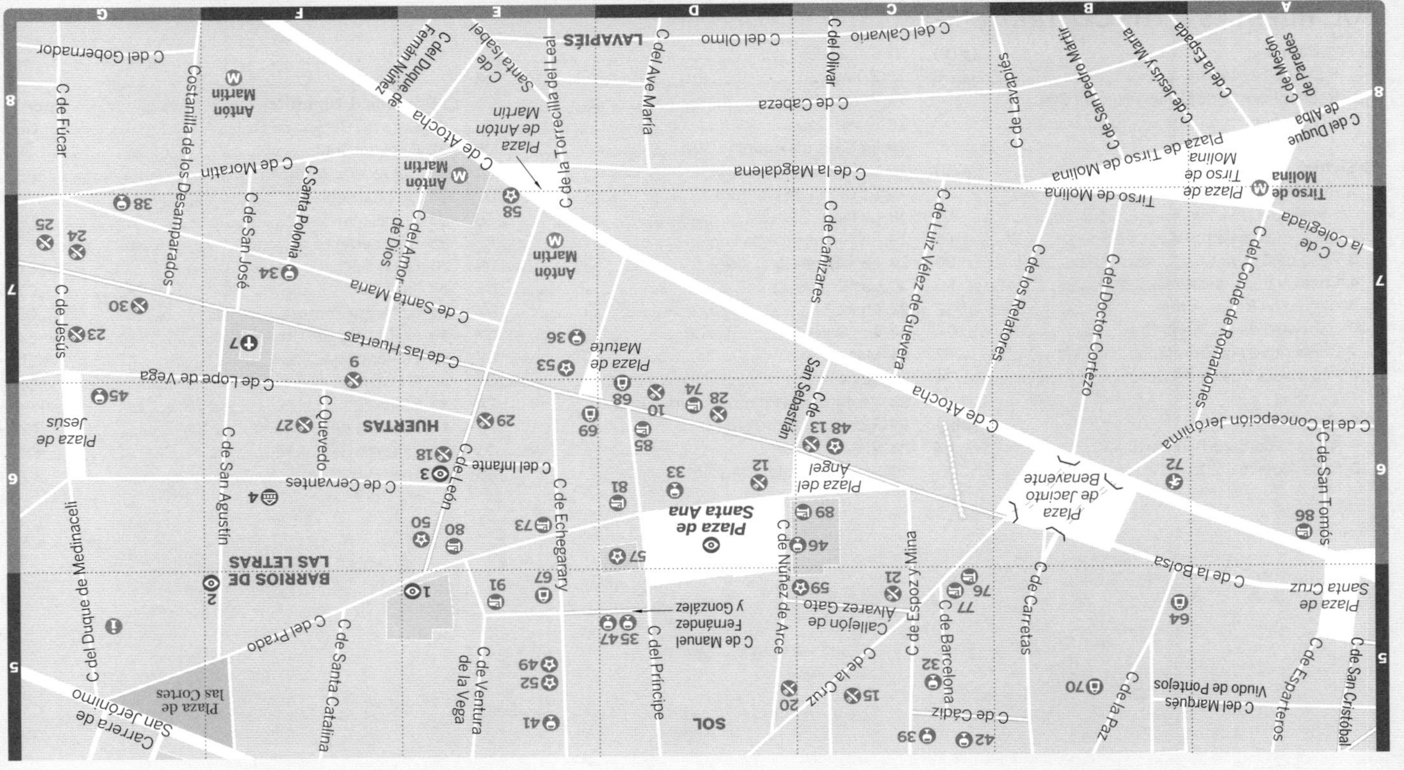

SOL, HUERTAS & THE CENTRE *Map on p242*

Top Sights (p78)
Plaza de Santa Ana ... D6
Real Academia de Bellas Artes de San Fernando ... D3

Sights (p79)
1 Ateneo Científico, Literario y Artístico de Madrid ... E5
2 Barrio de las Letras ... F5
3 Calle de Cervantes 2 ... E6
4 Casa de Lope de Vega ... F6
5 Circulo de Bellas Artes ... G2
6 Congreso de los Diputados ... G4
7 Convento de las Trinitarias ... F7
8 Plaza de la Puerta del Sol ... B4

Eating (p81)
9 A Tasca do Bacalhau Portugês ... F7
10 Casa Alberto ... D6
11 Casa Labra ... A4
12 El Lateral ... D6
13 Estado Puro ... C6
14 Fresc Co ... D2
15 La Casa del Abuelo ... C5
16 La Finca de Susana ... E4
17 La Gloria de Montera ... D2
18 La Piola ... E6
19 La Terraza del Casino ... E3
20 La Trucha ... D5
21 Las Bravas ... C5
22 Lhardy ... D4
23 Los Gatos ... G7
24 Maceiras ... G7
25 Maceiras ... G7
26 Restaurante Integral Artemisa ... E4
27 Sidrería Vasca Zeraín ... F6
28 Vi Cool ... D6
29 Vinos Gonzalez ... E6
30 Viva la Vida ... G7

Drinking & Nightlife (p84)
31 Café del Círculo de Bellas Artes ... G2
32 Café del Soul ... C5
33 Cervecería Alemana ... D6
34 Dos Gardenias ... F7
35 El Callejón ... D5
36 El Imperfecto ... E7
37 Glass Bar ... E4
38 Jazz Bar ... G7
39 La Negra Tomasa ... C5
40 La Terraza del Urban ... E4
41 La Venencia ... E5
42 Malaspina ... C5
43 Stella ... E4
44 Taberna Alhambra ... C4
45 Taberna de Dolores ... G6
46 The Roof ... C6

47 Viva Madrid ... D5

Entertainment (p86)

48 Café Central ... C6
49 Cardamomo ... E5
50 Casa Pueblo ... E6
51 Costello Café & Niteclub ... D2
52 La Boca del Lobo ... E5
53 Populart ... E7
54 Sala El Sol ... C2
55 Taquilla Ultimo Minuto ... B2
56 Teatro de la Zarzuela ... F4
57 Teatro Español ... D6
58 Teatro Monumental ... E7
59 Villa Rosa ... C5

Shopping (p87)

60 Casa de Diego ... B4
61 Casa de Diego ... A2
62 El Corte Inglés ... A3
63 Gil ... C4
64 José Ramírez ... B5
65 La Violeta ... D4
66 Lomography ... E4
67 María Cabello ... E5
68 México ... D6
69 México II ... E6
70 Santarrufina ... B5
71 Tienda Real Madrid ... B3

Sports & Activities (p89)

72 Hammam al-Andalus ... B6

Sleeping (p169)

73 Catalonia Las Cortes ... E6
74 Chic & Basic Colors ... D6
75 Hostal Acapulco ... B2
76 Hostal Adria Santa Ana ... C5
77 Hostal Adriano ... C5
78 Hostal Jerez ... C1
79 Hostal Luis XV ... C1
80 Hostal Sardinero ... E6
81 Hotel Alicia ... D6
82 Hotel de Las Letras ... E2
83 Hotel El Pasaje ... D4
84 Hotel Europa ... B3
85 Hotel Miau ... D6
86 Hotel Plaza Mayor ... A6
87 Hotel Senator ... D1
88 Hotel Urban ... E4
89 Me by Melía ... C6
90 Praktik Metropol ... C1
91 Suite Prado Hotel ... E5

PASEO DEL PRADO & EL RETIRO

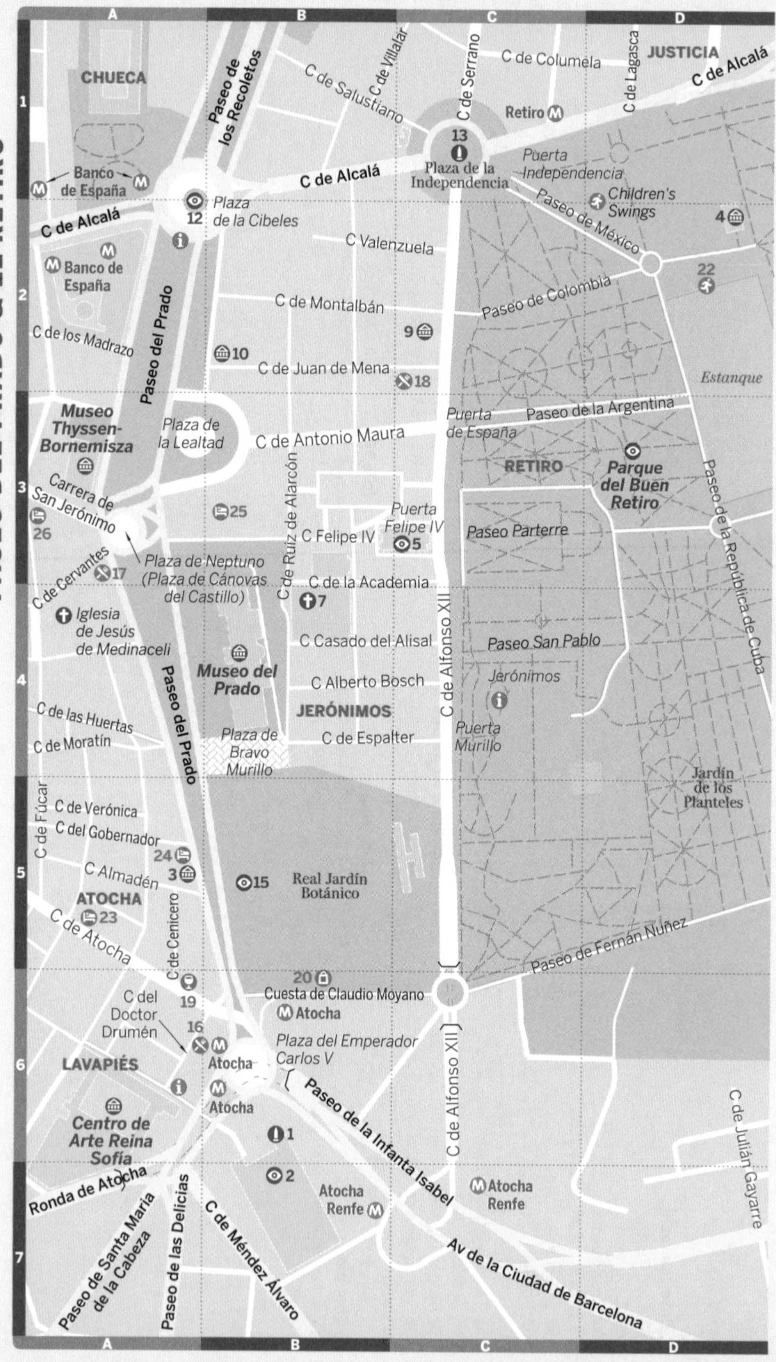

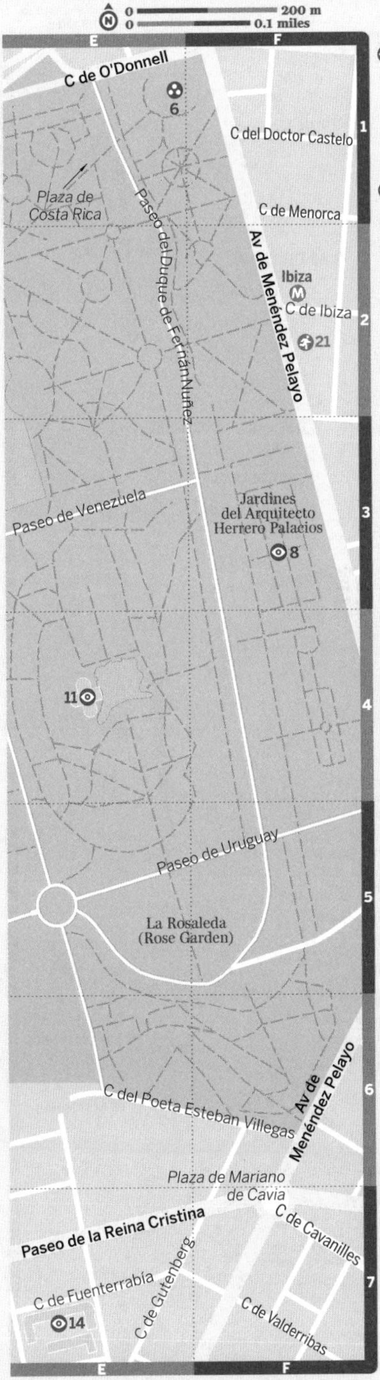

0 200 m
0 0.1 miles

E F

C de O'Donnell
6
C del Doctor Castelo
Plaza de Costa Rica
C de Menorca
Paseo del Duque de Fernán Nuñez
Av de Menéndez Pelayo
Ibiza
C de Ibiza
21
Paseo de Venezuela
Jardines del Arquitecto Herrero Palacios
8
11
Paseo de Uruguay
La Rosaleda (Rose Garden)
C del Poeta Esteban Villegas
Av de Menéndez Pelayo
Plaza de Mariano de Cavia
Paseo de la Reina Cristina
C de Cavanilles
C de Fuenterrabía
C de Gutenberg
C de Valderribas
14

1 2 3 4 5 6 7

E F

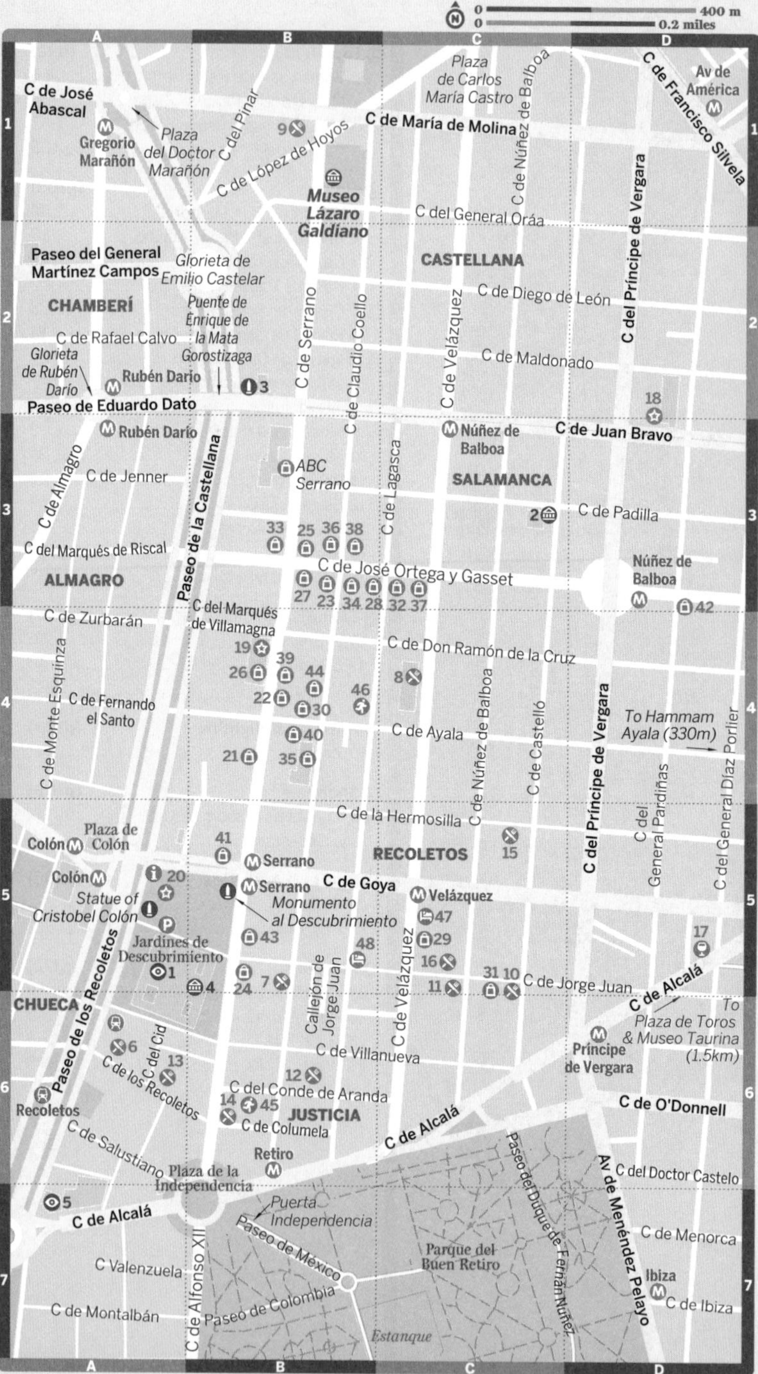
0 400 m
0 0.2 miles
C de José Abascal
Gregorio Marañón
Plaza del Doctor Marañón
C del Pinar
C de López de Hoyos
C de María de Molina
Plaza de Carlos María Castro
C de Núñez de Balboa
C de Francisco Silvela
Av de América
Museo Lázaro Galdiano
C del General Oráa
C del Príncipe de Vergara
Paseo del General Martínez Campos
Glorieta de Emilio Castelar
CASTELLANA
CHAMBERÍ
Puente de Enrique de la Mata Gorostizaga
C de Serrano
C de Claudio Coello
C de Velázquez
C de Diego de León
C de Rafael Calvo
Glorieta de Rubén Darío
Rubén Darío
C de Maldonado
Paseo de Eduardo Dato
Núñez de Balboa
C de Juan Bravo
C de Almagro
C de Jenner
ABC Serrano
C de Lagasca
SALAMANCA
Paseo de la Castellana
C de Padilla
C del Marqués de Riscal
C de José Ortega y Gasset
ALMAGRO
C del Marqués de Villamagna
C de Zurbarán
C de Don Ramón de la Cruz
C de Monte Esquinza
C de Fernando el Santo
C de Castelló
C de Ayala
To Hammam Ayala (330m)
C del General Díaz Porlier
C del General Pardiñas
C de la Hermosilla
Plaza de Colón
Colón
Serrano
RECOLETOS
C de Goya
Velázquez
Statue of Cristobel Colón
Monumento al Descubrimiento
Jardines de Descubrimiento
Paseo de los Recoletos
Callejón de Jorge Juan
C de Jorge Juan
C de Alcalá
CHUECA
To Plaza de Toros & Museo Taurina (1.5km)
Príncipe de Vergara
C del Cid
C de los Recoletos
C de Villanueva
C del Conde de Aranda
Recoletos
JUSTICIA
C de O'Donnell
C de Columela
C de Salustiano
Retiro
Plaza de la Independencia
Paseo del Duque de Fernán Núñez
Av de Menéndez Pelayo
C del Doctor Castelo
Puerta Independencia
Paseo de México
C de Menorca
C Valenzuela
Parque del Buen Retiro
Ibiza
C de Ibiza
C de Montalbán
Paseo de Colombia
C de Alfonso XII
Estanque

SALAMANCA

Top Sights (p113)

Museo Lázaro Galdiano ... B1

Sights (p114)

1 Biblioteca Nacional & Museo del Libro . A5
2 Fundación Juan March ... C3
3 Museo al Aire Libre ... B2
4 Museo Arqueológico Nacional ... B5
5 Palacio de Linares & Casa de América . A7

Eating (p115)

6 Al-Mounia ... A6
7 Biotza ... B5
8 El Lateral ... C4
9 José Luis ... B1
10 La Cocina de María Luisa ... C5
11 La Colonial de Goya ... C5
12 La Galette ... B6
13 Le Café ... A6
14 Mallorca ... B6
15 Restaurante Estay ... C5
16 Sula Madrid ... C5

Drinking & Nightlife (p117)

17 The Geographic Club ... D5

Entertainment (p118)

18 Almonte ... D2
Fundación Juan March ... (see 2)
19 Serrano 41 ... B4
20 Teatro Fernán Gómez ... A5

Shopping (p118)

21 Agatha Ruiz de la Prada ... B4
22 Bombonerías Santa ... B4
23 Burberry ... B3
24 Camper ... B5
25 Cartier ... B3
Chanel ... (see 28)
Cuarto de Juegos ... (see 10)
26 De Viaje ... B4
27 Dior ... B3
28 Dolce & Gabbana ... B3
29 Ekseption & Eks ... C5
30 Flamenco Chic ... B4
31 Gallery ... C5
32 Giorgio Armani ... C3
33 Gucci ... B3
34 Hermès ... B3
35 Isolée ... B4
36 Jimmy Choo ... B3
37 Lavinia ... C3
Loewe ... (see 43)
38 Louis Vuitton ... B3
39 Manolo Blahnik ... B4
40 Mantequería Bravo ... B4
41 Muji ... B5
42 Oriol Balaguer ... D3
43 Purificación García ... B5
44 Tous ... B4

Sports & Activities (p120)

45 Chi Spa ... B6
46 Lab Room Spa ... B4

Sleeping (p172)

47 Adler Hotel ... C5
48 Petit Palace Art Gallery ... B5

Key on p252

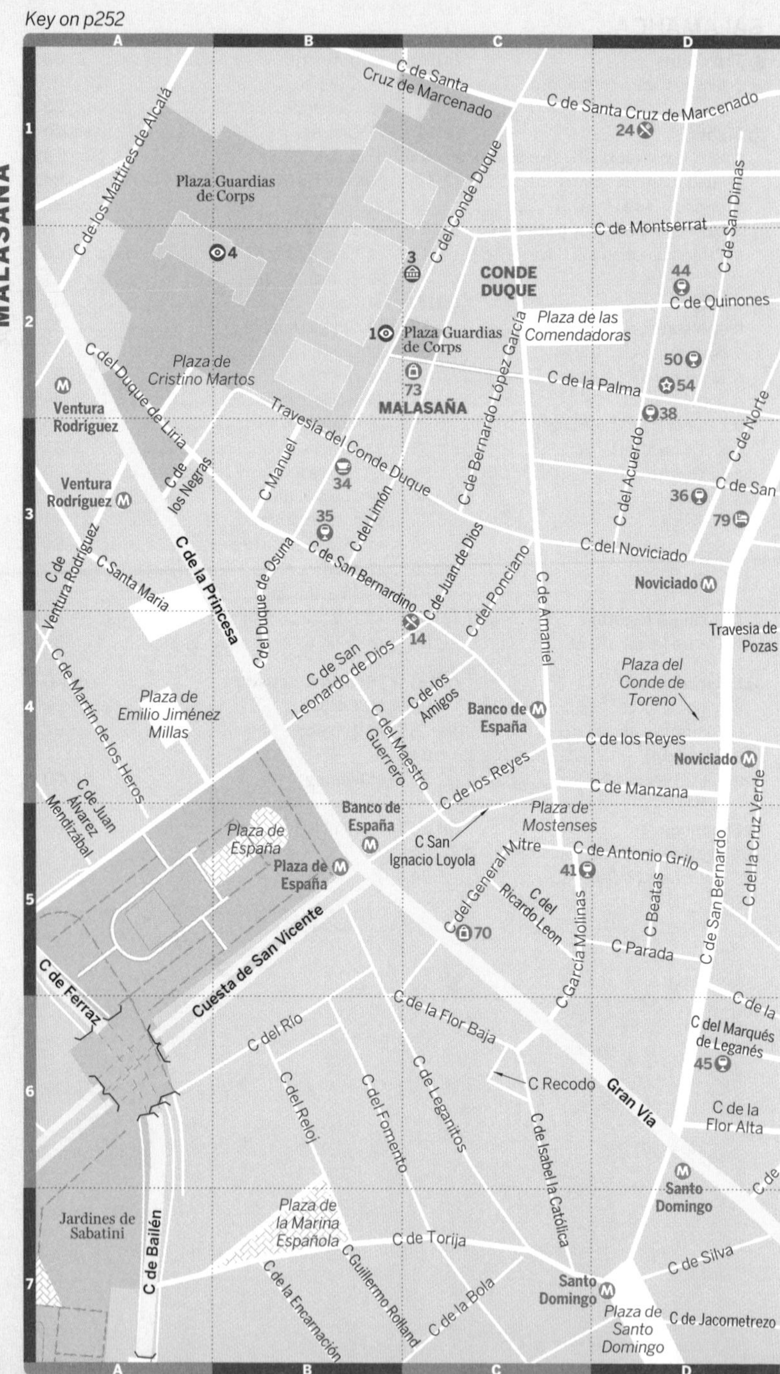
MALASAÑA
C de Santa Cruz de Marcenado
C de los Mártires de Alcalá
Plaza Guardias de Corps
C del Conde Duque
C de Montserrat
C de San Dimas
CONDE DUQUE
C de Quiñones
Plaza de las Comendadoras
Plaza Guardias de Corps
C de la Palma
Plaza de Cristino Martos
C del Duque de Liria
Ventura Rodríguez
MALASAÑA
Travesía del Conde Duque
C de Bernardo López García
C del Acuerdo
C de Norte
C de los Negras
C Manuel
C del Limón
C de San
C de San Bernardino
C del Noviciado
C de la Princesa
C del Duque de Osuna
C de Ventura Rodríguez
C Santa María
C de Juan de Dios
C del Ponciano
C de Amaniel
Noviciado
Travesía de Pozas
C de San Leonardo de Dios
Plaza del Conde de Toreno
C de Martín de los Heros
Plaza de Emilio Jiménez Millas
C de los Amigos
Banco de España
C del Maestro Guerrero
C de los Reyes
Noviciado
C de Manzana
C de Juan Álvarez Mendizábal
C de la Cruz Verde
Plaza de España
Plaza de Mostenses
C San Ignacio Loyola
C del General Mitre
C de Antonio Grilo
C de San Bernardo
C del Ricardo León
C Beatas
C Parada
Cuesta de San Vicente
C García Molinas
C de Ferraz
C de la Flor Baja
C del Marqués de Leganés
C del Río
C del Reloj
C del Fomento
C de Leganitos
C Recodo
Gran Vía
C de la Flor Alta
C de Isabel la Católica
Santo Domingo
Jardines de Sabatini
C de Bailén
Plaza de la Marina Española
C de Torija
C de Silva
C de la Encarnación
C Guillermo Rolland
C de la Bola
Plaza de Santo Domingo
C de Jacometrezo
24
44
50
54
38
36
79
3
4
1
73
34
35
14
41
70
45

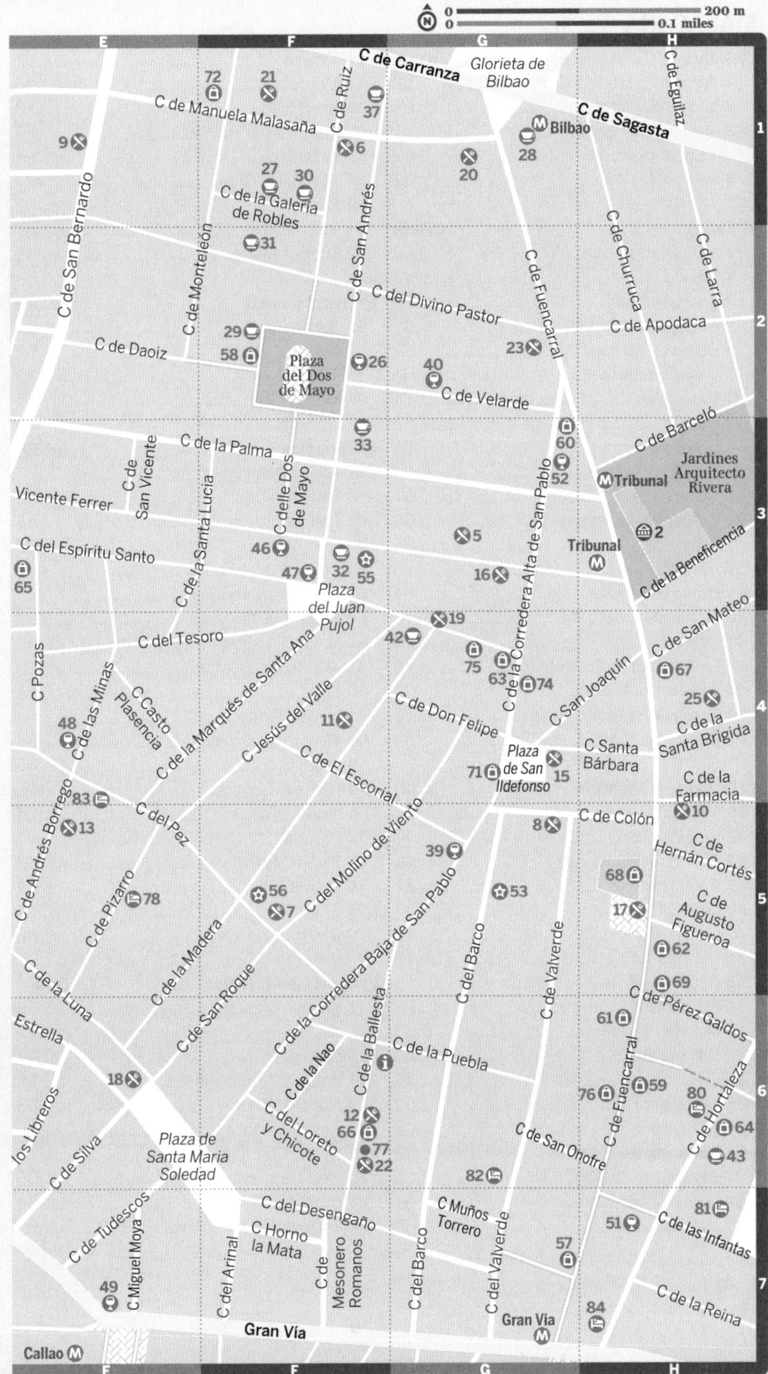

MALASAÑA
0 200 m
0 0.1 miles
Glorieta de Bilbao
C de Carranza
C de Sagasta
C de Eguilaz
Bilbao
C de Manuela Malasaña
C de Ruiz
C de San Andrés
C de la Galería de Robles
C de San Bernardo
C de Monteleón
C del Divino Pastor
C de Fuencarral
C de Churruca
C de Larra
C de Apodaca
C de Daoiz
Plaza del Dos de Mayo
C de Velarde
C de Barceló
Jardines Arquitecto Rivera
Tribunal
C de la Palma
C de San Vicente
Vicente Ferrer
C de la Santa Lucia
C delle Dos de Mayo
C de la Corredera Alta de San Pablo
C del Espíritu Santo
C de la Beneficencia
Plaza del Juan Pujol
C del Tesoro
C Pozas
C de las Minas
C Casto Plasencia
C de la Marqués de Santa Ana
C Jesús del Valle
C de Don Felipe
C San Joaquín
C de San Mateo
C de la Santa Brigida
Plaza de San Ildefonso
C Santa Bárbara
C de la Farmacia
C de El Escorial
C del Molino de Viento
C del Pez
C de Colón
C de Andrés Borrego
C de Pizarro
C de la Madera
C de la Corredera Baja de San Pablo
C del Barco
C de Valverde
C de Hernán Cortés
C de Augusto Figueroa
C de la Luna
C de San Roque
C de Pérez Galdos
Estrella
C de la Nao
C de la Ballesta
C de la Puebla
los Libreros
C del Loreto y Chicote
C de San Onofre
C de Hortaleza
C de Silva
Plaza de Santa Maria Soledad
C de Tudescos
C del Desengaño
C Horno la Mata
C Muños Torrero
C de las Infantas
C Miguel Moya
C del Arinal
C de Mesonero Romanos
C del Valverde
C de la Reina
Gran Vía
Gran Via
Callao

MALASAÑA *Map on p250*

Sights (p123)

1 Antiguo Cuartel del Conde Duque........B2
2 Museo de Historia........H3
3 Museo Municipal de Arte Contemporáneo........C2
4 Palacio de Liria........B2

Eating (p126)

5 A Dos Velas........G3
6 Albur........F1
7 Bar Palentino........F5
8 Bodega de la Ardosa........G5
9 Buenas y Santas........E1
10 Casa Hortensia........H5
11 Casa Julio........F4
12 Casa Perico........F6
13 Comomelocomo........E5
14 Con Dos Fogones........C4
15 Conache........G4
16 Crêperie Ma Bretagne........G3
17 El Lateral........H5
18 Home Burger Bar........E6
19 Home Burger Bar........G4
20 La Isla del Tesoro........G1
21 La Musa........F1
22 La Tasquita de Enfrente........F6
23 Le Pain Quotidien........G2
24 Peggy Sue's American Diner........D1
25 Ribeira Do Miño........H4

Drinking & Nightlife (p132)

26 Bar El 2D........F2
27 Café Ajenjo........F1
28 Café Comercial........G1
29 Café de Mahón........F2
30 Café de Ruiz........F1
31 Café Isadora........F2
32 Café Manuela........F3
33 Café Pepe Botella........F3
34 El Café Sin Nombre........B3
35 El Jardín Secreto........B3
36 El Naranja........D3
37 El Parnasillo........F1
38 La Palmera........D2
39 La Realidad........G5
40 La Vía Láctea........G2
41 Laydown Rest Club........C5
42 Lolina Vintage Café........G4
43 Mamá Inés........H6
44 Moloko........D2
45 Morocco........D6
46 Nasti Club........F3
47 Ojalá Awareness Club........F3
48 Picnic........E4
49 Sala Bash/Ohm........E7
50 Siroco........D2
51 Stop Madrid........H7
52 Tupperware........G3

Entertainment (p138)

53 BarCo........G5
54 Café La Palma........D2
55 Taboó........F3
56 Teatro Alfil........F5

Shopping (p139)

57 Adolfo Domínguez........G7
58 Baby Nest........F2
59 Camper........H6
60 Curiosite........G3
61 Custo Barcelona........H6
62 Divina Providencia........H5
63 El Templo de Susu........G4
64 H.A.N.D. Clothes & Accessories........H6
65 J&J Books & Coffee........E3
66 Kling........F6
67 Lurdes Bergada........H4
68 Mercado de Fuencarral........H5
69 Muji........H5
70 National Geographic........C5
71 Nest........G4
72 Popland........F1
73 Radio City Discos........C2
74 Retro City........G4
75 Snapo........G4
76 Uno de 50........H6

Sports & Activities (p130)

77 Kitchen Club........F6

Sleeping (p172)

78 Antigua Posada del Pez........E5
79 Flat 5 Madrid........D3
80 Hostal América........H6
81 Hostal Don Juan........H7
82 Hostal La Zona........G6
83 Hotel Abalú........E4
84 Petit Palace Hotel Ducal........H7

CHUECA *Map on p254*

Sights (p123)
1 Casa de las Siete Chimeneas ... C7
2 Galería Moriarty ... F5
3 Museo de Cera ... G4
4 Museo del Romanticismo ... B3
5 Palacio Buenavista ... E7
6 Plaza de Chueca ... C5
7 Sociedad General de Autores y Editores ... C3

Eating (p129)
8 Alma Lusa ... C7
9 Baco y Beto ... B5
10 Bazaar ... C6
11 Bocaito ... C7
12 Charlotte ... C5
13 El Original ... C7
14 Fresc Co ... C1
15 Gastromaquia ... B6
16 Home Burger Bar ... B6
17 Janatomo ... B7
18 Kim Bu Mbu ... C7
19 La Mordida ... D4
20 La Paella de la Reina ... C7
21 Le Cabrera ... E4
22 Magasand ... B3
23 Maison Blanche ... D5
24 Mercado de San Antón ... C6
25 Restaurante Extremadura ... C7
26 Restaurante Momo ... C7
27 Tepic ... B6
28 Un y 2 ... C6
29 Wogaboo ... D5

Drinking & Nightlife (p136)
30 Antigua Casa Ángel Sierra ... C5
31 Areia ... C4
32 Bar Cock ... B7
33 Black & White ... C5
34 Bristol Bar ... E5
35 Café Acuarela ... C5
36 Café Belén ... D4
37 Café-Restaurante El Espejo ... F5
38 Club 54 Studio ... B6
39 Del Diego ... B7
40 Diurno ... C6
41 El Junco Jazz Club ... D2
42 Gran Café de Gijón ... F6
43 La Bardemcilla ... D6
44 Le Cabrera ... E4
45 Liquid Madrid ... B6
46 Mercado de la Reina Gin Club ... B7
47 Museo Chicote ... B7
48 Pachá ... B2
49 Polyester ... C3
50 Splash Óscar ... B7
51 Stromboli ... C3
52 Why Not? ... B6

Entertainment (p138)
53 Bogui Jazz ... D5
54 El Búho Real ... C4
55 Libertad 8 ... C7
56 Zanzibar ... D3

Shopping (p142)
57 Aldaba ... C4
58 Biblioketa ... D3
59 Cacao Sampaka ... D2
60 Coorleone's Company ... B5
61 El Tintero ... C5
62 Elisa Bracci ... E4
63 Futuramic ... C5
64 Isolée ... B7
65 La Juguetería ... C3
66 L'Habilleur ... C5
67 Librería Berkana ... B5
68 Loewe ... B8
69 Lomography ... D3
70 Lurdes Bergada ... E5
71 MacChinine ... D7
72 Patrimonio Comunal Olivarero ... C2
73 Poncelet ... E2
74 Reserva y Cata ... E5
75 Salvador Bachiller ... C5

Sports & Activities (p130)
76 Apunto – Centro Cultural del Gusto ... C4

Sleeping (p173)
77 Albergue Juvenil ... B1
78 Casa Chueca ... B6
79 Hostal San Lorenzo ... B7
80 Hotel Óscar ... B7

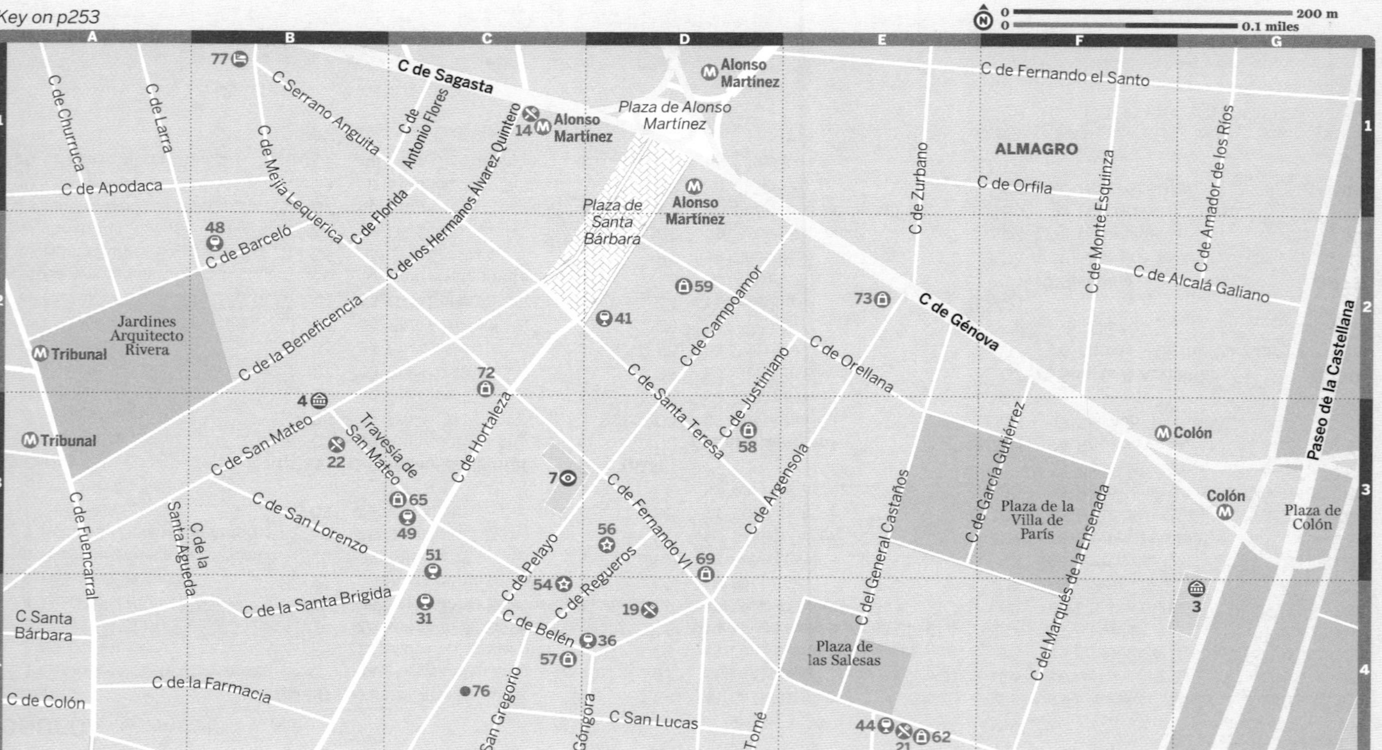
CHUECA
Key on p253
0 200 m
0 0.1 miles
C de Sagasta
Alonso Martínez
Plaza de Alonso Martínez
C de Fernando el Santo
ALMAGRO
C de Churruca
C de Larra
C Serrano Anguita
C de Antonio Flores
C de los Hermanos Álvarez Quintero
C de Mejía Lequerica
C de Apodaca
C de Florida
C de Barceló
Plaza de Santa Bárbara
C de Zurbano
C de Orfila
C de Monte Esquinza
C de Amador de los Ríos
C de Alcalá Galiano
C de Génova
Paseo de la Castellana
C de Campoamor
C de Orellana
Jardines Arquitecto Rivera
Tribunal
C de la Beneficencia
C de Justiniano
C de Santa Teresa
C de Hortaleza
C de San Mateo
Travesía de San Mateo
Colón
C de García Gutiérrez
Plaza de la Villa de París
C del Marqués de la Ensenada
Plaza de Colón
C de Fernando VI
C de Argensola
C del General Castaños
C de Fuencarral
C de la Santa Agueda
C de San Lorenzo
C de Pelayo
C de Regueros
C de la Santa Brigida
C Santa Bárbara
C de Belén
Plaza de las Salesas
C de la Farmacia
C de Colón
San Gregorio
Góngora
C San Lucas
Tomé

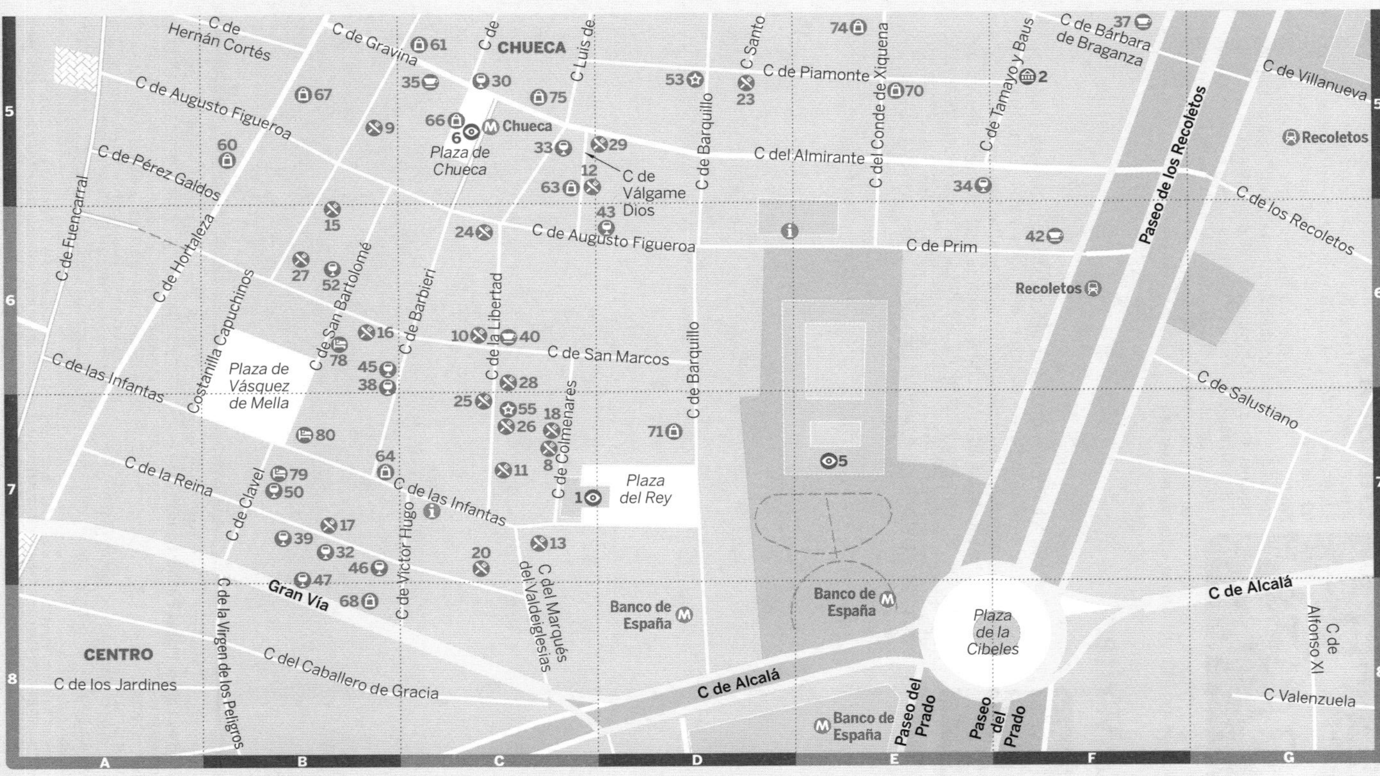
C de Hernán Cortés
C de Gravina
C de
CHUECA
C Luis de
C de Augusto Figueroa
Chueca
Plaza de Chueca
C de Pérez Galdós
C de Válgame Dios
C de Fuencarral
C de Hortaleza
C de Augusto Figueroa
C Santo
C de Piamonte
C del Conde de Xiquena
C de Tamayo y Baus
C de Bárbara de Braganza
C de Villanueva
Recoletos
C de Barquillo
C del Almirante
Paseo de los Recoletos
C de los Recoletos
C de Prim
Recoletos
Costanilla Capuchinos
C de San Bartolomé
C de Barbieri
C de la Libertad
C de San Marcos
C de Barquillo
C de las Infantas
Plaza de Vásquez de Mella
C de Colmenares
C de Salustiano
C de la Reina
C de Clavel
C de las Infantas
Plaza del Rey
C de Víctor Hugo
C del Marqués del Valdeiglesias
Gran Vía
Banco de España
Banco de España
Plaza de la Cibeles
C de Alcalá
C de Alfonso XI
CENTRO
C de los Jardines
C de la Virgen de los Peligros
C del Caballero de Gracia
C de Alcalá
Banco de España
Paseo del Prado
Paseo del Prado
C Valenzuela

CHUECA

Our Story

A beat-up old car, a few dollars in the pocket and a sense of adventure. In 1972 that's all Tony and Maureen Wheeler needed for the trip of a lifetime – across Europe and Asia overland to Australia. It took several months, and at the end – broke but inspired – they sat at their kitchen table writing and stapling together their first travel guide, *Across Asia on the Cheap*. Within a week they'd sold 1500 copies. Lonely Planet was born.

Today, Lonely Planet has offices in Melbourne, London and Oakland, with more than 600 staff and writers. We share Tony's belief that 'a great guidebook should do three things: inform, educate and amuse'.

Our Writer

Anthony Ham

In 2001 Anthony fell in love with Madrid on his first visit to the city. Less than a year later, he arrived on a one-way ticket, with not a word of Spanish and not knowing a single person. Having recently passed the 10-year mark in Madrid, he still adores his adopted city as much as the first day he arrived and considers this book his love letter to the city. When he's not writing for Lonely Planet, Anthony writes about and photographs Spain, Scandinavia, Africa and the Middle East for newspapers and magazines around the world.

Published by Lonely Planet Publications Pty Ltd
ABN 36 005 607 983
7th edition – April 2013
ISBN 978 1 74220 217 4

10 9 8 7 6 5 4 3 2 1
Printed in China